TEACHING FOREIGN LANGUAGES

2ND EDITION

TEACHING FOREIGN LANGUAGES

FRANK M. GRITTNER

Specialist in Foreign Language Education
with the Wisconsin Department of Public Education

HARPER & ROW

New York, Hagerstown, San Francisco, London

Sponsoring Editor: Michael E. Brown
Project Editor: Eleanor Castellano
Designer: Gayle Jaeger
Production Supervisor: Will C. Jomarrōn
Compositor: Santype International Limited
Printer and Binder: Halliday Lithograph Corporation
Art Studio: Vantage Art Inc.

TEACHING FOREIGN LANGUAGES, Second Edition
Copyright © 1969, 1977 by Frank M. Grittner

Library of Congress Cataloging in Publication Data

Grittner, Frank M
  Teaching foreign languages.

  Includes bibliographies and index.
  1. Languages, Modern—Study and teaching—
United States. 2. Language and languages—Study
and teaching. I. Title.
PB38.U6G7 1977   418'.007'1073   76–22709
ISBN 0–06–042524–5

To Rilla

CONTENTS

INDIVIDUALIZED INSTRUCTION 177

THE PATTERN DRILL 209

LEARNING THE FOUR SKILLS IN A CULTURAL CONTEXT 238

PREFACE

The title page to a foreign language research report issued by a Swedish pedagogical university in the early 1970s included a summarizing epigram stating that "all methods are the best method." This statement quite aptly sums up the conclusion arrived at by many contemporary foreign language educators with respect to the past claims of doctrinaire methodologists. That is, there is an increasing skepticism with respect to people who profess that they have discovered a "pedagogical breakthrough" or that they are in possession of some "new key" to teaching languages, which outmodes and makes laughable all previous instructional approaches. If the methodologist has become more modest, it is perhaps because—as Churchill once said of a political opponent—"He has a lot to be modest about." For neither the practical results nor the research findings of the past two decades have lent strong support for any of the particular pedagogical schools that were based on various mixes of linguistic theory, psychological principles, and administrative practice. As the flaws of doctrinaire approaches to methodology became apparent, language teachers tended to discard the pursuit of methodological panaceas in favor of a more pragmatic, eclectic approach. With such an approach, one examines the entire repertoire of available teaching techniques and selects those which work in a given situation regardless of whether or not they are consistent with certain linguistic, psychological, or administrative dicta. For example, a teacher may reject in principle the particular methodological school that is based upon structural linguistics and Skinnerian psychology and still feel perfectly comfortable using a pattern drill, which is derived from that method. The teacher would do so on the grounds that his/her practical experience showed that such drills have proven useful in helping students gain mastery of certain grammatical structures or syntactical patterns. With this eclectic approach, the final test of value for any technique is not its respectability in the eyes of theorists, but rather its demonstrated value in helping the target population of students achieve the goals of the course in the particular environment in which instruction must take place. In fact, in working with teachers in various in-service projects during the mid-1970s, I found them generally unresponsive to theory of any kind unless that theory could be closely tied to specific techniques that worked in real classrooms with real students. Thus, much of the new material in this edition is derived directly from classroom sources. As for orientation, both the eclectic attitude and the sequential arrangement of material chapter by chapter have been maintained in the new edition. However, the chapters have been expanded and updated to give the practitioner a broader theoretical perspective and a wider selection of practical examples from which to choose in coping with the everyday demands of classroom instruction.

Other goals toward which the book is directed and content that it emphasizes are as follows: (1) Historical material dealing with the nature and function of foreign language instruction in America is dealt with in Chapter 1 and elsewhere as appropriate. Such material is intended to help the teacher of languages gain a sense of identity with an old and respected tradition. It may also help teachers to better evaluate those kind of bandwagoneering movements that profess to be innovative but that, in reality, are nothing more than "old wine in new bottles." (2) Various rationales for learning a second language are discussed in Chapter 2. Among the items included are the pros and cons of basing foreign language programs on humanistic and utilitarian goals. A discussion of the advantages and limitations of the career education movement has been added in the new edition. (3) Chapter 3 deals with the relationship of the various schools of linguistics to foreign language teaching. The new edition includes a discussion of pedagogical approaches derived from generative grammar as well as those derived from structural linguistics and traditional grammar. (4) Chapter 4 has to do with the restraints placed on the American learner by environmental factors. School factors such as scheduling, length of study, age at which study is begun, and teacher competence are among the areas included. (5) Establishing goals and objectives for the foreign language program constitutes the principal subject matter of Chapter 5. Performance objectives and bilingual education are among the areas added in the new edition. (6) Chapter 6 deals with various psychological factors as they relate to second-language learning. The chapter has been expanded to include classroom-tested examples of motivational techniques that have been effective in getting students to learn basic language material. (7) Chapter 7 is completely new in this edition. It deals with the history, theory, and practice of individualizing and personalizing foreign language instruction. The pros and cons of large-group, small-group, and individual instruction are included, as are specific examples of how to use such groupings for teaching language and culture. Among these examples—which are drawn from successful programs—are items to help teachers construct unipacs (LAPS) and to help students become more directly involved in expressing their own ideas and feelings via the target language. (8) Chapter 8 presents a detailed discussion of pattern drills and includes scores of examples of such drills. Also included is a discussion of how they can be used in the classroom and laboratory. (9) Chapter 9 has been greatly expanded in the new edition to include sections on the teaching of culture and literature. Suggestions for the preparation and use of culture capsules, culture assimilators, and cultural minicourses are dealt with in considerable detail, with examples. Among other things, the literature section contains a rationale for the teaching of literature along with many practical suggestions for teaching various genre. (10) Chapter 10 discusses the use of language laboratories and other electronic and electromechanical devices that have proven useful in the instructional process. Considerable new material has been added here in the new edition. (11) Finally, Chapter 11 on testing and evaluation has been expanded to include suggestions for evaluating communicative competence in the various language skill areas. In addition, a textbook evaluation form has been added.

Despite these many additions and changes, the overall purpose of the revised, expanded edition remains the same as before. As was noted in the first edition, this book is an attempt to bring together, in a unified fashion, the chief areas of knowledge that are directly relevant to the teaching of foreign languages and to present that knowledge in a readily comprehensible form. The deletions and additions were made in response to feedback from teachers in the field who have been willing to comment quite frankly on the changes in administrative policies, student attitudes, and school programs that have taken place in the 1970s. The new material attempts to respond to these changes. However, there is also an attempt "not to throw the baby out with the bath." There has been a tendency in American education to discard perfectly sound traditional practices in favor of new and, therefore, supposedly better ones. Since I do not subscribe to the belief that newness automatically equates with improvement, I have retained those portions of the first edition that teachers still find useful.

As was the case with the first edition, the present volume is aimed at the prospective teacher of foreign languages and at the teacher in the field— that is, at people who, within severe time constraints, are seeking to establish a bridge between the many disparate fields of knowledge upon which instructional methodologies and the process of instruction itself are based. Users of the first edition have expressed the view that the book did, indeed, serve that purpose. It is hoped that the revised edition with its many added sections and updated bibliographies will continue to be of use to the profession.

Frank M. Grittner

A NOTE ON BIBLI- OGRAPHIES

The bibliographies in this book consist mainly of items that are likely to be available in the average college library or which can be obtained at nominal cost from the ACTFL Materials Center, 62 Fifth Avenue, New York, New York 10011. It is assumed that the foreign language methods instructor will direct all prospective teachers to the bibliography of significant professional publications that has been developed under the sponsorship of the American Council on the Teaching of Foreign Languages (ACTFL). It was written by Emma Marie Birkmaier and Dale L. Lange and was published under the title "A Selective Bibliography on the Teaching of Foreign Languages, 1920–1966," *Foreign Language Annals* 1 (May 1968), pp. 318–353. In the words of the authors, "This bibliography may be considered the prologue to the ACTFL *Bibliography*, an annual listing that began in *Foreign Language Annals* 1 (October 1967)."

A further source of bibliographies (recommended for every language teacher's library) are the various editions of the *ACTFL Review of Foreign Language Education* and the pedagogical journals of the professional language organizations and conferences.

Also worthy of note is the Educational Resources Information Center (ERIC). *Foreign Language Annals* contains the ERIC Clearinghouse on the Teaching of Foreign Languages. This section of the journal deals with the teaching of the commonly taught languages—French, German, Italian, Russian, Spanish—and the classical languages, Latin and Ancient Greek. Abstracts of selected ERIC accessions appear in *Annals*; a complete listing of accessions appears in the regular ACTFL Bibliography mentioned above. In view of the availability of such bibliographies with their built-in policy of updating, the author chose to limit his bibliographical selections to the most basic items.

TEACHING FOREIGN LANGUAGES

1

■ *He who does not learn from the past is condemned to relive it.* SANTAYANA

■The historical roots of foreign language teaching in America

The new "American Method" did not come into existence by spontaneous generation. Much of what is happening in our foreign language classes today is closely tied to the past. However, a large proportion of present-day methodology is a deliberate renunciation of goals and practices which were long held sacred. Over a period of several decades, the proponents of change have created a whole new school of thought regarding how languages should be taught and what should be learned. The ideas of the new school have, in a relatively short time, brought drastic changes in teaching procedures and objectives. What was the old? How does the new differ from the old? What changes in language instruction have taken place through the centuries? What brought about the changes, past and present? These are a few of the questions which must first be answered if the present is to be viewed in the proper perspective.

THE CLASSICAL LANGUAGE HERITAGE

Hear how learn'd Greece her useful rules indites,
When to repress, and when indulge our flights....

    . . .

Those rules of old discovered, not devised
Are Nature still, but Nature methodized....

    . . .

Learning and Rome alike in empire grew;
And Arts still followed where her Eagles flew;
From the same foes, at last, both felt their doom,
And the same age saw Learning fall, and Rome.
ALEXANDER POPE (1688–1744)

It is often said that Western civilization began with the Greeks; yet they are only indirectly responsible for the creation of foreign language study as a separate discipline. The Greeks themselves attached little value

1

to any language but their own. It was the Romans who first established knowledge of a foreign language—the language of the conquered Greeks—as the mark of an educated gentleman. The magnificence of Greek letters apparently overwhelmed the Romans. In fact, so great was their enthusiasm that they eventually set up Hellenic literary forms as the only models worth imitating. In their emulation of the Greeks, Roman poets came to create a great literature of their own in Latin. In addition, centuries of Roman rule produced a vast legacy of practical writings in such areas as law, engineering, architecture, medicine, and military tactics. And so it was that long after the collapse of Roman political power, Latin continued on as the language of philosophy and religion, as the repository of significant knowledge, as the means of communication of the educational elite of Europe. Throughout the Middle Ages, Greek was largely eclipesd by Latin, a language whose conquest of the educational world was to continue on into the present century.

A thousand years after the fall of Rome, a surprising number of Greek and Latin manuscripts were still extant. By that time of course, the languages themselves were "dead." That is, almost no one was learning Latin or classical Greek from childhood on as the means of everyday oral communication. By the sixteenth century, national tongues such as English, French, German, and Spanish had taken shape, and men who spoke them were producing significant writings in the vernacular. Yet European men of letters and science continued to draw heavily, if not exclusively, upon the Greek and Roman classics for knowledge and for literary models. This process of extracting knowledge from ancient writings was not without its critics. Montaigne, the famous sixteenth-century French essayist, had learned Latin as a child by a "natural" conversational method. Nevertheless, he was impelled to say: "No doubt but Greek and Latin are very great ornaments, and of very great use, but we buy them too dear."[1] In reference to bookish studies in Latin grammar and composition to which many a boy was subjected, Montaigne added: "Men are quick to inquire, 'Does he know Greek or Latin? Does he write in verse or in prose?' But whether he has become better or more prudent, which is the principal thing, this receives not the least notice. . . . If his soul be not put into better rhythm, if the judgment be not better settled, I would rather have him spend his time at tennis."[2]

Yet, despite Montaigne's dissatisfaction with the teaching methodology of his day, there were few who challenged either the practical or the cultural value of knowing Latin and Greek. The term "Renaissance" itself is a form of tribute to the study of the classical writings. For without such study a major portion of the knowledge upon which Western civilization is based could not have been transmitted to later generations of Europeans and Americans. The great figures of the Renaissance realized

[1] Michel de Montaigne, *Essays*, Book I, chap. 25, *Great Books of the Western World*, Encyclopaedia Britannica, Inc., Chicago, 1952, p. 77.
[2] Ibid., chap. 24., pp. 57–58.

the incalculable importance of the ancient languages. Erasmus went so far as to say, "When I have money I will first buy Greek books and then clothes." Rabelais indicated his respect for classical learning by having his hero, Gargantua, study ancient languages. Like Erasmus, Rabelais favored Greek, which had fallen into discredit in the Middle Ages. "Now all disciplines are restored, and the languages reinstated," he writes. "Greek (without which it is a shame for a person to call himself learned), Hebrew, Chaldean, Latin."[3]

The Renaissance established classical languages in a position of preeminence, which they were to hold for centuries. Yet it was during this period that forces were set in motion that would lead to the ultimate decline of Latin and Greek. One force was the great literature being produced in the vulgar languages, which would later serve as the base for the establishment of competing disciplines. A still greater force was the Protestant Reformation. As one writer expressed it:

In making man responsible for his own faith, and in placing the source of that faith in the Holy Scriptures, the Reform contracted the obligation to put each one in a condition to save himself by the reading and understanding of the Bible. . . . The necessity of explaining the Catechism, and making comments on it, was for teachers an obligation to learn how to expound a thought, and to decompose it into its elements. The study of the mother tongue and of singing, was associated with the reading of the Bible (translated into German by Luther) and with religious services.[4]

Acceptance of the belief that a Christian should read the Bible in his own language set up a chain of circumstances that profoundly influenced education in the Western world. It provided a powerful motive for commoners to become literate in the vernacular languages. It established a reason for the creation of primary schools. Ultimately, it led to the belief—in twentieth-century America—that a man could be ignorant of foreign languages and still consider himself adequately educated; a view which had been rejected by educated men in the Western world since the early days of the Roman empire.

FOREIGN LANGUAGES IN AMERICA BEFORE THE CIVIL WAR

The brief historical outline of foreign language learning in Europe can only hint at the educational traditions that the colonists had brought with them to the New World. For the field of foreign languages, two aspects of that tradition are of central importance. First, the link between literacy and salvation helped to establish the need for general primary education with particular emphasis on the ability to read English. Second, the need for professional men—particularly clergymen and lawyers—led to the establishment of secondary and higher education. For education beyond the three Rs, the traditions of past centuries dictated that Greek and Latin were

[3] Gabriel Compayre, *The History of Pedagogy*, Boston, Heath, 1886, p. 95.
[4] Ibid., p. 113.

3

indispensable. English and other modern spoken languages were still considered as unsuitable subjects for serious scholarship. The situation at Harvard University in the early 1800s typifies the shaky position of modern languages in the pre-Civil War period. "The course of study was designed to turn out right-thinking members of a New England society, and for the most part it did just that. Latin and Greek were the languages that were considered important. Modern foreign languages were tolerated."[5]

Ticknor, one of Harvard's first great professors of modern language (Spanish and French), was highly critical of the shabby treatment accorded to his field. Shortly before his resignation, he issued a sweeping condemnation of the entire institution: "We are neither a university—which we call ourselves—nor a respectable high school—which we ought to be."[6]

Aside from the University of Virginia, it is difficult to find an institution of higher learning in the first half of the nineteenth century which placed heavy emphasis on modern language study. Under the guidance of Thomas Jefferson, Virginia adopted a program of studies that included French, Italian, Spanish, German, and Anglo-Saxon. So successful was the program that, in 1825, modern language enrollment equaled that of mathematics and exceeded that of the ancient languages.[7]

Another of the founding fathers, Benjamin Franklin, had also been a strong advocate of modern language study. As early as 1749, he had proposed that the trustees of the Charity School of Philadelphia should "with all convenient speed endeavor to engage Persons capable of teaching the French, German and Spanish languages."[8]

It appears, however, that Franklin and Jefferson were not as successful in swaying the educational policies of the time as they were in effecting political changes. For it was not until after the Civil War that modern foreign languages—specifically French and German—began to establish themselves as part of the American educational system. Spanish made little progress until well into the twentieth century.

If we review the history of the teaching of Spanish in the colleges and universities in the nineteenth century, it is clear that the language seldom formed part of the curriculum. In some cases, provision was made for studying it outside the classroom and no credit was given. . . . The usual salary of the instructors was $500 (yearly), hardly a living wage.[9]

French and German did not gain a respectable place in the curriculum without a struggle. Much of the teaching of modern languages before the nineteenth century was done by self-appointed professors who advertised

[5] Sturgis E. Leavitt, *The Teaching of Spanish in the United States*, New York, Modern Language Association, 1961, p. 311.
[6] Ibid.
[7] Ibid, p. 315.
[8] Reprinted by permission of the Modern Language Association from *The Teaching of German in the United States* by Edwin H. Zeydel, Modern Language Association, 1961, p. 288.
[9] Leavitt, op. cit., p. 316.

their services in the local newspapers. Such teachers might serve as tutors either in their own homes or in the residence of the student. Sometimes the instructor would set up a contract with a small group of students from whom he demanded payment in advance. In other instances, instruction was carried on in foreign language boarding schools. In general, modern language instruction in colonial America and in the early years of the Republic was viewed as a frill which, if needed, could be acquired outside of the educational establishment. However, as the nineteenth century progressed and the public high schools began to replace the earlier forms of secondary education, French and German found an increasingly more prominent place in the regular course of studies.

FOREIGN LANGUAGES FROM 1880 TO WORLD WAR I— THE YEARS OF PROMISE

In the first hundred years of American history (roughly from 1780 to 1880), opposition to modern languages had come from professors of the classical languages. English and other living languages were considered too easy and too utilitarian to serve the high purpose of developing the intellectual faculties. Yet despite the resistance of the educational elite, German, French, and English gradually infiltrated the college and secondary curriculum. By 1883, these forces had grown strong enough to found the Modern Language Association, an organization that has survived and flourished down to the present. However, to gain academic respectability, the modern language forces felt compelled in the beginning to adopt the methods and objectives of the more highly regarded classical languages. The resulting emphasis upon grammatical analysis and the translation of prestige literature is manifested in the teaching of modern languages even today. The first major change in language teaching, then, came in the form of an alliance between the classical humanists and teachers of the modern languages. By the end of the eighteenth century, English had become firmly established as the common language of the colonies. French had become known worldwide as the language of diplomacy. This, coupled with the popularity of French Enlightenment authors and Revolutionary sympathy for France, made a compelling case for the study of the French language. German established itself as the most popular modern foreign language for somewhat different reasons. It had survived the first mild setback after the Revolution, when public reaction against the Hessian mercenaries caused the discontinuance of several established programs.[10] However, the large influx of German immigrants during the nineteenth century resulted in the existence of many communities and sections of larger cities in which German was the native tongue; English, the foreign language. As late as 1857, the school reports in Pennsylvania and Indiana were published in both English and German; in New Jersey this practice

[10] Zeydel, op. cit., p. 289.

persisted until 1888. And in 1870 the U.S. Commissioner of Education reported that "the German language has actually become the second language of our Republic, and a knowledge of German is now considered essential to a finished education."[11] As a further impetus, the highly regarded German universities of the late 1880s drew thousands of American students who brought back a zeal for German idealism as reflected in the writings of the great seventeenth-and eighteenth-century German authors and philosophers. France and England too had produced great literatures, and on this basis a compromise with the classical humanists was possible. Literary monuments of the past could all be studied in the same way, whether modern or classical. Grammars based on the Latin and Greek models could be written, and the fortress of high intellectual standards could thus be held against the onslaught of the sciences, technology, and other useful subjects.

The voices of those who saw modern languages as "useful" subjects went unheeded as had the suggestions of Ben Franklin and Thomas Jefferson in an earlier period. In the compromise with the classics, modern languages lost much of their modernity, while Latin ultimately lost in comparative enrollments. For several decades, modern languages claimed an ever-larger share of the growing high school enrollments as the following statistics indicate.

■1

FOREIGN LANGUAGE ENROLLMENT TRENDS PRIOR TO WORLD WAR I

| Year | Total enrollment | Latin | Modern language | | | |
			Total	French	German	Spanish
1890	202,963	34.7%	16.3%	5.8%	10.5%	
1895	350,099	43.9	17.9	6.5	11.4	
1900	519,251	50.6	22.1	7.8	14.3	
1905	679,702	50.2	29.3	9.1	20.2	
1910	915,061	49.0	34.3	9.9	23.7	0.7%
1915	1,328,984	37.3	35.9	8.8	24.4	2.7

Source: William R. Parker. The National Interest and Foreign Languages, *3rd ed., Washington, D.C., GPO, U.S. Deparment of State Publication 7324, 1961, p. 85.*

While these enrollment increases are impressive, they tell only part of the story. Equally as important as a head count of high school students are the answers to the following questions:
1   At what age did the students begin their study of the foreign language?
2   How long did students continue the study of the language in an uninterrupted sequence?
3   What was the total number of exposure hours to the language?
4   How well coordinated were the programs from year to year?
5   What methods were being used?
6   How well prepared were the foreign language teachers?

Reports and surveys from this era provide some of the answers to these questions. Considerable progress was made, for example, toward establishing an earlier beginning and a longer sequence of foreign language study. Tens of thousands of grade school youngsters were studying foreign languages in the early part of this century in Toledo, New York City, Milwaukee, Buffalo, Cincinnati, San Francisco, and many other cities and towns.[11] Some of the elementary programs became well established, while others were dropped after a few years of experimentation. Buffalo, for example, was unable to cope with the problem of setting up a sequential course of study.

. . . instruction in the elementary schools was poorly administered and badly given. It consisted mainly of reading a given pensum, without regard to control or teaching of vocabulary. Drill in pronunciation and speaking was haphazard, and a syllabus non-existent. After six years of this type of hit-or-miss instruction, the children took a uniform examination covering as much as might be achieved in an ordinary one-year high school course. . . . Of the 10,000 enrolled . . . fewer than 400 took an examination for advanced credit. As the report points out: "Measured by these results, nearly 10,000 pupils are taught by 67 teachers in 43 schools in order that approximately 400 may get what they would have been able to obtain under two or three teachers in one year of the high school course."[12]

Also during this period, a number of modern language teachers had begun to break with the grammar-reading-translation syndrome inherited from the alliance with the classics. The famous *Committee of Twelve Report* published in 1899 by the National Education Association, described some teaching techniques then in use, which sound strikingly like the methods that gained currency in the 1960s. Also mentioned in this report were the so-called "natural" and "direct" methods. These two approaches were doomed to limited success because of the fourth variable mentioned above—the teacher.

These methods require a native teacher with great energy, enthusiasm, and skill, almost exclusive use of the foreign language by teacher and pupil, much repetition, and an approach to the written word not by means of grammar but through oral-aural means. The method had many opponents from the start; they claimed that it is too time-consuming, that it encourages glibness, rather than depth, and treats adolescent and adult as though they were children.

In spite of the drawbacks of the system, it left its mark upon modern-language teaching in the United States once it had been developed into the Direct Method. Insofar as they stress the spoken word and the oral-aural approach and represent a reaction to the grammar translation method . . . the Natural and Direct method are similar. But the latter is less radical. It exploits the methodology of its predecessors eclectically, does not throw grammar overboard yet never teaches it for its own sake, and follows a well constructed plan of presentation.[13]

According to a contemporary observer, an ever-growing number of teachers had realized the need for a change of method.

[11] Zeydel, op cit., pp. 295–298.
[12] Ibid., p. 298.
[13] Ibid.

Even if reading the foreign language is held to be the legitimate aim of teaching, the need was felt by progressive teachers for a more active control of the vocabulary and grammar than could ever be won through the mere learning of rules, paradigms and translation. The Direct Method suggested that this could be accomplished by developing language material, usually a connected passage, by means of questions and answers. This procedure had long been utilized in the elementary schools, but now began to grow important in high school classes.[14]

A canvass of eighty high schools in 1894 also revealed a development favorable to the improvement of foreign language instruction. Two-thirds of them were offering a three- or four-year sequence of instruction in at least one foreign language.[15]

In an attempt to solve the problems of changing methods, lengthening sequences of study, and college entrance requirements, The National Educational Association Committee of Ten, in 1893, set down a series of recommendations. The ideal program was designated as four years of elementary school plus four years of high school. If the elementary program were not feasible, then four years of high school study were recommended for certain types of secondary schools, while two years were considered adequate for other types. This, according to Zeydel, was a fatal weakness of the *Committee of Ten Report:*

... in order not to interfere unduly with the courses in Latin and Greek, it provided for the notorious two-year modern foreign language course, which has been the bane of foreign-language teachers ever since. As the number of subjects and courses offered in the American high school increased by leaps and bounds in the next few generations, soon mounting to well over four hundred, and with the expansion of the high school into areas never dreamed of in the nineteenth century, less and less room remained in the curriculum for so "academic" a subject as modern languages. Hence the schedule makers, overlooking the fact that the two-year course was only an expedient suggested for exceptional cases, so as not to interfere unduly with the vested interests of Latin and Greek, treated the two-year course as the norm, which it was never meant to be. The final step, then, was to discredit the teachers of the languages because they could not accomplish in two years what requires at least four (in England, France, Germany, and almost any other country six or more).[16]

In all fairness it should be pointed out that the Committee actually went on record in favor of a four-year program for those students who stayed in high shcool through to graduation. In fact, the Committee went so far as to recommend that more than one language should be included in certain courses of study.[17] The "Classical" course called for four years of Latin *plus* three years of either French or German *plus* another two years of Greek. In the "Latin-Scientific" course the student was to study four years of Latin plus two years of either French or German. The "Modern

---

[14] Ibid., p. 298.
[15] Ibid., p. 296.
[16] Ibid., p. 295.
[17] Edward A. Krug (ed.), *Charles W. Eliot and Popular Education*, Classics in Education No. 8, New York, Teachers College, Columbia University, 1961, pp. 90–93.

Languages" course included French and German, one of which was to be studied for four years the other for three. Finally, in the "English" course, the student was to study Latin, German, or French for four full years.[18] Thus, in their intentions, the Committee of Ten was highly favorable to the study of foreign language, listing it among "the principal fields of knowledge" and suggesting that most youngsters could profit from such study.[19]

A report by the Committee of Twelve, which appeared in 1899, was perhaps more thorough and helpful than the *Committee of Ten Report*. However, the method of teaching advocated was the same: extensive reading-translation of graded texts and the study of grammatical principles with some oral drill work. It approved elementary foreign language study, but only if a truly competent teacher were available. On the whole, the *Committee of Twelve Report* exercised a great deal of influence on foreign language study in America.

Its proposals were widely discussed and adopted, and even the less well prepared teachers did their best to modify their soul-deadening translation procedures in accordance with it. For it also proved to be, and was used as, a handbook of method. . . . Most of the universities and colleges soon adopted the recommendations of the Committee, especially that of the establishment of three national grades of preparatory instruction, and in 1901, when the College Entrance Examination Board was set up, they were put into effect.[20]

Yet, despite its positive influence, this report also tended to fortify the notion that foreign language study should be a short-sequence affair. As Professor Zeydel expresses it: "So far as the pernicious over-emphasis of the two-year course and its gradual acceptance as the standard are concerned, this report was no better than its predecessor."[21] Yet, when everything is considered, the two reports *had* recommended the four-year course of study; and, in spite of their shortcomings, they had suggested alternative methods and had, in other ways, allowed sufficient breadth for positive development. One can only guess what their ultimate influence might have been had the climate for foreign language study remained favorable. But, unfortunately, the climate was about to change.

FROM U-BOAT TO SPUTNIK—THE BLEAK YEARS

On May 7, 1915, a German submarine sank the Lusitania off the coast of England. Among the 1198 people who went to the bottom with the British liner were 128 Americans. Submarine warfare and the subsequent American participation in World War I were to have a disastrous effect upon the study of foreign languages in the United States. In the years

[18] Ibid.
[19] Ibid., p. 89.
[20] Zeydel, op. cit., p. 296.
[21] Ibid.

9

between 1910 and 1915, as high as 80 percent of all high school students were in foreign languages; one-fourth in German. French was holding its own and Spanish was beginning to catch on. Latin still outnumbered all modern languages by a few percentage points. Then came 1917, and

... in the spring of that year, when the United States declared war on Germany, all hell broke loose. The propaganda, which had concentrated upon the German emperor, his army and submarines, with many allegations of atrocities, turned immediately, now that we were at war, against the language, its literature as a whole and, in some cases, even against its teachers who were confronted with the sweeping accusation of being "pro-German." Groups of vigilantes visited the libraries and removed German books; others came to the departmental offices in the universities and confiscated textbooks containing pictures of Emperor William II or equally "subversive" material....

State legislatures (twenty-two in number ...) and a score of cities vied with one another in forbidding the teaching of German in the public elementary and high schools, or even in prohibiting the speaking of German.[22]

But German did not suffer by itself. Like noncombatant passengers on a torpedoed ship, French and Latin went down with German. Forty years later, when the downward plunge finally ended, only Spanish had improved its percentage of enrollments over the year 1917. This was small consolation; it meant only that Spanish had won the largest share of a very small slice of pie. For in the mid 1950s, a little more than 20 percent of all students were now electing foreign languages as compared with 80 percent before World War I. Again, let the enrollments tell their own story.

■2

FOREIGN LANGUAGE ENROLLMENT TRENDS AFTER WORLD WAR I

| Year | Total enrollment | Latin | Modern language | | | |
			Total	French	German	Spanish
1915	1,328,984	37.3%	35.9%	8.8%	24.4%	2.7%
1922	2,230,000	27.5	27.4	15.5	.6	11.3
1928	3,354,473	22.0	25.2	14.0	1.8	9.4
1934	5,620,625	16.0	19.5	10.9	2.4	6.2
1949	5,399,452	7.8	13.7	4.7	.8	8.2
1954	6,582,300	6.9	14.2	5.6	.8	7.3

Source: William R. Parker, The National Interest and Foreign Languages, 3rd ed., Washington, D.C. G.P.O., U.S. Department of State Publication 7234, 1961, p. 86.

The zeal and energy with which Americans attacked the problems of World War I quickly turned sour when the fighting was over. Not only did this country reject the League of Nations; everything "foreign" was held

[22] Ibid., p. 298.

in contempt. Apparently the process of anglicizing the many disparate groups from non-English-speaking lands had not been completed satisfactorily. The norm for true-blue Americans had been stated in an old slogan: "To be Americanized is to be anglicized." And this meant speaking the "American language" with no trace of an accent. Certainly, the ability to use a foreign language of any kind was no very great or worthwhile accomplishment. A visiting evangelist at Peoria, Arizona summed up the prevailing attitude in a 1926 sermon: "If I had my way there would be no language taught in the United States except English, and any foreigner coming here would be immediately sent back if he could not speak our language. I am 100% American."[23] Vituperation was not limited to language and national background alone. Even entertainment had to be Americanized, if one can judge from an editorial in the New York *American Standard*, 1926.

The Metropolitan Opera House is the most thoroughly foreign institution in this country. Standing at the back of the house and surveying an operatic audience, one can scarcely find an Anglo-Saxon face. Jews and Italians predominate, with a liberal proportion of Germans, Slavs, and miscellaneous dregs of the Mediterranean and Levantine races. . . . Genuine Americans have no real feeling for it (Opera), and can neither produce operas nor act in them. To imagine George Washington, Benjamin Franklin, Thomas Jefferson, or any such representative American pay to witness the horrors and sensualities of grand opera is to imagine the impossible. . . .[24]

Students at the University of Arkansas were somewhat more tolerant of Germans and Slavs. In voting for "the world's greatest musician of all times," they assigned second place to Beethoven. Paderewski tied for third with Henry J. Tovey, Director of the Musical Department of Arkansas University. The title of the "world's greatest musician of all time" was awarded to Paul Whiteman.[25]

Some have blamed isolationism, super-Americanism, and anti-intellectualism for the decline in foreign language study. Whatever the causes, the decline took place. Not only did enrollments shrink, but elementary-school courses and advanced study programs vanished. Research in the 1920s showed that 83 percent of all high schools offered only two years of foreign language instruction.[26] To the language teachers of the day, one thing was clear: With so little exposure to language instruction, it was futile to attempt to teach students how to understand, read, write, and speak a foreign language. Or at least this was the conclusion reached by the most famous of a series of investigations conducted by grants from the Carnegie Corporation. Known as the "Coleman Report," this publication had a profound effect upon the teaching of

[23] Quoted by H. L. Mencken (ed.), *Americana 1926*, New York, Knopf, 1926, p. 9.
[24] Ibid., p. 147.
[25] Ibid., pp. 11–12.
[26] William R. Parker, *The National Interest and Foreign Languages*, p. 87.

foreign languages. According to Parker, ". . . it is a fact that from 1929 until World War II most modern language instruction in American schools and colleges stressed the 'reading aim' and produced a generation largely unable to speak French, German, or Spanish, or even to read a newspaper or magazine article in these languages beyond the ability of a fifth-grade pupil in English.[27]

Between the two world wars the climate grew increasingly inhospitable to foreign language study. The causes for the antilanguage trend are difficult to trace and harder to prove. Among the reasons often cited are antiintellectualism in American society, utilitarianism in education, isolationism in politics, and the immigrant's tendency to reject the culture of the "old country" and (in the second generation) the non-English language of the parents. Also, the rather narrow objectives and limited methodology employed by many foreign language teachers of the period may have contributed greatly to the deterioration. Further, the absence of any strong, organized group representing the interests of the foreign language profession at the secondary level, as well as the resulting inability of many scattered and isolated language teachers to contend with a changing high school curriculum, may partly explain the downfall. But, whatever the causes, the decline continued even beyond World War II, reaching such catastrophic proportions by the 1950s that over half the high schools in America offered no modern language during the postwar decade. In these bleak years, foreign languages tended to be referred to as "peripheral" subjects or were simply ignored. As late as 1950, a book on secondary education contained the following statement:

It is difficult to justify languages for all youth. True, languages can help students nderstand various cultures. A great deal of instruction in language, however, is concentrated with reading and speaking skills, and in face of so many urgent needs, use of the time and effort necessary to master these skills is questionable. . . . The time saved might be used for study of the current social problems completely overlooked by the classical curriculum. . . . Actually, about the only valid justification the authors can find for inclusion of foreign languages in the high school curriculum is that of satisfying the intellectual curiosity of a few students who are interested in developing their linguistic interests and abilities.[28]

With the exception of a few notable programs, such as the "Cleveland Plan" in Ohio, elementary school foreign language and the teaching of listening and speaking skills went by the board after World War I. The few programs that remained were not sufficient to maintain continuity of development within the profession, and, as a result, a total rebuilding program was subsequently necessary. Although the actual reconstruction did not start in earnest until the late 1950s, the foundations for it were laid well before America's involvement in World War II.

[27] Ibid., p. 87.
[28] J. G. Saylor, *Secondary Education: Basic Principles and Practices*, 1950 quoted by Parker, op. cit., p. 90.

Few laymen and a surprisingly small number of language teachers have a clear conception of either the origin or nature of the misnamed "Army Method." When Pearl Harbor suddenly wrenched America loose from its isolationism, and the need for foreign languages became associated with the war effort, a group of Army officers—so it seemed—had put their heads together and had devised a miraculous way of converting monolingual GIs into fluent speakers of Japanese, Chinese, Russian, German, or any other language for which there was a need. What is more, these skills could be acquired with only nine months of instruction! By contrast, the graduates of our schools and colleges, after two to six years of study, could only stammer hesitantly in language that was loaded with incorrect forms and antiquated vocabulary. A professor of languages visiting abroad once received a dubious compliment: "You speak very well," he was told, "for a character out of a nineteenth-century novel." The story is also told of an American professor of French who refused to speak that language with a visiting French woman. When she persisted in using her native tongue, the Professor is said to have replied testily, "Madame, I told you I *teach* French; I did not say that I *speak* French." It seemed clear that our schools and universities had failed to provide even the rudiments of genuine language learning. How was it, then, that boys from the corn belt could, in less than a year, be trained to interrogate prisoners, carry on espionage, and even successfully monitor low-fidelity radio transmissions in a foreign language?

The answer to this question can be summarized by describing four main characteristics of the Army Method:

Selection. The young men were selected on the basis of intelligence, aptitude, and willingness to participate in the program. In short, a group of bright young men with the proper attitudes could recieve special recognition for doing something they liked and come away with the feeling that they were serving their country in time of need in the process. Motivation could hardly have been better.

Time. The "nine months" of training was in reality a dawn-to-dark schedule of intensive study. If equated in terms of exposure hours, the time was more than equivalent to two years of high school plus four years of college.

Teaching conditions. Instruction was carried on in small groups by native or near-native instructors. The entire program was under the close surveillance of specially trained linguists who made adjustments in the program as it went along. Moreover, the language was used as the means of communication from breakfast to bedtime. A native "informant" was usually at hand to supply the correct expression when it was needed. Then too, the program was blessed with a liberal wartime budget, which allowed for the latest in instructional materials and facilities.

Well-defined objectives. Rapid and perfect comprehension of the spoken language plus the ability to speak with a good accent were the chief objectives of the program. Reading and writing were secondary in importance, and the literary and cultural objectives were largely replaced by an emphasis upon contemporary customs and the way-of-life of the people whose language was being studied. The college student had read poems by Villon or the prose of Cervantes. The military trainee learned to relate oral messages about gun emplacements, to convert miles into kilometers, or to eat holding his fork in the left hand.

It should be quite apparent to anyone that the course of instruction described above could not be applied directly and in toto to the college or high school program. Quite predictably, the first attempts to do so met with disappointment and frustrations. For more than a decade following the war, efforts were made to adapt the intensive Army Method to the nonintensive academic programs. By 1960, texts, tapes, and other audio-visual materials had been developed and were ready to market on a large scale. *Modern Spanish*, developed by the Modern Language Association, was the first major college text that was fully representative of the new American Method. The so-called "Audio-Lingual Materials" developed in Glastonbury, Connecticut with a federal grant from the U.S. Office of Education became the prototype for the new direction in secondary instruction. In the early 1960s, a commercial publisher acquired the rights to the materials and began publishing versions in French, German, Italian, Russian, and Spanish. Soon other publishers began producing their own audiolingual textbooks in the commonly taught modern languages. The more skeptical publishing houses made gestures in the direction of the new methodology by slightly revamping their old grammar-reading texts and providing tapes to accompany them. "Change comes slowly," ran the old adage, "it takes at least twenty years for a new educational idea to take hold once it has become widely known." But this time the adage did not hold true. Within three years, millions of students were being taught by one or the other of the new texts. More than $30,000,000 had been expended for 6,000 high school language laboratories. Tens of thousands of teachers had been run through a pedagogical version of the intensive military programs in the form of summer training institutes financed by the federal government. And where there had been only three states with foreign language supervisors in 1957, by 1964 the number had grown to 70 supervisors in 40 states, most of them sympathetic to the objectives of the American Method.[29] It seemed that a small group of Army officers had really started something big; or had they?

In plain truth, the main credit, as far as the military men are concerned, lay in their willingness to accept and apply a theory of linguistic analysis and language instruction that had lain dormant for several decades. Edward Sapir and Otto Jespersen had written books in 1923 that pointed the direction. C. C. Fries and a Frenchman, Joseph Vendryes, had also

[29] Frank Grittner, "The Influence of the State Foreign Language Supervisor upon Foreign Language Instruction in America," *Modern Language Journal 49* (February 1965), pp. 91–94.

done pioneer work later in the twenties, as had Leonard Bloomfield in the thirties, and Bernard Bloch and George Trager in the forties. However, the real catalytic agent behind the Army Method was the American Council of Learned Societies (ACLS). Even before the war, ACLS had put a number of linguists to work analyzing certain neglected foreign languages and developing methods for teaching them with the greatest efficiency. In addition to advocating longer exposure to the language, utilization of electronic equipment, use of native speakers, and emphasis upon speaking and listening skills, the ACLS theorists rejected the age-old practice of organizing language study around conventional Latinizing grammar. A new way of identifying points of grammar was suggested, and the points were to be learned functionally by drill in the foreign language rather than by analysis in English. It was these two aspects of the Army Method— the new linguistic analysis and the view of grammar as habit formation— that were to have an important influence in shaping the American Method.

For more than a decade after the war the ideas continued to incubate. The development of the wire recorder and then the tape recorder made it possible to store spoken-language material effectively and to reproduce the voices of native speakers inexpensively and with good fidelity. This appeared to solve one of the blocks to implementing the new ideas. Where the Army Method had called for expensive native informants to work with small groups of students, native voices could now be provided on tape at relatively low cost. The first full-fledged language laboratory was developed in 1947 at Louisiana State University. By 1957, 240 institutions of higher learning had some sort of language laboratory. (Significantly, there were only about 60 high school language laboratories in 1957, one year before the federal government had passed a law appropriating funds for the purchase of such equipment. Five years later, with federal aid, this number had exploded to 6,000.)

Many colleges and universities continued experimenting with the less technological applications of the new linguistic theory. Meanwhile, conditions outside the profession began to change in favor of modern languages. Well-known personalities such as Mrs. Roosevelt, General Eisenhower, and Mr. Dulles, as well as important people in business and education began to speak out in favor of language study. Within the Modern Language Association a well-organized group had already formulated the basic tenets of reform. By 1956, these rebels had written up specific proposals for turning their cause into a movement; all that was lacking was adequate support. Then, in 1957, the Russians shot their first Sputnik into orbit, and support for foreign language study was quick in coming. The bleak years, which had begun with advances in German submarine technology, came to an end with the development of Soviet rocketry. While most language people were unable to trace a clear cause-and-effect relationship between rocket thrust and foreign languages, they were happy that foreign languages had regained a place in the sun. In a few years, when the full implications of the new prosperity became apparent, many began to wonder if the enrollment gains had not been bought too dearly.

On the eve of the Sputnik launching, Imogene Montgomery, an Ohio foreign language teacher, had written an article for *The Bulletin* of the National Association of Secondary School Principals.[30] In her article she noted the continuing decline in high school foreign language enrollments, which, through the 1950s, she attributed to the failure on the part of language teachers to adjust to "a more pupil centered classroom" filled with young people who are "conditioned to personal consideration, to working in groups, and to pupil activity."[31] Thus, she argued, it has been difficult for languages to compete with the more attractive "activity subjects," such as band, photography, dramatics, art, and typing, which call for little homework and "allow for self-expression."[32]

She went on to list a series of recommended changes that she felt would make language programs more relevant in terms of student interests and career aspirations. With minor modifications, the article would have fit nicely into the professional journals and books of the 1970s, which contained many similar analyses and exhortations.[33] As it happened, however, Montgomery's advice turned out to be incompatible with what subsequently occurred. For, during the ensuing decade, the impetus for change came from external forces such as the infusion of federal money into language programs (see Chapter 2). An additional factor was the optimistic world outlook and the enthusiasm for international affairs which characterized the Eisenhower and Kennedy administrations. For various reasons, all of this led to a curriculum that was subject matter oriented and an instructional approach that was teacher centered. According to the catchwords of that era it was "in the national interest" for school boards to put foreign languages back into the local curriculum, to lengthen the sequence, and to purchase up-to-date instructional equipment and materials. In the latter case, public schools were paid to do so under the matching-grant provisions of the National Defense Education Act (NDEA). It was also in the national interest for teachers to be retrained. Accordingly, they too were paid to attend NDEA summer institute programs aimed at improving their language skills and adding to their knowledge in the area of linguistics, culture, and methodology.

The apparent results of all this were dramatic. During the NDEA years (between 1958 and 1968) enrollments in modern languages soared at the high school and university levels. (Elementary school programs and

---

[30] Imogene Montgomery, "A Good High School Program in French and Spanish," *The Bulletin* (September, 1957), pp. 61–66.

[31] Ibid., p. 61.

[32] Ibid., p. 62.

[33] See for example the Northeast Conference Reports for 1970, edited by Joseph Tursi, entitled *Foreign Languages and the "New" Student*, Middlebury, Vt.: Northeast Conference, and the Central States Proceedings for 1973, edited by Frank Grittner, entitled *Motivation and the Foreign Language Teacher*, Skokie, Ill., National Textbook Company, 1973.

16

Latin studies showed initial growth but faded rapidly after 1964.) By the late 1960s, even many of the smaller high schools had four-year programs in French, German, Russian, or Spanish. In larger school districts, sequences of four years or more soon became the "norm." Through the sixties, national high school enrollment figures served as the profession's Dow Jones report. And, as each state reported in each year, the market seemed consistently "bullish." As the following figures indicate, the decade of NDEA subsidies appeared to have produced the desired effect in grades 9 through 12.

MODERN FOREIGN LANGUAGE ENROLLMENTS IN THE NDEA YEARS

Year	High school population	Modern foreign language students	Percent enrolled
1958	7,906,679	1,300,882	16.5
1968	12,721,352	3,418,413	27.7

Source: See Childers, below.

However, the enrollment gains which, at first glance, appear quite impressive, became somewhat less so when classical languages are figured in.

MODERN AND CLASSICAL LANGUAGE ENROLLMENTS IN THE NDEA YEARS

Year	High school population	Modern and classical language students	Percent enrolled
1958	7,906,679	1,920,722	24.3
1968	12,721,352	3,890,924	30.6

Source: Wesley Childers, Foreign Language Offerings and Enrollments in Public Secondary Schools, Fall 1958, New York, Modern Language Association, 1969, pp. 1–16.
Julia G. Kant, "Foreign Language Offerings and Enrollments in Public Secondary Schools, Fall 1968," Foreign Language Annals (March 1970), pp. 400–476.

In fact, an analysis of enrollments in certain key years shows a rapid decline for Latin, the language that had been dominant through most of the history of the high school:

Year	Latin students Grades 9–12	Percent of high school population
1958	618,222	7.8
1968	371,977	2.9

Source: See Children and Kant, above.

The message is clear. The new-found prosperity of the modern languages was to a considerable extent realized at the expense of Latin.

17

And there were those who suggested that few new inroads into the public school population had actually been made. According to this view, the enrollment increases could quite plausibly be explained as nothing more than a reflection of the old elitism, which held that only college-bound students were considered to "need" a foreign language. Modern language enrollments had perhaps showed an increase chiefly because many more students were at the moment classifying themselves as "college preparatory," and they were—for various reasons—enrolling in modern rather than classical languages. Their reasons for choosing to study a language at all may have had more to do with the entrance and degree requirements in higher education than with the alleged values of the subject matter or the ostensible contributions of language to national defense. In the 1930s and 1940s, Kaulfers had spoken often of the high school teacher's dependence on the "subtle coercion" of the university requirements.[34]

And he had gone on to suggest that "certainly the high school teachers of foreign language deserve a more inspiring position in education than that of tagging doggedly at the heels of the university. . . ."[35] Kaulfers had recommended that an "integrated" language curriculum designed primarily for the terminal student should replace the college preparatory program, which, in his view, had resulted in a "very limited, stereotyped two-year course which could not possibly serve the varied life needs and interests of . . . young people. . . ."[36]

In the 1960s such advice seemed quaintly out of date, a reflection of the "soft pedogogy" of the defunct progressive education movement. And, in any case, a majority of high school students were now preparing for college and many were choosing the longer sequence of foreign language offerings. It seemed to have occurred to few people that the frequent result of this may have been (to paraphrase Kaulfers) a very limited, stereotyped four-year course which could not possibly serve the varied life needs and interests of young people. And the illogic of accepting federal funds to promote national defense and international understanding through language study, while at the same time causing the de facto elimination of half the future citizenry from such study, also seems to have eluded nearly everyone. Yet throughout the sixties a sort of "gentlemen's agreement" persisted among principals, teachers, counselors, parents, and students to the effect that foreign language study was only for the "chosen" who identified themselves as "college prep" students. In those schools where language enrollments remained low, the standard explanation by local personnel was usually something like: "Well, you know, this is a working class neighborhood; very few of our kids go on to college." In effect what this suggests is that language courses had inadvertently fallen into the curricular designation as an exclusive subject

[34] Walter V. Kaulfers, *Modern Languages for Modern Schools*, New York, McGraw-Hill, 1942, p. 347.
[35] Ibid., p. 348.
[36] Ibid., p. 359.

for middle-class students whose parents were affluent enough to send them to a four-year college. The idea that language courses could or should be modified to appeal to other groups seemed incomprehensible.

There were other problems in the sixties, of course, but they seemed solvable. For example, with rapidly expanding enrollments there was much talk about the "teacher shortage problem." Colleges and universities responded by creating or expanding foreign language education centers, which prepared teachers to staff elementary, secondary, and graduate school programs. Also, a reappearance of the so-called "articulation problem" was inevitable in the decentralized American school system (see page 9 of this book). As sequences lengthened, serious dislocations developed between junior high schools, senior high schools, and colleges. Teachers on the upper rungs of the sequence ladder began complaining that students from the "feeder" institutions did not fit into their established courses. And the usual countercharge from the "feeder" schools was that the established courses at the upper levels were inflexible and out of date. As the years wore on, the conflict too often went unresolved, and enrollments began to suffer.[37] The author has found senior high schools in which virtually no upperclassmen were enrolled in foreign languages. This attrition was often directly traceable to the inability of junior and senior high school teachers to work together in the establishment of a continuous level-to-level program. In other cases, the conflict was summarily resolved by the local school board, whose members in exasperation (and with an eye to economy) eliminated entire programs below grade nine. This despite the fact that research had indicated a direct positive correlation between years of study and student achievement.[38] Thus, although the profession had everything to gain from establishing a smooth transition from level to level, it was often unable to do so, despite the efforts of several influential groups and organizations to cope with the proplem on a regional or national scale.[39]

It should be noted that not all junior and senior high school articulation attempts ended in failure. Even as late as the mid-1970s, five- and six-year high school programs were flourishing in some school systems, which attested to the fact that the secondary school articulation gap was bridgeable. However, between high school and college the gap was more like a network of chasms. And these began to widen and deepen as the decade wore on, making bridging increasingly difficult.

---

[37] Fred M. Hechinger, "Mix-Up in Planning Language Courses Slows Pupils Here," *New York Times*, 8 October, 1963.

[38] John Carroll, "Foreign Language Proficiency Levels Attained by Language Majors Near Graduation from College," *Foreign Language Annals* 1 (December 1967), pp. 131–151.

[39] See for example *Foreign Language Articulation in California Schools and Colleges* published by the California State Department of Education. Also note publications and activities of the American Association of Teachers of German and the Indiana Language Program, University of Indiana at Bloomington.

THE GREAT SOCIETY, VIET NAM, AND WATERGATE—A TIME OF DISENCHANTMENT

In the early years of the Johnson Administration (during the mid-sixties), a new wave of "Great Society" federal legislation began to overshadow the National Defense Education Act. However, throughout the 1960s, NDEA managed to coexist with the much larger Elementary and Secondary Education Act (ESEA), which, unlike the NDEA matching grant Title III progam, offered 100 percent grants in aid to local schools. Title I of ESEA —by far the largest in terms of funding—was aimed at helping children whose academic achievement was low due to adverse socioeconomic conditions. ESEA Title II provided books and materials (but not equipment) for public and nonpublic school libraries. ESEA Title III was used to fund innovative and exemplary programs on a competitive basis. ESEA Title VII, added in 1968, was targeted toward various kinds of bilingual programs for children whose background included: (1) low academic achievement, (2) dominance in a language other than English, and (3) low family income. In short, the NDEA concept of promoting excellence in academic achievement was gradually superseded by the ESEA focus on remediation or special projects, most of which were unrelated to the existing foreign language programs. And, as the war in Viet Nam expanded, its spiraling costs tended to compete for federal subsidization with "low priority" educational programs. Inasmuch as the Johnson (and Nixon) administrations gave high priority chiefly to remedial education, the NDEA programs soon began to run into difficulties. The NDEA Summer Institute Program for foreign language teachers was first cut back, then transferred to the Education Professions Development Act (EPDA), and then, in 1970, eliminated entirely. The funding, which dealt with equipment and materials (NDEA Title III), lasted until 1976, but the money available was drastically reduced.

Meanwhile cataclysmic events on the domestic and international fronts began to be reflected in the behavior of many students at the high school and university levels. It would serve no purpose to recount the specific incidents of the period that were related to the escalation of the war in Southeast Asia, the massacres at home and abroad, the student riots, the ghetto riots, the assassinations, the Watergate proceedings, the resignation of the President and Vice-President, and the impeachment controversy. Suffice it to say, these events contributed to the various credibility gaps that developed between generations, racial groups, social class levels, and the sexes. To further complicate matters, the foreign language teacher shortage suddenly became a teacher surplus at all grade levels. Not only had teacher supply caught up to enrollment demand, but the birthrate had also begun to decline, thereby making the oversupply of teachers a long-term probability. And then, to make matters worse, increasing numbers of students began to opt out of foreign language study or to drop out of school and college altogether. Many of those who stayed in were reported to show a growing disinclination for sustained disciplined academic work.

In order to compete for the diminishing supply of reluctant students, the "overbuilt" universities began to reduce or eliminate foreign language entrance and degree requirements. This in turn had a negative effect on high school enrollments, particularly in those schools that had built their sole reason for being on the alleged needs of college-bound students. Inadvertently, foreign language study had often been presented in a negative light; that is, students were given the impression that it was something to be got rid of. High school students were told, in effect, that if they completed a certain amount of language in high school, they would have that much less to get rid of in college. However, when requirements were eliminated, the matter became much simpler; students could get rid of the language by opting out entirely. By 1970, a growing number of students were exercising that option. A Modern Language Association survey involving over half of all colleges and universities in the country indicated the following changes in enrollment between 1970 and 1972: French down 16.7 percent; German down 12.5 percent; Italian down 5.9 percent; Spanish down 5.4 percent; and Latin down 7.7 percent. The overall decline among all languages in higher education was 8.7 percent.[40] The same survey showed increases in Russian, ancient Greek, and some of the less commonly taught languages.[41] One of the few positive indicators with regard to commonly taught languages at the post–secondary school levels was in the junior colleges, where enrollments went up 3.8 percent between 1970 and 1972.[42]

There were reports from around the country of enrollement losses at the high school levels, but no accurate data were available. That fact in itself was indicative of the declining state of affairs, for it indicated that the Modern Language Association—which had conducted yearly enrollment surveys through the NDEA years—could no longer muster the funds for collecting and processing enrollment data.

Many people attributed the disaffection of students to the external social and economic factors mentioned above. But there were others who suggested that a good part of the problem was traceable to certain ill-conceived elements in the NDEA-inspired pedagogical movement. In her book, *The Psychologist and the Foreign Language Teacher*,[43] Wilga Rivers was the first to draw widespread attention to some of the practical shortcomings and theoretical question marks associated with the new, party line methodology. However, her concluding recommendations dealt with ways of modifying and improving the new pedagogical system rather than dismantling it.

Others—such as traditional and generative grammarians—were not so kind. They maintained that the reform movement was based on completely

[40] "1972 College Foreign Language Enrollment Survey," *MLA Newsletter* (May 1973), p. 1.
[41] Ibid.
[42] Ibid.
[43] Chicago, University of Chicago Press, 1964.

fallacious linguistic and psychological assumptions. Thus, by the late sixties, a methodological war had broken out between the "rationalist" Chomskyites, who attacked the reform movement, and the "empiricist" structuralists, who defended it.[44] Unfortunately for the empiricists, most of the empirical research efforts conducted during the sixties failed to support their pedagogical position. Various studies comparing traditional with audiolingual strategies at the high school and college levels had been inconclusive and the two-year *Pennsylvania Study* indicated that no better results were obtained with high school students taught by the newer methods, either with regard to skill development or improved attitudes.[45] Furthermore, the presence of a language laboratory appeared to make no difference in terms of observed student performance.[46] Perhaps most damaging of all to the reform movement was the finding that teacher performance on standardized test batteries failed to show a strong, positive correlation with student achievement.[47]

The teacher batteries were an expensive by-product of the NDEA-Summer Institute Program. The individual tests purported to measure teacher performance in the skills of listening, speaking, reading, and writing as well as their knowledge of linguistics, methodology, and culture. It was presumed that good scores in these seven areas would relate positively to good student performance in the classroom. Yet the findings did not so indicate. The investigators stated that "a comparison was made between the *MLA Teachers Proficiency Test* scores in all seven areas of eighty-nine French and German teachers and the mean of scores and mean class gain achieved by the students in their classes on two mid-year and six end-of-year achievement tests. No significant relationship was found to exist."[48]

In another section of the report the investigators noted, with apparent astonishment, that "classes taught by the *least* proficient French teachers often scored higher—sometimes markedly—on achievement tests. . . ."[49] What could have gone wrong? Both the student and teacher test batteries were certified as reliable and valid measurement devices, developed according to the best empirical measurement procedures. Why had all the results been so inconclusive? Could it be that the entire empirical approach to evaluation and testing was an expensive fraud? (There is, indeed, some evidence that a half century of this kind of allegedly empirical research in education has told us virtually nothing.)[50] Was one or the other of the instruments invalid? Had the investigators failed to take certain significant

---

[44] Karl C. Diller, *Generative Grammar, Structural Linguistics and Language Teaching* Rowley, Mass.: Newbury House, 1971.
[45] Philip D. Smith and Emanuel Berger, *An Assessment of Three Foreign Language Teaching Strategies Utilizing Three Language Laboratory Systems*, Washington, D.C., U.S. Office of Education, 1968.
[46] Ibid., pp. 130–131.
[47] Ibid.
[48] Ibid., p. 123.
[49] Ibid., p. 117.
[50] J. M. Stephens, *The Process of Schooling*, New York, Holt, Rinehart & Winston, 1967.

variables into account? Or, in the comparative study, were the differences between the various approaches basically so superficial that little difference in achievement could be expected? These and other questions were raised as students, teachers, and educators in general grew increasingly disenchanted with what was happening in the foreign language classroom.

Faced with the possibility of another serious setback, foreign language educators began to search for new solutions to the old problem of dwindling enrollments, student apathy, and lack of public and governmental support. The individualization movement was the first major attempt at reversing the trend away from language study (see Chapter 7). Still others saw the "systems approach"—a management system based on industrial models—as the answer.[51] There were also those who advocated humanization of the curriculum, career education, exploratory courses, noncredit courses, interdisciplinary approaches, literature in translation, student projects, and interest-centered minicourses as ways of drawing students back into foreign language study.[52] Yet by the mid-1970s none of these movements or curricular innovations had succeeded in pointing the way for the profession to go. However, in some ways the profession was in a better position to cope with the rapidly changing educational picture than it had been in the past. The American Council on the Teaching of Foreign Languages (ACTFL) had been founded in 1967. Although its membership had not grown at the anticipated rate, it did result in the establishment of a national pedagogical organization for drawing together the many disparate foreign language groups across the nation and for strengthening state level foreign language associations. Another sign of strength was the retention of the foreign language consultant positions in most state educational agencies. A few such positions were eliminated, but most of them survived the budget cuts of the early 1970s.[53] By 1973 there were signs that the enrollment picture in the secondary schools was stabilizing and, in some cases, even increasing.[54] Yet for most people in the profession, the seventies continued to be a time of uneasiness, a time of searching for guidelines to cope with an uncertain and ever-changing future.

BIBLIOGRAPHY

The books and articles listed below are suggested as a minimal bibliography for anyone with a serious interest in the history of foreign language education in America. The items are listed in the order in which they might most profitably be read.

[51] Bela H. Banathy, "The Design of Foreign Language Teacher Education," *Modern Language Journal*, 52 (December 1968), pp. 490–500.
[52] Joseph M. Vocolo, "What Went Wrong in Foreign Language Teaching in High School?" *Educational Leadership* (January 1974), pp. 294–297.
[53] The National Council of State Supervisors of Foreign Language (NCSSFL) showed a membership of 81 in 1968; the figure was 72 in 1973.
[54] Frank Grittner, "German Studies in the American High School: A Status Report," *Die Unterrichtspraxis* 6 (Fall 1973), pp. 1–8.

General

Parker, William R., "The National Interest and Foreign Language," 3rd ed., Washington, D.C., GPO, U.S. Department of State Publication 7324, 1961, 159 pp.

By Language

The following reports of surveys and studies in the teaching of modern foreign languages are available from the Materials Center, Modern Language Association, 62 Fifth Ave., New York, N.Y. 10011.

Leavitt, Sturgis E., H_{37} "The Teaching of Spanish in the United States"— A historical survey, 1961, 18 pp.

Watts, George B., H_{38} "The Teaching of French in the United States"— A historical survey, 1963, 165 pp.

Zeydel, Edwin H., H_{36} "The Teaching of German in the United States"— A historical survey, 1961, 23 pp.

The following books offer a more detailed view of pedagogical movements of the past:

Bayster-Collins, E. W., *Studies in Modern Language Teaching,* New York, Macmillan, 1930.

Handschin, Charles H., *Modern Language Teaching in the United States,* New York, Harcourt Brace Jovanovich, 1923.

Hesse, M. G., ed., *Approaches to Teaching Foreign Languages,* New York, American Elsevier Publishing Co., 1975.

Original source material from 22 commentators on foreign language teaching from Comenius to Berlitz.

Kaulfers, Walter V., *Modern Languages for Modern Schools,* New York, McGraw-Hill, 1942.

Kelly, Louis G., *25 Centuries of Language Teaching,* Rowley, Massachusetts: Newbury House, 1969.

A remarkably complete and impeccably documented compendium of pedagogical techniques in the field of foreign language instruction ranging from 500 B.C. to 1969. Kelly makes a good case for his thesis that language pedagogy is cyclical and that the basic corpus of ideas available to language teachers has not changed in 2000 years. Bandwagoneers are seen as unoriginal enthusiasts who "follow the successful innovators like sheep, accepting as received doctrine what is really a transitional stage."

■Why should Americans study a foreign language?

A discussion of foreign language teaching methods can make little sense if it is not accompanied by a clear statement of what the methods hope to accomplish. And the objectives of foreign language study, in turn, are closely related to the reasons for including the subject in the curriculum in the first place. The present-day proponents of foreign languages give reasons ranging from national survival to getting a better job. Entire books have been written listing in great detail the many advantages, both educational and practical, which come to the person who has studied a foreign language (see bibliography at the end of this chapter). While such lists provide valuable information regarding the current uses to which foreign languages are put, they do have several limitations. One of these is the tendency to give equal treatment to highly unequal items. For example, the need that PhD candidates have for a reading knowledge in a foreign language is given equal status with foreign language study for the general education of *all* children who are attending school, despite the fact that few persons out of every thousand in a given age group ever earn the doctorate.

In the interest of reorganizing the mountains of disproportionate facts into some meaningful pattern, this writer has attempted to identify the main reasons currently given for foreign language study in contrast with attitudes that have existed from the early beginnings of foreign language study in America, some of which are evident even today.

MENTAL DISCIPLINE AND GREAT BOOKS

From the more conservative classicists, the modern language profession inherited a tradition that might be summarized by the term "grim humanism." The word "grim" is used in reference to an attitude that characterizes the learning process as consisting necessarily of hard, unpleasant work. In many foreign language teachers this attitude is associated with a fierce devotion to literary and philosophical monuments of the past, especially those that have a high obscurity quotient. Naturally, the inclination toward literary content can exist separately from the predilection for subjecting students to hard labor. For example, there are those who believe in the laborious study of grammar for grammar's sake and there are others who believe in presenting literary masterpieces through pleasurable methods of instruction. The advocates of rigorous learning activity believe that mental dexterity is developed by such traditional language exercises as the memorization of rules, verb conjugations, and noun declensions and by other activities such as reconstructing sentences in the foreign language from English and translating sentences into English from the foreign language. In the pursuit of such exercises, the mental discipline advocate may look upon works of literature merely as convenient sources of material for parsing, decoding, and other forms of mental gymnastics. In this view, literature becomes merely a part of a long obstacle course through which raw *Homo sapiens* must be run in order to convert them into cultivated human beings. Thomas Huxley, in an essay on science and education, points up the absurdity of using difficulty for its own sake by applying the grim schoolmaster's language-teaching method to scientific content.

It is wonderful how close a parallel to classical training could be made out of that palaeontology to which I refer. In the first place I could get up an osteological primer so arid, so pedantic in its terminology, so altogether distasteful to the youthful mind, as to beat the recent famous production of the headmasters out of the field in all these excellences. Next, I could exercise my boys upon easy fossils, and bring out all their powers of memory and all their ingenuity in the application of my osteogrammatical rules to the interpretation, or construing, of these fragments. To those who had reached the higher classes, I might supply odd bones to be built up into animals, giving great honor and reward to him who succeeded in fabricating monsters most entirely in accordance with the rules. That would answer to verse-making and essay-writing in the dead languages.[1]

The great-books advocates from the older humanistic school will tend to focus more upon the literature and its content than upon the process of learning. This group tends to see the literary monuments as sources of truth and beauty; the foreign language itself must be learned only insofar as that learning is necessary to make these transcendent sources available to the student. As a rule, the emphasis is upon the "universal ideas," and this tends to place the language itself in a position of secondary importance. More often than not the student's exposure to the spoken language is passive, and the bulk of this active participation involves speaking or writing in English. All this gives rise to a seemingly logical question: If the chief activity of the student is to discuss the panhuman ideas in English, then would it not be better to bypass the foreign language entirely? An

[1] Edward A. Krug, *The Secondary School Curriculum*, New York, Harper & Row, 1960, p. 92.

enormous amount of time is lost in having the students laboriously produce their own inept translations from original texts. Why not have them instead read expertly translated versions of the classics, thereby enabling the students to cover more ground and leaving more time free for discussion?

MODERN HUMANISM AND ANTHROPOLOGY

The writings of Sapir and Whorf and the investigations of various cultural anthropologists have produced a new humanistic rationale for the study of languages. In essence, the Sapir-Whorf hypothesis asserts that (1) the native language determines how a person views the world and (2) the person is unaware of his or her mental entrapment if he or she remains monolingual. Thus Americans who grow up speaking only English are never conscious of how thoroughly their ability to think is circumscribed by the way their language compels them to structure their thoughts. Just as a deep-sea creature would be unaware of the nature of water because it has never experienced nonwater, monolingual Americans are unaware of the nature of English because they have had no significant contact with non-English. Their ethnocentric mind-set traps them into believing that English is the only reasonable way to express reality. Actually, English, like all languages, causes distortions by the way it structures expression. For example, the language of the Hopi Indians is more accurate than English in expressing certain natural processes. In English we say,

John is dying.

The Hopi language, by contrast, would say something like,

Dying is taking place in John.

The Hopi more accurately expresses the fact that John is really not doing anything, whereas the Anglo-American, by the very nature of how his language symbolizes actions in the "real" world, is forced to attribute agent power to John even though John is passively, and perhaps unwillingly, in the process of dying.

From the Sapir-Whorf hypothesis it follows that the study of a second language is essential to understanding what language is all about. The American student can develop a clearer understanding of his native English by comparing it with a non-English communication system. But this understanding can come only by means of a thorough immersion in the language of a non-Anglo-Saxon culture. A sampling of "general language" will not suffice—language is far too complex to be profitably sampled. American students must be taught to communicate through direct immersion in a totally new system of oral and written symbols. They must to some degree become conversant in the mother tongue of some non-Anglo-American culture.

Just how powerful this attachment to the mother tongue is was

27

demonstrated by the riots in India during the winter of 1965, when Prime Minister Shastri signed a parliamentary decree making Hindi the sole official language. According to newspaper reports at the time, Tamil-Bengali-speaking citizens reacted with such violence that more than seventy people were killed in the rioting and over two million dollars worth of property was destroyed. In an effort to calm the angry mobs, Shastri proposed elevating English to the status of an associate language. This only served to infuriate the one group that had theretofore remained calm. The 40 percent of India that speaks Hindi was incensed at the prospect of elevating an alien tongue to such a position of recognition. They began rioting, burning English books, and effacing signs written in English. Similar incidents have occurred in Europe, Africa, and the Middle East over the imposing of a nonnative language on a large segment of a country's population. It would seem from all this that the hope to establish any one language as a universal tongue is highly visionary.

Among those who cite the anthropological value of language study are people from a variety of disciplines. William R. Parker, whose background is English, comments as follows: "Learning a foreign language is an educational experience. By acquiring even a limited skill, which may or may not be retained, the individual finds himself personally breaking the barriers of a single speech and a single culture—experiencing another culture at first-hand in the symbols through which it expresses its realities."[2]

Marshall J. Walker, a professor of physics, says: "The main value to education of the study of a foreign language lies in its unique contribution to an understanding of the principles of the communication of thought. A basic aim of all serious education is a comprehension of the distinction between a concept and the words, or symbols, used to describe the concept. The person with only one language is at a hopeless disadvantage in such a task."[3]

The author, G. H. Fisher, puts it more strongly: "The American will never really penetrate the thinking of people in a new country until he has first penetrated the language which carries, reflects, and molds the thoughts and ideas of that people."[4]

While the anthropological value of languages provided a new impetus for foreign language study, it also placed heavy demands on the profession to change its ways. The exclusive focus on belles lettres was no longer defensible, particularly in the beginning courses. Neither could the preoccupation with the written word be defended nor the heavy emphasis on the disinterment of the dear dead past. The foreign language profession was called upon to relate itself to the present; to teach the language as spoken by people now living and within a contemporary cultural context. Moliere, Cervantes, and Goethe must share the stage with classified newspaper ads,

[2] William R. Parker, *The National Interest and Foreign Languages*, 3rd ed., Department of State Publication 7324, 1961, p. 8.
[3] Ibid.
[4] Ibid.

motion pictures of the marketplace, and taped discussions about the every-day life of ordinary people. And, since all of this was to be done in the target language, the profession was given a powerful reason for existing.

The change to a modern humanistic outlook did not come overnight. In fact, the old-line humanists are still entrenched in all levels of instruction. However, the new, or modern, humanism spread rapidly, and by the mid-sixties had come to dominate the secondary school curriculum.[5]

The word "modern" as it is used here refers to a willingness to change, to experiment, and to accept contemporary material along with the tried-and-true documents of the past. In fact, the modern humanist does not limit foreign language content to written documents alone; material reproduced on films, tapes, and records can also serve. But the insistence upon the fullest possible cultivation of human abilities—particularly the intellectual—remains an end in itself. Foreign language study is seen as an indispensable link in the chain of human intellectual development. In an article entitled "Foreign Languages and the Humanities," one writer states that the humanist's task is

. . . to break down [students'] narrow horizons and make them partake of the existence of the world. It is their task, also, to struggle against the invasion of technology and machines, by reminding them that man's ideal does not consist solely in enslaving matter for his needs but also to multiply his powers of life, through the acquisition of a better nourished thought, a more delicate sensibility, and a more fraternal soul. . . . It is their task to make others understand that humanity is not limited to a single moment—the present—nor to a single nation—however powerful it might be; rather, it is while preserving both the memory and the cult of the desperate shouts, songs of love, hymns of hope, epics, comedies, dramas, which the most divine of the sons of men, geniuses, have scattered in space and time.[6]

Foreign language teachers and professors have historically belonged to one humanist camp or the other. The more forward-looking humanists have no objection to their students using their command of language to discuss business, ballet, films, or philosophy but they would be aghast at a

---

[5] Compare this attitude with the following ideas expressed in Germany in the 1950s, which Friedrich Schubel refers to in his widely read book *Methodik des Englisch-unterrichts*, Verlag Moritz Diesterweg, 1960, pp. xi ff. *"Es liegt sogar im Sinne des von A. Bohlen kürzlich dargestellten 'modernen Humanismus,' bei der notwendigen Vor-bereitung 'auf das Leben der Gegenwart' auch die 'Vermittlung von Kenntnissen und Fertigkeiten, ohne die der gebildete Mensch das Dasein unserer Zeit nicht zu meistern vermag,' zu pflegen."* And also, *"Will man an den echten Geist eines fremden Volkes herangelangen, so kann das nur durch dessen unmittelbarsten Ausdruck—die Sprache—geschehen."* (Schubel here alludes to A. Bohlen's "Modern Humanism," which asserts that in preparing students to live in the present, certain skills and areas of knowledge must be mastered. Without these, the educated man will not be able to cope with the contemporary world. The second quotation states that, if one wishes to make contact with the genuine nature of a foreign people, such contact can only be made through the most direct expression of that nature; that is, through the language.)

[6] Georges J. Joyaux, "Foreign Languages and the Humanities," *Modern Language Journal* 49 (February 1965), p. 105.

university course called "ballet French," "cinema German," or "business Spanish." A properly taught language course will have equipped students with (1) a fundamental control of the language and (2) a flexibility of mind that will enable them to expand and apply their knowledge to meet the demands of any situation that might arise.

UTILITARIAN OBJECTIVES

Anyone who views education *primarily* as a way to get a better job or to improve his social standing or to solve economic or social problems has a nonhumanistic outlook. The same might be said of politicians who see education as a cure-all for unemployment; admirals who see its purpose in terms of producing better crews for atomic submarines; government officials who relate foreign language learning to the improvement of international understanding; or anyone who cites some utilitarian goal or national need, however noble, as the reason for learning something. Through most of its history, the foreign language community kept the nonhumanists on the outside. A story is told about a businessman who questioned a classical scholar regarding the practical value of Latin. "Thank God it has no value," the professor replied.

The time arrived, however, when the language people themselves—perhaps out of self defense—took up the habit of ascribing utilitarian values to the learning of a language. By the middle of the twentieth century —when language study had reached an all-time low—the modern language community showed itself willing to compromise with those who hold the nonhumanistic viewpoint. The new orientation is indicated by the title of a bulletin prepared by William Riley Parker called *The National Interest and Foreign Languages*. Mr. Parker explains that "What really happened was this. Beginning in 1952 the profession of modern foreign language teachers in the United States organized itself to discover and to meet its new responsibilities to American Society, and this constructive move coincided, providentially, with a growing public awareness that language study was being tragically neglected in American Education."[7] Mr. Parker, himself a Milton scholar, is able to reconcile the humanistic tradition with the national interest. "What is now most needed," he writes, "is an American Objective in language study; a goal or goals clearly seen, and the costs seen just as clearly, with the national interest put firmly above the vested interests of either foreign language teachers or their competition in our thousands of schools and colleges."[8]

The Modern Language Association, whose membership consists largely of college and university professors of English and modern foreign languages, also exhibited a wide tolerance for nonhumanistic objectives

[7] Parker, op. cit, p. 8.
[8] Ibid., p. 9.

30

when it pushed for the inclusion of foreign languages in the National Defense Education Act of 1958. The first Russian Sputniks had been launched in October and November of the previous year. This event led to widespread criticism of America's schools and focused public attention upon education in Russia and America. Comparisons were drawn in such a way as to show that schools in the United States were far behind in the teaching of mathematics, science, and modern foreign languages. Almost at once, Congress began working on a law that would provide federal funds to stimulate the improvement of these areas.

On September 2, 1958, President Eisenhower signed the National Defense Education Act into law. With full approval of the leaders of the foreign language community, America launched a foreign language improvement program backed by tens of millions of dollars. There was nothing new in the principle of having the federal government supply money in support of schools, colleges, or individuals. The government in Washington has been a major influence in shaping local education from the very beginning.

Most of the states were first organized as territories in all of which Congress provided for public school systems. Thus the majority of our state school systems were initiated by the federal government. Starting in 1785 with grants of federal land for public education in the Northwest Territory, the land grant program has since then aided all levels of education in the states and Alaska by federal grants.[9]

The first aid was in the form of land grants for the general support of education. Subsequent aid was usually earmarked for special purposes or for special subject areas. The Morrill Act (1862) was directed largely at state agricultural and mechanical colleges. Later Acts reveal a similar concern for practical education: agricultural experiment stations (1887); resident instruction in land grant colleges (1890); agricultural extension service (1917); vocational rehabilitation (1920); school lunch program (1946). In addition, billions of dollars have been expended to individuals and educational research. The best-known personal aid program was Public Law 346, popularly referred to as the "GI Bill of Rights."

Yet there was something novel about the National Defense Education Act (NDEA). Previous school aids had been largely directed at utilitarian subjects or at practical matters such as school lunch. First came foreign languages, mathematics, and science; later, English, reading, history, civics, economics, and geography were added. The implication behind the Act is that improvement of instruction in the eight areas is in the national interest. Thus, by legislative action, a new reason why Americans should study foreign languages was created. The new "American objective" which (as Parker expressed it) puts "the national interest . . . firmly above" other considerations was widely publicized in language gatherings and in post-Sputnik publications. Within a few years, entirely new sets of objectives in

9 Hollis P. Allen, *The Federal Government and Education*, New York, McGraw-Hill, 1950, p. 3.

foreign language learning had found their way into curriculum guides across the nation. And, if we were to have a new American objective, clearly a new American method was called for to fit the objective. A brief survey of the chief reasons currently given for studying a foreign language will help to illustrate the new attitudes that have shaped the new American Method.

NATIONAL DEFENSE

At the opposite end of a value scale from the humanistic ideal of developing the intellect, lies the very specific goal of physically destroying the human body. Yet, to a certain extent, this was one of the purposes of the much-publicized Army Specialized Training Program (ASTP) during World War II. Specialists were needed to monitor enemy broadcasts, interrogate prisoners, and otherwise obtain information that could be used to shoot down aircraft, sink submarines, and drop bombs and artillery shells on infantrymen with maximum accuracy. Present-day Americans engaged in espionage and brushfire wars still have need of such skills, although the number of such specialists needed is relatively small. The modern concept of foreign languages for national defense has been broadened to include all contacts that Americans might have with any foreigner either in his or her country or in ours. The late Secretary of State, John Foster Dulles, expressed it as follows:

Each of you has a task in foreign policy. Foreign policy isn't just something that is conducted by secretaries of state and by ambassadors in different parts of the world; every one of you has got a part in making a successful foreign policy for the United States, because whether or not we peacefully succeed will largely depend upon the demonstration you make as to the value and productivity of liberty. . . . The heart of a successful foreign policy is our national conduct and example, and that is a matter for every individual and not just the diplomats.[10]

Others relate foreign language and national defense to the poor impression made by monolingual employees of the federal government, particularly in critical positions such as the Diplomatic Corps and Foreign Service Offices. A best-selling novel, *The Ugly American,* emphasized this theme throughout. To document their case, the authors included a "Factual Epilogue" in which they cited examples of American linguistic ineptitude. They summarize the case with the statement, "Think for a moment what it costs us whenever an American representative demands that the native speak English or not be heard. The Russians make no such mistake. . . ."[11] The authors also quote John Foster Dulles: "Interpreters are no substitute. It is not possible to understand what is in the minds of

[10] Parker, op. cit., p. 68.
[11] William Lederer and Eugene Burdick, *The Ugly American*, New York, Fawcett, 1958, pp. 232–233.

other people without understanding their language, and without understanding their language it is impossible to be sure that they understand what is on our minds." The enormous danger of failing to communicate in the modern world is dramatically illustrated by the circumstances surrounding the bombing of Hiroshima. There is evidence that the first atom bomb might never have been dropped if a Japanese translator had not erred in the translation of one word. The word *mokusatsu*, used by the Japanese cabinet in their reply to the Potsdam surrender ultimatum, was rendered "ignore," rather than, correctly, "withholding comment pending decision." Thinking the Japanese had rejected the ultimatum, the Allies went ahead with the nuclear bombardment.[12]

Foreign language courses aimed at fulfilling the "national needs" outlined above have a very large task to accomplish. For they imply the ability to comprehend rapid native speech even under adverse listening conditions, to speak the language skillfully without committing social or cultural blunders, to write the language, and to read it. Further, all this must be done with full awareness of the fine nuances of meaning carried by utterances, gestures, tone of voice, or selection of vocabulary. Clearly, all this will not be accomplished in the typical high school course, but under satisfactory conditions, a good start can be made. As an absolute minimum, the early work in foreign languages should not tend to inhibit learning of the language at a later date if national defense is the primary objective of language study. Such "later date" foreign language courses for federal employees is a large-scale enterprise.

More than 40 languages, including those generally offered in the Nation's schools, are being taught intensively in Government training programs. An interagency committee of language and area specialists. . . . listed 106 different languages needed in Government over a 5-year period by people with competence in other fields. That committee's personnel estimates have been found to be much lower than the actual needs. For example, the Army annually requires 3,000 specialists in various languages; the Air Force 1,500.[13]

INTERNATIONAL UNDERSTANDING

There are many who object to the identification of foreign language learning with making (or preventing) war. Harold Taylor, former President of Sarah Lawrence College, objects to a policy "which deliberately assumes that education is an instrument of national policy." He recommends, instead,

. . . a return to the concern for communication with other people in the use of foreign languages in order to break through to other cultures, to penetrate the consciousness of humanity at large, and to bring the world closer together rather

[12] Lincoln Barnett, *The Treasure of Our Tongue*, New York, Knopf, 1964, p. 292.
[13] Marjorie Johnston, "Language Needs in Government," *School Life*, Official Journal of the Office of Education (April 1957), p. 14.

than to devise educational means through which one can add language study to the list of techniques of defense. In place of the ideals of military security I suggest the ideal of the Peace Corps, in which the study of foreign languages has a social and moral purpose.[14]

The purpose given here is nobler, but it is still essentially utilitarian. If the goal of language learning is to understand people from another culture, who speaks a different language, the skills needed are essentially the same whether you are trying to destroy them or get along with them.

FOREIGN LANGUAGE AND BUSINESS

Inasmuch as the dollar value of American exports is greater than the total value of imports, a case could probably be made for maintaining the economic well-being of the nation through better foreign language programs. The usual approach here, however, is to appeal to personal vocational interests rather than the national economic interest. In a book called *Foreign Language Careers*, Theodore Huebner discusses the many hundreds of job opportunities for those with language skill. The $35 billion export-import business is only one of the many fields of opportunity mentioned. Another section of the book contains an alphabetical listing and discussion of twenty-two vocations in which a knowledge of foreign language is useful. Included in the list are airlines, advertising, hotel service, librarians, missionaries, scientific research, travel, and tourism.[15]

Dr. Roeming, editor of the *Modern Language Journal*, summarizes the vocational application of foreign language study as follows:

. . . to be a member of an export department of an industry a girl must at least be a good secretary, with skills in typing and shorthand; as for a man, he must be trained in business administration unless he wants to be an ordinary clerk. An airline stewardess must first have the qualities to make her one, with or without language; at one time it was a requirement that she have nurses' training. A foreign sales representative must be a salesman, that is quite simple and obvious. Everywhere one turns the answer is consistently the same. A primary vocational skill may be enhanced by competence in a foreign language, but the latter is never the primary skill sought by the employer.[16]

The humanists have traditionally regarded foreign language training for specific practical purposes as appropriate only for vocational schools, or else they have held that such training should be paid for by the individual or his employer. The secondary schools, following the example of higher education, have also avoided vocational foreign language courses. The resulting vacuum has been filled by governmental institutes and private

[14] *Modern Language Abstracts*, 15 (November 1964), abstract 801, p. 14.
[15] Theodore Huebner, *Opportunities in Foreign Language Careers*, New York, Universal Publishing and Distributing Corp., 1964.
[16] Robert F. Roeming, "Traditional," *Modern Language Journal* 48 (February 1964), p. 99.

enterprises of various sorts. A multimillion dollar business has grown up around the latter type of activity. The Berlitz Schools alone are said to gross $8,000,000 yearly.[17] There is some indication, however, that certain elements within the business community want a larger percentage of their employees to come equipped with at least minimal language skill. A subcommittee report at the September, 1963, White House Conference on Export Expansion made this the first of its five recommendations: "The Committee recommends that teaching of foreign languages in the public schools be started at the earliest practical age and that schools of business encourage proficiency in at least one foreign language."[18]

Despite such statements of support over the years, there is little evidence that career needs (real or imagined) have ever played a significant role in shaping the language curriculum or the instructional process in most American schools. In fact, the historical pattern in England and America has been to remain aloof from the whole question of languages and careers. This is in sharp contrast to practices in certain non-English-speaking countries.

In the nineteenth century, the industrial revolution in Europe gave considerable impetus to the growth of commerce and travel among people of different languages. However, the value of language study in relationship to international commerce was perceived differently by the various European commercial powers. According to Handschin, England "deemed it unnecessary to make concessions to any other linguistic tradition; so the system of teaching modern foreign languages in England remained backward until near the end of the century."[19] France and Germany, on the other hand, put great emphasis upon communication with foreign peoples. In fact, Germany was one of the first modern nations to deal adequately with the teaching of foreign languages for cultural and commercial purposes. By the end of the nineteenth century, German entrepreneurs were selling goods in many countries, "using always the language of the country itself as the means of communication."[20] This practice has been suggested as an important factor in Germany's phenomenal commercial growth prior to 1914 and its rapid recovery of foreign markets after World War II. Also, the acceptance of language study as a valuable cultural and intellectual asset (as well as a commercially useful tool) would explain why foreign languages have been so widely implemented as required subjects in German schools and universities. This acceptance carried with it a commitment on the part of many German methodologists to teaching listening and speaking as well as reading and writing skills. For several decades preceding World War I, American foreign language teachers were strongly

[17] Edwin H. Zeydel, "The Teaching of German in the United States from Colonial Times to the Present," *The German Quarterly* 37 (September 1964), p. 359.
[18] Donald Walsh, "Foreign Language Program Notes," *Newsletter of the Modern Foreign Language Association* (Summer 1964), p. 3.
[19] Charles H. Handschin, *Modern Language Teaching*, New York, Harcourt Brace Jovanovich, 1940, p. 7.
[20] Ibid.

influenced by those German (and French) pedogogical theories that strongly emphasized direct acquisition of all language skills. However, in the postwar era American educators tended to move away from the "fourfold aim of skill development" in favor of exclusive attention to reading skill development. With regard to career applications of foreign language skills "practical businessmen" in America moved toward the British view that a speaking knowledge was not needed for trading purposes because of the belief that "it is generally possible to use English in carrying on business with foreign countries."[21] To some degree the statement was true up until the mid-1960s. International businessmen reported that government officials in many countries were often proud to have their name on trade and manufacturing agreements written in English. However, in the mid-sixties this began to change. A wave of nationalism led to a situation in which the local officials said, in effect, "If you want to deal with us, do it in our language."[22] Felix Toussaint, a businessman with the multinational Williams Company, has noted that foreign languages are of vital importance in carrying on their business in such varied areas as pipeline construction, chemical fertilizer sales, foods production, auto parts distribution, and many other areas of commerce across the world. Two solutions to the problem of non-English communication involved the use of company interpreters and written translations prepared through contracted services with large translation companies. However, these options often produced highly unsatisfactory results due to the specialized nature of the business terminology.[23] Toussaint saw as a preferred solution "the development of a staff of executives, engineers and other specialists who are fluent in languages." Unfortunately, in his experience, "crash" foreign language courses for such specialists usually did not do the job. In Toussaint's opinion, what is required for the 1980s and beyond is "to bring America out of its linguistic isolationism." He summarized the problem and its solution as follows:

American business, or at least a large number of American businesses, are involved in international business operations. In the present state of renewed national awareness of peoples throughout the world, American business, wanting to preserve or develop its position in the global market place, is attaching more and more importance to foreign languages, and is looking to our educators for a helping hand.

There will always be a place for the translator and the interpreter, and it is definitely one aspect the foreign-language teacher should be aware of. But it will only be fair for the teacher, while guiding his students toward such a career—if that is their choice and inclination—to make sure that they are fully aware of the limitations that are inherent to such a career.

We, in the business world, see a much-higher-level requirement in modern

[21] Ibid., p. 60.
[22] Felix J. Toussaint in an unpublished address given at the Fourth General Session of the Central States Conference on the Teaching of Foreign Languages, Milwaukee, Wis., 20 April 1974, p. 1.
[23] Ibid.

international business transactions for the multi-lingual executive—be he an engineer, business manager, or the like—who, in his own right, is valuable to international business as a specialist in his field, but who becomes the more valuable the more languages he speaks.

Such desired polyglotism would, I believe, have better chances of flourishing if we made a long-term commitment to develop conditions under which it would have the best chances for growth. Learning from those West-European countries where such polyglotism is quite common, we would conclude that our constant efforts should be directed, first, to making bilingualism in our education the norm, not the option; and second, to gradually but unrelentingly lower the age at which our children are exposed to a second language.[24]

In a similar vein, *The Wall Street Journal* reported on a number of business disasters in various foreign enterprises that were traceable directly to the foreign language ineptitude of Americans.[25] The existence of such problems, along with pressures from business competitors in countries like Germany and Japan (where language instruction is taken more seriously), has produced a "boom in corporate business at language schools across the country."[26] For example, Berlitz Schools report that language training for corporate executives has risen from a negligible level 20 years ago to make up well over half its present business. American University reports that corporate requests for language training have increased tenfold in two years. The Inlingua Schools of Languages, which was formed in 1967, had developed 130 branches by 1973. Representatives of this company noted that the cost of bringing a businessman and his wife to fluency in a second language averaged about $3,000. However, the *Journal* noted that this was often a small price to pay. Lack of knowledge of foreign languages and cultures had often produced business losses far in excess of any possible training costs. In one instance, an American aerospace company lost more than $500,000 when it was forced to close a project because none of its technicians could communicate with people in the target culture. As the *Journal* expressed it, "It was only after that debacle that the company sought language training.[27]

THE CAREER EDUCATION MOVEMENT
AND FOREIGN LANGUAGE EDUCATION

In the early 1970s, an ill-defined, but much talked-about, educational movement called "career education" began to receive increased attention in professional journals. It had the endorsement of President Nixon, Sidney Marland (then Commissioner of Education), and a number of prominent educators including a few in the foreign language field. What it did *not* have behind it was the kind of massive funding that had propelled

[24] Ibid., pp. 2–3.
[25] Michael Wines, "As More Companies Send Men to Foreign Lands, Language Schools Thrive—and Help Solve Problems," *The Wall Street Journal* 20 August 1973, p. 20.
[26] Ibid.
[27] Ibid.

into prominence and had sustained other programs emanating from the U.S. Office of Education. Nevertheless, its goals were ambitious. It was supposed to become an integral part of the curriculum in kindergarten through college and beyond. It was to touch teachers in all disciplines, which, presumably, meant everyone teaching anything to anyone anywhere.[28]

According to one of its leading proponents, "The basic rationale for career education is found in the need to restore the work ethic as a viable and effective force in American society."[29] The need to do this was substantiated by the claim that, while we were losing the work ethic, Russia and China had found it and were, therefore, threatening to catch up to the United States as the leading world power. This was accompanied by the remarkable statement that the loss of the work ethnic had led to the decline and/or fall of such varied civilizations as Persia, Egypt, Greece, Rome, Spain, Portugal, France, and England! It was further noted that "there is no reason to believe that the United States of America is exempt from this historical pattern."[30]

Thus, foreign language teachers were to share with teachers in other disciplines the responsibility for imbuing all young people (not merely a college-bound minority) with a respect for all kinds of labor. In addition, teachers were to be responsible for helping young people to identify "clusters" of occupations for which foreign languages would be useful. A further goal was to help students to know themselves better so that they could make reasonable choices with respect to their appropriate future role in the world of work.

Underlying the whole movement was an implicit belief in the need for extrinsic motivation. Relevance was defined in terms of enhancing occupational goals, which, in turn, means earning more money. Also, "knowing oneself" was not the Socratic goal of building a strong, autonomous personality. Its function was rather that of identifying and assessing one's skills so as to achieve optimum placement in a burgeoning technocracy. Thus students who had an interest in and a talent for languages could help themselves economically while at the same time helping their country keep ahead of Communist-bloc competitors in the political realm and Western competitors in the economic arena. As Florence Steiner expressed it, "Career education can provide the basis for reform that is needed in the teaching of foreign languages. We need citizens who can communicate with those of another culture."[31]

Steiner was one of the first within the language teaching profession to take a clear stand on career education and to suggest what it should involve. Among other things she suggested deemphasis of the traditional

[28] Kenneth B. Hoyt, *Career Education Resource Guide*, Morristown, N.J., General Learning Corporation, 1972, p. 6.
[29] Ibid., p. 2.
[30] Ibid.
[31] Florence Steiner, "Career Education and its Implications," *Modern Language Journal* 58 (April 1974), p. 189.

belletristic, college-oriented curriculum. In her opinion, this should be replaced by a "common content area" involving culture. "Such content must show how people live, function and exist within their own societies, and provide the student with insights into a way of life that differs from his own."[32]

Many people in the profession are unenthusiastic about career education as a primary motivational device. In fact, the late William Riley Parker stated that talk about vocational values "is quite irrelevant to discussions of whether or not foreign languages should be required as part of a BA program."[33] In an editorial in the *Modern Language Journal* the author suggested that career education could easily become a somewhat overrated bandwagon.[34] This designation of career education brought an angry response from a supporter of the movement. (This reader's reaction and the author's response appeared in the March 1974 issue of the *Modern Language Journal.*) What underlies such disputes is the basic question whether foreign language study is primarily an instrument to some other end or whether it is something worth doing for its own sake. Reinert, in contrast to career educationists, opts for the latter approach. In his words, "When our students ask what is the purpose of learning another language, let us answer that from language comes the power to understand and the power to communicate. From the power to understand comes our hope of controlling our environment and our destiny. Such control is what we call freedom."[35]

Extrinsic Versus Intrinsic Motivation

The above examples are illustrative of the tendency on the part of academically oriented educators to reject the use of vocational outcomes as *primary* motives for learning traditional disciplines. The underlying reason for this attitude is the belief that external motives tend to inhibit the educational development of the individual. For example, if someone convinces a student that he or she might want to become a bookkeeper, then the student is likely to look at a subject such as mathematics and ask, "Just how much mathematics do I need to become a bookkeeper?" This very process may limit the individual's potential to become anything else. On the other hand, if the individual had been encouraged to view the field of mathematics as something that can be a highly satisfying and worthwhile activity in itself, then the individual would tend to gain control of the discipline in such a way as to render it more than adequate for bookkeeping while, in addition, not closing the door to hundreds of other occupations

[32] Ibid., p. 186.
[33] William Riley Parker, "Why a Foreign Language Requirement?" Jame Dodge (ed.) pp. 17–25 in *The Case for Foreign Language Study: A Collection of Readings*, New York, Modern Language Association Materials Center, 1971, p. 19.
[34] Frank M. Grittner, "Barbarians, Bandwagons and Foreign Language Scholarship," *Modern Language Journal* 57 (September–October 1973), pp. 241–248.
[35] Harry Reinert, "Truth in Packaging . . . for Foreign Languages," *Modern Language Journal* 56 (April 1972), p. 209.

(such as engineering) in which a deeper knowledge of mathematics is required. Some would even go so far as to say that for academic disciplines to be useful they must be learned without reference to narrow career applications, for learning them well involves emotional commitment to the discipline itself. It is difficult to get an emotional commitment to something that is looked at merely as a minimal prerequisite to some external goal. Thus, in education, we sometimes find ourselves in the paradoxical situation of discovering that certain learnings are more useful to a given profession if they are not acquired for the specific purposes of the profession in question.

In the field of foreign languages we have a classic example of this paradox. I have personally known doctoral candidates who had allegedly acquired a "reading knowledge" of one or two foreign languages. The purpose of acquiring this skill was ostensibly to enable the individual to read scholarly materials in other languages. Yet it is common knowledge that a large portion of successful PhD candidates are incapable of reading even the simplest prose in any of the languages in which they have been certified as competent. Also, studies into the question have shown that very few people with a PhD have subsequently used their language skills for research purposes. The people who can and do read material in languages other than English after graduation are those who found intrinsic satisfaction in the learning of the language in the first place. There is no question in my mind that the same applies to virtually every area of human learning. Almost everyone who is making successful career use of science or mathematics or public speaking or athletics or English language skills was originally motivated to learn it simply because he was "turned on" by the subject matter itself. Furthermore, there is a very strong possibility that such individuals could actually have been *prevented* from making use of such skills by having the career applications of a given subject identified too early and too emphatically. Apparently, the crippling effect of extrinsic motives can even affect monkeys. Harlow, the renowned psychologist who works with anthropoids, found that monkeys enjoyed solving certain kinds of puzzles. They became very good at it simply by pursuing the activity of puzzle solving for its own sake. Initially, the rewards consisted only of the intrinsic satisfaction that the monkeys got from solving the problems inherent in the puzzles. Then, as an experiment, Harlow introduced food as an extrinsic reward for solving the puzzles (which the monkeys had originally done without extrinsic rewards). However, as the rewards were withdrawn, the animals progressively lost interest in the process of puzzle solving. Ultimately they stopped solving the puzzles altogether when the rewards were totally removed. The point here is that self-sustaining, intrinsically stimulating activities can be choked off by introducing rewards that are inherently unrelated to the activity itself.

This raises the distinct possibility that the career education movement could be dysfunctional to its own purposes if young people are systematically made to look upon learning not as something that is worth doing in itself, but something that is tied to specific utilitarian outcomes. The

40

profession could find itself in the position of promising material rewards that it is unable to give and finding students—like Harlow's monkeys—"turning off" on school even more than they are presently doing, simply because the promised rewards were either not forthcoming or were so remote in the future as to be nonreinforcing.

It seems to me, in view of the above, that certain risks are involved in the career education movement. For example, the prospect of having grade school children planning their curricular choices around predetermined commitments to become bookkeepers, doctors, cowboys, or airline stewardesses is somewhat frightening. The dangers of this are at least as great as with the practice of prescribing subject matter for students and telling them in effect, "You will learn it because it is good for you; and you will like it!" These, of course, represent extreme attitudes. Actually, few people in the career education movement are advocating predetermination of one's lifework by the sixth grade. And few present-day academicians are claiming today that their subject matter can only be good if it is totally irrelevant.

Underlying this discussion is a problem that educators have struggled with since Socrates—that is, if education is too narrowly focussed on short-term practical outcomes, it paradoxically becomes impractical. Specific skills acquired for specific utilitarian ends are highly limited in value simply because the individual may subsequently not find himself in the situation for which he was specifically trained. This is especially true in our rapidly changing contemporary society. On the other hand, if education becomes too disassociated from present-day realities, it tends to become demotivating because students fail to perceive its relevance. Hence it would probably be a mistake for the foreign language profession to choose sides so that one is forced either to reject career education entirely or, on the other hand, to reject the humanistic concept of "learning how to learn" and of acquiring knowledge for its own intrinsic worth. It would seem that both concepts can be encompassed under the idea of education as a means to personal self-fulfillment. This concept does not exclude the obvious need that a person has to make a living, nor does it exclude the idea that the individual must ultimately perceive a reason for living in the first place.

Relevance in Language Education

In effect, what I am attempting to do here is to show how humanistic ends can be reconciled with career goals even in a subject like foreign languages, which, in this country (if nowhere else in the world), is viewed as the rather special property of the middle-class college-bound student. In this regard, it may be useful to examine the concept of *relevance*, which is so glibly espoused by critics of education. Relevance is a highly individualistic phenomenon that does not exist outside of a specific context. One cannot say, for example, that English as a foreign language has career relevance for all Japanese (although all Japanese children are required to learn it). We can say with resonable assurance that English is highly relevant to a Japanese airline pilot who is making his landing approach at the Los

Angeles airport. It is probably also safe to say that the Japanese workman on the Toyota assembly line does not perceive his knowledge of English to be relevant to that situation. But the problem is that neither of these individuals, when they began the mandatory study of English in grade school, could have known whether that foreign language would ultimately be relevant to the occupation in which he subsequently found himself.

The study of foreign languages has a high level of relevance as far as thousands of occupations are concerned. Occupations in areas like international banking, government service, international travel, hotel service, and the military services, to name but a few, are enhanced by a knowledge of languages. Yet the pedagogical relevance level is rather low insofar as the individual student is concerned, simply because few students know what occupations they will be pursuing during that period when their ability to learn is at the optimum level. Hence from the *pedagogical* standpoint, the relevance of language study must be presented in terms of more immediate rewards. Careers are too remote to serve as *primary* motivators for the large majority of students. In practical terms, this means that foreign language teachers should first emphasize the personal-development or self-fulfillment potential of language study and then *secondarily* make students aware of the many careers that can be enhanced by such study.

This is not to say that the career implications of language study can be safely neglected. In fact, foreign language teachers and guidance counselors in this country have done their pupils a great disservice by concentrating almost exclusively upon the career needs of those students who aspire to a college education. In some instance, the non-college-bound student will find a more pressing need for foreign language skills. Some airlines, for example, require at least one foreign language as a precondition for employment for stewardesses and other personnel. In some cases, the screening process includes a test of oral proficiency, which the candidate must pass in order to be considered for employment. In other occupations, advancement within the employing company or agency is contingent upon demonstrated language skill. Even though there are tens of thousands of nonacademic jobs that can be obtained or enhanced through the knowledge of a second language, this information has not been widely disseminated to students. In fact, the myth is still prevalent that only the college-bound student has any need for studying a language other than English. Language teachers themselves have tended to treat all students as if they were incipient language majors, despite the fact that the demand for language as the *primary* skill is very small.

SUMMARY

In conclusion, it seems advisable to summarize the reasons given for foreign language study, while at the same time putting into perspective the relative importance of each reason as reflected in the textbooks and classroom applications.

The Anthropological-Humanistic Reason

Diversity of language is a fact of human existence; seven-eighths of the world's people do not speak English natively. Even if they have learned English as a second language, they still cherish their mother tongue as an essential means of communication. Therefore, people who have failed to acquire minimal proficiency in at least one foreign language have missed an experience that is essential to understanding the world they live in. Being monolingual, they cannot grasp the nature, function, and social importance of languages, both English and foreign. In their ignorance, they tend to assume that all languages convey meaning in much the same way as does English. This fundamental error leads to gross misunderstandings regarding the actions, customs, and beliefs of other peoples, an ignorance the modern world can ill afford. Also, many of the great monuments of human thought have been expressed in a foreign language. Some writings have not been translated, and, in any case, much is lost when foreign writings are translated into English. In this view, foreign language study is essential to the full development of an individual's latent potentialities as a civilized human being.

The Utilitarian Reason

Students may or may not find a direct practical application for the knowledge and skill they have acquired in learning a foreign language, just as they may never use the skills gained in the chemistry laboratory or apply the insights resulting from the study of algebra or geometry. Almost never does education produce a set of skills or a body of knowledge that is applied directly in toto to some real-life situation. Yet in some way, broadly educated people have developed a knack of understanding new situations and of communicating their ideas to others, which they would not have had without benefit of schooling. Indeed, the multibillion dollar investment in education is based upon the belief that what is learned in school will transfer to situations that the student will later face in life. In this sense, the study of languages is "practical," because it reinforces the development of verbal skills in English. (It would not be an adequate substitute for the study of English, however, as some enthusiasts have implied.) The most direct transfer, of course, would be to the learning of still another foreign language should the need arise later in life.

Many of the other reasons so often given might be considered more as fringe benefits or by-products of language study. The doctor or the pharmacist may find that his or her knowledge of Latin has been useful in the writing and filling of prescriptions. The businessman may suddenly find that his four years of high school Spanish was the deciding factor in his being selected to manage a new branch factory in South America. The scientist may draw information from French, German, or Russian scientific journals and thus gain knowledge that would have required needless months of experimentation and study. Any American may find great satisfaction in communicating with a visitor from overseas or in speaking a foreign language during his or her vacation abroad. In the age of jets, internationalism, world trade, and communications satellites, the list of conceivable applications of foreign language skill is practically endless. In this regard, it is certainly better to have the skill and not need it than to need the skill and not have it.

BIBLIOGRAPHY

Alter, Maria P., *A Modern Case for German,* Philadelphia, American Association of Teachers of German, 1970.
Dodge, James W., (ed.), *The Case for Foreign-Language Study: A Collection of Readings.* Northeast Conference, 1971.
Copies of this publication are available from the Materials Center, MLA–ACTFL, 62 Fifth Avenue, New York, N.Y., 10011. Price: single copies $1.75 each, 50¢ handling charge on orders under $5.00. Payment must accompany all orders under $10.00.

Grittner, Frank M., "Barbarians, Bandwagons and Foreign Language Scholarship," *Modern Language Journal* 57 (September–October 1973), pp. 241–248.
Grittner, Frank M., (ed.), *Careers, Communication and Culture in Foreign Language Teaching,* Skokie, Ill., National Textbook Company, 1974.
Honig, Lucille J., and Richard I. Brod, "Foreign Languages and Careers," *Modern Language Journal* 48 (April 1974), pp. 157–185.
Reprints are available from the MLA Publications Center, 62 Fifth Avenue, New York, N.Y. 10011. Cost: single copy 75¢; 10–49 copies, 50¢ each; 50 copies or more, 25¢ each. Topics include "Language as Auxillary Skill" for business and commerce, executive and managerial positions, technical and engineering positions, banking and financial positions, personnel, secretarial and clerical positions, civil service, education, law, library science, journalism, radio and television, film production, publishing, science, health services, social work, religious occupations, social sciences, travel and tourism, hotel work, transportation industries. "Language as a Primary Skill" involves mainly foreign language teaching as well as interpreting and translating. The article is directed primarily to the present or potential student of foreign languages. It can also be used by parents, teachers, guidance counselors, administrators, and other persons.

Latimer, John F., *The New Case for Latin and the Classics,* Occasional Paper Number Nineteen (January 1973), Washington, D.C., Council for Basic Education.
The address for the Council for Basic Education is 725 Fifteenth Street N.W., Washington, D.C. 20005. Cost for a single copy is 50¢.

Lederer, William, and Eugene Burdick, *The Ugly American,* New York, Fawcett, 1958, pp. 232–233.
Nash, Robert J., and Russell M. Agne, "Career Education: Earning a Living or Living a Life?" *Phi Delta Kappan* 54 (February 1973).

Steiner, Florence, "Career Education and Its Implications at the National Level," *Modern Language Journal* 58 (April 1974), pp. 186–191.

Turner, Paul R., " Why Johnny Doesn't Want to Learn a Foreign Language," *Modern Language Journal* 58 (April 1974), pp. 191–196.

3

■ *"When I use a word," Humpty Dumpty said, in a rather scornful tone, "it means just what I choose it to mean—neither more nor less." "The question is," said Alice,, "whether you can make words mean so many different things." "The question is," said Humpty Dumpty, "which is to be master—that's all."*
LEWIS CARROLL

■What is language? The new linguistics

The long reign of the Latin language over the intellectual world did more than influence the content and method of teaching languages. According to many structural linguists, the Latin grammar books of past centuries have tended to create and perpetuate a series of myths about language in general and grammar in particular. The cornerstone of this myth—say the linguists—is the belief that Latin was a universal and perfect form of language. Therefore, once grammar books had been written for Latin, it was considered a simple matter to apply the rules and terminology to English or any other lesser language. Once the basic fallacy was established, hundreds of subfallacies were built around it. The modern linguists look upon some of these misconceptions as mere annoyances; others, they feel, have had a disastrous effect upon the teaching of both native and foreign languages. A few samples of those that are considered to have been the most damaging are:

1 The fallacy that language is logical.
2 The fallacy that language is based on writing.
3 The fallacy that language is good or bad or that some language is right while other language is wrong.
4 The fallacy that language should be studied by learning rules of correctness.
5 The fallacy that present-day vernacular speech is a deterioration of an earlier more perfect language.
6 The fallacy that the language of one region is somehow better than the language of another.

These attitudes are by no means the exclusive property of Americans. During a study tour of German schools and universities, the author and four other educators from the United States were somewhat chagrined to learn that the language of educated Americans was considered "substandard" by many Germans. In one German high school, the head of the university system from a western state of the U.S. was asked to read a story about Buffalo Bill to an English class. He had hardly begun to read when the students broke out laughing. The German youngsters had been indoctrinated to believe that British "received English" (similar to Oxfordian English) was the only "good" English. The sudden shock of hearing an important, scholarly man "mispronouncing" his A's startled and amused the German teenagers. Charles Dickens ran into a similar reaction from American audiences in the nineteenth century when he toured the United States giving oral readings from his better-known books; many people were disappointed to hear their favorite stories read with a "foreign accent."

As a scientist of languages, the modern linguist rejects such insular and moralistic attitudes toward the way people speak a language. The purpose of linguistic science is to *describe*; not to *prescribe* one type of language and *proscribe* another. For example, if someone is out of money in America, a second person might comment on that fact in any one of several ways:

He don't have no money.
He ain't got no money.
He's broke.
He doesn't have any money.

Since all of the above expressions do, in fact, occur, and since all of them convey *with equal certainty* that the man has no money, the linguistic scientist has no choice but to record each. Furthermore, because he has no evidence that anyone has ever used "two negatives to make a positive" in this sort of situation, he rejects that rule as an example of school-teach-erish folklore. It should be quite evident from these examples that the new linguistic science reflects a greatly changed attitude toward the analysis and application of grammar. When a recent edition of Webster's unabridged dictionary also applied this philosophy to its treatment of words, many highly literate people were incensed. To them, the scientific approach to language appears blatantly permissive and anarchistic. To others who are a bit more knowledgeable, it represents little more than a superimposition of new terminology upon facts that have long been obvious. However, to the modern language community in the second half of the twentieth century this approach has supplied the main rationale for sweeping changes in the manner of analyzing and teaching foreign languages. What, then, are the main features of the new linguistics, and how have they influenced language teaching?

IS LANGUAGE LOGICAL?

Language, like mathematics, is man-made. Both language and mathe-matics are used to represent things, concepts, relationships, and qualities. Mathematics, for the most part, transcends time, place, language, and culture. It has even been stated that mathematics "represents a universal language which could be recognized by rational beings wherever they may exist. It is for this reason that the radio astronomers who are making a conscientious attempt to contact life elsewhere in the universe send their contact messages out in mathematical code."[1]

Perhaps the ways of eating, the method of mating, even the manner of breathing might be different in other rational creatures. Despite this, the mathematician will insist that his language is so pure, so unencumbered with emotionalism and provincialism, and so universal in nature as to be comprehensible and applicable to any world that may exist anywhere. The proof that mathematics is a universal language in the broadest sense will have to await further space explorations. For our purposes it is sufficient to observe that the science of mathematics has developed a notation system that is clearly understandable to educated persons regardless of culture, language, politics, or religion. The symbols below will convey the identical message to the knowledgeable Japanese, American, East Indian, German, Italian, Arab, or Russian.

$$.. + :: + ::. \quad = 2 + 4 + 5$$
$$2 + 4 + 5 \quad = a + b + c$$
$$a + b + c \quad = \sqrt{4} + \sqrt{16} + \sqrt{25}$$
$$\sqrt{4} + \sqrt{16} + \sqrt{25} = .. + :: + ::.$$

While the mathematician would have no trouble communicating across cultures with written symbols, his communication would break down the moment he began to vocalize the little black marks, for then he would be compelled to fall back on language. And it is virtually impossible to find a consistent pattern in one language that recurs with equal consistency in a different language. Notice below that other languages can be made to look chaotic if systematic aspects of English are used as a basis for comparison:

English	French	German	Spanish
I am young.	Je suis jeune.	Ich bin jung.	Soy joven.
I am cold.	J'ai froid.	Mir ist kalt.	Tengo frío.
I am glad.	Je suis content.	Ich freue mich.	Estoy contento.
I am fond of him.	Je l'aime.	Ich habe ihn lieb.	Quiero a él.
I am sorry.	Je regrette.	Es tut mir leid.	Lo siento.
I am hungry.	J'ai faim	Ich habe Hunger.	Tengo hambre.

From this it might be concluded that English is a more logical language than any of the other three. Such a conclusion, the linguist would say, is typical of the type of false logic that led previous grammarians into basing the study of other languages upon Latin grammar. As a matter of fact, any language can be made to appear as the most logical if it is the one

[1] Harry L. Phillips and Marguerite Kluttz, *Modern Mathematics and Your Child.* Publication no. 29047, Washington, D.C., U.S. Office of Education, 1963, p. 1.

that is chosen as the base of comparison. The German verb pattern shown below is regular; the English, erratic in form:

Es *muß* gehen.   *It must go.*

Es *mußte* gehen.   *It had to go.*

And both Spanish and German have a consistent pattern of comparing adjectives, while English uses now one, now the other:

Spanish (*adj.* + más)	English	German (*adj.* + -er)
grande—más grande	*big—bigger*	groß—größer
inteligente—	*intelligent—*	intelligent—
más inteligente	*more intelligent*	intelligenter

If we used Spanish as the logical basis for comparing things and people we would have to say in English:

He is more smart than I.
His car is more fast than mine.
I am more tall than you.

If German were considered the logical language, we would say "smarter," "faster," and "taller." However, we would also have to say "resource-fuller" and "reliabler." Similarly, if French were set up as the model of logic, we would have to use a different form of verb in the sentence "I allow my boy *to go*," than we use in the sentence "I want my boy *to go*." In French (and in Spanish) it seems logical to use a subjunctive verb form and a different sentence structure to express that you want another person to do something. English and German do not consider this to be logical.

WHAT IS WRITING?

Writing, linguists tell us, is a partial and highly incomplete representation of language. Language itself consists of highly complex arrangements of sounds, including pauses, stresses, rhythms, and the like. Once a person has learned to make the appropriate noises, then he can learn to attach meaning to the little black marks that partially symbolize the sounds he has learned to produce. The native speaker of a language has acquired the sounds without conscious effort, usually well before the first year of school. The writing system can be mastered in the first few years of school if the language provides graphic symbols that are used consistently to represent the same given sounds. Italian and Hungarian have this near one-to-one correspondence between writing and sound. As a result, Italian and Hungarian children are able to master their respective spelling systems while they are still in the early primary grades. Spanish- and German-speaking children take a bit longer. Many Americans never learn to spell at all. The forty sounds of English are represented not by forty written symbols but by a chaotically complex and irregular maze of letters and letter groupings. For example, English spelling permits one symbol to stand for five different sounds:

Same symbol	Sample word	Different sound
-ough	through	[oo]
-ough	though	[oh]
-ough	cough	[awf]
-ough	rough	[uff]
-ough	plough	[ow]

In other cases, eight graphic symbols are used to represent a single sound:

Different symbol	Sample word	Same sound
-o	go	[ō]
-ow	tow	[ō]
-oe	toe	[ō]
-ough	dough	[ō]
-eau	beau	[ō]
-ew	sew	[ō]
owe	owe	[ō]
oh	oh	[ō]

The purpose of this section is not merely to show that English spelling is frustratingly inconsistent and unpredictable (which it is), but rather to emphasize the fact that written symbols (or graphemes) are highly incomplete representations of language even in those languages that have a consistent orthography. To speak a language "exactly as it is written" would reduce the effectiveness of communication, the linguists tell us. The human mind actually depends upon the slurring of vowel sounds to provide clues to the meaning of the complete utterance. This is why some people who speak perfectly all right become nearly incomprehensible when they begin to read aloud. In their desire to articulate every sound clearly they give undue importance to the little black marks on the paper. Such readers have not learned that writing is a pale, incomplete, and highly imperfect representation of language. Those who read well, such as radio and TV commentators, have learned to treat the little black marks as "clues" from which they automatically reconstruct a more or less normal flow of speech sounds. They have—perhaps intuitively—grasped the idea that language is primarily sound; or, as the linguists express it, "language is an arbitrary system of vocal symbols." Writing is the shorthand for that complex system of sounds.

STRESS, PAUSE, AND INTONATION

Suppose someone asked you to read aloud the following series of capital letters printed on a card:

J I N V U

If you are like most people you will pronounce each of the letters with equal emphasis and will allow a very definite pause of approximately the same length between each letter. Also, in your mind, the letters will remain separated as isolated meaningless utterances. Now, however, let us take the series of sounds that these letters represent and indicate that you are talking to a very successful man named Jay. Let us suppose also that you are a close friend of his and that you are going to tell him that you are envious of him. You could take the same sounds represented by the letters of the alphabet above and utter them in the same sequence:

Jay, I envy you.   *[J I N V U]*

This may seem like childish word play, but it helps to illustrate one of the favorite ideas of modern linguistics; namely, that language is much more than a series of vocabulary items strung together in a certain order. If you speak English natively, you would automatically modify your way of speaking when you conceive of the five sounds in terms of communication. For example, you add certain pauses and you stress certain syllables more than others. The result cannot be represented adequately in print, but it would come out something like this:

Jay—I ^{en}vy y$_{o_u}$.

This pattern will be repeated unconsciously by the native speaker whenever he makes a simple statement directly to an acquaintance. The elements of this pattern are just as much a part of communication as are the segments of sound that make up the words themselves. For we have seen that sounds can be read mechanically with the same stress on each syllable and the same pause between each utterance without communicating any idea whatever. In simple terms, the main characteristics of the above pattern are: (1) use of pause, (2) placement of main stress, and (3) use of a falling intonation at the end of the sentence. The words may change, but the pattern will not.

John—we ex^{pect} you $_{to}$ $_{come.}$

Mary—he ^{is} ^{leav}^{i}$_n$$_g$ $_{n_{o_w.}}$

It is usually not possible to change the stress and intonation pattern of a sentence without altering the meaning considerably. For example, our original sentence could be stressed on the first and last syllables:

I $_{envy}$ y$^{o^{u?}}$ *(For what possible reason ?)*

In this case the rising end-intonation and the stress on the first-person pronoun would convey doubt; perhaps even sarcasm. Similarly, the main stress could be placed on the first word:

I ^{e}$_{nvy you.}$ (Even if no one else does.)

In some cases, misapplication of intonation can produce a comical effect:

What are we having for dinner, fa$t^{he^{r?}}$ (*cannibalistic implications*)

By slightly modifying the pause after the word "dinner" and by using a falling rather than a rising intonation, this sentence means what it was intended to mean. With similar modifications the following sentence can signify either that the husband is asking his wife about the entire morning menu or that he wants information about what is being served with his toast:

What are we having for breakfast, honey?

The key to the meaning centres around the intonation used with the final word and the pause that precedes it.

It is easy for many people to lose patience with such discussions, particularly if they are still conviced that the written language is of predominant importance. To the native speaker of English the facts seem obvious and hardly worth belaboring. In any case, what does it all have to do with learning a foreign language? The comparative linguist, as usual, has an answer: Languages differ in their use of rhythm, intonation, stress, pause, and pitch just as they differ in their respective use of sounds, words, and word order. An extreme example of this would be Chinese compared to English. What would seem to be one word in English can have four different meanings in Chinese depending on the pitch of the speaker's voice. Some faint notion of how Chinese words sound can be conveyed by humming the scales. Although each "hum" is the same "word" the mind may be registering the meaning associated with the musical symbols "do," "re," "mi," "fa," etc. However, it is not necessary to go into Asiatic languages to find a reason for concentrating on such matters. Even the closely related European languages differ in their use of stress, rhythm, intonation, and the like. In one language, a level intonation may indicate boredom; in another it may register normal interest. At the other extreme, the placement of stress can indicate enthusiasm or excitement in one language, while it is the normal pattern in another. The problem comes when the American student tries to put foreign language words together using the speech mannerisms that are characteristic of American English. The results can be insulting, ludicrous, or baffling; they may even be totally unintelligible. The novice student of Spanish will often place the accent on the first syllable in accordance with the predominant English pattern. As a result he may say,

¿Sra. Gomez, esta lista?"   (*Mrs. Gomez, this list?*)

when he wants to say,

?Sra. Gomez, está lista?   (*Mrs. Gomez, are you ready?*)

Similarly, a Frenchman whose command of English is less than perfect may carry over an interrogative pattern from his own language; he may ask,

Is it za left ^{door} or za right $^{door?}$

rather than,

Is it the ^{left} door or the ^{right} door?

The American listener who is trying to help the French visitor may be just as badly misled by the wrong intonation as by the mispronunciation of individual sounds. The same lack of communication results when the American applies his native intonation to the French language.

A German example can be drawn from lesson one of almost any textbook most of which contain a greeting such as:

Guten Tag, Herr Schumann.

The American student will invariably overstress the word *Tag* by applying the English pattern to German.

He^{llo} *Mr. Schumann.*

If the German intonation pattern is used in English it seems to convey a tone of indifference and distinterest that the speaker did not intend.

According to the linguist, there are several implications as far as language teachers are concerned:

1   They should be aware of the main points of conflict between English and the target language.
2   They should concentrate oral drill work—preferably using native models—on these areas of differences.
3   They should see to it that students develop an awareness of each trouble spot so that they will be able to detect and correct their errors when the teacher is no longer present.
4   They must provide drill work that involves complete utterances; for even if students know how to pronounce flawlessly many thousands of individual words, they will still not know how to combine them into complete, understandable units of thought unless they are taught specifically to do so. Without proper instruction they will be inclined to pronounce each syllable mechanically, or, worse, they will apply the intonational and rhythmic patterns that characterize their native way of speaking. In either case, communication will be blurred.

PHONEMES AND MORPHEMES—THE GRAMMAR OF SOUND

Highly literate speakers of English can be incredibly naive in their statements concerning the sound system of the language they manipulate so well. A much-published author writing a popularized version of the history of the English language commented that "A further stride in the direction of simplicity came with the adoption of the letter 's' to indicate the plural form of all nouns." In reality there are three main plurals in spoken English, only one of which is the letter *s* (as represented by the *s* in the word *hiss*). The plural forms of three animals will illustrate the point:

cats   *[s]*
dogs   *[z]*
horses   *[iz]*

It is very simple to prove that these two plurals have different end sounds; one only needs to add the sounds to the same stem:

hiss
his

The change of sound in these two one-syllable words completely alters the meaning. The spelling difference is of no relevance; small children who have not yet learned to read or write can tell the difference with perfect ease, even though they may never have heard of double versus single *s*. For when normal 6-year old Americans enter school they have already spent many thousands of hours in hearing and speaking English. After they learn to read, they may even accept the fallacious statement that "Nearly all English plurals are formed by adding *s*." In any case, they will continue to use the three plurals as the situation requires (as in cork*s* [s], bottle*s* [z], and glasse*s* [iz].) Their ignorance is of little consequence in their use of English.

However, the same misconceived rule proves disastrous to a person who is learning English as a second language, particularly if his or her native tongue does not contain words that end with a voiced sibilant (that is, the final sound in the word *his*). For example, the nonnative will ask:

Where are the docks? [s]

when he means:

Where are the dogs? [z]

Or he will say:

I need some carts, [s]

when he means:

I need some cards [z]

American students of French, German, or Spanish make comparable blunders when their English speech habits interfere with their attempts to speak in the target language. One of the chief functions of the linguist is to identify such pitfalls or conflict points and to construct oral drills aimed at minimizing their effect upon the student's attempts to speak the target (or foreign) language.

In analyzing the foreign language, the linguist identifies the minimal

54

signficant sound contrasts which may or may not be characteristic of the student's native language.

Again, for economy of time and efficiency of learning, the emphasis must be upon the pitfalls of pronunciation. To do an adequate job, the teacher must have a thorough understanding of both the native and the target language. If he is teaching English to those whose native language is Spanish, he must be aware that the student will hear no difference between words such as:

hash	*hatch*	*wash*	*watch*
cash	*catch*	*lash*	*latch*

The consonant clusters *sh* and *tch* are two phonemes of English; however, in Spanish no such meaning contrast exists. As a result, to the Spanish-speaking student, these word pairs sound identical. If someone asks him,

Where is my watch? or *Where is my wash?*

he may not know in either case whether the speaker is asking about laundry or a timepiece. The same sort of thing happens to Americans when they encounter sound contrasts that do not exist in English but that are phonemes of the target language. A South American friend of the author heard a college instructor teaching his students a Spanish sentence that meant:

The Korean hasn't come yet,

when he wanted to say:

The mail hasn't come yet.

The teacher had not mastered a basic sound contrast, namely, the single-trilled *r* versus the multiple-trilled *rr.* His students were inadvertently learning *Coreo* for *correo*. In French, a similar confusion can result if the student pronounces *ils viennent* with undue nasalization and is understood as saying *il vient*. In German, pairs such as *Stadt* and *Staat* are nearly impossible for the American to differentiate. Even *schön* and *schon* are troublesome for some students.

Once the difficult sounds have been singled out, drills must be devised that teach the student first, to identify them; second, to imitate them correctly; third, to apply them in sentences that make sense; and fourth, to use the sounds correctly and without hesitation whenever the speaking situation calls for them. In addition, the drills must account for any elisions or merging of words that take place in normal speech, as well as any of the matters of stress or intonation that were discussed earlier.

Just as the term "phoneme" is used to refer to each significant sound contrast, the term "morpheme" is used in reference to minimal units that carry meaning. For example, the word *dogs* has two morphemes:

dog *is a "free" morpheme—it can stand alone.*

s *is a "bound" morpheme—it has meaning in that it shows plurality,*
                       but it cannot stand by itself.

As is the case with phonology, the morphology of each language shows great areas of difference. For example, English and German commonly use separate free morphemes to express person and number: e.g., I eat; *ich esse.* Spanish, on the other hand, will regularly combine the morpheme showing person with the morpheme referring to eating: e.g., *como.* The stem *com* carries the meaning "eat" and the ending *-o* indicates that person is "I." However, the important thing about the new linguistic analysis is not in the jargon used, but in the attitude toward the target language. The linguist attempts to describe each language scientifically. He avoids such statements as "Spanish does it backwards" or "In Spanish the pronoun is part of the verb." Such statements tend toward the traditionalist fallacy of using one language as the model; the other as a quaint deviation from the norm.

TRADITIONAL GRAMMAR VERSUS MODERN GRAMMAR

The linguist shies away from the normative approach to grammar, which sets up rules of correctness based upon the speech of a certain period or of a certain geographical area. Even a well-educated person may use a variety of language forms depending upon the formality of the situation in which he finds himself. Thus, at a formal tea, he may say:

A cup of coffee, please.

while at a crowded corner snack bar he may say:

Hey, how 'bout a cuppa coffee?

Changes of this sort are not corruptions of "good" language, but are looked upon by the linguist as normal features of all languages. The importance of recognizing such changes is particularly relevant to the teaching of listening. Since normal native speech contains numerous contractions, omissions, and elisions, the language student must be trained to comprehend the language as it is, rather than expecting it to conform to some arbitrary standard of correctness.

Methods based upon traditional grammar were also ineffective for teaching students to *speak* a foreign language, say the linguists, because they tended to treat language as a list of words to be strung together according to cookbooklike formulas. Many teachers had the notion that the major difficulty in learning a foreign language was remembering the meaning of words. Yet linguists tell us that whereas we should aim at virtually 100 percent control of pronunciation (learning the phonemes), possibly 50 to 90 percent control of grammar (the morphemes), we might get by with only 1 percent of the vocabulary.

Preschool children who have acquired a tiny fraction of their total potential vocabulary can carry on rather lucid conversations in their native language. By age 5 or 6, normal children will control most of the sounds, structures, and word-order arrangements that are characteristic of informal speech. By contrast, a nonnative adult may have acquired a far larger vocabulary but may find that, lacking control of pronunciation, structure, and word order, his vocabulary is more of a hindrance than a help.

The following note from a Chinese firm to a New York importer illustrates what can happen when the nonnative speaker attempts to put words together according to grammatical rules.

As an auspice of beatitude to the community, as an omnipotent daily utilized novelty, as a pioneer of the scientifical element, as a security to metal, as agent to economy of both time and money, is the newly discovered wonderful Polishing Powder that is to be heartily welcomed wheresoever. Despite the heavy sacrifice of capital and the consumption of brains, we have thereby succeeded in researching out the usage of this Polishing Powder. We lose not promptitude in taking this opportunity to recommend to the attention of the Community. This Polishing Powder is the conqueror.[2]

In summary, what the Chinese translator was trying to say was, "Your firm has produced a useful, effective polishing powder. We have just finished trying it out; it's great!" Instead, however, the Chinese translator came up with a classic example of the limits of the traditional grammatical method. He has carried over into the English, elements of Chinese style and misconceptions of English word order. Further, he is unable to distinguish between antiquated forms (wheresoever) and appropriate vocabulary items (conqueror) in reference to a polishing powder.

Traditional grammarians have looked upon the new linguistics as an invitation to anarchy, as a departure from those rules that delimit meaning and thus make clarity of communication possible. Linguists reject this static view of language. Instead, they attempt to describe how language works rather than prescribing rules of correctness for how it should be used. While patterns do exist in all languages, there is no underlying logic on which they are based. That is, each national group uses certain arbitrarily selected auditory signals to represent its version of reality. Each culture selects only certain vocal symbols and arrangements of them, rejecting all other possibilities. However, the utterances are not fixed and stable; they are modified with time, place, social station, and even with regard to whether they are used in a formal or an informal situation. Any given word is either an accidental creation or else is the offspring of an earlier accident. For example, there is no logical reason why English *the spoon*, German, *der Löffel*, and Spanish *la cuchara* happen to stand for a certain type of eating utensil. Neither is there a logical reason why "spoon" is masculine in German, feminine in French and Spanish, and neuter in English. The question, "Why do the French refer to a spoon as a 'she'?" makes no sense to the descriptive linguist. The only answer is that many nouns that refer to inanimate objects use the same forms that are used for nouns that refer to female human beings. This is true simply because that is the way the French speak.

At this point one is tempted to ask the following questions, which

---

2 Alfred Aarons (ed), *The Florida Foreign Language Reporter* (January 1965), p. 14.

lead us out of the realm of the linguistics scientist and into the fields of applied linguistics and foreign language education. The answers are those most frequently given since World War I . Earlier language educators had given different answers.

Which Frenchmen do we use as models for imitation?	*Educated speakers of the foreign language.*
Of what historical period?	*Of the twentieth century.*
What topics of their conversation do we emphasize?	*Any topics that they normally read about, write about, or talk about.*

THE WAR OF THE WORDS—STRUCTURAL LINGUISTS VERSUS GENERATIVE GRAMMARIANS

The influence of structural linguists on foreign language teaching remained strong through most of the sixties as did their recommended psychological approach. Perhaps it was the empiricist orientation of the descriptive school of linguistics that prompted many linguists to accept a rather limited form of behaviorist psychology to accompany structuralist theorizing and to explain how languages are acquired. After all, the linguists worked with a corpus of material drawn from the overt speech behaviors of native speakers. It was quite natural for them to gravitate toward a then-popular form of empirical behaviorism in psychology, which was based on the manipulation of observable overt behaviors. For if language is viewed as nothing more than patterned oral responses to external stimuli, then it is a rather easy step to a pedogogical dictum that language instruction *should* involve the elicitation and reinforcement of verbal patterns that closely approximate those of the target culture. This, in effect, is what appears to have happened in the 1960s in the field of language pedogogy. That is, linguists who prided themselves on their nonprescriptive, empirical approaches to *linguistic phenomena* suddenly became highly prescriptive and proscriptive in areas where they had little, if any, expertise, namely in *psychological* and *pedagogical* matters. The irony of this situation seems to have escaped nearly everyone including the linguists themselves. Also, in retrospect the language teaching profession's acceptance of theoretical taxonomies as blueprints for classroom instruction appears naive, to say the least. A biologist who would take a taxonomic explanation of human life and who would attempt to build a live human being from it would be considered crazy; the insufficiency of the descriptive model would be obvious to everyone. Similarly, it should have been obvious that the structuralist-behaviorist rationale was an inadequate base upon which to build a living, working model of language instruction. Nevertheless, toward the second half of the decade, structurally oriented materials had come to dominate the secondary school programs of the nation. The "takeover" was less complete at the college level, but even there, by 1967, a substantial portion of college teachers reported that, to some degree,

58

"class materials were based on modern structural linguistic analysis."[3] Thus it was somewhat of a shock to the profession when Chomsky speaking before the 1966 Northeast Conference stated that he was "frankly rather skeptical about the significance, for the teaching of languages, of such insights and understanding as have been attained in linguistics and psychology.[4] This was perhaps the opening shot in the "war of words" among linguists, which was subsequently waged in books, articles, editorials, and book reviews during the late sixties and early seventies.[5]

Despite Chomsky's pessimism regarding the relevance of linguistics to language teaching, many of his disciples made use of his theories to discredit the "empiricists" (that is, the structuralist-behaviorist school) and to advocate a revival of the "rationalist" approach to second-language instruction.

The Rationalist Case
Against Behaviorist Empiricism

On the negative side of the argument, representatives of the rationalist school asserted that language is *not* basically speech, as the structuralists had claimed. Language, they said, is merely a means of symbolizing the much more complex process of thought, which takes place within the mind. As evidence, there are cases of totally mute people who are able to communicate and receive written messages without ever having uttered a sound. Even one of the early advocates of new key methodologies presented evidence that "Thought is central and language is a symbolic system that refers incompletely to it in various ways."[6]

Since language is basically an inner cognitive process, the structuralists are said to have misconstrued the matter by insisting on the primacy of externally derived speech patterns. According to the rationalist school, it was this fallacy that led to the classroom practice of subjecting students *ad nauseum* to mindless oral repetitions of dialogs and pattern drills. Language is simply not an arbitrary set of conventions that the speaker stores and retrieves from a computerlike brain in order to communicate. Instead, language is "creative and stimulus free." That is, it is an *active*, *internal* process on the part of human individuals, who, by nature, seek to organize their perceptions of the world in terms of innate linguistic concepts. Also, inasmuch as language is species-specific, psychological principles derived from an analysis of animal behavior are totally irrelevant.

[3] Ann F. Gut, "A Survey of Methods and Materials in French Language Programs of American Colleges and Universities," *Modern Language Journal* 51 (December 1967), p. 471.

[4] Noam Chomsky, "Linguistic Theory," in Robert G. Mead, Jr. (ed.), *Language Teaching: Broader Contexts*, Middlebury, Vt., Northeast Conference Reports, 1966, p. 43.

[5] It should be noted here that outside the foreign language field, the battle had begun much earlier. For example, Chomsky's devastating review of Skinner's *Verbal Behavior* appeared in *Language* 35, January–March, 1959.

[6] Robert Lado, "Language Thought and Memory in Language Teaching: A Thought View," *Modern Language Journal*, 54 (December 1970), p. 582.

Even mentally defective children acquire language without being taught. Yet normal chimpanzees can learn a limited form of sign language only after careful planning and extensive training by human experimenters.[7] Thus, to characterize language as nothing more than "verbal behavior" is to imply that learning a language is only quantitatively different from the process of conditioning animals and birds to behave in certain specified ways. For example, Skinner's pigeons could be taught to play Ping-Pong by a careful rewarding of selected responses. Skinner's theory of language acquisition is merely an extrapolation from the kind of operant-conditioning process that he used in the laboratory with birds and rats. From the Chomskyan viewpoint, this is absurd. A human being does not learn "language behavior" any more than a pigeon learns "flying behavior." There are some things that are simply part of a creature's genetic equipment. Where man is concerned, language is posited as being somehow innate. Thus for speakers of all specific languages there is an underlying universal grammar, or set of "deep structures" that manifest themselves in the sounds and "surface structures" of the particular language community in which the child happens to be raised. (Presumably there is also a common semantic base that lies beneath deep structure and which, if we could ever have access to it, would eliminate misunderstandings that arise from differences in language, dialect, or cultural background.)

Limitations in All Grammatical and Linguistic Theories

All of this discussion about the nature of language, thought, and meaning has raised more questions than it has answered. Does language come from hereditary endowment, or is it a product of environmental conditioning? Is language acquisition, therefore, basically involved with "creative" problem solving and individual hypothesis testing (and never mind correctness in the early stages)? Or is language best acquired by means of intensive drill work in which the student is rewarded in proportion to his ability to produce correct responses based on descriptions of native speech patterns? To the language teacher who is expected to cope with five or six large classes of reluctant students each day (and who, in the space of a little over a decade has been confronted with three conflicting approaches to grammatical analysis) the rhetoric of the language war may well appear to be little more than an updated version of medieval scholasticism. "Is it phonemic angels or transformational demons with which we are concerned? And how many of each can dance on the head of a semantic pin?" How significant is it to second language learning that surface structure differs from deep structure? For example, the following sentences are said to have the same surface structure:

A. *John is easy to please.*
B. *John is eager to please.*

[7] D. O. Hebb, W. E. Lambert, and Richard Tucker, "A DMZ in the Language War," *Psychology Today* 6 (April 1973), p. 56.

Yet, at a deeper level, sentence A means "Someone pleases John," while sentence B means "John pleases someone." From the standpoint of teaching English as a foreign language, an understandable question is "So what?" The sensitive teacher will attempt to get students to expand pattern A with adjectives like "hard", "impossible," and "difficult." The teacher may also have students substitute infinitives like "to fool," "to understand," and "to get along with" and may show them how the various elements can be interchanged to produce a relatively large number of sentences with somewhat different meanings. Similarly, he or she would lead students to expansions of pattern B, which would involve infinitives such as "to help out," "to join up," "to participate," and so forth. Further, the teacher will help the student to develop a sensitivity to meaning in connection with language patterns so that the student will intuitively avoid combinations such as

John is easy to join up.   or   *John is eager to get along with.*

Long before structural linguists and generative grammarians began debating such matters, many foreign language teachers considered the cultivation of this sensitivity to the relationship between form and meaning to be an important indicator of the student's progress in learning the language. (It was referred to as *Sprachgefühl*.) It is, therefore, highly questionable to insist that the successful language teacher must be a linguistic theorist, as Diller has stated.[8] This is almost like saying that a potter (who is dealing with movement, inertia, and momentum) must first master the niceties of Newtonian and Einsteinian physics before beginning his work in ceramics. In the real world a more sensible procedure is usually followed, one which requires the aspiring potter to work with one who is experienced in converting raw clay into finished ceramic products. Similarly, the aspiring language teacher may have more to learn from close contacts with one successful classroom teacher than from hours of course work involving all the conflicting and changing theories of all the contemporary linguists and grammarians. This skepticism as to the pedagogical value of linguistic science is shared by many linguists. One has gone so far as to suggest that we have reached the "end of the linguistic era" in language teaching.[9]

The views of various linguists with respect to the value of applying theoretical linguistics to language teaching include remarks to the effect that there is little if any relevance to linguistic theory, that past results have been almost completely negative, that there is no logical connection between linguistics and language teaching, that uncritical reliance on theory is dangerous, that it is a classic example of the tyranny of irrelevant expertise, that it is foolhardy to look to linguistics for applications, and

---

[8] Karl C. Diller, "Linguistic Theories of Language Acquisition," in Ralph Hester (ed.), *Teaching a Living Language*, New York, Harper & Row, 1970, p. 6.
[9] Terence J. Quinn, "Theoretical Foundations in Linguistics and Related Fields," pp. 329–353, in Gilbert A. Jarvis, (ed.), *Responding to New Realities*, Skokie, Ill., National Textbook Company 1974, p. 329.

61

that it is impossible to base teaching materials or a teaching methodology on linguistics.[10] What emerges from Quinn's review of the matter is not whether or not linguistics might be useful to language teaching. Instead, the choices seem to relate to whether linguistic theory has been irrelevant to teaching practice or whether it has been actually harmful. Quinn concludes his review with the hesitant suggestion that, nevertheless, language teachers should have "some sort of training in or at least exposure to linguistics."[11]

SUMMARY

Theoretical linguists and generative grammarians are concerned either with describing language or with devising theoretical models that are sophisticated enough to explain how human beings are able to use a finite number of sounds and structures to communicate spontaneously in a potentially infinite variety of novel situations. In their investigations of relationships between sounds, words, structures, and meanings, the various linguists and grammarians devise elegant rules of procedure. They set up new, highly specialized terminologies; and they use familiar words to describe unfamiliar phenomena. (For example the term "competence" as used by Chomsky means something far different from what it signifies in the expression "communicative competence" as used by methodologists.) Whatever message the linguists and grammarians have to convey tends to be accessible only to those who have the time and interest to be full-time scholars. And the focus of such scholarship is upon the internal functions of the investigatory system; pedagogical applications are seldom, if ever, a major consideration. Thus, while there is no question about the intellectual integrity of such theoretical pursuits, there is a question regarding what they have to offer to the classroom teacher of foreign languages. From the structuralist viewpoint the following principles are often given as the main points that linguistic science makes for facilitating the teaching of languages:

1   Language is a system of sound symbols. These sounds must be learned not only as individual entities but also in the manner in which they function in the normal flow of speech.

2   The process of learning to use the sound system must not be contaminated by improper introduction of the writing system. The two must be kept distinctly separate in the student's mind.

3   Intensive oral drill must be directed toward the conflict points. These are the sounds, structures, and word orders in the foreign language that differ greatly from those of English (or that are nonexistent in English) and that, therefore, present a major learning problem.

[10] Ibid., pp. 329–349.
[11] Ibid., p. 350.

As might be expected, the implications drawn from the rationalist approach to language analysis are in conflict with those of the empirically minded linguists. The following principles are representative of pedagogical applications derived from generative grammarians:

1   Language is rule-governed behavior. Hence the language student must learn to apply rules in all phases of language instruction including the learning of sounds. Mastery is achieved not by avoiding errors but by committing them, understanding them, and correcting them.

2   Language involves the creative expression of inner thoughts. Therefore mindless drill on externally devised material is both wasteful and un-natural. What is called for is meaningful practice in which the learner uses internalized principles actively to express personal thoughts and feelings or to actively comprehend a message in which he is interested.

3   Heavy initial emphasis on phonological drill has no valid basis. Also, the identification of linguistic pitfalls has little, if any, pedagogical value insofar as organizing the course of instruction is concerned. Instead, instruction should develop "naturally," beginning with an examination of language universals and proceeding from such basic concepts to the ever more complex manifestations of universal grammar that occur in the target language.

BIBLIOGRAPHY

Buchanan, Cynthia D., *A Programed Introduction to Linguistics,* Boston, Heath, 1963.
This self-teaching text provides an excellent introduction to phonology and phonemic transcription. It is also a good review for anyone who wishes to update his or her knowledge of phonetics and phonemics. An additional value of this text is that it can familiarize the reader with the techniques of Skinnerian programming, which have had considerable influence on current methods of foreign language instruction.

Chomsky, Noam, *Language and Mind: Enlarged Edition.* New York, Harcourt Brace Jovanovich, 1972.
A collection of six essays that attempt to clarify what the rationalist approach is all about. Terms such as "deep structure," "generative grammar," "universal grammar," and "the creative aspect of language use" are dealt with in considerable detail.

Diller, Karl C., *Generative Grammar, Structural Linguistics, and Language Teaching,* Rowley, Mass., Newbury House, 1971.
In his preface the author states that he favors "the rationalist theory of language learning as put forth by Noam Chomsky, and the tightly organized direct methods of language teaching which have been based on older versions of the same theory." He notes further that people in the profession "have not seen what the positive contributions of generative grammar might be. This book can be seen

63

as a statement of the implications which generative grammar should have for language teaching."

Hebb, D. O., W. E. Lambert, and G. Richard Tucker, "A DMZ in the Language War," *Psychology Today,* 6, (April 1973).
This article provides a middle position between the extreme nativist (rationalist) school and the extreme behaviorist (empiricist) school of grammar and linguistics.

Moulton, William G., *A Linguistic Guide to Language Learning,* New York, Modern Language Association Materials Center, 1966.
A summary of the structural linguist's view of language. According to the author, "This book has been written in the belief that there is a kind of linguistic sophistication which, once learned, will make the learning of any foreign language less arduous, more efficient—and probably also more enjoyable." It is clearly written and comprehensible even to the uninitiated.

Politzer, Robert L., *Teaching French, An Introduction to Applied Linguistics,* Waltham, Mass., Ginn Blaisdell, 1960.
Explanation of linguistic teaching method with detailed information on teaching pronunciation, morphology, syntactical patterns, and vocabulary.

Quinn, Terence J., "Theoretical Foundations in Linguistics and Related Fields," in Gilbert A. Jarvis (ed.), *Responding to New Realities,* Skokie, Ill., National Textbook Company, 1974.
An analysis of the relationship between language teaching and the various schools of linguistics ; extensive bibliography.

Savignon, Sandra J., *Communicative Competence: An Experiment in Foreign Language Teaching.* Philadelphia, Center for Curriculum Development, 1972.
An interesting field study in which many of the rationalist principles are put into effect and evaluated. In the author's opinion, "With the distinction between linguistic and communicative competence in mind, the FL teacher needs to take yet another look at current audiolingual practice and to ask himself to what extent methods of instruction and teaching reflect the professed but seldom realized goal : communication with native speakers of the language."

Valdman, Albert, "Grammar and the American Foreign Language Teacher," in Frank Grittner (ed.), *Student Motivation and the Foreign Language Teacher,* Skokie, Ill., National Textbook Company, 1974.
The author concludes his middle-of-the-road approach to the linguistics question by stating that "we must overcome the temptation to wander into areas that are marginal to our field. The goals of language teaching are to form incipient bilinguals and biculturals, not apprentice linguists or bargain basement cultural anthropologists."

4

■How well can Americans learn a second language ?

There are many factors that limit the extent to which the student can expect to become bilingual. Chief among them are the following : (1) The student : his or her age, environment, and motivation ; (2) the educational system : available contact hours, scheduling procedures, and financial structure ; (3) the teacher : his or her preparation and pedagogical orientation.

It is understood here that we are dealing with foreign language instruction not in some theoretical, idealized situation, but within the framework of American educational institutions as they are now formed and are likely to be formed in the foreseeable future. These educational facts of life tend to limit the degree to which instructional goals can be attained. They are included here simply because no meaningful discussion of methods is possible if they are not taken into account.

AMERICAN STUDENTS AND THEIR ENVIRONMENT

The natural way to learn a language is to grow up in a culture where the language is spoken. In many cases, highly proficient bilinguals have spent their childhood in a region where two languages of somewhat comparable status were used for everyday communication. Such individuals have not really learned a foreign language ; they have learned two native languages to refer to a single cultural context. Their acquisition of sounds, structures, word-order arrangements, and basic vocabulary takes place without conscious effort. Bilingual children may later enter bilingual schools where they begin the formal study of the two languages they have already learned to understand and speak. In elementary school they begin to use graphic symbols to express their thoughts in writing and to expand their knowledge of the world through reading. However, before the formal study of graphic language symbols begins, the children have already become quite proficient in the active skill of speaking and the more passive skill of listening to others.

In fact, these skills were acquired so automatically that the youngsters tend to take the listening-speaking aspects of the language for granted.

Because their first conscious study of language dealt with written symbolization, they identify language learning with learning to read and write. Thus, for example, bilingual children in New Hampshire might spend part of the school day writing compositions and reading stories in French with a French-speaking teacher and another part of the day studying spelling and reading with an English-speaking instructor. In the first situation they would listen and recite in French; in the second they would hear and speak English. But in either case, if they are asked what they are doing, they are likely to reply that they are learning to read and write French or English. It would usually not occur to them to mention that they were also hearing and speaking these languages as part of the learning process.

Unfortunately, American bilingual communities are limited in number and usually, where they do exist, educators have failed to capitalize on the language skills of the non-English-speaking segment of the local population. Too often, in fact, the ability to speak another language has been viewed as a mental disability. As a result, most Americans who learn a second language begin their study of it in the formalized atmosphere of the schoolroom. Also, the study of the second language is undertaken, in nearly every case, long after the pupil has learned to understand, speak, read, and write English. Accordingly, educators and parents should not expect pupils to achieve anything approaching full coordinate bilingualism even in school districts that offer foreign languages in the elementary school. According to contemporary learning theory, a number of factors make such expectations unrealistic. Chief among those that are often listed are the following.

Age and Monolingualism

The Americans' habitual manner of relating to the world about them is exclusively by means of the English language and the Anglo-American value system which this language reflects. The older they become, the less flexible they will be in adjusting to the different sets of values reflected by non-English-speaking cultures. Also, they will tend to assign American cultural values to vocabulary items in the foreign language. The fact that Americans generally begin the study of a language relatively late in life tends to magnify the adverse effects of monolingualism.

First-Language Literacy

American students of language are literate or semiliterate in English when their study of the second language begins. Thus, like the bilingual students, they will expect to read and write in the second language within a short time after they are introduced to it. However, unlike the bilingual students, they have not spent thousands of hours conversing in the second tongue. They will consequently be reading and writing a language they do not

66

control conversationally. As a result, their American-English habit system will cause considerable interference with their reading of the foreign language.

Opportunity for Using the Language

Unlike the bilingual student (or the student in some European countries), the American language learner has little opportunity to practice conversational skills in a natural manner. In this regard, a European educator visiting in American has observed:

In this country a student's contact with a foreign language is completely academic, divorced from any cultural feeling for it, cold. It is at best a necessary evil which somehow must be endured. In Europe, a child's approach to another language is an integral part of his life before he enters school. It is something he lives with daily and something he can continually read, due to the availability of foreign newspapers, films, even such an insignificant thing as a candy wrapper. To the European student, a foreign language never becomes a purely academic matter. It is a part of a culture different from his own which he respects and which he is eager to learn thoroughly. Language for him is alive.[1]

THE EDUCATIONAL ENVIRONMENT—
THE SYSTEM, THE SCHEDULE, AND THE TEACHER

Some of the more significant achievements in foreign language instruction have involved radical departures from (1) traditional scheduling procedures, (2) the manner of utilizing staff, and (3) the age at which language learning was begun. Less is known about a fourth departure—the replacement of the teacher with self-instructional devices; but there is some evidence to show that a rather large portion of the foreign language teaching task can be performed by machines. (This is discussed further in the chapter on individualized instruction.)

With regard to the question "How well can Americans learn a foreign language?", the factors of pupil age, schedule, staff, and instructional devices may be more significant than the instructional techniques per se. The stereotype of the ideal language teaching situation has twenty adolescent students meeting five one-hour periods weekly during four academic years (or more) with an instructor who has an academic degree in the target language. These matters are so firmly rooted in the established way of doing things that they are almost taken for granted. Yet there are many responsible language educators who feel that we do not attain our objectives in foreign language learning because we begin at the wrong age, make improper use of time, and employ the wrong type of teachers. Such factors apparently cannot be overlooked in a discussion of teaching techniques.

[1] "Learning a Foreign Language in Europe and America," *Indiana Newsletter* 12 (April 1966), p. 5.

THE AGE OF THE PUPIL

The profession is fond of assigning names to the different levels of foreign language study such as FLES (foreign language in the elementary school) and "Elementary College French." Someone has even suggested the term FLOP (foreign languages for older people). The designations "Conversational Spanish," or "Scientific German," are also in common use to differentiate course objectives. This sort of labeling misleads many people into believing that the schools are teaching many different varieties of the same language. The modern linguist deplores such clouding of the issues. To him, the French that a child needs to learn is essentially the same French that an adolescent or an adult should learn. The *way* they learn will perhaps be different, the amount of vocabulary they can acquire in a given period of time will be different, and the sophistication of content will necessarily reflect the age of the learner. But the French itself remains constant as a system of sounds that must be uttered in a certain unique way if communication is to take place. The same is true of any language. The learning process, regardless of the pupil's age, must be directed at the mastery of those sounds and word arrangements that are characteristic of the language being studied. The small child may learn better if the material is presented to him in songs, poems, games, and stories, while the adult may require a more sophisticated analytical process; yet, in the end, both must learn to attach meaning directly to the "strange" sounds that flow from the native speaker's mouth, and to form utterances of their own at a rather rapid rate—utterances that are pronounced and arranged in such a way as to be comprehensible to the native listener. And ultimately, both must learn to derive meaning from the little black marks on paper known as writing—the shorthand representation of speech—and to produce their own little black marks in an acceptable manner.

There is ample evidence that a well-motivated adult can, in a relatively short time, gain a functional command of a foreign language. Drawing upon his greater knowledge, his ability to organize his thoughts and discipline himself, and, having a clearer sense of purpose, the adult can cover much more ground in a given period of time than can the small child. Why, then, do we have FLES programs at all?

One reason is the element of time. While it is true that the adult *can* learn certain aspects of language more rapidly, he is generally so involved in the specialized business of adult life that he simply cannot fit into his schedule the several hundred hours of concentrated drill work that are necessary to acquire even minimal command of a language. However, the longer sequence of study, though important, is not the main reason advanced by the FLES advocates; instead, the rationale for FLES is rooted in the belief that the ability to learn a foreign language declines with age. As one FLES teacher expresses it:

Childhood is the ideal period for acquiring a native or near-native pronunciation. Medical evidence, experimentation, and objective observation have proven conclusively that children learn foreign languages more quickly and more accurately (at least as far as pronunciation is concerned) than adolescents or adults because of the flexibility of their speech organs, their lack of inhibitions that are typical of older persons learning a language, and their apparent physiological and psychological need to communicate with other children. To children a new way of expressing themselves, particularly if it is associated with a normal class activity, presents no problem. Children make no attempt to analyze a language as adolescents or adults do. They do not immediately compare what they hear or say in the new language to English. They experience no conflict because of similar or completely dissimilar language items in English. They do not look for difficulties. They even use the dreaded subjunctives as normally and naturally as they would use the present tense of the verb "to have."[2]

The medical evidence mentioned here refers to studies relating to the treatment of brain damage in children and adults. Several studies have indicated that there is a physical basis for advocating FLES programs.[3] When brain tissue in the speech areas of the adult cortex is damaged, only partial recovery of speaking ability is possible in most instances; but with children, it is another story. Doctor Wilder Penfield, the noted Canadian neurosurgeon, comments on this phenomenon as follows:

I had seen children under the age of ten or twelve lose the power of speech when the speech convolutions in the left hemisphere of the brain had been destroyed by a head injury or a brain tumor. I had seen them recover after a year of dumbness and aphasia. In time they spoke as well as ever, because the child's brain is functionally flexible for the start of a language. They began all over again and established a speech center located on the other side of the brain in what is called the nondominant hemisphere. (In a right-handed person, the left hemisphere is normally dominant—that is, it contains the specialized speech centers.)[4]

The adult's failure to recover full control of his speech after suffering brain damage is apparently "because he has by that time taken over the initially uncommitted convolutions of his brain for other uses. The uncommited cortex is the part of the human brain that makes man teachable and thus lifts him above all other species."[5]

The implications of the neurological evidence are that only a child of 10 or younger can ordinarily acquire a full coordinate system (see Chapter 5). One who grows to adulthood as a monolingual is compelled to superimpose the second language on speech areas already committed to his native tongue. He may become a skilled compound bilingual with a considerable vocabulary at his command, but his accent and intonation will forever betray him as one who began his study of language beyond the optimum age; that is, after the speech areas of the cortex had been committed to non-

[2] Mary Finocchiaro, *Teaching Children Foreign Languages*, New York, McGraw-Hill 1964, p. 4.
[3] Wilder Penfield, "The Uncommitted Cortex," *The Atlantic Monthly* (July 1964), pp. 77–81.
[4] Ibid., p. 78.
[5] Ibid.

speech functions. (Bilingualism is examined in Chapter 5.) If the validity of this evidence is accepted, then the goal of coordinate bilingualism becomes unequivocally linked with the objectives of elementary school education. Failure to provide adequate exposure to native patterns of foreign speech in the primary grades is tantamount to crippling a section of the child's brain. Whether it is done with the blow of a hammer, the slice of a surgeon's knife, or the apathy and ignorance of those who control educational policy, crippling will result if the first ten years of a child's life are allowed to slip by without implanting a second language in the "uncommitted cortex." Dr. Penfield states at the end of his essay:

What the brain is allowed to record, how and when it is conditioned—these things prepare it for the great achievement, or limit it to mediocrity. Boy and man are capable of so much more than is demanded of them! Adjust the time and the manner of learning, then you may double your demands and your expectations.[6]

Studies of FLES students' performance in high school foreign language programs have tended to support Doctor Penfield's contentions. When the program is a continuous, well-articulated course of study from the beginning point in the grades through to the senior high school, students with a FLES background have shown significantly better achievement than youngsters with a non-FLES background.[7] Studies have also shown that foreign languages can be added to the elementary school program without adversely affecting pupil achievement in other areas of the curriculum. A carefully controlled experiment at the University of Illinois showed that the "pupils in this study who engaged in learning a second language for twenty minutes each school day showed no significant loss in achievement in other subjects as measured by the Iowa-Every-Pupil Test of Basic Skills."[8] An earlier study had also indicated that "a strong FLES program is especially important to the slow learner, who finds it one of his areas of highest achievement."[9]

Despite the evidence to the effect that FLES programs can be effective, many such programs have not achieved satisfactory results. One obvious reason for the difficulties is the shortage of properly trained elementary school foreign language specialists. Dr. George Scherer has

[6] Ibid., p. 81.

[7] For example, a 1963 Title VI, NDEA report from the U.S. Office of Education showed the Somerville, N.J. FLES students achieving 67 points higher than average on the College Board Foreign Language Achievement Tests. Also, the FLES students were at least one year ahead of other high school students and showed no loss of achievement in other subject areas. Moreover, a much larger than average number of low-ability FLES youngsters elected foreign languages at the high school level.

[8] C. E. Johnson, J. S. Flores, and F. P. Ellison, "The Effect of Foreign Language Instruction on Basic Learning in Elementary Schools," *Modern Language Journal* 47 (January 1963), pp. 8–11.

[9] Paul C. McRill, "FLES in District R–1," *Modern Language Journal* 45 (December 1961), p. 370.

commented on some of the other reasons for the failure of the FLES programs: *Exactly what happened to me.*

The practice of having FLES graduates start all over again with seventh grade beginners must be vigorously condemned. There are several possible reasons for such a procedure, each implying lack of foresight. a) The outcomes of FLES are so minimal or so nebulous that there is no ongoing program in junior high with which the children can be adequately articulated. b) While the outcomes are entirely adequate, the FLES and junior high materials are not sequential. c) The school cannot afford a special track for the FLES graduates. d) The school is unable to arrange to join FLES graduates with junior high school beginners who have advanced to the second or third year of study. Any of these reasons, or any combination thereof, means that there has been a lack of planning for articulation. And without such planning, the program should never have been initiated. The failure to provide for progressive continuity can only mean serious educational waste.[10]

THE SCHEDULE

In most of the writings on foreign language teaching below the college level, the schedule—if it is mentioned at all—is treated as a constant rather than as a variable. It is assumed that 20 to 30 students will meet with the same teacher each day, 5 days a week, for 50 to 60 minutes in a rather traditional-type classroom. In his book, *Language and Language Learning,* Nelson Brooks devotes one paragraph to a description of the traditional schedule. He concludes the paragraph by stating, "Whatever variants of this pattern may be found serve only to emphasize its basic sameness."[11]

Since the class period is viewed as a constant, improving the schedule is usually seen in quantitative terms: A year of language study consists of 36 five-day weeks (rougly 180 hours for the school year). To improve the schedule a school can, for example, set four such years of study as the minimum in place of the traditional two. Contact hours with the language are thereby doubled without changing the "basic sameness" of the schedule or of the classroom situation.

The schedule remains highly resistant to change mostly for reasons that have little to do with the learning process. Administrative expedience appears to be the chief reason for having divided a day into the "egg-crate" pattern; allotting equal daily modules to each area of the instructional program is the simplest way of proceeding. And the egg-crate pattern is resistant to alteration because it has become built into the method of defining the quality of secondary school education within various regions of the United States. The 5-hour school week (multiplied

[10] George A. C. Scherer, "The Sine Qua Nons of FLES," *German Quarterly* 37 (November 1964) pp. 9–10.
[11] Nelson Brooks, *Language and Language Learning*, New York, Harcourt Brace Jovanovich, 1964, p. 46.

by 36 weeks) constitutes the school year for grades 9 through 12. Completion of a school year carries one unit of credit. According to accrediting agencies, a "good" school offers a certain pattern of such units in various subject areas. Thus a school might not be fully accredited if it fails to show 2 units of foreign language, 4 units of English, 4 units of mathematics, and so forth. It is presumed that the units have meaning in terms of what a student has learned in these subject areas as a result of having spent a certain number of hours in the classroom.

Colleges and universities lend support to the practice of assigning quantitative value to units of credit. College language departments apparently presume that the instructional goals of the high school are identical with those of the college but that the pace of instruction is approximately half that of the college. Accordingly, it has long been the practice to equate two years of high school foreign language with one year of college instruction. Students who have completed two or four years of high school languages are thus credited with one and two years of college work. (One and three are often considered less desirable as units of credit since they are not readily divisible by two.) There have been sporadic attempts to modify the egg-crate schedule and the credit system during the first half of this century. Such efforts have not been fully satisfactory in the eyes of many educators. As a Minnesota administrator expresses it:

The schedule often has come to dominate the students, the teachers, the administrators, and the curriculum. We see around us a struggle which has been left at a stalemate. By employing makeshift devices such as dropping required courses, conducting early morning or late afternoon classes, teaching during the lunch periods, students are allowed to take "extra" electives such as foreign languages. These devices are hardly the answer.[12]

The answer, as viewed by some educators, is to change the method of organizing the curriculum so that the instructional goals become the constant factors and everything else becomes variable. That is, the staffing policies, time allotment, class size, and pace of instruction are all adjusted to conform to the needs of the instructional objectives. This method of reorganizing the curriculum is often referred to as "flexible scheduling." Those who advocate flexible scheduling assume that such basic changes in the approach to teaching can and should be made. The most basic tenet of flexible scheduling is that the student should be directed toward attaining certain clearly defined educational objectives rather than toward serving time in a rather inflexible pattern of courses. The problems resulting from having daily variations in class size, period length, and staff utilization can be solved—it appears—through use of the computer. In fact, dozens of schools throughout the nation have operated successfully on computer-generated schedules produced by the Stanford School Scheduling

[12] Almon Hoye, "Can Flexible Schedules Affect Foreign Language Enrollments," *Minnesota Foreign Language Bulletin* 6 (May 1966), pp. 1–2.

System.[13] Two of the Stanford advocates of this system comment as follows upon the possibilities and limitations of computer-generated schedules:

School schedules are the result of the simultaneous availability of three basic elements: (1) teachers, (2) students, and (3) rooms, within well-defined limits of time. The nearly infinite number of combinations of these factors far exceed the capacities of the most astute educator. A sophisticated computer, however, has a memory capacity that will investigate millions of possible combinations within a few seconds. Consequently, the availability of teachers, rooms, and student requests for each class can be determined at each stage of schedule development. Thus, a high percentage of student requests can be satisfied. There are, however, important things that a computer cannot do. A computer is an intricate box of switches that is controlled completely by a logically designed program. The computer and the programs of control are logical and systematic procedures; there is no mystique—no magic. The computer cannot create needed rooms, additional teachers, or expand time available for a program. The limits of reality have not been altered, but the ability to manipulate the factors within these limits has been greatly enhanced.[14]

There is, of course, much more to flexible scheduling than the specification of educational objectives and the use of the computer. Enthusiasts of this type of instructional reorganization make certain assumptions regarding (1) use of staff, (2) allotment of time, (3) size of class, and (4) pace of instruction. By itself, changing the schedule will have little positive impact on foreign language learning unless major changes are made in these four areas. The four basic assumptions, as they apply to foreign language learning, are outlined below:

Assumption Number One: Staff Flexibility
A significant amount of student learning is possible without the professional teacher being physically present in the classroom or laboratory, even though some aspects of language learning require the presence of a highly skilled professional.
Corollary a:
Certain types of drill can be performed as well or better with audiovisual devices and programmed materials.
Corollary b:
Nonprofessional native speakers can direct small-group conversational practice sessions.
Corollary c:
A nonprofessional librarian-technician can perform routine laboratory functions in such a way as to make foreign language drills available to the student on an open-hour basis as an alternative procedure. Remote-access equipment can provide drill in a similar fashion by means of a dial or push-button system.

[13] Dwight W. Allen and Donald DeLay, "Flexible Scheduling, a Reality," *Stanford University School of Education* (May 1966), p. 3.
[14] Ibid., p. 10.

73

Corollary d:
A hierarchy of staff members is implied by all this. A professional teacher directs the instruction for each language, and assigns instructional tasks to native-speaking teacher aides, interns, clerks, and other members of the instructional team. The number of people needed in each category will, of course, vary according to the size of the school.

Assumption Number Two: Time Flexibility
The length of the class period should be varied in accordance with the nature of the learning task.
Corollary a:
Certain learning activities may require a continuous period of time in excess of the traditional 60-minute class period.
Corollary b:
Other activities may be more adequately performed in smaller modules of time.

Assumption Number Three: Class-Size Flexibility
The size of a class group should vary from day to day and from class to class according to its purposes.
Corollary a:
Some learning activities can be carried on effectively with groups as large as 100 or more.
Corollary b:
Other types of learning are better carried on in groups of six to eight students.
Corollary c:
On still other occasions, total individualization is desirable.

Assumption Number Four: Pacing Flexibility
All students in a foreign language program need not be studying the same material at the same time.
Corollary a:
Some students can reach the instructional goals at a much faster rate than permitted under the present scheduling system.
Corollary b:
Other students who are now failing or doing poorly can reach the instructional goals if more time is allowed for them to do so.
Corollary c:
Each step in the learning process should be scheduled in such a way as to permit students to go faster or slower in accordance with their ability with respect to the learning problem in question.
Corollary d:
The proposed goal-oriented curriculum can be established in the existing time-oriented system. (This presumes that each student's level of achievement can be converted into credit units for graduation from high school and to semester hours of credit for college entrance.)

At this writing, several dozen schools throughout the nation had tried flexible scheduling with varying degrees of success. An evaluation of the more successful programs shows that the flexible schedule reduces the psychological pressures on the student and allows him a wider choice of elective subjects. In one school, the introduction of flexible scheduling was accompanied by a three-fold increase in foreign language enrollment within a four-year period.[15] At worst, the introduction of flexible scheduling can produce virtual chaos. The most common causes for instructional breakdowns resulting from the schedule are:

1 Failure to feed workable scheduling data into the computer; result: an unworkable schedule.
2 Failure to provide adequate self-instructional materials.
3 Failure to provide adequate laboratory facilities so that the students can use the self-instructional materials without teacher supervision.
4 Failure to staff properly or to reorient the staff to the instructional changes required by the flexible schedule.

THE TEACHER

As often the case, the key to the success or failure of schedules—flexible or otherwise—lies with the teachers and their skill or lack of skill as trained professionals. According to a nationwide study of teacher preparation in America, there is little cause for optimism in this direction. For, if 30 semester hours of study in a given foreign language are accepted as the equivalent of a major in that language, then less than half the foreign language teachers in the country are teaching in their major field of study.[16] Immediately the question arises, "What does the term 'major' mean with regard to the person's effectiveness as a teacher?" For a partial answer we can turn to the findings of the Foreign Service Institute of the Department of State with respect to the average time required for adults to achieve functional mastery of a foreign language. In preparing federal employees for assignment overseas, 600 classroom contact hours were found to be the required time in the commonly taught languages.[17] Converting 30 semester hours into classroom contact hours produces a figure of 540; 60 hours fewer for the college major than for the federal employee. A narrow interpretation of these figures could lead one to conclude that over half the foreign language teachers in America have not even had the opportunity to become proficient in the language they are teaching

---

[15] Hoye, op. cit., p. 3.
[16] Donald D. Walsh. "The Préparation of Modern-Foreign-Language Teachers," *Modern Language Journal* 48 (October 1964), pp. 352–353. This article based on a nationwide survey shows 55.2 percent of all foreign language teachers with less than 30 semester hours; 15 percent with less than 17 hours.
[17] Marjorie C. Johnston and Elizabeth Keesee, *Modern Foreign Languages and Your Child*, Washington, D.C., GPO, 1964. p. 29.

because they lack even minimal contact with that language. However, there are other factors that may alter the picture somewhat. Many teachers have traveled in foreign countries and have engaged in special kinds of remedial work, which may not appear as semester hours on the survey forms.[18] On the other hand, many of the nation's language teachers—including those with more than 30 semester hours—received their college training during the grammar-reading-translation era; the semester hours gained during that period can scarcely be equated with the hours spent in the intensive programs of the Foreign Service Institute. In view of the facts available, it appears safe to assume that a rather large proportion of the nation's foreign language teachers are not very proficient in the languages they are called upon to teach. If the majority of our teachers are in reality highly limited compound bilinguals, how realistic is the goal of coordinate bilingualism? In short, can the student achieve a higher degree of language proficiency than his teacher possesses? There are those who feel that, with proper use of audiovisual devices, he can. As Patricia O'Connor expresses it, "The notion that only a teacher with a wide range of conversational fluency can successfully conduct aural-oral practice in the classroom is a common error and reflects a mistaken impression of the function of a teacher of a beginning foreign language."[19] The teacher, in Miss O'Connor's view, is needed to diagnose student problems, to direct the amount and type of drill work needed to overcome such problems, to motivate, and to perform many other important teaching duties. However, the machine can make up for much of the teacher's linguistic deficiency, if good materials are available and if they are used intelligently.

In an effort to cope with the problems created by a shortage of well-prepared teachers, many schools have employed educated native speakers. However, even when they are fully bilingual, such persons do not always prove effective. Sometimes the failure is traceable to cultural differences; that is, the foreign speaker is simply unable to adjust to the American way of doing things. In other instances, the problem seems to be his inability to identify the problems confronting the English-speaking student. In short, the native speaker, having learned his language the "natural way," cannot understand why anyone should have any trouble learning it. As a result, he fails to realize that even the simplest items can be major learning problems. (For example, the native teacher of English as a foreign language may fail to realize that those who speak Spanish cannot hear the difference between such word pairs as "hit" and "heat" or "watch" and "wash.") Therefore, the native speaker must receive thorough advance instruction in the linguistic, cultural, and psychological problems of teaching his own tongue to nonnatives. With suitable training, the native can become a highly competent instructor. The problems involved in such a training program are discussed in a letter to the Modern Language Association.

[18] Walsh, op. cit., p. 356.
[19] Patricia O'Connor, *Modern Foreign Languages in High School: Prereading Instruction*, Washington, D.C., GPO, 1960, p. 3.

No individual is inherently prepared to teach his own language—sometimes contrary to his own belief. In our some thirteen Peace Corps language programs we have dealt with close to forty language informants. Never have we been quite so successful as we have in this program for Afghanistan. Upon their arrival, they were plagued with the common adult misconceptions of language and how it is learned. Their concepts and attitudes toward their native language, Farsi, have changed. Their preconceived ideas of how to "tell" someone about their language and thus impart language skills have been obliterated. Their insistence that language is words no longer persists. Their recognition that language is pattern and must be thoroughly drilled is exemplified in the classroom by good classroom practices.[20]

SUMMARY

The fullest realization of the objectives of the American method is hindered by many factors. Chief among them are:
1 The difficulty of motivating students to become partial bilinguals when they live in a monolingual society.
2 The short sequence of study provided by an inflexible curriculum.
3 The tendency to delay language learning beyond the optimum age.
4 The lack of well-trained foreign language teachers at all levels.

Educators are experimenting with new instructional approaches which may provide partial solutions to such problems. Among those now being investigated are:
1 The team approach to language instruction, which enables the school to draw upon the strong points of native speakers, American-born teachers, and language laboratory drill sessions.
2 More flexible scheduling practices, which provide longer sequences of study and which make language study available to more students.
3 Individualized programs that can minimize continuity problems, thus enabling the high school to capitalize upon language skills acquired in the elementary and junior high school.
4 Electronically reproduced models of native speech presented in such a way as to allow the student to acquire a better accent than that of his nonnative instructor.

BIBLIOGRAPHY

Agard, F. B., and H. B. Dunkel, *An Investigation of Second-Language Teaching,* Boston, Ginn, 1948.
Allen, Dwight W., "Individualized Instruction," *CTA Journal* (October 1965), 28 f.

[20] David Burns, Language Coordinator, *Experiments in International Living*, 30 November 1963, quoted in "Foreign Language Program Notes," Spring Issue, 1964, p. 2.

Allen, Dwight W., and Donald DeLay, "Flexible Scheduling, a Reality," *Stanford University School of Education* (May 1966).

Allen, Dwight W., and Robert L. Politzer, "Flexible Scheduling and Foreign Language Instruction: A Conference Report," *Modern Language Journal* 50 (May 1967), 275 ff.

Bush, Robert N., and Dwight W. Allen, *A New Design for High School Education: Assuming a Flexible Schedule,* New York, McGraw-Hill, 1964.

Frank, J. G., "Can One Really Learn a Foreign Language at School?" *Modern Language Journal* 42 (May 1958), pp. 379–381.

Hoye, Almon, "Can Flexible Schedules Affect Foreign Language Enrollments," *Minnesota Foreign Language Bulletin* 6 (May 1966), pp. 1–5.

Kettelkamp, G. C., "Time Factor in Beginning Foreign Language Classes," *Modern Language Journal* 45 (February 1960), pp. 68–70.

Penfield, Wilder, "The Uncommitted Cortex," *The Atlantic Monthly* (July 1964), pp. 77–81.

5

■ *"Would you tell me, please, which way I ought to go from here?" said Alice to the Cheshire-Puss. "That depends a great deal on where you want to get to," said the Cat. "I don't much care where—" said Alice. "Then it doesn't matter which way you go," said the Cat.*
"—so long as I get somewhere" *Alice added as an explanation. "Oh, you're sure to do that," said the Cat, "if you only walk long enough."* LEWIS CARROLL

■Goals of foreign language instruction: minimum essentials

In a world more rational than Wonderland, Alice would have known her destination and would then have requested precise directions as to how to arrive there. Similarly, in those real human enterprises that are subject to rational restraints, it is common practice to determine one's objectives and then to do whatever is necessary to reach them. An automobile manufacturer, for example, does not settle for an assembly line that turns out vehicles sans motor, sans fenders, sans steering wheel. The requirements of economic survival dictate that the production goals be achieved. Accordingly, the manufacturer hires staff and purchases equipment needed to arrive at those objectives with maximum efficiency. Failure to achieve the goals means economic loss and, ultimately, the dissolution of the enterprise.

But in the teaching of foreign languages in our schools and colleges, such restraints appear not to operate. Generations of Americans have enrolled in courses called French, German, and Spanish without having learned French, German, or Spanish. American language ineptitude continues to be a rich source of international humor. Apparently, we have not staffed and equipped our language teaching enterprise to accomplish results that native speakers consider adequate. What is more, the language teaching profession has failed even to agree upon what those results *ought* to be. There are those who would be satisfied with the reading-translation goals of the post–World War I era. On the other hand, a substantial segment of the profession advocates the teaching of all four language skills—listening, speaking, reading, and writing. Moreover, the advocates of the fundamental-skills objective generally insist that the foreign language be learned in such a way that the student is able to communicate directly in the target language. This implies at least a limited degree of bilingualism in the learner; a sharp contrast with the older reading-translation objective, which required the student only to talk about the foreign language in English and to decode written material from the foreign language into English. Thus, in the relatively short post-Sputnik era, the expectations of many high school language programs have changed drastically. Publications of the major American educational organizations state that ability to communicate in the foreign language should be a primary objective of the foreign language curriculum. California, New York, and other high-population states list similar objectives in their state curriculum guides.[1] And, as was noted in the second chapter, a rather high level of language proficiency is deemed necessary if foreign language study is to have significant educational value according to contemporary standards. All of this raises a very practical question regarding what degree of bilingualism is actually attainable within the framework of American education. This, in turn, calls for clarification of what bilingualism really is.

WHAT IS A BILINGUAL?   DISAGREE

A person who has some degree of facility in more than one language is a bilingual. That is obvious enough. However, researchers tell us that the method of acquiring the two languages and the conditions under which they are learned can be so different as to produce significantly divergent types of dual-language behavior. The two extremes have been labeled *coordinate bilingualism* and *compound bilingualism*. To indicate what is implied by these terms it might be helpful to cite conditions of the sort that have produced various degrees and types of bilingualism. (Although these are hypothetical cases, they do have living counterparts which differ only in the specific details.)

In the case of the coordinate bilingual, imagine a person who had spent one half of his early childhood in Chicago; the other half in Paris, and that, as a result of this dual residence, he is able to function as a Frenchman in France and as an American in the Midwest without being distinguishable as a foreigner in either culture. Such a person is a coordinate bilingual in the fullest meaning of the term. His use of language gesture, and other behavior patterns will reveal a perfect sensitivity to the cultural referents of either Paris or Chicago.

In contrast, imagine a man who has achieved bilingualism without ever having left the northeastern section of the United States. He is equally fluent in French and English, but he has learned his French within a Franco-American cultural context. After high school, he studied French at an Eastern University under the tutelage of a native Frenchman so that his accent is flawlessly Parisian. The resultant bilingual is identifiable in the East as a man who speaks American English; in Paris, he is identifiable as an American who speaks excellent French.

Both types described here are bilingual. Yet there is a basic difference. One uses two languages to communicate in two different cultures, while

---

[1] See foreign language bulletins from the Bureau of Secondary Education, State Department of Education, Sacramento, Calif.; and from the Bureau of Secondary Curriculum Development, New York State Education Department, Albany, N.Y.

the other uses two languages to communicate in one culture. The dual-residence bilingual views such common phenomena as home, food, family, and school as being highly dissimilar in the two cultures. He will tend automatically to associate different images with the different words and expressions used to symbolize phenomena that are culturally divergent. However, the single-residence bilingual will be compelled to associate the same home, food, family, and school with the words that stand for these items in both languages. He can discuss everyday happenings with people who speak exclusively in one language or the other, but his cultural referents are largely the same in English as in French. Thus he has developed a *compound* system insofar as he ascribes the same meaning to words in the two languages, but he may be said to have a *coordinate* system to the degree that neither language dominates or interferes with his efforts to communicate in one language or the other. He is not confused by sounds, grammatical forms, or word arrangements as he shifts from one language to the other. But the shift, for example from the French word *famille* to the English *family* is an interchange of two words that refer to the same type of family organization, rather than two words symbolizing two ethnically distinct social institutions. The single-residence bilingual may be consciously aware that differences exist, but his knowledge of divergence represents vicarious rather than direct experience. (See the figure for an illustration of three varieties of bilingualism.) The student who has learned his French exclusively by translation to and from English is an example of the totally compound bilingual. Since all meaning in French is defined through English equivalents, he perceives no meaning in the foreign language until all the words and expressions have been translated into English and interpreted through the Anglo-American value system. A three-way process is followed for both active and passive skills. The sequence for listening and reading is: *French expression* to *English* to *meaning*. Similarly, with speaking and writing, the compound bilingual can only express his thoughts in the foreign language by reversing the three-way process so that communication flows from *meaning* to *English* to *French expression*. Nelson Brooks describes the compound system as one in which "the mother tongue is not relinquished, but continues to accompany—and of course to dominate—the whole complex fabric of language behavior."[2] For the totally compound bilingual, all referents—whether linguistic or semantic—are through the mother tongue. Brooks goes on to discuss ways "to establish in the learners in our classrooms a dual system of verbal symbolism in which mother tongue and second language are co-ordinated but not compounded."[3] Like most proponents of the new methodology, Brooks suggests that limited bilingualism of the coordinate type is feasible in American schools. Presumably this refers to the second type of coordinate system in which semantic referents to the target culture are either compound or vicarious. (That is, the language referents are either to

[2] Nelson Brooks, *Language and Language Learning,* 2nd ed., New York, Harcourt, Brace Jovanovich, 1964, p. 49.
[3] Ibid., p. 50.

81

BILINGUAL WITH DUAL-RESIDENCE BACKGROUND

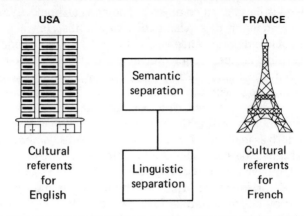

USA

FRANCE

Cultural referents for English

Semantic separation

Linguistic separation

Cultural referents for French

BILINGUAL WITH SINGLE-RESIDENCE BACKGROUND

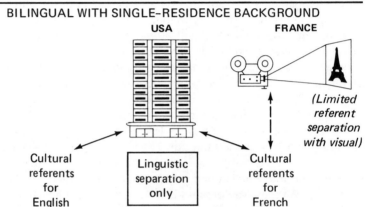

USA

FRANCE

(Limited referent separation with visual)

Cultural referents for English

Linguistic separation only

Cultural referents for French

BILINGUAL WITH TOTALLY COMPOUND SYSTEM
(All foreign language meaning filtered through English)

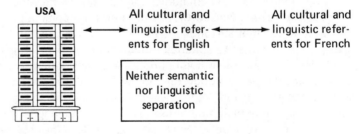

USA

All cultural and linguistic referents for English

All cultural and linguistic referents for French

Neither semantic nor linguistic separation

the American culture or to a visualization of cultural phenomena in the target culture.)

Judging from past experience with dual-language learning in this country, it appears that few American students will ever become full co-ordinate bilinguals. In the areas of culture and vocabulary the American can, for example, gather knowledge about the Mexican home, the German school system and the French family. But such knowledge, whether gained through reading, lecture, or visualization, provides only a pale, distorted, in-

82

complete expression of reality as viewed by a native speaker who grew up in the culture. Vicarious experiences—valuable as they appear to be—cannot be expected to duplicate the experience that one gains, for example, by living as a child in a Mexican home, attending a German *Volksschule*, or growing up in a French family.

However, the Army Specialized Training Programs and certain post-Sputnik experiments have demonstrated that, under certain conditions, Americans can achieve a degree of fluency that resembles coordinate bilingualism of the single-residence variety. That is, students can develop considerable skill in expressing their version of reality through the foreign system of auditory symbolization. But that symbolization, however, skillfully it is manipulated, will be strongly influenced by the fact that the learner grew up in an American family and attended an American school. His or her essential outlook is likely to remain Anglo-American regardless of the degree of fluency and correctness which he or she acquires in the new language. In the final analysis, the serious student of language—whatever system is used—must approximate, to some degree, the language performance of a literate native.

Table 3 summarizes and categorizes the essential learning objectives that are applicable to any of the commonly taught European languages. Assuming that oral and written communication is the ultimate goal of instruction, it is evident that the student must be able to produce all the sounds, grammatical structures, and word-order sequences of the new language and be able to recognize all auditory and graphic symbols as they are used in writing and in the normal flow of native speech. It is also clear that learning a considerable number of "content words" is a matter of high priority, perhaps second in importance only to the mastery of phonology, morphology, and syntax. Many would insist that the vocabulary be acquired with a clear understanding of the cultural implications carried by the foreign words. For example, peninsular Spanish has four patterns of pronouns and/or verb endings to express the idea of "you" while English uses one predominate pattern to express the second person. But the choice of the familiar forms (*tu—vosotros*) versus the polite forms (*usted—ustedes*) requires an understanding of Spanish attitudes toward age and social status. Certainly, more is involved here than the mere matching of vocabulary items from one language to the other. For this reason, Table 3 includes "Culture" in the horizontal headings. The column labeled "Ultimate Goals" refers to the synthesis of the five essentials that must take place in the student's mind if genuine communication is to take place. The vertical listing of the four skills is necessary because there are distinctly different objectives and learning problems for each skill. For example, the vocabulary that one uses for active speaking is vastly different in type and scope from the vocabulary that one recognizes in the more passive process of listening. A similar divergence exists between reading and writing. The instructional goals must reflect such differences. The final category entitled "Concept" is based on the belief that mastery of the four skills must be accompanied by a grasp of certain basic generalizations and concepts.

ESSENTIALS FOR COMMUNICATION

Skills and concepts	Phonology	Morphology	Syntax
Listening: the ability	to hear all the meaningful sound contrasts of the foreign language when it is spoken at a normal rate in complete utterances.	to hear all the changes of meaning caused by modifications of word forms when the language is spoken at a normal rate in complete utterances.	to hear the foreign language without being confused by syntactical arrangements.
Speaking: the ability	to produce all the significant sounds and intonation patterns of the foreign language in a manner acceptable to native speakers.	to express one's ideas orally using appropriate grammatical forms.	to express one's ideas orally using word order which is characteristic of the spoken language
Reading: the ability	to associate the appropriate graphic symbols with the sounds for which they stand.	to draw meaning directly from the printed page through recognition of changes in meaning caused by modifications in structure.	to read directly in the foreign language without being confused by syntactical arrangements.
Writing: the ability	to spell the graphic symbols which stand for the sounds of the language.	to express one's ideas in writing using appropriate grammatical forms.	to express one's ideas in writing using the appropriate word order of the foreign language.
Concept: the ability	to understand the relationship between sound symbols and written symbols (i.e., "phonemes" versus "graphemes").	to understand how the foreign language uses such devices as gender, number, case, agreement, verb endings, and other modifications of oral and written forms to express meaning.	to understand how the foreign language uses variations in word order to express meaning.

Source: The preliminary edition of the German Curriculum Guide, Madison, Wis.,

Vocabulary	Culture	Ultimate goals
to hear and understand words in normal conversational contexts.	*to detect nuances of meaning relating to social position, family relationships, customs, national traditions, literary classics, etc.*	*to comprehend aurally new arrangements of familiar material when spoken at normal tempo and with normal intonation and rhythm.*
to acquire an active speaking vocabulary appropriate to the age, maturity level, and capacity of the student and one which is appropriate for communication in the modern world.	*to use culturally acceptable forms appropriate to the age, social standing, and occupation of the person addressed and to reveal some knowledge of the heritage of those who speak the foreign language.*	*to recognize familiar vocabulary and grammatical forms and to apply them to new situations using pronunciation and intonation in a manner acceptable to a native speaker.*
to recognize in context a wide range of vocabulary items with sensitivity to the differences between spoken and written vocabulary and between contemporary and older literary forms, words, and expressions.	*to be able to read everything from newspapers to works of literature. This implies a basic knowledge of the history, literature, current world position, etc. of countries in which the language is spoken.*	*to read directly without constant recourse to a bilingual vocabulary list.*
to express one's ideas in writing using vocabulary which is appropriate to the occasion.	*to use the appropriate style according to the nature of what is being written.*	*to express one's ideas —idiomatically and freely—in writing.*
to understand that the semantic range of foreign words usually differs from that covered by the nearest English equivalents.	*to evaluate the foreign culture objectively and on its own merits rather than from the standpoint of Anglo-American culture.*	*to apply spontaneously everything one has learned to new situations.*

Department of Public Instruction, 1968.

85

WHAT IS BILINGUAL-BICULTURAL EDUCATION ?

The discussion to this point referred to teaching a second language to speakers of English who have been rather completely assimilated into the Anglo-American culture. There are people in the United States who have not been assimilated into the so-called "dominant" culture. These include speakers of Spanish, French, Chinese, Portuguese, and American Indian languages, and others who have remained culturally and linguistically distinct from the Anglo majority. During the late sixties and early seventies increasingly larger allocations of federal, state, and local moneys were made available for the education of school-age children whose background included linguistic and cultural influences other than those of the dominant culture. The type of bilingual-bicultural educational programs that evolved as a result could be defined as a process that uses the student's primary language as the principle vehicle of instruction, while at the same time systematically and sequentially teaching him the language of the predominant culture.

The design of the more extensive programs include pupils ranging from preschool levels through high school. One of the characteristics of the well-developed bilingual-bicultural program is that the program includes schools in which the student hears and is free to use both English and the primary language as best fits his needs as a learner. Another characteristic is that children who are truly dominant in a second language learn to read first in that language. Learning to read in English is postponed until the child is ready to read in that language. The reverse is also true. That is, students who are dominant in English learn to read in English first and then, after they have practiced listening and speaking in the language of their heritage, are taught to read the language. Those who are in the program from kindergarten through grade 6 will have the opportunity to become not only bilingual but to become literate in two languages. That is, they will be able to do reading, arithmetic, science, social studies, and other activities in both English and the second language.

As far as sequence is concerned, the comprehensive bilingual-bicultural program offers junior and senior high school programs as well as programs at the elementary school level. Thus, a youngster having completed a bilingual program in the elementary school is not cast adrift. On the contrary, he has the opportunity to learn more about the language of his heritage and the heritage itself. Also, the secondary school program usually includes such components as bilingual guidance services, special help in reading development, and courses such as French for speakers of French, Spanish for speakers of Spanish, and so forth. In the later case, students who already have considerable knowledge of their ancestoral language can further develop it without having to sit through courses that were designed for Anglos. For example, in a bilingual-bicultural program for Spanish speakers, American history and Hispanic culture may be studied bilingually (that is, either in English or Spanish or both).

One of the most significant elements of a program of this kind is that students are encouraged to use their dominant language in the school. To people who have only recently become exposed to bilingual education this may not sound very revolutionary. However, in the past, the policy of many schools around the country was to ban the use of any language other than English. The implication was that the students had to learn by means of English whether they knew it or not. Thus, making instruction available in the language of one's cultural heritage is an important aspect of a bilingual-bicultural program. The reasons for doing this are quite subtle and the values derived from it are not easy to document, prove, or measure. Basically, it has to do with something that educators refer to as "positive self-concept." This means simply that for people to do well in school or in life in general they have to feel good about themselves and about their background. If the language, culture, and the historical heritage that the students bring with them from the home are neglected or even looked down upon in school, then this tends to damage the students' view of themselves and to cause them to reject the educational institution and everything that it has to offer. The people who advocate bilingual education are often quite sensitive about not referring to it as "remedial education." The reason for this is that the term "remediation" seems to imply that there is something wrong with the student's cultural background; that it needs to be eliminated or reformed. For this reason the stance of many bilingual educators is "developmental," which means that the student's background is to be treated as something positive, something worth being further developed.

Another question that frequently comes up relates to biculturism. One of the very sensitive issues in this regard has to do with staffing. Questions have arisen both from opponents and supporters of bilingual education asking to what extent the program is bilingual-bicultural if teachers in the program represent only one cultural background. This question is far from being resolved. (Should staff members be exclusively from the cultural group of the students, or should there be a mix of Anglo and non-Anglo staff members?) Many misunderstandings have arisen due to the lack of understanding of the nature and purpose of bilingual education. Let me suggest a few basic ideas that need to be conveyed:

1   Few, if any, proponents of bilingual education contend that the student should *not* learn English as part of the bilingual program. On the contrary, a well-designed bilingual program will enable students to learn English as well as other subject matter.
2   The bilingual program is not intended to make the student less able to function in the dominant English-speaking culture.
3   The bilingual program is oriented to the concept of pluralism. In simple terms this means that an individual can function in the dominant culture without having to give up his or her ties *to* and feelings *for* a culture that has a different language and a different set of cultural patterns.

In 1974, while driving through a large city in the Midwest, where the question of local funding of a bilingual program was in the public view, I was listening to the car radio when an announcer from that city came on with an editorial denouncing bilingual education. He said that, after all, people have to live and work in this country and this requires them to speak English. They should not waste their time, he said, studying other languages and cultures. In effect, his opinion was that bilingual education would leave students worse off than they were before. This man was simply assuming that the intent, or at least the result, of bilingual education would be to make people so different from English-speaking Americans and so deficient in English that they would be unable to survive in an English-speaking, North American community. He was apparently unaware that some bilingual programs have actually resulted in *higher* achievement in both languages and a better understanding of both cultures. So it is clear that people who are advocates of bilingual education need to make a much greater effort to explain what its purposes are and to emphasize the good results that can come from this kind of a program.

THE CONTENT OF THE FOREIGN LANGUAGE PROGRAM

Each European language has a finite number of phonemes, morphemes, graphemes, and syntactical arrangements in the standard dialect. By one means or another, the student must gain functional mastery of these elements insofar as they apply to the skills of listening, speaking, reading, and writing. Most high school programs attempt to "cover" all the principal aspects of phonology during the first year (180 classroom hours) of instruction. The basic aspects of morphology and syntax are frequently not presented in their entirety until the second or third years of instruction. The learning of vocabulary and culture is, of course, never completed. Attempts have been made to identify the basic vocabulary items for the commonly taught languages, but these efforts have never been fully successful. As a result, most specification of vocabulary becomes a matter of arbitrary judgments based upon little more than common sense. In establishing priorities for learning, two categories of word types are often identified. First, there are a certain number of "function words" (that is, articles, prepositions, conjunctions, auxiliary verbs, and so on), which are used constantly by all native speakers. Most of these basic items are relatively easy to identify. Secondly, there is an unlimited reservoir of "content words." Here we can only guess at certain categories of vocabulary that the language learner is most likely to need for daily communication. Basic lexical items pertaining to home, numeration systems, colors, and other everyday words will normally receive priority consideration along with the function words. Current practice in the European nations is to deemphasize vocabulary building as such until the student has a good control of phonology, morphology, and syntax. In Russia, for example, as few as 300 new words are introduced during the first year's instruction. American foreign language programs typically attempt to teach between 1000 and 2000 new items during the beginning levels. This could be an unrealistically high expectation in view

good idea

of the concurrent emphasis upon phonology and grammar during the early years. In this regard, it appears that much research needs to be done in the direction of establishing reasonable content standards for the secondary school program. The course content tables which appear in this chapter are intended to serve as *samples* of minimal goals for a full four-year program in each of the commonly taught languages (French, German, and Spanish). It is a well-established fact that a few students could master the content of this four-level course in two years or less while others would need five or six years to gain even limited control of the suggested items. To cite but one example of rapid individual learning, we can take the case of Robert Baker of Indiana University who is said to have learned Russian by himself when he was a junior in high school. While manning a fire tower for the U.S. Forest Service in South Dakota, he completed a year and a half of high school Russian in 75 days.[4] However, despite the pace, or the sequence, or the manner of learning, there are certain aspects of each language that must somehow be mastered if the student is to claim with justification that he has learned French, German, or Spanish. Tables 4, 5, and 6 attempt to summarize the most basic items and to suggest the optimum sequence of presentation for each year of a four-year sequence. The scope of this book obviously does not permit a comprehensive listing of all conceivable course content for each language. It is hoped, however, that the tables will prove useful as a guide for helping teachers and students to focus their attention away from peripheral textbook items and toward a more balanced approach to the acquisition of fundamental language skills and concepts. Ideally, each school would develop its own curricular goals and would carry out the program in somewhat the following manner:

1 Determine the ability of local students to master a desired course of study.
2 Establish a continuous sequence of language study with enough contact hours to enable youngsters to progress from their usual state of total monolingualism to one of partial bilingualism (perhaps of the single-residence variety).
3 Staff and equip the language program to whatever extent is necessary for the achievement of the stated instructional goals.
4 Test students regularly to determine whether the goals are being achieved.

To do less than this is to encourage aimless, unfocused activity rather than systematic language learning. And, unlike Alice in Wonderland, a publicly financed educational enterprise cannot forever explain where it is going with some version of Alice's reply to the Cheshire Cat: "We don't much care where we are going, so long as we get somewhere." If it is to flourish, any educational enterprise must indicate its instructional goals in rather precise

[4] T. R. St. George (ed.), "Indiana's Russian Institute," *Education Age* 3 (September-October 1966), p. 9.

■4

I. FRENCH LEVEL I: MINIMAL COURSE CONTENT

A. Phonology
1. Listening and speaking skills
   a. all vowels, particularly, u, eu ; nasals in, on, an, un
   b. consonants and semiconsonants, especially l, r, gn, oui, ui, ail
   c. stress and absence of stress; 3 patterns of intonation, liaisons
   d. produce all of the above sounds accurately
   e. make obligatory liaisons
   f. reproduce short sentences with correct stress and intonation
2. Reading and writing skills
   a. all vowels, nasals, consonants, and semiconsonants, particularly e and mute e
   b. liaisons (obligatory and impossible)
   c. syllable and word boundaries
   d. stress and intonation
   e. various orthographic representations
   f. all vowels, nasals, consonants, and semiconsonants, mute e
   g. silent consonants
   h. m for nasals before p and b
   i. liaisons
   j. understand that French and English differ considerably in sounds and stress orthographic representations of sounds

B. Morphology
1. Listening and speaking skills
   a. determinatives (articles)
(1) definite	(4) possessive
(2) indefinite	(5) demonstrative
(3) partitive	

   b. nouns
(1) singular	(3) masculine
(2) plural	(4) feminine

   c. adjectives
(1) singular	(4) feminine
(2) plural	(5) interrogative
(3) masculine	

   d. pronouns
(1) demonstrative	(4) reflexive
(2) interrogative	(5) personal (subjects and objects)
(3) possessive	

   e. verbs (3 regular groups)
(1) être	(5) present
(2) avoir	(5) future
(3) faire, etc.	(7) imperative
(4) infinitive	(8) reflexive

2. Reading and writing skills
   Content as above plus an understanding that nouns, adjectives, determinatives agree with each other and with verb forms. There is generally one verb form to each person.

C. Syntax
1. Listening and speaking skills
   a. basic word order in statements (affirmative and negative)
   b. questions and commands (sp. qu'est-ce que c'est . . .)
   c. position of adjectives
   d. position of personal pronouns

I. FRENCH LEVEL I (Continued)

2. Reading and writing skills
   Content as above plus an understanding that word order differs from English especially in questions (several interrogative patterns coexist) with adjectives and with pronouns.

D. Vocabulary
1. Listening skill   (approximately 1000 words and expressions)
2. Speaking skill   (approximately   500 words and expressions)
3. Reading skill   (approximately 1200 words and expressions)
4. Writing skill   (approximately   500 words and expressions)
   a. content words
      (1) greetings
      (2) leave-taking
      (3) classroom, including conversational terms
      (4) numbers
      (5) colors
      (6) clothing
      (7) clock time
      (8) calendar time
      (9) school building
      (10) members of family
      (11) family life
      (12) meals
      (13) weather
      (14) Christmas
      (15) house parts
      (16) functions of body
   b. nouns, verbs, adjectives, adverbs pertaining to these subjects as well as function words such as et, ou, mais
   c. emphasis should be placed on concrete descriptive vocabulary connected with reality familiar to the students.
   d. in spoken and written form, words make up a language; to communicate in that language, one must grasp the meaning, isolated or in context, without conscious reference to English.

E. Culture
1. Introduction to French culture should be an integral and natural part of teaching French but should not take the place of teaching the language. The environment. of the classroom, French books, magazines, tapes, films, records, pictures, should stimulate the students' interest in learning about the following cultural items:
   a. French names
   b. forms of address
   c. courtesy patterns
   d. French school day and school year
   e. 24-hour clock
   f. French houses
   g. some typical foods and table manners
   h. French holidays—especially Christmas and Easter
   i. rhymes
   j. songs and music
2. The units of vocabularly are obviously linked closely to the study of culture As much of this as possible is done in French.
3. Cultural items are an integral part of a language. In listening to or reading the language, one must be aware of the nuances of cultural forms. To speak or write the language correctly also means to use culturally acceptable forms.

II. FRENCH LEVEL II: MINIMAL COURSE CONTENT

A. Phonology
1. Listening and speaking skills
   a. further work towards the mastery of sounds, especially those that differ most from English, r, u, etc.

      b. *rhythm and melody of sentences*

      c. *French pronunciation requires clearer enunciation, more articulation* (*tension is more sustained with lips but breath has less force*).

  2. *Reading and writing skills*

      a. *association of all French sounds with the right orthographic representations*

      b. *cognates*

      c. *homonyms* (*real and deceptive*)

      d. *technique in word attack*

      e. *accent and syllabication*

      f. *rhythm and melody of sentences*

      g. *writing emphasis on mute letters and groups of letters*

      h. *homonyms*

      i. *adjectives denoting nationality or city are capitalized*

B. *Morphology*

  1. *Listening and speaking skills*

      a. *prepositions and adverbs*

      b. *personal pronouns* (*indirect object*) + en, y, on, *and stressed forms*

      c. *verbs,* passé composé

        (1) *imperfect*   (5) *past infinitive*

        (2) *pluperfect*   (6) *immediate future*

        (3) *future perfect*   (7) *recent past*

        (4) *irregular imperative*

      d. *irregular verbs*

      e. *relative pronouns* qui, que

  2. *Reading and writing skills*

      a. *the same as above plus* passé simple (*used mostly in writing*)

      b. *tense functions almost always differ in French and English. There are many more verb endings in French than in English, also more irregular verbs.*

      c. *range of meaning of prepositions differs in French and in English.*

C. *Syntax*

  1. *Listening and speaking skills*

      a. *position of adverbs*

      b. *position of personal pronouns*

      c. *position of negative particles* (ne . . . pas, rien, plus, personne) *with auxiliary verb*

      d. *verb construction* (*direct or indirect objects or with infinitive verb with or without preposition*)

      e. *causative* faire

      f. *various ways of expressing possession*

      g. *pattern,* c'est . . . qui, c'est . . . que

  2. *Reading and writing skills*

  Content as above plus an understanding that the position of direct and indirect objects will be different according to whether they are nouns or pronouns; note also, complex and rigid word order in negative patterns with various particles.

D. *Vocabulary*

  1. *Listening skill*   (*approximately 1000 words and expressions*)

  2. *Speaking skill*   (*approximately 800 words and expressions*)

  3. *Reading skill*   (*approximately 1200 words and expressions*)

  4. *Writing skill*   (*approximately 800 words and expressions*)

  a. content words

(1) daily routine	*(10) transportation*
(2) telephoning	*(11) city*
(3) shopping	*(12) landscape*
(4) money	*(13) countryside, farming*
(5) sizes	*(14) travel, customs*
(6) letters and post office	*(15) animals*
(7) restaurants	*(16) holidays*
(8) doctor, dentist	*(17) sports*
(9) community	*(18) entertainments, arts*

  b. vocabulary should include functional words such as:
   (1) que
   (2) aussi longtemps que
   (3) même si
   (4) alors que
   (5) current idiomatic expressions
  c. words and expressions in French are sometimes closely related to English but almost always differ in range and meaning; vocabulary is influenced by historical background, social customs, and other factors, Beware of cognates (false or true).

 E. Culture
  1. Visual and audio stimuli as well as the topics of vocabulary should suggest the following cultural items for study at the second level.
   a. forms of letters
   b. types of urban life
   c. types of rural life
   d. relationships (family, friends)
   e. France:
    (1) landscape in regions
    (2) main rivers and cities
    (3) highlights of economy, industry, and present political situation
    (4) holidays
    (5) entertainments
    (6) folklore
    (7) proverbs
    (8) music, popular and classical
    (9) current events
  2. In listening and speaking, reading and writing, cultural patterns are obvious and must be observed by a native or nonnative speaker of the language.

III. FRENCH LEVEL III: MINIMAL COURSE CONTENT

 A. Phonology
  1. Listening and speaking skills
   a. introduction of regional differences
   b. increased length and speed of utterances
   c. nuances associated with different stresses and intonations
   d. perfecting pronunciation with increase in speed of utterance
   e. greater awareness of minute pronunciation differences
  2. Reading and writing skills
   a. perfecting of reading skill with increase in fluency and expression
   b. perfecting of writing skill with attention to individual needs

      c. *not all French-speaking people pronounce sounds alike but French as it is spoken in the Loire Valley, considered the purest, is understood by all French-speaking people.*

B. *Morphology*
  1. *Listening and speaking skills*
    a. *comparisons (adjectives, adverbs)*
    b. *relative pronouns* lequel, dont, où
    c. *conditional, present perfect*
    d. *subordinating conjunction with indicative*
    e. *more irregular verbs*
  2. *Reading and writing skills*
    Content as above, plus the second form of the past conditional; also an understanding that various nuances of meaning result from tense variations of verbs in subordinate clauses.

C. *Syntax*
  1. *Listening and speaking skills*
    expressions of duration: e.g., il y a . . . que, cela fait . . . que
  2. *Reading and writing skills*
    Content as above plus an understanding that time and duration are expressed with different word order and word forms than is characteristic of English.

D. *Vocabulary*
  1. *Increase in vocabulary cannot be stated in figures.*
  2. *Spoken and written vocabulary differ in volume and kind. The command of a large vocabulary can be achieved only through constant listening, speaking, reading, and writing practice.*
  3. *Passive vocabulary will be larger than active, but extent of both will depend on students' ability to speak and read French.*
  4. *A variety of graded readers may be used at this level. Much of the passive vocabulary will depend upon the selection of reading materials and textbooks.*
  5. *A vocabulary suitable for writing letters, outlines, reports, compositions should be developed.*
  6. *Topical vocabulary should include:*
    a. *current events*
    b. *education*
    c. *government*
    d. *history*
    e. *biography*
  7. *Emphasis should be placed on:*
    a. *more abstract vocabulary connected with intellectual activity, criticism, judgment*
    b. *vocabulary designed to express emotions and feelings*

E. *Culture*
  1. *Cultural items studied at the third level should include:*
    a. *France*
      (1) *government*
      (2) *educational system*
      (3) *recreation*
      (4) *highlights of history*
    b. *other French-speaking countries*
      (1) *Belgium*

        (2) Switzerland

        (3) French Canada

    c. French influence in:

        (1) Africa

        (2) America

  2. The cultural study is done mainly in French with some supplementary reading in English. It includes:

    a. listening to recordings and viewing films, filmstrips, and slides

    b. discussing what has been heard or read

    c. reading graded readers, periodicals, poetry, and literary prose

    d. writing letters, reports, compositions—revealing an understanding of the French culture

IV. FRENCH LEVEL IV: MINIMAL COURSE CONTENT

  A. Phonology

    1. Listening and speaking skills

      a. poetic variations in the language, in phrasing, rhythm, intonation

      b. perfecting pronunciation with attention to individual needs

    2. Reading and writing skills

      a. perfecting reading skill with increase in speed

      b. perfecting writing skill

        (1) punctuation

        (2) apostrophes

        (3) syllabication

      c. poetic forms of the language may differ from everyday French. In turn, spoken French differs from written French. French requires strict punctuation.

  B. Morphology

    1. Listening and speaking skills

      a. special uses of conditional

      b. subjunctive (present, imperfect)

      c. passive voice

      d. subordinating conjunctions and verbs with subjunctive

      e. direct and indirect discourse

      f. tense correspondence between main clause and subordinate clauses

      g. knowledge of the fact that the passive voice is used much less in French than in English and that on-forms or reflexive forms will often be used instead of the passive.

    2. Reading and writing skills

    Content as above plus the past and pluperfect forms of the subjunctive; also, students gain an understanding of the importance of the subjunctive in French along with the tendency to avoid forms other than the present.

  C. Syntax

    1. Listening and speaking skills

      a. word order in passive

      b. inversion of subject and verb in sentences other than questions

      c. word order with series of objects

      d. there are many patterns but each of them is specific

      e. emphasis is often conveyed by use of specific pattern (as well as by use of different intonation, as is mostly the case in English

    2. Reading and writing skills

    Content would be essentially the same as for listening and speaking skills.

D. *Vocabulary*
   1. *Amount of active and passive vocabulary is a matter of student's individual progress. A high rate of active vocabulary should be aimed for through a wide range of conversational topics, giving the student the ability to communicate in the modern world.*
   2. *Choice of litterary works is up to the teacher but should be based on the ability, interest, and maturity of the students, developing in them a sensitivity to the differences between spoken and written vocabulary and between contemporary and older literary forms, words, and expressions. Consideration may also be given to the grouping of college-bound and terminal students for selective reading.*
   3. *A writing vocabulary appropriate to the occasion should be mastered.*

E. *Culture*
   1. *The increased ability of the students to communicate in French, to read everything from newspapers to works of literature, makes it possible for them to gain an appreciation and understanding of French contributions to:*
      a. *literature*
      b. *painting*
      c. *sculpture*
      d. *architecture*
      e. *dramatic arts*
      f. *music*
      g. *sciences*
   2. *Current events are listened to, viewed, discussed, read, and written about. Books, periodicals, tapes, films, slides, records, and pictures are resource materials used directly by the students. The choice of these materials is up to the teacher who should take into consideration the age, maturity, ability, and interest of the student*
   3. *A knowledge of cultural forms and of the French heritage is a part of learning the French language. Works of literature can be appreciated best in the language in which they were written.*

■5

I. GERMAN LEVEL I: MINIMAL COURSE CONTENT

A *Phonology*
   1. *Listening and speaking skills*
      a. *short and long vowels*
      b. *pure and umlauted vowels*
      c. *difference between certain consonants in German and English, especially l, r, ch, (ich, ach sounds)*
      d. *word accent*
      e. *intonation and rhythm in statements, questions, commands*
   2. *Reading and writing skills*
      a. *short and long vowels*
      b. *pure and umlauted vowels*
      c. *diphthongs au, ai, äu, eu, ei*
      d. *consonants ch, chs, ck, dt, j, l, r, s, sch, st, sp, ß, th, v, w, z; silent h; final b, d, g*

　　　e. *off-glide,* er ; *final* e, *word accent*
　　　f. *intonation of sentences*
　　　g. *capitalization of nouns;* ich *is not capitalized*

B. *Morphology*
　1. *Listening and speaking skills*
　　　a. *agreement of subject and verb* (*especially important in speaking*)
　　　b. *definite and indefinite articles in nominative, accusative, dative*
　　　c. *personal pronouns in nominative and accusative*
　　　d. *predicate adjectives*
　　　e. *possessive adjective in nominative, accusative, dative*
　　　f. *interrogative and reflexive pronouns*
　　　g. *present tense of regular and irregular verbs and* haben, sein, werden *and* wollen, müssen, können
　　　h. *imperative of regular verbs*
　2. *Reading and writing skills*
　　　a. *nouns with definite and indefinite articles in nominative, accusative* (*dative: reading only*)
　　　b. *personal pronouns in nominative and accusative*
　　　c. *predicate adjectives*
　　　d. *possessive adjectives in nominative, accusative. dative*
　　　e. *interrogative and reflexive pronouns*
　　　f. *present tense of regular and irregular verbs and* haben, sein, werden *and*
　,　　wollen, müssen, können
　　　g. *imperative of regular verbs*
　　　h. *nouns and pronouns in agreement with present tense of regular and irregular verbs and* haben, sein, werden, *and* wollen, müssen, können
　　　i. *predicate adjective*
　　　j. *possessive adjectives in nominative and accusative*
　　　k. *interrogative and reflexive pronouns*

C. *Syntax*
　1. *Listening and speaking skills*
　　　a. *normal word order and inverted word order after* dann, hier, *etc.*
　　　b. *word order in questions and commands and statements*
　　　c. *word order with modals*
　　　d. *position of reflexive pronouns*
　　　e. *position of* nicht
　2　*Reading and writing skills*
　　　a. *normal word order and inverted word order after* dann, hier, *etc.*
　　　b. *word order in questions, commands, and statements*
　　　c. *word order with modals*
　　　d. *position of reflexive pronouns*
　　　e. *position of* nicht

D. *Vocabulary*
　1. *Listening skill*　(*approximately 1000 lexical items*)
　2. *Speaking skill*　(*up to 800 words and expressions*)
　3. *Reading skill*　(*approximately 1200 lexical items*)
　4. *Writing skill*　(*up to 800 words and expressions*)
　　　a. *basic items*
　　　　(1) *definite and indefinite articles in nominative, accusative, dative*
　　　　(2) *personal pronouns in nominative and accusative*
　　　　(3) *possessive adjectives*

97

I. GERMAN LEVEL I (Continued)

    (4) interrogative and reflexive pronouns
    (5) wollen, müssen, können
    (6) und, oder, aber, hier
    In addition, appropriate nouns, verbs, and adjectives are needed as they pertain to the adjoining categories of content words.

  b. content words

(1) greetings	(9) school building
(2) leave-taking	(10) house
(3) classroom	(11) members of family
(4) numbers	(12) parts of body
(5) colors	(13) common foods
(6) clothing	(14) weather
(7) clock time	(15) Christmas
(8) calendar time	

E. Culture

  1. Introduction to German culture should be an integral and natural part of teaching German but should not take the place of teaching the language. The environment of the classroom, German books, magazines, tapes, films, records, pictures, should stimulate the student's interest in learning about the following cultural items:

    a. German names
    b. forms of address
    c. courtesy patterns
    d. German school day and school year
    e. regional costumes
    f. 24-hour clock
    g. German houses
    h. some typical foods
    i. German holidays—especially Christmas, Advent
    j. rhymes
    k. songs and music

  2. The units of vocabulary are obviously linked closely to the study of culture. As much of this as possible is done in German.

II. GERMAN LEVEL II: MINIMAL COURSE CONTENT

A. Phonology

  1. Listening and speaking skills
    a. combination of sounds pf, qu, zw
    b. glottal stop
    c. foreign words with ch, tion, initial c, initial ps
    d. rhythm and melody of sentences
    e. production of all sounds in German words and in words adopted into German
    f. rhythm and melody of sentences
    g. accent in all types of words

  2. Reading and writing skills
    a. association of all German sounds with the right graphic symbols
    b. cognates (real and deceptive)
    c. foreign words
    d. accent and syllabication
    e. rhythm and melody of sentences
    f. learning to spell
    g. capitalization of polite "you" in all forms
    h. adjectives denoting nationality are not capitalized

B. Morphology
  1. Listening and speaking skills
    a. personal pronouns in dative
    b. demonstrative adjectives in nominative, accusative, dative
    c. adjective and adverb prepositions with accusative, dative, dative-accusative
    d. verbs (*including all modals, separable and inseparable verbs, and imperative of irregular verbs*)
      (1) past
      (2) present
      (3) perfect
      (4) future
  2. Reading and writing skills
    a. personal pronouns in nominative, accusative, dative
    b. demonstrative adjectives in nominative, accusative, dative
    c. prepositions with accusative, dative, dative-accusative
    d. verbs in past, present, perfect, and future tense (*including all modals, separable verbs, and imperative of irregular verbs*)

C. Syntax
  1. Listening and speaking skills
    a. position of direct and indirect objects (*nouns and pronouns*)
    b. inverted word order after adverbial and prepositional phrases
    c. word order in present and perfect tense
    d. word order in future tense
    e. word order with separable verbs
  2. Reading and writing skills
    a. position of direct and indirect objects (*nouns and pronouns*)
    b. word order in present, perfect, and future tenses
    c. word order with separable verbs
    d. inverted word order after adverbial and prepositional phrases

D. Vocabulary
  1. Listening skill   (*1200 lexical items above level I*)
  2. Speaking skill   (*1000 lexical items above level I*)
  3. Reading skill   (*1500 lexical items above level I*)
  4. Writing skill   (*1000 lexical items above level I*)
    a. content words

(1) daily routine	(9) city (German, American)
(2) telephoning	(10) landscape
(3) shopping	(11) travel
(4) letters	(12) animals
(5) post office	(13) holidays
(6) restaurant	(14) fairy tales
(7) community	(15) legends
(8) transportation	

  b. vocabulary should also include:
      (1) personal pronoun in dative
      (2) demonstrative adjective
      (3) prepositions with dative, accusative, dative-accusative dürfen, mögen, sollen
      (4) separable verbs
      (5) some foreign words

E. Culture
  1. Visual and audio stimuli as well as the topics of vocabulary study should suggest the following cultural items for study at the second level:
    a. forms of letters

99

II. GERMAN LEVEL II (Continued)

    b. German restaurants
    c. places in a German city
    d. Germany:
        (1) landscape in regions
        (2) 4 to 5 rivers
        (3) 10 to 12 cities
        (4) highlights of economy, industry, and
            present political situation
    e. holidays, festivals, fairs
    f. fairy tales
    g. legends
    h. folklore
    i. proverbs
    j. music—popular and classical
    k. current events

III. GERMAN LEVEL III: MINIMAL COURSE CONTENT

A. Phonology
  1. Listening and speaking skills
    a. introduction to difference between standard German and dialects
    b. aural comprehension of longer and more rapidly spoken utterances
    c. perfecting pronunciation with increase in speed of utterance
    d. greater awareness of minute pronunciation differences
  2. Reading and writing skills
    a. perfecting reading skill with increase in fluency and expression
    b. introduction to Fraktur
    c. perfecting writing skill with attention to individual needs
    d. adjectives made from city names are capitalized

B. Morphology
  1. Listening and speaking skills
    a. nouns with articles in all cases
    b. personal pronouns in all cases
    c. relative pronouns in nominative
    d. all types of adjectives in all cases
    e. prepositions with genitive
    f. comparative and superlative
    g. special nouns like Herr
    h. adjectives and verbs as nouns
    i. es as subject
    j. use of present and past participle
    k. adjectives from city names
    l. all tenses of verbs in indicative
    m. use of helfen, lassen, etc., with verbs
  2. Reading and writing skills
    a. nouns with articles in all cases
    b. personal pronouns in all cases
    c. all types of adjectives in all cases
    d. prepositions with all cases
    e. comparative and superlative
    f. special nouns like Herr
    g. adjectives and verbs as nouns
    h. es as subject

    i. relative pronoun in nominative
    j. use of present and past participles
    k. adjectives from city names
    l. all tenses of verbs in indicative
    m. use of helfen, lassen, *etc. with verbs*

  C. Syntax
    1. Listening and speaking skills
       a. position of verbs in all tenses (including modals and double infinitives)
       b. word order in clauses with coordinating and subordinating conjunctions and relative pronouns
       c. position of genitive before and after noun
       d. position of adverbial expressions of time, manner, and place
       e. participial constructions (in listening only)
    2. Reading and writing skills
       a. participial and extended adjective constructions (in reading only)
       b. position of verbs in all tenses (including double infinitive and modals)
       c. word order in clauses with coordinating and subordinating conjunctions and relative pronouns
       d. position of genitive before and after noun
       e. position of adverbial expressions of time, manner, and place

  D. Vocabulary
    1. Increase in vocabulary cannot be stated in figures.
    2. Passive vocabulary will be larger than active, but extent of both will depend on student's ability and willingness to speak and read German.
    3. "Basic (Spoken) German Word List," by J. Alan Pfeffer is suggested as guide for active vocabulary.
    4. A variety of graded readers may be used at this level. Much of the passive vocabulary will depend upon the selection of reading materials and textbooks.
    5. A vocabulary suitable for writing letters, outlines, reports, compositions, should be developed.
    6. Topical vocabulary might include:
       a. current events
       b. sickness and doctor
       c. education
       d. government
       e. history
       f. biography

  E. Culture
    1. Cultural items studied at the third level might include:
       a. Germany
          (1) government
          (2) educational system
          (3) recreation
          (4) highlights of history
       b. other German-speaking countries
          (1) Austria
          (2) Switzerland
       c. German influence in America
          (1) famous German immigrants
          (2) Americans of German descent
          (3) German settlements

2. The cultural study is done mainly in German with some supplementary reading in English. Activities might include:
   a. listening to recordings and viewing films, filmstrips, and slides
   b. discussing what has been heard or read
   c. reading graded readers, periodicals, poetry, and literary prose
   d. writing letters, reports, compositions—revealing an understanding of the German culture.

IV. GERMAN LEVEL IV: MINIMAL COURSE CONTENT

A. Phonology
   1. Listening and speaking skills
      a. poetic variations in the language of phrasing, rhythm, intonation, and in word forms (i.e., contractions, and the dropping and adding of syllables)
      b. perfecting pronunciation with attention to individual problems
   2. Reading and writing skills
      a. perfecting reading skill with increase in speed
      b. perfecting writing skill
      c. punctuation
      d. apostrophe
      e. syllabication

B. Morphology
   1. Listening and speaking skills
      a. passive voice
      b. substitutes for passive
      c. subjunctives (I and II)
      d. conditionals
      e. infinitive with or without zu
      f. relative pronouns in all cases
      g. all forms of negation
      h. all ways of forming nouns
      i. plurals
      j. indirect discourse (in listening)
   2. Reading and writing skills
      a. passive voice
      b. substitutes for passive
      c. subjunctives (I and II)
      d. conditionals
      e. indirect questions and quotations
      f. infinitive with or without zu
      g. relative pronouns
      h. all forms of negation
      i. all ways of forming noun plurals

C. Syntax
   1. Listening and speaking skills
      a. wenn clauses with subjunctive; and omission of wenn in such clauses
      b. word order after all relative pronouns
      c. all infinitive constructions
   2. Reading and writing skills
      a. word order in indirect questions and quotations
      b. wenn clauses with subjunctive; omission of wenn in such clauses
      c. word order after all relative pronouns
      d. all infinitive constructions

102

D. *Vocabulary*
1. *Amount of active and passive vocabulary is a matter of student's individual progress. A high rate of active vocabulary should be aimed for through a wide range of conversational topics giving the student the ability to communicate in the modern world.*
2. *Choice of literary works is up to the teacher but should be based on the ability, interest, and maturity of the students, developing in them a sensitivity to the differences between spoken and written vocabulary and between contemporary and older literary forms, words, and expressions. Consideration may also be given to the grouping of college- bound and terminal students for selective reading.*
3. *A writing vocabulary appropriate to the occasion should be mastered.*

E. *Culture*
1. *The increased ability of the students to communicate in German, to read everything from newspapers to works of literature, makes it possible for them to gain an appreciation and understanding of German contributions to:*
   a. *literature*
   b. *painting*
   c. *sculpture*
   d. *architecture*
   e. *dramatic arts*
   f. *music*
   g. *sciences*
2. *Current events are listened to, viewed, discussed, read, and written about. Books, periodicals, tapes, films, slides, records, and pictures are resource materials used directly by the students. The choice of these materials is up to the teacher who should take into consideration the age, maturity, ability, and interest of the student.*
3. *A knowledge of cultural forms and of the German heritage is a part of learning the German language, works of literature can be appreciated best in the language in which they were written.*

■6

I. SPANISH LEVEL I: MINIMAL COURSE CONTENT

A. *Phonology*
1. *Listening and speaking skills*
   a. *Spanish vowels:* a, e, i, o, u
   b. *all consonant sounds*
   c. *initial and intervocalic:* d, g, b
   d. *differentiate between systems of stress in Spanish and English*
   e. *intonation and rhythm in statements, questions, and commands*
   f. *dental and velar* n
   g. *develop auditory discrimination among verb tenses (present to preterite, future, etc.)*
   h. *diphthongs*
   i. *produce and differentiate the sounds listed above*
   j. *produce liaisons between like vowels and consonants*
2. *Reading and writing skills*
   a. *associate sounds of the language with written symbols, especially:* l, ll; qui, que; ca, co, cu, ch; h; r, rr; n; ga, go, gu, gue, gui
   b. *read aloud with proper pronunciation and intonation*

      c. knowledge of proper syllabication and placement of accents

      d. spell vowel and consonant sounds correctly, especially: l, ll ; qui, que ; ca, co, cu, ch ; h ; ua, ue, ui, uo

      e. formulate meaningful sentences in Spanish

      f. write complete sentences correctly in Spanish

      g. basic principles of stress (hablo, habló, estas, estás)

B. *Morphology*

    1. *Listening and speaking skills*

      a. familiar and polite (*pronoun, verb contractions* al, del)

      b. regular present of ar, er, ir *verbs*

      c. present of ser, *and* estar

      d. possession with de

      e. imperatives

      f. personal a

      g. articles, nouns, and adjectives (*gender, number*)

      h. placement of no

      i. placement and agreement of adjectives

      j. present with future meaning

      k. cardinals and ordinals

      l. pronouns with prepositions

      m. stem-changing verbs

      n. object pronouns (*form and position*)

      o. possessive adjectives

      p. preterite

      q. imperfect

      r. demonstratives, adjectives, and pronouns

      s. present progressive

      t. comparison of adjectives and adverbs

      u. future and conditional

      v. relative pronouns: gustar, faltar

      w. indefinite pronouns

      x. interrogative pronouns: por *and* para

    2. *Reading and writing skills*

      a. use of and exposure to above in reading—especially number and gender of nouns and adjectives, number and person of verbs and pronouns

      b. agreement of adjectives with nouns and verbs with their subjects

      c. use of preterite and imperfect

      d. comparison of adjectives and adverbs

      e. use of above in writing

      f. knowledge of gender and number of adjectives and nouns

      g. person and number of verbs and pronouns

      h. agreement of verbs with their subjects

      i. write answers to questions stressing correct spelling and agreement

      j. write simple text from dictations and narratives

      k. capitalization

C. *Syntax*

    1. *Listening and speaking skills*

      a. statements, interrogatives, and imperatives

      b. position of adjectives

      c. word order to denote possession

      d. negative sentences (*the concept of the double negative*)

      e. position of pronoun, including affirmative commands, infinitives, and gerunds

      f. difference between positions of demonstrative pronouns and adjectives

I. SPANISH LEVEL I (Continued)

    2. Reading and writing skills
- a. expose students to additional basic forms or word order by introducing them to additional short readings
- b. provide more complex sentences where students encounter basic word order in a more varied context
- c. rewrite statements in the form of questions and commands
- d. change affirmative statements into negative ones
- e. written exercises requiring an understanding of:

(1) adjectives	(5) demonstrative pronouns
(2) negatives	(6) indefinite pronouns
(3) articles	(7) word order in comparisons
(4) object pronouns	

D. Vocabulary
    1. *Listening skill*   (approximately 1000 lexical items)
    2. *Speaking skill*   (up to 800 words and expressions)
    3. *Reading skill*   (approximately 1200 lexical items)
    4. *Writing skill*   (up to 800 words and expressions)
- a. basic items
  Samples of all forms listed under Morphology: that is, definite and indefinite articles, interrogatives, verbs ser and estar in present tense, suitable examples of regular verbs, etc.
- b. content words

(1) greetings	(8) calendar dates
(2) leave-taking	(9) school building
(3) classroom	(10) family
(4) numbers	(11) parts of body
(5) colors	(12) common foods
(6) clothing	(13) weather
(7) clock time	(14) Christmas

E. Culture
    1. Patterns of behavior typical of the culture, characteristics of the people who speak Spanish such as:
- a. greeting
- b. showing respect (tu and usted)
- c. introducing friends
- d. la piñata
- e. la siesta
- f. el patio
- g. names of married women

    2. Student participation in the activities mentioned above. Teachers should try to obtain student participation by asking questions in Spanish about the materials covered.
    3. Selections from children's literature, singing, etc.
    4. Units of cultural content clarifying special points that vary between English and Spanish-speaking cultures.
    5. Meals, holidays, etc.

II. SPANISH LEVEL II: MINIMAL COURSE CONTENT

A. Phonology
    1. Listening and speaking skills
- a. vowel clusters, emphasizing diphthongs
- b. fusion of vowels (dónde estás)

105

      c. linkage (los alumnos)

      d. phrases emphasizing the production of vowel clusters, diphthongs, fusion of vowels, and linkage

      e. sounds involving the points listed above—always with practical materials in complete meaningful sentences

    2. *Reading and writing skills*

      a. vowel clusters, diphthongs, fusion of vowels, and linkage in reading selections

      b. practice reading sounds represented by the following spellings: ll, y; qui, que; ca, co, cu; b, v; j; ge, gi, ga, go, güe, güi, gue, gua, guo

      c. observe accents that break diphthongs: caído, traído, Raúl

      d. dictations and other written exercises emphasizing knowledge of written symbols for sounds listed above

  B. *Morphology*

    1. *Listening and speaking skills*

      a. imperfect vs. preterite

      b. progressives and perfects

      c. reflexive verbs and pronouns

      d. nominalization of:

        (1) adjectives

        (2) possessives

        (3) indefinites

        (4) articles

      e. por *vs.* para

      f. passive voice

      g. present and imperfect subjunctive

      h. indicative vs. subjunctive

      i. sequence of tenses

      j. hacer *with expressions of time*

      k. change from present to imperfect subjunctive

      l. passive voice with se *and* ser

      m. si *clauses in the subjunctive*

    2. *Reading and writing skills*

      a. supplementary readings involving the subjunctive in as many forms as possible

      b. graded readers or other material incorporating the basic grammatical forms listed above

      c. give students contexts requiring them to choose between the imperfect and preterite, indicative and subjunctive, sequence of tenses, por *and* para, *the correct use of the passive-voice construction.*

      d. additional written exercises involving the use of the grammatical forms listed above

  C. *Syntax*

    1. *Listening and speaking skills*

      a. position of reflexive pronouns

      b. word order with gustar, faltar, parecer, *etc.*

      c. word order with passive voice

      d. word order with hacer *in expressions of time*

      e. use of subjunctive in subordinate sentences

      f. position of indefinite pronouns

      g. word order in comparisons of adjectives and pronouns

      h. position of relative pronouns

II. SPANISH LEVEL II (Continued)

    2. Reading and writing skills

        a. expose students to supplementary readers where basic word order is found in new context. Provide more complex reading in order that students encounter basic word order in varied contexts.

        b. write short sentences in which word order is stressed.

        c. give the infinitive of reflexive verbs or expressions requiring the subjunctive.

        d. change active to passive voice.

        e. cues requiring the ruse of gustar, faltar, etc.

        f. all material written by the students should be in complete and meaningful sentences.

D. Vocabulary

    1. Listening skill   (1200 lexical items above level I)

    2. Speaking skill   (800 lexical items above level I)

    3. Reading skill   (1200 lexical items above level I)

    4. Writing skill   (800 lexical items above level I)

        a. basic items

        Necessary vocabulary to understand simple statements incorporating the basic grammatical forms outlined for Levels I and II within contexts utilizing the most functional patterns and vocabulary: verb forms like gustar, faltar; use of the imperfect and preterite; future and present progressive; use of object pronouns.

        b. content words

(1) daily routine	(8) transportation
(2) telephoning	(9) city (Latin American
(3) shopping	vs. North American)
(4) letters	(10) travel
(5) post office	(11) animals
(6) restaurant	(12) holidays
(7) community	

E. Culture

    1. Expose students to selected topics presented in short conversations and illustrated by films, slides, tapes, records, and guest speakers; use questions in Spanish about the materials covered. Topics suggested at this level inlcude:

        a. songs

        b. music

        c. childhood literature

        d. games

        e. climate

        f. cultural heritage

    2. Elementary supplementary readings emphasizing cultural content.

    3. Written exercises requiring students to use the key words illustrating their knowledge of patterns of behavior and culture.

    4. Develop an appreciation and understanding of the patterns of behavior and units of culture characteristic of Spanish-speaking peoples.

    5. Create an atmosphere in the classroom which fosters an interest in furthering knowledge about Spanish-speaking countries.

III. SPANISH LEVEL III: MINIMAL COURSE CONTENT

A. Phonology

    1. Listening and speaking skills

        a. reinforce intonation patterns in statement, questions, and commands

        b. reinforce auditory discrimination among verb tenses studied

        c. review dental and velar n, initial and intervocalic d, g, b *d.* review vowel clusters, liaison, and linkage

       e. production of intonation patterns in statements, questions, and commands

       f. oral discrimination among verb tenses

       g. production of r, rr; *initial, intervocalic, and terminal* r

       h. stressed and unstressed vowels

  2. *Reading and writing skills*

       a. recognition of stress patterns and accentuation

       b. review qui, que; ca, co, cu, ch; ga, gue, gui, go, gu, gua, guo, güi, gue; j; ge, gi (je, ji); h; *initial* r *and* rr

       c. read aloud with proper pronunciation and intonation

       d. spell correctly vowel and consonant sounds listed above

       e. take dictations in the foreign language emphasizing the representation of these sounds

       f. written exercises using material previously illustrated

       g. reinforce the knowledge of the relationship between sounds and written symbols in Spanish

       h. listen and speak with respect to breath groups and meaningful phrases

  B. *Morphology*

    1. *Listening and speaking skills*

       a. Expansion of the knowledge of the following points:

         (1) *all pronouns*

         (2) ser *and* estar

         (3) *imperatives*

         (4) *gender and number of articles, pronouns, and adjectives*

         (5) *most commonly used irregular verbs*

         (6) *cardinals and ordinals*

         (7) *negative words*

         (8) *form and use of the subjunctive (recognition)*

       b. reinforce ability of student to change person and number of verbs and pronouns; change number and gender of nouns and adjectives

       c. use of the subjunctive

       d. use of negatives

       e. reinforce points listed above in conversation

    2. *Reading and writing skills*

       a. exposure to readings in which the above-mentioned structures are emphasized

       b. reinforce ability to write answers to questions requiring the use of gender and number of adjectives and nouns, person and number of verbs and pronouns

       c. write simple sentences and do other written exercises requiring knowledge of the basic grammatical forms listed in listening and speaking

  C. *Syntax*

    1. *Listening and speaking skills*

       a. reinforce use of the form and position of personal pronouns, adjectives, and indefinite pronouns

       b. comparisons of adjectives and adverbs

       c. utilization of the above items in meaningful utterances related to daily situations

       d. auditory discrimination with respect to the above items

       e. expand ability to distinguish between basic word order in statements, questions, commands, and negatives

    2. *Reading and writing skills*

       a. expose students to additional forms and word order by the continued use of supplementary readings

      b. provide more complex sentences where students encounter word order in a more varied context

      c. reinforcement of the use of the items in listening and speaking with emphasis upon written exercises

      d. rewrite statements in the form of questions, commands, and negatives

  D. Vocabulary

    1. Increase in vocabulary cannot be stated in figures.

    2. Passive vocabulary will be larger than active but extent of both will depend on student's ability and willingness to speak and read Spanish.

    3. A variety of graded readers may be used at this level. Much of the passive vocabulary will depend upon the selection of reading materials and textbooks.

    4. A vocabulary suitable for writing letters and compositions should be developed.

    5. Topical vocabulary might include:

      a. current events

      b. sickness and doctor

      c. education

      d. government

      e. history

  E. Culture

    1. Cultural items at the third level might include:

      a. Spain

        (1) government

        (2) educational system

        (3) recreation

        (4) historical highlights (especially the conquest of South and Central America)

      b. South and Central American nations (topics similar to those for Spain)

      c. Spanish influence in North America

    2. The cultural study is done mainly in Spanish with some supplementary reading in English. Activities might include:

      a. listening to recordings and viewing films, filmstrips, and slides

      b. discussing what has been heard or read

      c. reading of various kinds including graded readers, periodicals, poetry, literary prose

      d. writing letters, reports, or compositions

IV. SPANISH LEVEL IV: MINIMAL COURSE CONTENT

  A. Phonology

    1. Listening and speaking skills

      a. reinforce the contrast involving unstressed vowels vs. stressed vowels

      b. reinforce auditory discrimination of all consonant sounds

      c. review and reinforce liaison and linkage

      d. develop proper liaison and linkage in speaking at near-native speed

    2. Reading and writing skills

      a. read materials aloud with proper pronunciation and intonation at normal speed

      b. concentrate on words that exemplify the ways in which changes in phonology affect meaning

      c. reinforce ability to associate written symbols with sound

      d. have students paraphrase in writing what they hear (short dialogues or stories)

      e. give dictations incorporating the more difficult spelling: h, j, ge, ji, (je, ji) gue, gui, y, n, ll, rr, v., b, diphthongs, silent vowels in linkage

IV. SPANISH LEVEL IV (Continued)

B. Morphology

1. Listening and speaking skills
   a. review use of the subjunctive, imperfect vs. preterite, por and para, the passive voice, stem-changing verbs
   b. progressive and perfect tenses, comparisons of adjectives
   c. reflexive verbs
   d. reinforce understanding of verbs like gustar, faltar, parecer, etc.
   e. use of the above items in speaking at near-native speed and in contexts that are understandable to native speakers
2. Reading and writing skills
   a. use of the above items in written exercises according to a specific grammar point, using the passive voice, por, and para
   b. imperfect and preterite, subjunctives, comparison of adjectives, progressive and perfect tenses, gustar, faltar, etc.
   c. stem-changing verbs, reflexive verbs

C. Syntax

1. Listening and speaking skills
   a. reinforcement of knowledge with respect to the word order in sentences with gustar, faltar, parecer
   b. passive voice
   c. comparison of adjectives
   d. use of subjunctive in subordinate clauses
2. Reading and writing skills
   a. provide supplementary readings stressing the importance of basic word order as outlined above
   b. have students write sentences and do other written exercises according to specific points of word order, position of pronouns, passive voice, use of subjunctives in subordinate clauses
   c. comparison of adjectives
   d. gustar, faltar, parecer, etc.

D. Vocabulary

1. Students should be able to understand almost any word in standard Spanish in normal conversational contexts.
2. Students should have an active speaking vocabulary appropriate to their age and capacity enabling them to communicate in Spanish with considerable fluency.
3. Students should recognize in context a wide range of vocabulary items. If they are planning to continue Spanish in college, they should do extensive outside reading to familiarize themselves with many literary forms, words, and expressions.
4. Students should have a writing vocabulary that is appropriate to the occasion.

E. Culture

1. Students should listen with understanding to audio stimuli and detect nuances of meaning relating to common aspects of Hispanic culture.
2. Students should speak and write in culturally acceptable forms and in their speech and writing reveal some knowledge of the heritage of the people who speak Spanish.
3. Students should read everything from newspapers to works of literature with an understanding of its place within the Spanish culture.
4. Students planning to continue their studies of Spanish in college should familiarize themselves with literature in their field of interest.

110

terms, and then must find the best way to achieve those goals. It is hoped that Tables 4, 5, and 6 will suggest ways to specify the content aspects of the language curriculum with greater clarity.[5]

BEHAVIORAL OBJECTIVES, HUMANISTIC AIMS, AND COURSE CONTENT

From time to time in American education, movements have arisen based upon the belief that educational problems could be solved through the process of stating one's objectives in accordance with certain narrowly prescribed principles. In the 1920s Bobbitt used "activity analysis" in an attempt to determine empirically everything of importance that people did in society. Having collected a mass of data describing what people *did*, he then attempted to build a curriculum prescribing what students ought to learn.[6]

For various reasons the efforts of Bobbitt and others who attempted to apply scientific management theories to education were soon abandoned. The problems inherent in identifying and prescribing specific, standardized output behavior for future generations were apparently overwhelming. Nevertheless, an effort was made to do precisely that again in the 1950s. In fact, one project resulted in the publication of thousands of objectives covering not only the three Rs but also some of the more minute details of daily personal behavior. One objective, for example, is worded as follows: "Wears (if a girl), with growing self-assurance, appropriate foundation garments and clothing properly styled for the maturing figure."[7] Other areas covered by French's objectives included such diverse items as not being gullible about flying saucers; accepting the democratic way of life; knowing how to spell; and avoiding drinking, sex, and fast driving.[8]

In the late 1960s and early 1970s, a new variation of the older movements became widely visible in pedagogical circles. One difference in the "new" approach to stating objectives lay in its heavier emphasis upon traditional subject matter rather than upon personal "life adjustment" behaviors. Another difference had to do with its wide acceptance by local, state, and federal educational agencies as an accountability tool. Just as combat units in the early stages of the war in Viet Nam were expected to produce weekly body counts (as indicators of having met subobjectives in

[5] The items in Tables 4, 5, and 6 are selected excerpts from the French, German, Spanish Curriculum Guides published in preliminary form by the Department of Public Instruction, 126 Langdon Street, Madison, Wis. The native-born consultants were: Miss Gertrud Meyer of Wauwatosa Public Schools, Wauwatosa, Wis. (German); Dr. Aldo Busot of Wisconsin State University, Whitewater, Wis. (Spanish); and Mrs. M. D. Hage of Paris, France (French).

[6] Franklin Bobbitt, *How to Make a Curriculum*, Boston, Houghton Mifflin, 1924.

[7] Will French, *Behavioral Goals of General Education in High School*, New York, Russell Sage, 1957, p. 118.

[8] Ibid., pp. 102, 103, 97, and 116 respectively.

111

a war of attrition), teachers were expected to produce periodic indices of improvement in the form of "measurable student output behaviors." In some federal programs, funding was contingent upon stating one's curricular goals in this format. Some state education agencies attempted to force the approach on to local school districts by making the receipt of state educational aids contingent upon stating local goals in behavioral terms. Also, many local school districts began requiring teachers to state their curricular goals in behavioral terms. In some school districts an attempt was made to make payment for instruction depend upon the degree to which the specified behaviors were successfully elicited. Such efforts, however, were not shown to result in improved instruction.[9]

What are behavioral objectives? Basically, the behavioral objective movement is an attempt to make broad, practical classroom applications of the techniques used earlier by experimenters in programmed instruction (see Chapter 7). Behavioral objectives are sometimes referred to as "specific performance objectives" and "desired terminal behaviors," (although the latter term was seldom used after the mid 1960s). Behavioral objectives carry with them the assumption that most, if not all, educational outcomes can and should be state explicitly in advance. (It should be noted in passing that this assumption is rejected by several major schools of psychology, linguistics, and pedagogy; see Chapter 3.) Another presupposition is the belief that learning involves the sequential acquisition of measurable behaviors that lead stepwise to mastery of the whole learning task. That is, the "whole" (for example, learning a second language) is viewed as the sum of its behavioral parts. Inner thoughts, feelings, and perceptions are functionally nonexistent to the empirical behaviorist. Hence all such alleged inner mental states are to be dealt with operationally, in the form of manifested overt actions. The suggested format for specifying all elements of the curriculum behaviorally generally includes the following:

1 behavior to be elicited
2 conditions of elicitation
3 minimum acceptable performance level
4 method of measurement

To illustrate, let us specify (1) "the behavior to be elicited" as "the ability to use esperanto verbs correctly in the present tense." We could then set (2) the "conditions" as follows: "Given six line drawings of various activities (see illustrations in Chapter 6), the student will respond orally and in a complete utterance describing correctly that which is depicted." As for (3) "the minimum acceptable performance level," it is customary to establish 80 percent as the bottom level. Item (4) "measurement" would, in this case, involve teacher assessments of live or taped student responses. This would include vocabulary items, verb endings, pronunciation, and word order. If the student is able to produce at least eight out of ten right, with

[9] Ellis B. Page, "How We All Failed at Performance Contracting," *Phi Delta Kappan* 54 (October 1972), pp. 115–117.

respect to these elements, he is said to have performed at the criterion level. He has met the behavioral objective.

Advantages of Behavioral Objectives

Teachers and administrative personnel who favor behavioral objectives often cite the following advantages with respect to their use:

1   *Behavioral objectives help us to look at student performance rather than teacher activities.* This is based on the belief that language teachers have tended to focus too heavily on their own behaviors without regard to whether or not it makes a difference in the learner.

2   *Learner-oriented outcomes help the teacher to develop a better balance in the material to be learned.* Interaction analyses of student-teacher activities in the classroom have revealed an overbalance in the direction of teacher talk and teacher-dependent responses (see Chapter 2). By specifying what the *student* should be doing, instructional staff members can turn their attention toward student performance on all the essential elements of language acquisition, thus achieving more active student participation.

3   *Evaluation of the language program is facilitated by having outcomes stated in advance.* By pinning down with great precision the exact language behaviors that each student is supposed to exhibit, an evaluator can, in theory, at least, determine the congruity that exists between what was attempted and what was achieved. This will tell the staff whether it is meeting its overall goals with a majority of the students. It can also help the staff to diagnose and correct problems with individual students early in the school year before the situation becomes hopeless.

Problems with Behavioral Objectives

As in the past, the approach to "human engineering," which is based on "a precise statement of objectives," became popular with school administrators, educational bureaucrats, and a variety of other educationists. However, at the height of its popularity, there was little empirical evidence (other than extrapolations from animal behavior) to sustain the movement on a theoretical level. On a practical level there were also a number of questions left unanswered. The following are illustrative of the difficulties involved:

1   *How do we determine what to specify?* This is a problem. If we look only at the "Minimal Course Content" for Spanish Level I listed above we find over 200 conceptual items (not to mention over 1000 lexical items). If each of these were to be developed according to one of the behavioral objective formats, the result would be an encyclopedic and repetitious listing. A similar problem would exist for levels II, III, and IV. Yet if we settle for general goals only (see "Essentials for Communication," Table 3 above), then specificity and measurability are lost,

which is the reason for having the "specific performance objectives" in the first place.

2 *Where does the teacher find the time and expertise to prepare the objectives in some usable form?* This question has never been satisfactorily answered. University researchers have spent many years attempting to develop and refine objectives for one year's instruction at the university level without completely satisfactory results.[10] Secondary school teachers have little time allotted to such activities. Behavioral objective "banks" have not been much help; other people's objectives simply cannot be borrowed and "plugged in" locally.[11]

3 *What is the significance of performing at the criterion level; and what does the teacher do with students who fail to reach the 80 percent criterion level?* Theoretically he/she is supposed to individualize instruction so that each person arrives at the prestated objective at an individual rate in an individual manner. Yet very few schools have been able to set up an adequate program to achieve this end. Even where such a program has been established there is some question as to its value. Do students retain the material learned in this manner? Does material acquired in this way enable the student to apply his/her knowledge to a genuine communications situation? The answers to these questions are by no means clear. It has been suggested, however, that behavioral objectives, because of their arbitrary, artifical format, can be learned, checked off by the teacher as mastered, and then quickly forgotten by the student.

4 *How do we specify behavioral outcomes for feelings, emotions, and aesthetic appreciation?* There are those who say that the so-called "affective domain" is behaviorally specifiable; there are others who disagree. Recently an educator paraphrased E. B. Browning's line: "How do I love thee; let me put that on a nine-point scale," (contrasted with the original, "How do I love thee; let me count the ways.") Those who believe that the paraphrased version makes sense will probably accept as feasible the behavioralization of affective outcomes.

PERFORMANCE OBJECTIVES AND THE STUDENT

Despite the limitations of behavioral objectives discussed in the preceding paragraphs, there is some evidence that their discriminate use when integrated into the regular classroom procedures can have a beneficial effect

[10] Albert Valdman, "Programmed Instruction versus Guided Learning in Foreign Language Acquisition," *Unterrichtspraxis* 1 (1968) pp. 1–14.

[11] Herbert M. Kliebard, "Bureaucracy and Curriculum Theory" in Vernon F. Haubrick (ed.), *Freedom, Bureaucracy, and Schooling*, Washington D.C., National Education Association, 1971, pp. 89–91.

upon instruction. In the view of this writer, behavioral objectives have been discredited mainly in those situations where educational administrators have attempted to relate them too closely to some elaborate system of account-ability. The reason for the failure of this approach is that very few, if any, public schools have the technical resources to validate thousands of objec-tives in each subject matter area. Neither do they have the resources to en-gage in the kind of research that would enable the school district to control all the relevant variables relating to such things as student intelligence, socioeconomic background, and teacher competency. Unless this can be done, it is impossible to identify the variables that accounted for improve-ments in student achievement. Thus the teaching staff has no way to deter-mine which procedures to modify in order to improve "the behavioral output products." In addition, many people in the humanities object to the rather simplistic analogy in which the student is treated as a piece of raw material to be processed on an educational assembly line.

In my experience the use of performance objectives has been of value when the following criteria were met:

1   The objectives are used only in those areas where actual student per-formance can be realistically observed, but not to the exclusion of nonobservable outcomes.
2   The local school administration has provided ample time to prepare the objectives.
3   The objectives are made available to the learners themselves in such a way that students can see their relevance to the course of study. An even better approach is to have learners involved in the preparation of objectives.
4   The objectives are used in a positive way to help the student learn the material and are not used in connection with punitive measures (such as classifying students through curve grading, threatening students with failure, and so on).
5   The objectives are not set aside as a separate compendium of goals but are worked into and are related to the ongoing instructional activities.

Ideally, such objectives would be part of a student manual or guide that relates directly to all texts, tapes, and other materials used in the everyday program. The wording used to state the objective varies. Sometimes the objective is stated, for example, with a phrase such as "By the end of this chapter you will be able to do the following. . . ." Some teachers use the first person format, which, by its very nature, helps to personalize the objectives. Since many books have been written on this topic, it would be inappropriate to go into great detail here on the various formats for behavioral objectives (see the bibliography at the end of this chapter.) Hence the following are simply representative samples from the many thousands of objectives that have been written. The two lines at the right of each objective are for the following purpose: the student puts a check mark on the first line when the student thinks he or she has mastered the objective in question; the teacher puts a check mark on the second line when he or she feels that the student has achieved an acceptable level of mastery of the directive in question.

Sample Performance Objective

1   *I can ask people what their name is in Spanish and can respond appropriately when they ask me what my name is.*   _____   _____
2   *I can pronounce the following four French vowels correctly: u, eu, in, on.*   _____   _____
3   *I can ask, "How are you?" in German and can respond correctly regarding my health and the health of members of my family.*   _____   _____
4   *I can write a paragraph in Spanish identifying the main steps in the Spanish bullfight and the sequence in which they occur.*   _____   _____
5   *After listening to native speakers bargaining in a Mexican market, I can summarize what happened in English.*   _____   _____

Objectives such as those listed above can be extremely useful in a program of individualized instruction.[12] If such objectives are to be of any value in the more traditional classroom setup (which still predominates), then obviously the teacher will have to modify his or her instructional techniques accordingly. Basically this means that the teacher will have to use periods of supervised study or will have to set up the small group interaction situations within the classroom in order to observe and validate whether or not the student can, indeed, perform in accordance with the performance objectives. Unless this is done, the students will very quickly cease to take the performance objectives seriously. For example, if evaluation consists of written quizzes and final exams, most students will find no good reason to take the listening and speaking work seriously. As class size becomes larger and larger, the teacher will find it increasingly difficult to manage more than a few performance objectives on each of the chapters or units of work. In this situation, it is advisable for the teacher to select only a few of the most basic items for personal monitoring. Some teachers have successfully used peer teaching and peer evaluation for the other objectives. That is, working in pairs or in small groups, students can attest to the successful completion of various performance objectives by fellow students. In this situation the teacher functions as a roving consultant to the various groups or pairs of students. For a number of reasons, some teachers are unable to cope with paired and small-group work. Usually it is for lack of knowing what techniques to use or knowing how to manage a more open classroom situation. (For suggestions on individualizing instruction, see Chapter 7).

[12] Frank Grittner and Fred LaLeike, *Individualized Foreign Language Instruction*, Skokie ,Ill., National Textbook Company, 1974, chap. 2, pp. 25–28.

116

SUMMARY

American educators appear to be highly susceptible to the lure of panaceas. Frequently these are manifested in the form of bandwagon movements that are drawn from practices in business and industry. Thus in the technological era of the seventies, public school educators were subjected to pressures that urged them to adopt a technological, production-line model of education. Through this analogy the student was viewed as a piece of raw material with crude or primitive behaviors who, when subjected to educational "inputs" was supposed to respond by evidencing the desired behavioral "outputs," which could be measured and evaluated. These outputs were to be thought of as educational "products," which, if the school "factory" was efficient, could be produced at minimal cost. However, it has been pointed out that, unlike the raw material in an automobile assembly line, human students may talk back, may have nervous breakdowns, may become truants, or may simply choose to ignore both the inputs and outputs that the teachers wish them to take seriously.

Furthermore, education has to do with the quality of human beings who emerge from the schooling process. These qualitative effects of education may be long-term—that is, they may not become evident until several decades after the schooling process has actually been completed. A further difficulty lies in determining any direct cause and effect relationship between what the teacher has done in the school and how the student subsequently performs. (For example, a given student's fluency in Spanish may have had more to do with the family vacation in Mexico than with the efforts of the teacher.) Even though questions of this type have been raised and have gone unresolved, there is evidence that the sensible use of objectives can help the teacher to focus on the performance of students, which, in the final analysis, is an important part of what foreign language instruction is all about. There is some evidence to indicate that foreign language teachers simply do not know when to stop talking and let the students perform. It appears to be an occupational hazard. Thus the discriminate use of performance objectives in appropriate areas of learning can be helpful in getting students more actively involved in the direct use of the target language. In most cases, the successful use of objectives will be relative to such factors as the availability of time to prepare them and the ability of the teacher to modify instructional procedures and evaluation techniques so that these are congruent with the objectives that are prepared.

The question of how to relate course content to instructional goals is a difficult one. Obviously, the language teacher wants the students themselves to do something with the foreign language curricular material. In any foreign language program of several years duration students are expected to gain sufficient control of linguistic elements to enable them to express and receive ideas and feelings by means of the second language. However, since we do not fully understand the process of second language acquisition (see Chapter 3), it is not clear how explicit we can be in prescribing "behaviors to be elicited" without actually inhibiting the language-learning process. If it is true that language performance is "creative and stimulus-free," then it would follow that the instructional process should involve students in acquiring internalized generalizations that can be applied creatively to a virtually infinite variety of communications contexts. With the possible exception of learning phonology, this would preclude highly specific behavioral objectives as being irrelevant to language performance. For, if language use is creative and idiosyncratic, students should be taught to apply to unanticipated situations functional principles that they perceive to be relevant rather than being expected to meet arbitrarily stated objectives based on someone else's formulations of reality. This means, in effect, that such things as grammatical forms, syntactical patterns, and vocabulary items should be treated not as specific, behavioralizable learning "outputs" but rather as tools for receiving and communicating thoughts and feelings. With this orientation, course objectives tend toward outcomes that require students to synthesize and integrate what they have learned rather than to recite from memory totally predetermined responses. For example, for a unit of work that contains greetings, vocabulary about people's health, certain basic verbs, grammatical principles, and cultural information, the objectives might include the following expectations:

1   To be able to greet and correctly address a fellow student playing the role of either a close friend or a respected adult
2   To inquire about the health of such persons and their relatives using correct pronouns and verb forms
3   To answer questions correctly about the health and well-being of real people in one's own family.

There are a number of advantages to objectives of this kind. First, instead of having to formulate scores of atomistic and unrelated behavioral outputs dealing with correct student use of verbs, pronouns, interrogatives, social conventions, case and gender endings, and the like, the teacher lists a small number of expectations that require the student to apply such items to a unified, sense-making communications situation. Hence students are more likely to see a reason for learning the isolated elements of language, not because they will be tested on them per se but because they can see how the parts are relevant to a whole act of communication. Secondly, because objectives are reduced to a manageable number, the teacher can work with the whole class (and with pairs and small groups within the class) on a problem-solving, task-oriented basis. From the student's standpoint the question becomes: "What grammar, vocabulary, and cultural knowledge do I need in order to perform relevant communications acts; that is, acts which have a wide range of potential future applications?" A third advantage of this approach to stating goals is that evaluation can be accomplished either by means of conventional testing or by having students actually perform in an impromptu situation or by both. The type of evaluation activity that requires the student to hear, speak, read, or write the target language for communications purposes in unanticipated contexts is essential. Without it, students will tend to rely on rote memory and to avoid the kind of practice that requires them to recombine and to apply what they have learned for purposes of communication. And communication—either productive or receptive—is what language is all about.

BIBLIOGRAPHY

Born, Warren C. (ed.), *Goals Clarification: Curriculum, Teaching, Evaluation,* Middlebury, Vt., Northeast Conference, 1975.
Lange, Dale L., and Charles J. James (eds.), *Foreign Language Education: A Reappraisal,* ACTFL Review of Foreign Language Education, vol. 4, Skokie, Ill., National Textbook Company, 1972.
Peters, R. S., *Education as Initiation,* London, Harrap, 1970.
Steiner, Florence, *Performing with Objectives,* Rowley, Mass., Newbury, 1975.
Strasheim, Lorraine A., "Foreign Language : Part of a New Apprenticeship for Living," *The Bulletin of the National Association of Secondary School Principals,* 54, (January 1970), pp. 87–107.
Valette, Rebecca, and Renee Disick, *Modern Language Performance Objectives and Individualization: A Handbook,* New York, Harcourt Brace Jovanovich, 1972.

6

■Psychology
and language
learning:
motivation
and method

■ *Work without hope draws nectar in a sieve, And
hope without an object cannot live.* SAMUEL TAYLOR
COLERIDGE ■ *As drill sessions succeed each other with
relentless regularity, ... many students begin to tire or
to lose interest ... ; boredom sets in.* FROM A STUDY
ON THE EFFECTIVENESS OF THE AUDIOLINGUAL METHOD.
■ *All authorities agree that the discernment of relationships is the genuinely intellectual matter; hence the
educative matter. The failure arises in supposing that
relationships can become perceptible without experience. ...* JOHN DEWEY

There are indications that a rather large segment of the language teaching
profession has, for the most part, accepted the goals listed in Chapter 5. It is
also fairly safe to state that linguists have identified the priority items for the
commonly taught languages. In fact, even before the linguists of today were
well known, many teachers of language had successfully identified the
sounds and structures that had to be learned for the purpose of communication in the commonly taught languages. However, even where there is
general accord on matters of instructional goals and course content, there
still remain some definite areas of disagreement about the language
learner and the process by which he learns. In this regard it might be
helpful to refer to a continuum of theories on how languages are acquired
and use the two extremes as a means of identifying the principal schools of
thought. On such a continuum we would find the cognitive-code-learning
advocate on one end, the operant-conditioning enthusiast on the other.
The "cognition" school insists that the use of grammatical generalizations
is an essential part of language learning. The "conditioning" school tends
to minimize the importance of conceptualization and to insist on developing
correct language habits in the student through a long series of carefully
planned stimuli designed to elicit only correct responses. There is also a
middle-of-the-road, or "eclectic," school consisting of those who
believe that language learning involves some cognition and some conditioning depending on which aspect of a language is being learned. In fact, a
careful review of the professional journals and books on methodology will
reveal that there are few purists in either of the first two schools mentioned
above. Apparently there is a considerable reluctance among language
teachers to abandon the cognitive process, particularly where morphology
and syntax are concerned. Even the newest textbooks usually make some
provision for the learning of grammatical generalizations. However, here
again there are widely differing views on the *manner* of learning the generalizations.

120

To illustrate the problem more clearly, we have selected a type of language pattern in French, German, and Spanish that presents essentially the same learning problem for those who speak English natively. The following sentences show the English pattern; the conflict point is underscored:

He is a professor.
He is a student.
He is a salesman.
    (and so on for any occupation)

Notice that the comparable pattern in French, German, and Spanish omits the article:

French	German	Spanish
Il est professeur.	Er ist Professor.	(Él) es profesor.
Il est élève.	Er ist Student..	(Él) es alumno.
Il est commerçant.	Er ist Kaufmann.	(Él) es vendedor.

The psycholinguistic problem here is to teach American students to omit the article (*un, une, ein, eine,* and so forth) when referring to any profession or occupation in any form of the pattern:

Il est _____.
Er ist _____.
(El) es _____.

Further, we want language students to be able to apply the pattern to any appropriate situation in the language that they are learning. In conversing, they must automatically leave a "blank" between the verb and the word referring to a profession or an occupation. Generalized, the pattern becomes:

SUBJECT + VERB *to be* + (   ) + OCCUPATION OR PROFESSION (*unmodified*)

As they learn new words referring to occupations and professions and as they gain control of new forms and tenses of the verb, students should *not* have to relearn the concept of nonuse of the article. Thus, if they have learned the generalization properly, they will be able to generate any number of sentences in the target language to express ideas such as:

He was a farmer.
Pablo wants to be a bullfighter.
Heinrich will be an engineer when he grows up.
Madeleine would have been a teacher if she had not married.
Do you want to be a bum?

If the generalization has been properly mastered, students will not be confused by new verb tenses or moods, more complex sentence structures, or other possible distractions. Instead they will perceive the basic pattern in any of the infinite variations of sentences that they may subsequently need for purposes of communication. Moreover, they will have eliminated

121

the compulsion to use the French, German, or Spanish equivalent of the English articles (a, an) to refer to human occupations, but will use the articles freely where they are appropriate (that is, in reference to objects, in reference to people where no occupation is involved, in reference to occupations that are preceded by an adjective, and so forth).

If we apply this specific question to the entire area of language learning, the question then becomes: How does the teacher induce the student to learn the basic problem sounds, structures, and word-order sequences so that he can apply them unhesitatingly to new situations, while avoiding the pitfalls created by interference from his native English? This is a very large question, and it will probably never be answered to everyone's satisfaction. Yet each year, teachers are faced with decisions relating to the selection of texts, tapes, and visual materials and the utilization of these materials in the instructional process. It is therefore imperative for them to develop a definite point of view on the psychology of language learning. Without such orientation, textbook selection becomes a game of chance; and teaching procedures tend to become aimless, unfocused activities. The following discussion attempts to identify a few of the key psychological premises underlying the more widely used texts and methods and to comment upon their soundness in the light of psychological theory.

GRAMMATICAL GENERALIZATIONS VERSUS ROTE MEMORIZATION

One of the most basic, practical problems faced by the language teacher relative to the question of language learning and cognition is whether the student should memorize a foreign language utterance without understanding how each element of that utterance functions or, on the other hand, whether the student should only commit to memory those expressions for which a grammatical explanation is immediately supplied or learned? That is, how much language material will the pupil be required to learn by rote without knowing such things as, how a verb ending relates to the whole pattern of verb structure, why a familiar noun suddenly has a different ending, or why a newly acquired pronoun comes before the verb instead of after it? The difficulty arises when the language teacher's desire to teach many useful expressions in a short period of time comes into conflict with his belief that language must be presented in an orderly fashion. For example, during the first weeks of instruction the teacher, wishing to use French or Spanish for giving classroom instructions, may say to the class:

I want you to learn this for tomorrow.

Yet in most high school texts more than a year will pass before the student sees a systematic presentation of the grammatical principles necessary to make that type of statement in French or Spanish. Similarly, in German it is common practice to begin the first day with dialog material such as the following:

Hello, Hans. How are you? Guten Tag, Hans. Wie geht's?
Fine, thanks, and you? Gut, danke, und dir?

Even this simple exchange of greetings contains grammatical problems that will not be dealt with for several months in the typical high school German course. The same might be said of a large part of the material commonly taught in French, German, and Spanish classes everywhere. In each of these languages during the first week, youngsters are often required to memorize such conversational exchanges as:

My name is Carlos
What is your name?
My father's name is John.

These seemingly simple structures are loaded with pitfalls for the student who has learned them only by rote memorization. This is because the verbs, the possessives, and other structural elements function differently in each language from the way they do in English. Therefore, while students *can* say from memory:

What is your name? or *My father's name is John,*

they are often unable to ask such questions as:

What is your father's name? or *Is your name John?*

The student who has memorized only a few pat utterances pertaining to peoples' names does not know how to change them for application to new situations. To perform the latter task he must first learn to manipulate with great rapidity all relevant verb forms, possessives, and other peculiarities of the language as they relate to asking and telling what someone's name is.

In short, the student must ultimately master the *general system* used for naming people rather than learning, parrotlike, a few *specific examples* such as those given above. On this point, most knowledgeable language theorists agree. After all, the possible variations of the naming system above are nearly infinite in number if one thinks in terms of specific sentences for memorization. (For example: What's your name? What was her name before marriage? What would her name be if she had not married? I know his name. Do you know their names? and so forth, ad infinitum.) The same is true of hundreds of other situational dialogs. It is quite obviously unrealistic, therefore, to use the tourist-phrase-book approach as the sole method of learning a language. First, it is mathematically not possible to identify and tabulate all the conceivable word combinations in a given language. Secondly, it would not be psychologically reasonable to expect anyone to memorize them all if they were available. Yet second-language learning does demand a considerable amount of memory work simply because the learner must acquire a basic vocabulary. Thus it becomes a question of how much rote memorization is desirable throughout the language course, particularly at the beginning levels where problems of student motivation are often most acute. Another problem relates to the sequence of introducing the student to grammatical structures; that is, should the presentation be orderly or random?

RANDOM PRESENTATION OF LANGUAGE STRUCTURES

There are a number of recently published texts that present the foreign language lessons as a series of situational dialogs that the student is expected to memorize by rote. Although, in some instances, these books are supplemented with attractive visual aids, they frequently do not lend themselves easily to a systematic attack on grammatical structures. Frequently, the authors of such texts have chosen to concentrate on presenting genuine idiomatic utterances that fit the conversational situation rather than on presenting grammatical structures in an orderly fashion. In extreme cases, complex structures will appear in the very first lesson, while elemental ones may be scattered throughout the text. Other such texts present their situational dialogs in a less capricious manner, making certain that the more basic structures are presented in their entirety in the first few lessons while withholding the more difficult ones until later. With this latter approach, the teacher can, at various points, stop and focus the students' attention on critical structural elements after they have been memorized in dialog form. When this is done, grammatical generalizations serve to organize and integrate material that the students may have previously viewed merely as a series of specific sentences without pattern. On the other hand, the inexperienced teacher may plod through a text in which structures are presented in random order without ever stopping to determine whether or not the student has grasped the generalizations contained in the specific sentences. Success in such a course is almost entirely a matter of brute memory.

THE SEEDED DIALOG APPROACH

The manner of presenting structure that is most characteristic of the new American Method is to combine situational dialogs with structure drills. Seeded into each dialog are selected examples of fundamental grammatical structures. Each lesson begins with a "basic dialog," which, typically, involves the memorization of a supposedly appealing conversational exchange between two or more teenage youngsters from the target culture. The basic dialog is supposed to serve as follows:

1   In the process of hearing and saying the basic dialog sentences, students learn to imitate the individual sounds and intonational patterns of the target language.

124

2   In learning the sentences they are, hopefully, also learning vocabulary items in a meaningful context; they are not asked to memorize isolated items from a word list.

3   Where possible, the dialogs contain situations that point out sharp contrasts between the target culture and American culture.

A disadvantage of the basic-dialog approach is that a number of "advanced" structures invariably appear in the early dialogs simply because the conversational situation demands them. Students are told to learn these as if they were unstructured idioms and not to ask questions; "An explanation will be provided in a later chapter," they are told. Meanwhile, they are permitted to concentrate on a few sentences from the basic dialog that contain selected structural elements. These serve as models for drill on phonology, morphology, and syntax. And the drills, in turn, provide material on which to base a systematic presentation of grammatical generalizations. However, as is the case with the random presentation of structure, the seeded dialog approach requires that a large part of the learning process be devoted to the learning of utterances without a full understanding of how those structures are organized in the target language. Opponents of the seeded-dialog approach contend that the motivational value of the situational dialogs wanes rapidly after the first few months. For students eventually discover that many sentences that they have memorized with great effort are useless to them for the purpose of communication. They simply do not know how to transform these specific sentences to meet the demands brought forth by an unanticipated conversational situation. Consequently, students begin to resist an approach that requires still more memorization of utterances of questionable utility.

MONOSTRUCTURAL PRESENTATION OF LANGUAGE STRUCTURES

There are several prominent foreign language educators who completely reject either of the previously mentioned polystructural approaches to morphology and syntax. There are even some who insist that phonology must be presented one phoneme at a time. Through the mid-1960s such monostructuralists formed a small but highly vocal segment of the foreign language profession. However, as we shall see in a later chapter, the monostructural approach is highly adaptable to self-instructional methods of teaching. Therefore, it may well be expected to assume greater importance in the future if the present educational trends toward automated learning and individualized study continue. Then too, there are several new texts that adhere rather closely to a monostructural presentation of grammar. It is possible that these have been overlooked or misunderstood by the profession. In any case, it seems advisable to examine this approach from the standpoint of the psychology of second-language learning.

125

Monostructural courses, with a few exceptions, are not "mono" in the strictest sense of the word. Beginning lessons will usually contain several structures simply because they are needed in order to create sense-making utterances and to elicit seminatural responses from the student. However, the number of new elements introduced in each lesson is severely limited, and the sequence of introducing grammatical elements is carefully planned. Moreover, every effort is made to focus the student's attention on the structure to be learned and to keep him from being distracted or confused by extraneous material. Accordingly, the monostructural approach makes heavy initial use of simple, concrete vocabulary items and nondeceptive cognates. Thus, for example, the first lesson of a monostructural course in Spanish would aim at teaching the masculine and feminine singular. The students would learn selected sentences containing the four singular articles (*un, una, el, la*). The teacher could use items from the classroom environment to teach all the basic elements.

Lesson I. Masculine and Feminine Singular

Masculine indefinite articles

Es *un* libro.	*(It's a book.)*
Es *un* lápiz.	*(It's a pencil.)*
Es *un* papel.	*(It's a paper.)*
etc.	etc.

Feminine indefinite articles

Es *una* pluma.	*(It's a pen.)*
Es *una* regla.	*(It's a ruler.)*
Es *una* tiza.	*(It's a piece of chalk.)*
etc.	etc.

Masculine definite article

Es *el* libro, lápiz, papel. *etc.*

Feminine definite article

Es *la* pluma, regla, tiza. *etc.*

Interrogation

¿ Es *un* libro ?

Affirmative reply

Si, es *un* libro.

Negative reply

No, no es *un* libro ; es *una* pluma.

Students and teacher can hold up articles (or point to them) saying :

¿ Qué es esto ?   *(What's this ?)*

Es *un* libro, es *una* pluma. *etc.*

126

Each of the foregoing structures would be drilled thoroughly as isolated phenomena. Later, masculine and feminine forms would be intermixed in the same utterance; (that is, un libro y una pluma*). Subsequent lessons would build upon the earlier ones using as little new vocabulary as possible. Among the succeeding lessons would be:*

Lesson II. Learning the Plurals

el libro	los libros
el lápiz	los lápices
la pluma	las plumas

Lesson III. Agreement and Word Order— Noun with Adjective

el libro rojo	*(the red book)*
los libros rojos	*(the red books)*
la pluma amarilla	*(the yellow pen)*
las plumas amarillas	*(the yellow pens)*

The well-conceived monostructural approach has logic on its side. Each new lesson builds upon that which went before, and in this process of reentry, the retention of previously learned material is strengthened through constant reinforcement. From the very outset, the student is able to use the new language to relate to the world that most immediately surrounds him. However, much of the early application of language structure to the real world is necessarily oversimplified and unnatural. Students may spend many weeks discussing yellow pencils, new books, brown tables, and low chairs. The teacher, meanwhile, may feel convinced that she or he is introducing sounds and structures in the most logical sequence; but will the students see it this way? Too often, they do not, particularly with the inexperienced teacher. And, if the youngsters cannot be made to see how each lesson is moving them another step closer to controlling the new language, they will begin to resist the course and the teacher. The resistance may manifest itself overtly in the form of discipline problems or covertly in the form of lethargic student responses. But some form of resistance is very likely to appear during the first few months of a monostructural course unless the teacher is a skillful motivator.

Thus, a polystructural approach using high-interest situational dialogs may show initial high motivation followed by gradual student disillusionment. Conversely, the monostructural approach runs the risk of losing the learners' interest before they have reached the point where they can be intrinsically motivated by the thrill of learning to express themselves in the target language. On the other hand, the monostructural approach can produce a progressive growth of student confidence if the teacher knows how to capitalize on the strengths of the system. For at each step the students know what they are doing and why. Ideally, they also know how to *apply* all the vocabularly and grammar they have learned. At each step the emphasis is on application of generalizations rather than on rote memorization. Moreover, learning is cumulative, and most new vocabulary can, therefore, be integrated into the prelearned system of structures. Theoretically, the association of new material with old should improve the retention of both.

PHONOLOGY AND OVERLEARNING

In the native speaker, phonology might well be explained in terms of stimulus-response conditioning. The tongue, lips, and lungs appear to function automatically to produce those vibrations in the air which carry meaning to the ear of anyone who belongs to the same speech community. At the same time nonphonemic sounds are automatically avoided. The monolingual speaker does not have to decide, for example, between the trilled *r* of Spanish, the uvular *r* of French and German, or the retroflex *r* of English. Native speakers simply use the sound system they were raised with. Pronunciation problems do arise by accident or occur when speakers attempt to modify the language of their childhood to conform to what they believe is a higher-status dialect. Thus, in the forties, an announcer introduced a radio play on a national network by saying, "Tonight we bring you that popular musical, 'Noo Meeoon.'" He had intended to pronounce the word "new" using the "elegant" vowel of an east-coast dialect, which would differentiate between the vowels in "new" and "moon." Instead, he inadvertently reversed the sounds using the pronunciation of "new" which was standard in his midwestern dialect and transforming "moon" into a caterwauling sound that belonged to no American dialect whatever. Accidentally garbled or misplaced phonemes can be amusing. For example, there is the story of a general who pompously announced to his troops that "We will deliver the enemy a *blushing crow*." (He meant to deliver, of course, a *"crushing blow*.") But while such phonemic and allaphonic misplacements, humorous or otherwise, occur rarely with native speakers, they are a constant plague to persons who have imperfect command of a second language. For, in addition to all the problems involved in selecting meaning, vocabulary, word order, word endings, and the like, nonnatives are constantly fighting the interference of their native sound system. This writer has observed that interference in the area of phonology becomes strongest when the nonnative speaker is fatigued or under emotional stress. Thus, when accuracy is most important (such as when meeting influential people or when addressing a large audience), mistakes in phonology are most apt to occur. For example, the author has heard South Americans use the words "bitch" and "bowels" when they meant to say "beach" and "vowels." The results were embarrassing both to the speaker and to the audience. What is worse, the speaker of Spanish does not know what he has done wrong and the American listener is often unable to explain it to him.

It would seem, therefore, that in the teaching of phonology a strong case can be made for overlearning correct responses to the extent that all *combinations* of conflict-point phonemes are made part of the second-language habit system. It must be emphasized that certain *combinations* of phonemes are more difficult than phonemes in isolation. For example, many students of Spanish learn the single-flap *r* in the word *toro* with relative ease, but are unable to pronounce the same *r*-sound in the high-frequency lexical item *tarde*. In some cases, simple explanations and devices help the student to contort his speech organs into the positions needed for correct articulation. Below are a few examples of commonly used devices.

1. Using approximate English points of articulation

Example A
PROBLEM: *German initial (ts) as in* zehn
SOLUTION: (*1*) *Pronounce the phrase "cats and dogs."*
        (*2*) *Omit* ca, *and pronounce the remnant "ts and dogs" until fluent.*
        (*3*) *Transfer English utterance to meaningful German phrases:*
            zehn Männer
            Zehn und eins ist elf.
            Der *Zug* ist schon hier.

Example B
PROBLEM: *Spanish word* tarde
SOLUTION: (*1*) *Pronounce the English word "totter" closely followed by the word "they" (that is, "totter-they").*
        (*2*) *Practice, noting, if necessary, the tongue positions behind upper teeth and then between teeth.*
        (*3*) *Drill in meaningful contexts from simple to difficult expressions:*
            Es muy *tarde.*
            por la *tarde*
            Buenas *tardes*
            todas las *tardes*

2. Using approximate target language points of articulation

Example A
PROBLEM: *German uvular* [r]
SOLUTION: (*1*) *Pronounce German word* Hau *with force of articulation directed far back against roof of mouth until uvular vibration is created.*
        (*2*) *Say* Hau-Frau *repeatedly until* r-*sound is produced in the word* Frau.
        (*3*) *Repeat the process with other words (for example,* Heu-freu, *and so forth).*
        (*4*) *Use in meaningful utterances:*
            Das ist *Frau* Schmidt.
            Es *freut* mich.

129

Example B
PROBLEM: *French uvular* [r]
SOLUTION: *The above procedure could be followed with* hâle-râle.

3. *Using charts and diagrams*

Example A. Charts of speech organs
> *Some students find it helpful to see a cutaway view of the oral cavity so that they can locate the correct points of articulation for subsequent practice on the difficult sounds. (It is desirable for the teacher to have a fairly good knowledge of the phonetics and phonemics of the native and target languages before attempting such an approach.)*

Example B. Intonation diagrams
> *Increasingly, the new texts indicate foreign language intonation patterns with lines, dots, or musiclike scales. These diagrams can be helpful, especially in conjunction with taped native voices.*

At this point a word of caution seems in order regarding the dangers of overexplaining phonology. Diagrams and mnemonic devices are valuable only insofar as they enable students to *locate* the points of articulation for the problem phonemes. Their skill in *manipulating* the phonemes automatically whenever they speak is the final measure of their control of those phonemes. And the acquisition of this skill seems to call for a great deal of rote memorization and overlearning. However, this appears to be in conflict with other aspects of language learning. For there is some evidence to the effect that rote learning of stereotyped responses actually interferes with the process of free application of language structures.[1]

There are a number of ways to minimize the negative effects of overlearning. The following two are most common.

Use of Nonparadigmatic Forms

Select expressions that contain the desired phoneme combinations, but that also are nonparadigmatic. These are expressions that function more or less as conditioned responses in the target language. For example, in American-English:

Sure enough!	*See you later.*
You bet!	*That's for sure.*
How do you do?	*What's new?*
Hello.	*Okay.*
Not yet.	

Most of the above expressions either do not fit a pattern or else their essential meaning will change if they are placed in a pattern. For example, it is possible to set up a paradigm:

How do I do?	*How do we do?*
How does he do?	*How do they do?*
How does she do?	

---

[1] Wilga M. Rivers, *The Psychologist and the Foreign Language Teacher*, Chicago, University of Chicago Press, 1964, p. 67.

But none of these are semanitc variants of the greeting, "How do you do," used when one American is introduced to another. "How do you do" is a complete, self-contained, stereotyped response that may justifiably be taught to a foreign student of English simply because the phrase can be used repeatedly in precisely that form whenever the student is introduced to an American or Englishman. The expression can therefore be used, not only for its own value, but also to teach certain phonemes that it contains.

Use of Irregular Forms

Similarly, an entire class of irregular forms can be used to teach phonology if there are not too many of them. Forms that deviate from a main pattern tend to require rote memorization rather than extension of a pattern. Thus in Spanish the familiar singular commands would serve:

Utterance	Examples of phonemes
Ten cuidado.	frontal [t], intervocalic [d]
Ven acá.	bilabial consonant

In German, the *ich* and *ach* sounds could be taught in conjunction with an irregular familiar singular command form:

Benimm *dich* gut.
Nimm *dich* in *Acht*.

Even a quotation from Goethe could be used to present a number of problem phonemes (for example, *l, r, ch*).

"Edel sei der Mensch
Hilfreich und gut."

Other pat expressions containing irregular singular commands can serve the double purpose of learning high-frequency vocabulary along with essential sounds.

In French, the following irregular or stereotyped forms contain problem sounds such as the contrast between *ou* and *u*, the nasal *ent* liaison between *comment* and *allez*, syllabification, and intonation.

Comment allez-vous?
Viens ici.
Où vas-tu?

If a course of study is carefully planned, the more difficult phonemes will be introduced gradually lesson by lesson. It would seem as unwise to cluster all the conflict sounds in the first few lessons as it would to begin a diving class by expecting novice students to execute a jackknife from the highboard. Phonology is clearly the most difficult aspect of language learning for the adolescent and postadolescent learner. (Few late learners of a second language ever eliminate all traces of first-language phonemes even decades after having mastered the morphology and syntax of the adopted language.)

131

PHONOLOGY AND FLES

It appears that small children in the school environment are able to learn phonology better than adults (see Chapter 4), but are less able in the areas of morphology and syntax. Thus, the elementary school foreign language program would seem to be justifiable only if this aspect of language learning shows good results. Certainly a FLES program that produces substandard pronunciation is of questionable value. Therefore, although the small children may sing songs, play games, engage in folk dancing, and present playlets, the adults directing the enterprise must be aware that the underlying purpose of the FLES program, insofar as foreign language education is concerned, is to develop good habits of pronunciation. Parents and high school language teachers should be quite satisfied with a FLES program if it accomplishes little more than good control of the "problem" phonemes, learned within a limited framework of vocabulary items and grammatical structures (see also Chapter 4).

OVERLEARNING MORPHOLOGY AND SYNTAX

It appears that the muscular reactions of the speech organs must be trained by some process of conditioning to contort rapidly into those unaccustomed positions that are necessary to produce the sounds of the target language understandably and without hesitation. Long hours of student practice must be devoted to correct positioning of tongue and lips with regard to the problem sounds. Exhaustive drill work must then follow until all phoneme combinations can be produced without effort and without conscious thought. It seems that a relatively large number of language educators can accept noncognitive training where phonology is concerned. However, there are fewer who would agree that grammar as well as phonology should be learned "out of awareness." Yet a number of influential language educators look upon the learning of grammatical forms as a process of conditioning. For example, Robert Lado contends that the student's attention should actually be drawn *away* from the problem structure during certain kinds of drill work.

This may seem paradoxical, but it is in effect a highly important feature of pattern practice. When the student expects a change at the crucial point, his attention is upon it, and his habit system is not involved. By fixing the attention elsewhere, the teacher forces the student to focus his attention away from the crucial point, and to carry the pattern increasingly through habit responses.[2]

In direct opposition to Lado's opinion is a statement by Paul Glaunde: "Should we not adopt as a cardinal principal that the student be kept aware of each structural point throughout drill on this point?"[3] Both men are

[2] Robert Lado, *Language Teaching: A Scientific Approach*, McGraw-Hill, 1964, p. 106.
[3] Quoted from the introduction of the bulletin, *Curricular Change in the Foreign Languages*, College Entrance Examination Board, 1963, p. x.

prominent foreign language educators, yet one appears to believe that awareness of structure interferes with the development of oral proficiency, while the other indicates that awareness is essential to the development of such proficiency. Behavioristic psychological theories favor the first view on the grounds that human reaction time is not swift enough to allow a cognitive process to regulate the flow of rapid speech. However, proponents of the cognitive theory contend that speech is far too complex to be explained by a series of conditioned responses alone. Thought processes must precede the actual production of speech according to this hypothesis, with desired word order and grammatical structures being determined in advance, then stored momentarily in the brain's "memory banks," and finally being released as needed to sustain the rapid flow of conversation. This theory would perhaps account for what happens when a person is interrupted midway through a statement and then is unable later to pick up the thread of conversation. The chain of thought making way for subsequent articulation is broken and replaced by a different, unrelated sequence of ideas. The speaker cannot resume until he reestablishes the severed link in the chain of thoughts that had been directing his speech. The interruption of simple habitual activities does not ordinarily cause this type of confusion. The person who has been interrupted simply continues automatically with what he had been doing. The expert swimmer, for example, whose path is crossed by a moving rowboat, simply stops and treads water for a moment and then swims on when the path is clear. The stroke-kick sequence, which the swimmer resumes automatically, can be plausibly accounted for as a series of conditioned reflexes. But spontaneous conversation is hardly in the same category. The swimmer does not invent new strokes as he goes along; his reaction pattern is fixed and recurrent. When two people are speaking freely on the same general topic (as opposed to reciting from memory as in a play), a much more complex and amazingly rapid process of decoding and encoding takes place. That is, each participant in a free conversation must receive an auditory message, which he then reacts to by producing his own appropriate message orally. Among other things this response involves:

1   Deciding upon meaning to be conveyed
2   Selecting suitable vocabulary from a vast repertoire of items
3   Determining word order, word endings, and word forms
4   Articulating the sounds in such a manner as to produce an intelligible message

In this regard, Lambert believes that a thought process runs several steps ahead of the actual production of the message. Taking his cue from the theory of brain-cell assemblies developed by Hebb, Lambert comments:

Apparently some word ordering and grammatical sequencing must first be decided on, then rapidly scanned and found appropriate, and finally set in motion while active thought moves on ahead to the next phase. This whole chain of processes is remarkably fast and "automatic" in the native speaker, making a

133

sharp contrast with the novice in a language who slows the process way down and makes evident to listeners that his thought and speech are running nearly in parallel.[4]

Following the implications of such cognitive theories, one could conclude that students should first understand the grammatical generalization before they aim at rapidity of response. That is, they should begin by mastering very short utterances in patterns whose functions they comprehend completely. The longer and more complex utterances would be developed through a similar grasp of the general principles on which the structures are built. All drill work would involve a conscious understanding of the underlying generalizations. Also, drill exercises would require intellectual alertness; they would force the students to respond orally to unanticipated stimuli that require them to make basic structural changes almost instantly. To the cognitive theorist, language learning is problem solving. Conversation skill is achieved by speeding up the problem-solving process, not by bypassing it. Thus the cognitive theorists tend to disagree with the practice of having students memorize entire blocks of basic-dialog material from the very beginning of the course; there are simply too many underlying generalizations for the student to grasp. And if they are articulating without thinking, little or no language learning is taking place above the level of phonological training. To support this contention, advocates of the cognitive-code learning theory point to recent studies of how small children learn their first language. These studies of infant language learning seem to indicate that children do not acquire language by imitating complete utterances from adult speech. Instead they appear to draw selected lexical items from the language environment and to manipulate these items according to simple grammatical rules. Thus, according to this line of thought, the fractured language called "baby talk" is different from adult speech precisely because children are following basic—if somewhat primitive—patterns in applying their limited repertoire of words. Their ability to combine these items into all sorts of nonadult patterns indicates that they are applying rational principles rather than merely imitating adult speech. The fact that they can form hundreds of meaningful utterances from a few dozen words seems to attest to that fact.[5] A number of linguists suspect that children possess an innate capacity for producing the basic structures of language. For example, McNeill comments

". . . that the general form taken by grammatical rules and the general distinction between rules of formation and rules of transformation are part of children's

[4] Wallace E. Lambert, "Psychological Approaches to the Study of Language," *Modern Language Journal* 47 (February 1963), pp. 58–59.
[5] David McNeil, "Some Thoughts on First and Second Language Acquisition," from a paper presented to the Modern Foreign Language Title III NDEA Conference, Washington, D.C., May 24, 1965. Preparation of this report was supported in part by a grant from the National Institutes of Health, No. 5–TI–GM 1011–03 to Harvard University, Center for Cognitive Studies.

134

linguistic capacity. . . . Indeed, it is possible that all the linguistic universals are part of the general capacity to acquire language; at least, this has been argued by Chomsky (1965) and Katz (1965)."[6]

The traditionalist grammarians will often leap on any shred of evidence to the effect that language learning is a rational process and use this to justify the learning of prescriptive grammatical rules. Yet in effect what they are often advocating is the replacement of one kind of rote memorization with another. In terms of student boredom, the memorization of grammatical rules, conjugations, and word lists can be at least as deadly as the memorization of unrelated dialog sentences. And furthermore, the memorization of grammatical rules appears to have negligible influence upon actual communication. This has been a well-known fact among educators in the field of English for half a century. Generations of American youngsters have been subjected to long years of memorizing rules about the evils of double negation, misuse of *will* and *shall*, and the "wrong" use of *I* and *me*. Yet as virulent as ever are expressions such as:

I don't have no book.
I will be there later.
It's me; me and John.

At the other extreme from rule learning is an approach that calls for the learning of patterns without conscious analysis. In support of nonanalysis, it is often pointed out that small children can produce most of the structures of their native language but are unable to explain the underlying rule for the operation of those structures. Even more significant, they can creatively apply the rules to unanticipated situations. For example, any normal 5-year-old can demonstrate his or her control of grammar in test situations such as the following:

Adult: Today I am glinging. I did the same thing yesterday; What did I do?
Child: You glinged. (Or, "You glung.")
Adult: (Holding up picture of an imaginary creature.) This is a gick. Now I have two of them; what do I have?
Child: You have two gicks.

The first reply shows that the child has mastered the system for changing regular verbs to the past tense. The second example demonstrates an ability to form regular plurals. The fact that the child can perform these operations with nonsense words proves that he has not merely memorized the forms from the adult speech community. The child has never heard of a "gick," nor has he ever seen anyone "glinging." At age 5 he has also not been introduced to the grammatical folklore that nouns are "the name of a person, place or thing" and that verbs show "action or state of being." Yet

[6] Ibid., p. 28.

135

he quite correctly and instantly treats "gick" as a noun and "gling" as a verb. Similarly, a German 5-year-old would have no trouble answering the first question in his language with,

Sie haben geglingt.　or　Sie haben geglungen.

A Mexican child could easily answer the second question with,

Vd. tiene dos guiques.

In both languages a child unhesitatingly will select the culturally acceptable pronouns (*Sie* instead of *du; Vd.* instead of *tu*) and will use word forms, word endings, and word order as the situation demands. In fact, it appears that all normal children develop this ability to integrate new (or imaginary) lexical items into the native language system, which they have largely mastered audio-lingually during the first five years of life. This ability for instant analogy will sometimes lead them astray (e.g., "He brung it," or "I don't got any"), but in the great majority of cases, preschool children have developed a listen-speak communications system that is infinitely expandable to all the tens of thousands of vocabulary items that exist in their language and those that will later be created during their lifetime.

　　In the early stages of second-language learning, a basic problem is that of getting the young adult or adolescent to acquire at least a rough approximation of the analogizing skill of a 5-year-old. Proponents of the American Method generally advocate an inductive approach to the learning of grammar as the best method for developing this automatic control of base structure. This approach requires students first to manipulate basic structures, secondly to arrive at the underlying generalizations relative to how they function, and thirdly to apply the generalizations to create new sentences for expressing what they want to say. Students are permitted to phrase the generalizations in their own words so long as their grasp of concepts is accurate and functional. In fact, they are not tested on their ability to conceptualize but rather on their ability to produce acceptable word forms and word sequences. There are some modern methodologists who feel that the inductive approach to learning grammar is often slow and inefficient. They feel that it is sometimes better simply to give students the rule or generalization and let them get down to the business of drilling upon the structure in question. As a matter of plain fact, there is no body of research to prove which approach is more effective. In the next section, we have provided an opportunity for the reader to examine sample lessons illustrating both approaches and to learn several structures of a second language using both processes. The first lesson is one in which the learner helps to formulate his own rules; in the second lesson the rule is given to him in advance. The language used is a modified form of Esperanto, which we will call ME for simplicity. The problem of providing foreign language examples is a complex one. If the reader already has learned the language that is used for illustrative purposes, he or she very often will be unable to appreciate the difficulties encountered by the novice learner of that language. The same applies to examples given in English where most of the readers are native Americans. To overcome such difficulties, foreign language methods teachers often employ a "shock" language, which the students must learn (in part) so that they experience the psychological problem of coping with an entirely unfamiliar language. Quite often a seldom-taught modern language is used. For the purposes of this book it was felt that an invented language would be adequate.

APPROACHES TO LEARNING GRAMMATICAL GENERALIZATIONS— TWO SAMPLE LESSONS

The sole purpose of the following lessons in Modified Esperanto is to give the reader an opportunity to experience the two most common ways of presenting grammatical principles. This invented language was chosen in the belief that few readers would be familiar with it. Therefore, the value of this section would be somewhat reduced for a person who has already studied Esperanto. Since this section is not intended to illustrate other aspects of methodology, a number of shortcuts have been taken for the sake of efficiency. First, it is assumed that the phonology of the target language (Modified Esperanto) is identical with the phonology of English; a situation that never actually occurs in second-language learning. (However, phonology has been treated earlier and its reentry at this point would have produced needless complications.) Secondly, translation is used to a degree that would be unacceptable to many methodologists. Thirdly, an artificial, overly regular language has been used as a model. And finally, since the classroom situation obviously cannot be recreated in a book, it was necessary to employ a somewhat limited programming device. Despite these limitations, it is possible for the reader to follow the main steps of the inductive process and to gain some indication of how a creative teacher might use this process to draw generalizations from students in a live classroom situation.

Lesson I. Grammar Learned Inductively

Step One: Learning the pattern without analysis
To approximate the learning of a structure drill and to acquire the necessary minimal vocabulary, the reader may wish to learn the seven sentences in Step One. The Modified Esperanto sentences (hereafter referred to as ME) can be studied first in association with the English, then with the ME sentences covered by a card or folded sheet of paper. The sentences can be considered learned when the reader is able to produce them orally in 35 seconds by referring only to the English. English pronunciation can be used with the ME words, but care must be taken to get all endings and word forms correct. There should be no special effort to analyze the sentences at this time. The method calls for learning a pattern without prior analysis.

1   *The lady is sitting on the chair.*
            .... (On each problem place a card on the dashed line until after you
                    have responded. Then check your answer.)
        La sinyorino sidas sur la sajo.

137

2   *The teacher is sitting on the chair.*

     La instruisto sidas sur la sajo.

3   *The student is sitting on the chair.*

     La lernanto sidas sur la sajo.

4   *The boy is sitting on the chair.*

     La knabo sidas sur la sajo.

5   *The salesman is sitting on the chair.*

     La vendisto sidas sur la sajo.

6   *The secretary is sitting on the chair.*

     La secretarino sidas sur la sajo.

7   *The girl is sitting on the chair.*

     La knabino sidas sur la sajo.

Step Two : Learning generalizations about nouns

1   *In the seven sentences above there were eight nouns; say them (or write them) and then check your answers:*
     lady, chair, teacher, student, boy, salesman, secretary, girl.
     ------------------ (Remember to place card at dashed line.)
     sinyorino, sajo, instruisto, lernanto, knabo, vendisto, secretarino, knabino.

2   *What do all these nouns have in common ? Before responding, find two unique characteristics. Then check your answers below.*

     The eight nouns end with the vowel o.
     The eight nouns are all preceded by the word la. *(La is roughly equivalent to the English article* the.*)*

Step Three : Application of generalizations about nouns

Complete the following sentences and check your answers.

1   _____ bird _____ sidas sur la sajo. *(The bird is sitting on the chair.)*

     La birdo sidas sur la sajo.

2   _____ hund _____ sidas sur la sajo. *(The dog is sitting on the chair.)*

     La hundo sidas sur la sajo.

3   _____ Kat _____ sidas sur la sajo. *(The cat is sitting on the chair.)*

     La kato sidas sur la sajo.

138

4   ____ knabin ____ sidas sur la sajo. *(The girl is sitting on the chair.)*

La knabino sidas sur la sajo.

Note : *If all answers were correct in step three, you have achieved excellent control of the definite article and the nominative case of ME nouns.*

Step Four : Learning verbs without analysis.
Using the directions given in step one, learn the sentences below.

1   *The bird is flying. (flies, does fly)*

La birdo flugas.

2   *The dog is barking. (barks, does bark)*

La hundo boyas.

3   *The cat is mewing. (mews, does mew)*

La kato miowas.

4   *The salesgirl is chattering. (chatters, does chatter)*

La vendistino babilas.

5   *The student is studying. (studies, does study)*

La lernanto studas.

6   *The fish is swimming. (swims, does swim)*

La fisho najas.

Step Five : Learning generalizations about verbs.

1   *In the six ME sentences above there were six verbs; say them or write them, and then check your answers:*
fly, bark, mew, chatter, study, swim.

flugas, boyas, miowas, babilas, studas, najas.

2   *To what kind of actions do these verbs refer: to present actions ? to past actions ? or to future actions ?*

The verbs refer to present actions.

3   *What do all these verbs have in common ?*

The verbs all end in as.

4   *In the ME language, the forms* flug-, boy-, miow-, babil-, stud-, naj-, *are called verb stems. What must be done to these stems to make them refer to actions taking place at the present time ?*

To make verb stems refer to the present time, merely add as.

139

5   *Complete the following sentence:*
     La lernanto stud _____. *(The student is studying.)*

     La lernanto studas.

6   *Express the ME equivalent of the following English sentence:*
     The student studies.

     La lernanto studas.

7   *Express the ME equivalent of the following English sentence:*
     The student does study.

     La lernanto studas.

8   *In summary, it can be stated that the* _____ *language has three verb*
     forms to refer to present action while the _____ *language has only one*
     verb form for present action.

     The English language has three verb forms . . . while the ME language has
     only one form to refer to present action.

9   *The ME language expresses present action by adding* _____ *to the*
     verb _____.

     ----
     by adding as to the verb stem.

Step Six : Using generalizations to create new combinations

At this point, the reader who has mastered all the material in steps one through six
will be able to form dozens of new sentences simply by applying the generaliza-
tions to the vocabulary items. Some of the combinations that are grammatically
feasible would have to be rejected because they would be semantically
unacceptable (for example, La fisho studas*). However, most of the nouns can be*
combined with most of the verbs, and many of the people and animals could be
made to sit on one another instead of sitting only on the chair. In ME it is simply a
matter of filling in the pattern: La _____ sidas sur la _____. *Occasionally,*
absurdity can be employed to advantage. For example, if the teacher would say,
"La instruisto sidas sur la birdo," and the students responded by laughing, then it
can be assumed that a number of students understood what was said. Ideally,
however, the teaching process would not be restricted only to the passive
listening-reading skills. For communication to take place, the student must also
learn to make his own reapplications in the active speaking-writing skill areas.
One device for eliciting free application of generalizations from the student is to
show him a series of pictures that he can comment on using only the vocabulary
and knowledge of grammar at his disposal. This frees the student from depen-
dence on the native language and helps to minimize the effects of interference
from English. Another technique is to use English to describe a situation that the
student is asked to comment on rather than to translate. The reader who has
mastered the vocabulary in steps one and four can now test his ability to apply his
knowledge about the ME language by supplying oral responses in ME to the
situations described below. A reasonable oral fluency has been achieved if the
five sentences can be completed correctly in 60 seconds.

Using a simple sentence tell what each person is doing in the pictures below. In number 4, the actor will be a fish.

(Remember to place a shield card at the dash line and to check each response for correctness.)

1   *Comment on what he is doing.*

La knabo najas.

2   *Describe what he is doing.*

La vendisto babilas.

3   *Comment.*

La knabino sidas sur la hundo.

4   *Comment.*

La fisho flugas.

5   *Tell what she is doing.*

La knabino studas.

6   *Comment.*

La vendistino sidas sur la sajo.

142

Lesson II. Grammar by Application of Rules

To simplify this section we have drawn mainly upon prelearned vocabulary. Also, the format will change to the more traditional presentation of word lists and rules for application to the vocabulary items. This procedure should enable the reader to understand the two approaches more clearly, and to begin to form opinions about the pedagogical value of each.

Step One: Presentation of grammatical generalization

Learn the following rules, from the teacher or the text, regarding nouns, verbs, and adjectives in ME.
Rule one:
In the ME language, all nouns in the objective case add the ending n
The dog bites the boy. La hundo mordas la *knabon.*
The teacher helps the student. La instruisto helpas la *lernanton.*
Rule two:
In ME all nouns and adjectives form their plurals by adding y.
The train is full. La vagonaro estas plena.
The trains are full. La vagonaroy estas plenay.
Rule three: *Note that verbs do not change form in the plural.*
Rule four: *Singular adjectives end with* a, *plural adjectives with* ay.
Rule five: *All adjectives in the objective case add* n.
Rule six: *ME omits the use of the indefinite articles (a, an).*

Step Two: Learning vocabularly

Memorize the following words, and review the vocabulary from previous lessons.
vagonaro—*train*   estas—*am, is, are*

granda—*big*   havas—*have, has*
plena—*full*   helpas—*help, helps*
saga—*wise*   mordas—*bite, bites*
ni—*we*

Step Three: Learning the paradigms

Memorize the following noun and adjective declensions.

	Nominative case	*Objective case*
Singular nouns	vagonaro	vagonaron
	hundo	hundon
	birdo	birdon
Plural nouns	vagonaroy	vagonarony
	hundoy	hundony
	birdoy	birdony

	Nominative case	*Objective case*
Singular adjectives	granda	grandan
	plena	plenan
	saga	sagan
Plural adjectives	granday	grandany
	plenay	plenany
	sagay	sagany

Step Four: Drill exercises involving the new grammatical forms

Fill in the blanks in the sentences on the left. Check your answers by progressively uncovering the correct responses given on the right.

(Place shield at dashed line)
(Place shield at dashed line)

1	La knabo havas _____ *(a cat)*	katon
2	La vendistino havas _____ *(a dog)*	hundon
3	La hundo mordas _____ *(the boy)*	la knabon
4	La kata mordas _____ *(the girl)*	la knabinon
5	La knabino helpas _____ *(the teacher)*	la instruiston
6	Ni havas _____ *(trains)*	vagonarony
7	La kato mordas _____ *(the birds)*	la birdony
8	Ni helpas _____ *(the teachers)*	la instruistony
9	La instruistoy helpas _____ *(the students)*	la lernantony
10	La instruistoy estas _____ *(wise)*	sagay
11	La vagonaroy estas _____ *(full)*	plenay
12	La knaboy estas _____ *(big)*	granday
13	Ni havas _____ *(wise teachers)*	sagany instruistony
14	Ni havas _____ *(big trains)*	grandany vagonarony
15	Ni helpas _____ *(wise students)*	sagany lernantony
16	La knabo estas _____ *(big)*	granda
17	La sinyorino estas _____ *(wise)*	saga
18	Ni havas _____ *(a wise teacher)*	sagan instruiston
19	La kato mordas _____ *(a big dog)*	grandan hundon
20	La vagonaro estas _____ *(big)*	granda

144

Step Five : Drilling all forms through translation

Translate the following sentences applying what you have learned in steps one, two, three, and four. Check your answers.

1   *The boy has a train.*

    La knabo havas vagonaron.

2   *The boys have a train.*

    La knaboy havas vagonaron.

3   *The boys have the dogs.*

    La knaboy havas la hundony.

4   *We are big boys.*

    Ni estas granday knaboy.

5   *We help the big boys.*

    Ni helpas la grandany knabony.

Step Six : Testing application of rules to vocabulary

Translate the following sentences into ME. Check your answers.

1   *The dogs are biting the big boys.*

    La hundoy mordas la grandany knabony.

2   *The cat is biting the dog.*

    La kato mordas la hundon.

3   *The cats have the fish. (singular)*

    La katoy havas la fishon.

4   *The teacher is helping the girls.*

    La instruisto helpas la knabinony.

5   *The girls are wise.*

    La knabinoy estas sagay.

6   *We have a full train.*

    Ni havas plenan vagonaron.

7   *We have big trains.*

    Ni havas grandany vagonarony.

8   *The birds are sitting on the trains.*

    La birdoy sidas sur la vagonaroy.

145

9 *A wise student helps the teacher.*

Saga lernanto helpas la instruiston.

10 *We have big fish. (plural)*

Ni havas grandany fishony.

RULE MEMORIZATION VERSUS LEARNING BY INDUCTION AND ANALOGY

Anyone who has spent an hour or more on the sample lessons should be able to read hundreds of simple ME sentences and be able to produce a few dozen simple written sentences. According to advocates of the American Method, the reader should have found the first approach clearer and intellectually more stimulating than the second. To the traditionalist, on the other hand, the second approach is superior because students have the rules and vocabulary available from the outset. Therefore they know what they are doing at all times and can cover a great deal more material if they are only willing to work hard and to concentrate upon applying the rules to the vocabulary. As a matter of fact, both approaches appear to work equally well in actual practice if nothing more than the acquisition of the four language skills is taken into account. We will subsequently discuss other aspects of inductive learning versus rule application. First, however, a few words must be said about a third approach, namely one in which the student's attention is never drawn to the underlying generalizations either by means of induction or by rule. This is an extremely important point, because many teachers have assumed that students will automatically grasp grammatical principles and see relationships without having them pointed out. In the two ME lessons, a generalization was "seeded" into the drill material, but no rule was supplied for it, and no pattern drill or paradigm was set up to illustrate it. Thus if the reader has grasped this "hidden" rule while going through the sample lessons, he/she will at this point be able to supply ME words for "gentleman," "female dog" and "female cat," among others. Further, if told that the word "frato" means "brother," the reader should now be able to produce the word "sister" by simple applica-tion of principles he/she has already been exposed to. Chances are, however, that the generalization was not grasped by most readers simply because it was not pointed out in the lesson. If the principle has not been grasped, it should become evident in the first four exercises given below. By drawing simple analogies, the reader should be able to fill in all twelve blanks in items 2 through 7 below.

1	knabo	*(boy)*	knabino	*(girl)*
2	_____	( )	sinyorino	*(lady)*
3	hundo	*(male dog)*	_____	( )
4	kato	*(tom cat)*	_____	( )

146

5	_____	( )	onklino	(aunt)
6	frato	(brother)	_____	( )
7	patro	(father)	_____	( )

The simple analogizing power, which appears to operate below the level of consciousness in small children, can also operate with adults, although it may require the support of conscious analysis. Many adults and adolescents seem to feel the need to verbalize what they are doing and why they are doing it. In any case, the process of analogy should have produced the following answers to the above exercises:

2	sinyoro	(gentleman)
3	hundino	(female dog)
4	katino	(female cat)
5	onklo	(uncle)
6	fratino	(sister)
7	patrino	(mother)

If the reader now knows how to take the word for "Frenchman" (*Franco*) and change it to to mean "Frenchwoman" or transform the words "cow elephant" (*elefantino*) to mean "bull elephant," then the main lesson has been learned. Should a generalization regarding ME suffixes then be added as a means of consolidating what has been learned? Or should the rule about the masculine suffix -*o* and the feminine suffix -*ino* have been given in the first place, perhaps along with comparable English word pairs such as prince/princess, host/hostess, etc.? Or should the teacher merely proceed to the next lesson without making it clear to the student that all feminines are indicated by the -*ino* suffix and that all masculines and genderless nouns are indicated by the -*o* suffix? The weight of opinion in the field of educational psychology seems to favor the learning of generalizations rather than the mere learning of patterns. One psychologist quite emphatically states that "the teacher must . . . abandon outright that Herbartian variety of teaching, in which after the examination of a considerable number of concrete instances, the solution is assumed to roll out into clear sight . . . and to wait not for validation but only for 'application.'"[7] Thus, if it is generally agreed that generalizations must be learned, then the question becomes one of how best to learn them. A number of studies in foreign languages and other academic areas have attempted to answer the question as to whether better learning results are achieved by the application of memorized rules or by the application of generalizations that students have learned to formulate by themselves. Is it best for the teacher to give a clear initial statement of the generalization so that students understand what the drill work is all about? Or should students first learn some specific examples from which they formulate

[7] R. R. Palmer, "Straight and Crooked Thinking," in L. D. Crow and A. Crow (eds.), *Readings in Human Learning*, New York, McKay, 1963, p. 399.

their own generalizations for application to the subsequent drill work? One of the most elaborate studies ever conducted in the field of foreign language learning focused specifically upon this problem. The control group used the traditional rule-application approach. With the experimental group, however, the investigators report that grammar was taught after the fact, "and such generalization was never attempted before functional practice with new principles. However, nothing in our direictives to the instructors barred them from helping students to organize grammar, so long as this organization was made in retrospect."[8] At the end of the four-semester experiment, the 101 control students were not significantly different from the 128 experimental students in terms of overall proficiency in the four skills. The experimental audiolingual group did show better attitudes toward the foreign language and culture and were able to associate meaning more directly in the target language. However, all measures of the ability to read, write, speak, and understand the foreign language indicated no significant overall difference between the audiolingual and the traditional groups.[9] Other studies of the effectiveness of rule application versus inductive formulation of principles tend to follow the same pattern where the learning of skills is concerned. For example, in a study of different ways to learn to read Chinese characters, it was found that the symbols could be learned equally well and with equal rapidity by either approach.[10] One study in the field of science showed that better results were achieved if students were allowed to formulate their own concepts when compared to students who had learned the same material by rote memorization and verbalization of definitions.[11] However, other studies relating to the learning of skills in chemistry and arithmetic have indicated that students learned equally well by the rule-application method.[12] One investigator felt, however, that since both approaches worked equally well, it would be desirable for students to have the additional experience in learning generalizations. In the final analysis, it appears that the inclination toward the inductive process for learning generalizations is based more upon the belief that it is an important educational experience in itself rather than upon any proof that it is conducive to better learning of the language skills. The idea that the learner should discover by himself a large fraction of the material to be learned is at least as old as the "Socratic method." Lichtenberg, an eighteenth-century German physicist, endorsed the inductive approach when he wrote: "What you have been obliged to discover by

[8] George Scherer and Michael Wertheimer, *A Psycholinguistic Experiment in Foreign-Language Teaching*, New York, McGraw-Hill, 1964, pp. 85–86.
[9] Ibid., p. 245.
[10] C. L. Hall, "The Evolution of Concepts," in L. D. Crow and A. Crow (eds.), *Readings in Human Learning*, New York, McKay, 1963, pp. 119–133.
[11] W. R. Hatch and Ann Bennett, *New Dimensions in Higher Education, No. 2: Effectiveness in Teaching*, Washington, D.C., GPO, 1963, p. 22.
[12] Frances Colville, "The Learning of Motor Skills as Influenced by Knowledge of Mechanical Principles," in L. D. Crow and A. Crow (eds.), *Readings in Human Learning*, New York, McKay, 1963, p. 376.

yourself leaves a path in your mind which you can use again when the need arises." Similarly, Immanuel Kant in his *Critique of Pure Reason* stated that "Learning begins with action and perception, proceeds from thence to words and concepts, and should end in desirable mental habits." And, more recently, there is John Dewey who is often unfairly associated with certain abuses of the learning-by-doing approach to education. In reality, Dewey was as opposed to meaningless physical activity as he was to sterile, disembodied mental activity. In his book, *Democracy and Education*, Dewey comments that "Mere activity does not constitute experience. . . . Experience as trying involves change, but change is meaningless transition unless it is consciously connected with the return wave of consequences which flow from it."[13] Thus, according to Dewey, the actual "doing" is a step that must take place prior to or in connection with learning, because "the discernment of relationships is the genuinely intellectual matter; hence the educative matter. The failure arises in supposing that relationships can become perceptible without experience. . . ."[14]

In the minds of many great thinkers of the Western world it would not be a question of which approach developed the best control of language skills. Instead, the value of the entire language-learning process would be seriously questioned if it were to consist merely of applying rules for the purposes of developing skills and gaining knowledge. For, as Dewey expressed it, "Acquiring is always secondary and instrumental to the act of inquiring. . . . While all thinking results in knowledge, ultimately the value of knowledge is subordinate to its use in thinking. For we live not in a settled and finished world, but one which is going on. . . ."[15]

PROVING STUDENT MASTERY OF GENERALIZATIONS

In the final analysis, the value of learning generalizations must be measured by the psychological impact that that learning has upon the student's attempts to use the foreign language when he wishes to express himself freely either orally or in writing. As far as the student's ability to communicate in the language is concerned, this is a more relevant issue than the question of whether he learned the rule by himself or had it drawn to his attention by the teacher or the textbook. The author has seen students who are unable to perceive—much less apply—grammatical generalizations even after hundreds of repetitions of pattern drills. The ability to retrieve a series of grammatical forms only in response to specific prelearned stimuli is no proof that any genuine language learning has taken place at all. If students are unable to rearrange their repertoire of language forms in response to an unanticipated stimulus, then the value of what they have learned is questionable as far as genuine communication is concerned. At the other extreme are students whose knowledge of generalizations

[13] John Dewey, *Democracy and Education*, New York, Macmillan, 1961, p. 139.
[14] Ibid., p. 144.
[15] Ibid., p. 151.

149

prevents them from communicating effectively in the language because of the way they learned them. An example of this are the students who find it necessary to mentally run through four forms of the future before they can say "we will." (They may have learned the forms by chanting all eight persons beginning with the first person singular and ending with third plural.) However, this does not prove that students should not have learned the conjugation, but rather that they should not have memorized it as a numerical sequence. If they have properly grasped the concept of verb endings, then the sixth verb form in the conjugation should be just as instantly retrievable as is the first. Similarly, it does students no harm to know that the days of the week are listed in a certain order starting with Sunday. But their learning of vocabulary has been deficient if they are compelled to count to seven on their fingers before they can say "Saturday." Fluency is destroyed if students must mentally run through a sequentially organized system of rules, paradigms, and mnemonic devices before they can express an original thought. Thus, students of French or Spanish may have memorized the rules for the use of the present and past subjunctive, or they may have learned them by observation and induction; further, they may be able to produce all the present subjunctive endings in conjugated form. Yet all of this has little relevance if they are unable to automatically supply the right verb form when the flow of conversation calls for a response such as:

The teacher wants you to come *in early tomorrow.*

or

I would go if I had *the money.*

Thus, testing the students' grasp of generalizations about the subjunctive must relate to their speed and accuracy in supplying correct subjunctive forms in new and unanticipated combinations of familiar verbs. Knowing the rules is no guarantee that they will apply them; but applying them spontaneously is proof that they know them.

AIDS TO MEMORIZATION OF VOCABULARY

A certain amount of memorization is essential in the learning of a foreign language. Clearly students must not invent their own vocabulary, grammatical structures, sounds, and word order sequences. Instead, they must approximate to the best of their ability the language as it is used by educated native speakers. Some foreign language teachers have interpreted this fact to mean that all the basic language material must somehow be imposed upon the learners' mind by force of repetition before they are allowed to do anything creative. To make the process of repetition more palatable, modern textbook writers have presented vocabulary in the form of natural-sounding connected dialogs, which students can learn and retain more easily, than isolated words out of context, which were so often taught in the older traditional courses. Another aid to memory is the visual, which allows the student to associate meaning directly with a colorful cartoon or photograph that is projected on a screen or that appears in a book or on a large card. But, however dramatic and impressive dramatizations and visualizations may be, they still involve the imposition of material upon the mind of the learner. Yet if anything has been learned by decades of research in the field of learning psychology, it is that the mind is much more than a *tabula rasa* upon which knowledge is systematically imprinted by the teacher. It is quite generally agreed that optimum learning is seldom possible without positive emotional involvement on the part of the students. And the students' attitude is not likely to remain positive if they are never allowed to express their individuality.

One investigator found that children could memorize word pairs more effectively if they were allowed to create their own mediators. They were instructed to learn the words by fitting them into a sentence of their own creation. A second group was told to memorize the word pairs in isolation, and a third group was given for memorization the sentences created by the first group. Finally, all three groups were tested to see which method produced the best learning results. The group that was allowed to create its own memory mediators did significantly better than the two that had the material imposed upon them. In the words of the investigator, "The chief result is . . . that children who provide their own mediators do best— indeed, one time through a set of thirty pairs, they recover up to 95 percent of the second words when presented with the first ones of the pairs, whereas the uninstructed children reach a maximum of less than 50 percent recovered."[16] It may be that material that is organized in terms of a person's own interests and manner of thinking is material that is most likely to be recalled. In applying this principle to foreign language learning the problem is to keep the student's urge for originality within those bounds that are rather arbitrarily set by his limited knowledge of grammar, phonology, and vocabulary. Yet if the teacher makes the students wait until they have memorized "everything," she or he may find that the process of rote memorization has driven them into other electives that are more intellectually stimulating.

There are teachers who have devised ways to capitalize on the desire for originality, while at the same time overcoming most of the dangers of premature use of partially learned material. One technique involves the use of "formula sentences," which enable students to use newly acquired structures to refer to people and places within their realm of experience.

The name of my _____ is _____.
I live on _____ Street in _____, Illinois.
That car belongs to my _____, who is here on a visit from _____.
I would like my _____ to give me _____ for Christmas.
If I had a million dollars, I would _____.

16 J. S. Bruner, "The Act of Discovery," in L. D. Crow and A. Crow (eds.), *Readings in Human Learning*, New York, McKay, 1963, pp. 423–435.

This approach allows students to relate what they have learned to the world as they know it. The teacher helps to minimize error by structuring the nonpersonal aspects for the students. Theoretically students will be more willing to learn the material because it refers uniquely to them and because they have had a hand in producing it. However, before they commit the sentences to memory, the teacher (or a native-speaking teacher aide) must check each blank to make certain that acceptable structures have been supplied. Also, before using formula sentences, students must have reached the point where they can write with reasonable accuracy and can read aloud without undue distortion.

As the students progress in knowledge and experience, they can be required to create the entire dialog material for themselves using current and previous lessons for models. This technique seems to work best with small groups of two or three students who first create the dialog, then check it with the teacher for accuracy, and finally present it before the class. The only limitations are that the dialog must be in keeping with the materials currently being studied, and that each member of the team must learn each role in the dialog. The experience of one teacher who uses this technique tends to confirm Bruner's thesis that students learn best when they devise their own memory mediators. As he expressed it:

I have had some success with having students construct their own dialogues. These are then memorized and presented to the class in a rather competitive fashion. I have continued it because this is one thing my students thoroughly enjoy. . . . The learning takes place during the dialogue construction. The students seem to enjoy bits of conversation long after it has been presented.[17]

A further advantage of the self-produced dialogs relates to the problem of utterance length. The length of utterance that students can retain in the foreign language is far shorter than in their native tongue. During the first few months of instruction, eight to twelve syllables are as much as most youngsters can handle. Thus, students who produce their own dialogs for recitation in front of their classmates tend to be quite realistic about sentence length. The desire to sound adult and sophisticated will lead them away from infantile discourse, while the fear of floundering will help to prevent the introduction of overly complex sentences.

TOTAL EXCLUSION OF ENGLISH
FROM THE FOREIGN LANGUAGE CLASSROOM

Many people have confused the American Method with an approach to language teaching that is popular in Europe today and that had a considerable following in America during the latter part of the nineteenth

[17] Arnold Schaeffer, "Conversation-Promoting Techniques Used in Secondary Modern Foreign Language Classes," *Voice of the Wisconsin Foreign Language Teacher* 7 (1967), p. 30.

century. We refer here to all those methods that call for the total exclusion of the mother tongue from the foreign language classroom, and which, for the sake of simplicity, we can lump together under the designation "direct method." This approach is based on the belief that second-language learning must take place in total isolation from the native language. The student must draw meaning from the foreign language by direct exposure and never by reference to native-language equivalents, which, as we have seen, are seldom fully equivalent to words in the foreign language. The teacher may use a wide variety of techniques to convey meaning more efficiently. The following are among the more commonly used devices.

Visuals. Students see a still picture or motion picture and hear the teacher, the soundtrack, or some other audio source comment on the visual stimulus. Hopefully, students make the correct association between the picture that they see and the sound that they hear. They learn first by imitating the model sounds, then by responding to the visual stimulus without the sound. They have learned a given lesson when they can produce all the utterances in response to all the visual materials.

Charades. The teacher performs in various ways to illustrate the meaning of new words and expressions. For example, the arms may be flapped vigorously while saying, "I'm a bird." Then, while moving across the room, arms still flapping, the teacher may say, "The bird is flying."

Question and Answer. Interrogation usually occupies a large part of the direct-method teacher's time.

(Holding up a picture of a bird in flight)
Teacher: What is this?
 Pupil: It's a bird.
Teacher: What is the bird doing?
 Pupil: The bird is flying.

Paraphrase.
A house *is a building in which the family lives.*

Opposites.
Hot *is the opposite of* cold.

Gouin Series. The teacher goes through a series of actions while describing what she is doing as she is doing it. Then each pupil must do likewise.

I stand up. I walk to the window. I open the window. I put my hand out the window. I close the window. I walk to the chair. I sit down again.

A skillful direct-method teacher, given plenty of time, can achieve excellent results. In fact, there are some situations in which the direct method may be the most effective. For example, if the members of the class have a dozen different language backgrounds (as is often the case with adult classes for immigrants), then the teacher is compelled to use some sort of direct approach. (Clearly, it is unlikely that a teacher would be sufficiently well versed in twelve languages to be able to supply mother-tongue equivalents for all students.) Also, when the students of a new

153

language are located in the country where that language is spoken, the direct approach can be quite effective. For then the students are able to step from the classroom into direct contact with native speakers "on location" in the target culture. In this situation, the need for direct communication is obvious to the student during a large part of every waking hour.

However, students in the American comprehensive high school do not normally attend classes that demand the direct method, nor is the need for direct oral communication as apparent as with students who are studying abroad. Another problem is that the direct method requires a teacher who is highly skilled both in methodology and in the use of the foreign language, a combination of skills frequently unavailable to American education. And, unless conditions are ideal, the direct method can be highly inefficient. Often students will be unable to ascertain what the teacher is getting at despite the use of visuals, charades, and other devices. The result is either that they are confused about the meaning of an utterance or else they try to guess at the intended meaning. Since the teacher is forbidden to explain the meaning in English, students may go for months without having their guesses confirmed or corrected. (The author knows a girl who went through an entire semester in a direct-method course thinking that the French word for "notebook" meant "candy bar" because the visualization of the word was ambiguous.) And even if students are able to determine the general meaning of words, there is no guarantee that they will not draw false conclusions about their significance in the target culture. Thus, without recourse to English they may indeed learn words that refer to secondary education in France or Germany, but if they equate attendance in these institutions with the process of attending and graduating from an American high school, then they are very little wiser in the end than the student who has been told that *lycée* and *Gymnasium* mean "high school" and that the school-leaving certificates from these schools are "like high school diplomas." Apparently, where abstract, culturally loaded expressions are concerned, the direct method will often result in nothing more than a fluent mouthing of misconceptions. On the other hand, when referents are largely to the American culture or to generalized topics and vocabulary (for example, swimming, walking, books, pencils, trees, and so on), the psychological impact of having to rely solely on the foreign language can be enormously positive. Through total exclusion of English, some language teachers have been able to develop an esprit de corps among their students that carries beyond the confines of the classroom and even beyond the school itself. There is perhaps no sweeter music to the language educator's ear than the sound of students on the way home from school discussing yesterday's party or tomorrow's date in the foreign language. Indeed, this direct, spontaneous communication in the target language is the ultimate goal of most modern programs. The improper use of English is the deadly enemy of that objective. For if the students know they can always fall back on the native language, they are unlikely to take the target language very seriously as a vehicle for direct communication of ideas.

154

DISCRIMINATE USE OF ENGLISH
IN THE FOREIGN LANGUAGE CLASSROOM

Proponents of the American Method believe that the mother tongue has a very definite place in second-language learning, and that, under proper conditions, the use of English can greatly speed up the learning process for the American high school student who is studying a foreign language. On the other hand, they are aware of the dangers of indiscriminate use of English. The rule of thumb for proper and improper use of English in the foreign language classroom is rather simple: Any use of English that leads to more efficient and intensive practice *in the foreign language* by the student is good use of English; any use of English that leads the student *away* from the target language or that tends to make him a passive listener is bad use of English. The advocates of discriminate use of English base their thinking on the belief that young adults in America cannot possibly escape the influence of English as they undertake the learning of a second language. The English habit is so strongly ingrained that no amount of direct-method drill can override its influence. Therefore, according to this line of thought, it is better to capitalize on the student's knowledge of English than to pretend that it is not there. Although not all modern methodologists would agree on all points, the following uses of English are widely accepted.

English to Convey Meaning of Dialog Material

Students passively refer to English approximations as they first hear and then repeat the dialog sentences of the target language. They read the English but are never asked to recite or translate actively. Once the meaning of an utterance is fully grasped, the English is abandoned and the student concentrates on speed and accuracy in committing the foreign utterance to memory. The great danger here is that students may become too dependent upon English and may resist being weaned into full reliance upon the target language. To counteract this tendency, visual material can be used as the main stimulus for memorizing and recalling the dialog utterances. In this case English is used only to explain (and thus avoid) the trouble spots.

English to Explain Tests and Drills

Students could know their lesson thoroughly and still score badly on a test or do poorly on a drill simply because they failed to understand the directions. The danger of this happening is greatly increased when the directions are given in the foreign language. Thus it seems best to explain the mechanics of a drill or the directions for a test in English. This is particularly true when a new type of drill is being introduced for the first time. Another technique often used with drill work is to give both the English and the foreign language at the beginning, and then gradually to phase out the English with those types of instructions that are recurrent.

Throughout the course, new drill formats can first be introduced in both languages, then gradually replaced by exclusive use of the target language. It is felt that the time saved by using English so that students will always know what they are doing more than compensates for any loss in psychological conditioning that may result from the brief use of English.

English in Cues for Pattern Drills

In certain cases it seems advisable to put an English expression into sharp contrast with its foreign language counterpart. The English is then used as an auditory stimulus for evoking an oral student response. The purpose of such drills is to point up the fact that the target language uses a vastly different structure to convey a particular kind of meaning. Perhaps one example will serve to point out the difference between this use of English and the traditional translation exercise:

I forgot the book.
I forgot the novel.
I forgot the bread.
I forgot the newspaper.
I forgot the ice cream.

The purpose of this particular drill is to "reset" the students' minds so that they replace the English subject-verb pattern for expressing the idea, "I forget . . .," with the structure, *Se me olvidó. . . .* The student might find it helpful to realize that the Spaniard shifts the verb form into the third person, thus removing some of the implication of responsibility from himself when he has forgotten something. But the main intent of such drill is to replace "I" with *se me* plus the third person preterite. Hopefully, the drill will also prevent students from ever drawing a false analogy based on the logic of English that would lead them to the pitfall expression *Yo olvidé . . .* It would seem unwise ever to lead a student into producing an expression that is not used by native speakers (also see the chapter on pattern drills).

English for Cultural Notes and Grammatical Summaries

Some teachers provide brief explanations of culture and grammar as they appear necessary for the student to progress without wrong learning taking place. At the very early level, students may lack the vocabulary they need to grasp basic concepts about cultural and grammatical patterns if these are presented in the target language. For example, the familiar and polite forms of "you" carry cultural overtones that cannot be conveyed by pictures and gestures alone (and certainly not by the English words "you" or "thou"). Similarly, students may become confused when they hear that there are three common equivalents for "wife" in Spanish. A few lines in English can point out that a man will often use *esposa* or *mujer* to refer to his own wife, but would usually use the more formal word *señora* to refer to someone else's wife. The same would be true of grammar.

An example of the need for an explanation in several European languages would be the use of the present tense where English uses the present perfect tense (for example, *Ich bin zwei Wochen hier;* literally, "I am two weeks here"). To many teachers, the psychological loss resulting from brief English explanations is more than compensated for by the fact that such explanations tend to minimize the danger of implanting a serious cultural or grammatical error in the student's mind. In some of the most modern texts, these notes are written into each chapter so that no class time need be lost to the use of English. Thus students are able to spend maximum class and laboratory time productively manipulating the foreign language forms without being puzzled by seeming irregularities in the form or content of the material they are learning.

English to Dispel Students' Doubts

While some teachers will allow the student to *read* English and to *hear* English in class (and on the introductory segments of taped lessons in the laboratory), they will never allow the student to *speak* or *write* English in these situations. The underlying rationale for this limitation is the belief that the student must use every possible moment of the language class for active practice *in* the foreign language. Other teachers will allow several minutes at the end of the period for student questions in English. This enables students to clear up uncertainties that may have arisen during the period.

The experience of the past few decades has shown that many Americans have, in fact, learned a foreign language despite the use of the mother tongue in the instructional process. On the other hand, it is also true that many Americans have been subjected to years of something called "foreign language study" without developing any semblance of bilingualism. The critical factor may be not the exclusion of English from the instructional process, but rather its discriminate exploitation in that process. In general, this means using English for *passive understanding* of the precise meaning carried by foreign language utterances, while spending the majority of classroom and laboratory time in *actively practicing* those utterances. Studies of verbal learning have shown that visuals and certain direct-method techniques (especially the Gouin series) can produce excellent results as far as direct association of meaning with actions and concrete objects is concerned. As for the misuse of English, millions of Americans can attest to the results achieved by language instruction in which the chief activity is talking *about* the foreign language in English. Predictably, this system produces students who are able to talk about the foreign language in English.

LEARNING VOCABULARY IN CONTEXT

In the past, many people have considered the learning of vocabulary to be a relatively simple matter of identifying the high-frequency words and then committing them to memory. Studies have shown that approximately 95 percent of all conversation in European languages is carried on with only a few thousand separate word forms. There are, for example, several hundred thousand lexical items in English; yet "language surveys indicate that—95 percent of the time—we chose words from a library of only 5,000 to 10,000 words. The vast number of other words are rarely used."[18] On the basis of such word counts some people concluded that a foreign language could be learned simply by teaching the foreign language equivalents of the high-frequency words. There is a certain degree of logic in this. After all, the student must eventually acquire a content vocabulary. For, while the learning of phonology and grammar may have top priority at the outset, any language program that attempted to deal only with sounds and forms would soon lose its audience. And surely, once students have good control of the phonology. morphology, and syntax of the target language, it becomes essential for them to master the lexicon that is most often used by native speakers of that language. Why not, then, identify the high-frequency lexical items and commit them to memory in association with an English equivalent?

Linguists and methodologists give several reasons why words should not be learned in this manner. In the first place (as was noted earlier in the chapter on linguistics), each language has its characteristic rhythm, stress, and intonation patterns. Clearly, these aspects of language are lost or distorted if the student memorizes individual sounds or words rather than complete meaningful utterances. Then too, psychological studies have indicated that vocabulary items are learned and retained better in sense-making contexts than in isolation. But beyond the linguistic and psychological reasons is the question of semantics. This is perhaps the major flaw in the practice of learning vocabulary equivalents; for while there may be only 10,000 commonly used word items, each item may have dozens of meanings depending upon the context in which the item is used. Thus, the 10,000 high-frequency words actually represent untold tens of thousands of separate units of *meaning*.[19] And, since these meanings have few, if any, perfect matching pairs from one language to another, they cannot convey meaning in any useful way until they are placed in a specific context. For example, one can imagine the difficulties encountered by a lexicographer in attempting to provide matching pairs in French, German, or Spanish equivalents for so apparently simple an English word as "hit." A few samples of the semantic range of that word will perhaps illustrate the point. To a person learning English as a foreign language, such varieties in meaning can be highly perplexing, particularly if there are no equivalent terms in the native culture. Thus, the baseball term "hit" mentioned above presents few problems to the Japanese or Mexican student. Because

[18] Peter B. Denes and Elliot N. Pinson, *The Speech Chain*, Waverly Press, 1963, p. 12.
[19] An extreme example of how misleading a word count can be is the word "honey" in a famous Spanish word list. After the word had been included in a number of basic Spanish readers it was discovered that "honey" itself appeared seldom in literature. It was the expression *luna de miel* (honeymoon) which was in reality the high-frequency item.

Lexical item (verb or noun; singular or plural	Sample contexts in which the item may be used	Varieties of meaning
hit, hits	Don't hit him	blow with the hand or an object
	The stock market hit a new low.	reach or attain
	The bombers hit the assigned target.	successful attack
	This LP record contains the top hits.	popular songs
	The play was a hit.	great success, something or someone well received by public
	You hit it off well with him.	establish rapport
	I think you've hit upon something.	discover
	Hits, runs, and errors.	baseball term
	Hit the road, you bum.	command someone to leave
	Hit me again! (blackjack, card game)	request another card

baseball is a popular sport in their homelands, each will have an equivalent term in Japanese or Spanish. However, the German-speaking student, being unfamiliar with baseball, will not grasp the fine distinctions that differentiate the word "hit" from other baseball terms—such as, grounder, foul ball, fly-out, line drive, dribbler, bunt, and home run. On the other hand, the term "song hit" will be grasped quickly by the German teenager. This is because the German noun *Schlager* carries a comparable meaning and the verb *schlagen* has other points of correspondence with the English verb "hit." However, merely because German students of English might learn to pronounce and use the word in two of its contexts is no assurance that they will even recognize its meaning in any of the other eight contexts. In fact, there is even a question as to whether nonnatives should ever attempt to use the specialized or slang meanings of the more common words unless they are entirely familiar with the limits of acceptable usage within the target culture. For example, the term "Hit me again," is a fully appropriate way to request another card when playing blackjack in a barracks card game; it would be absurd in a ladies' bridge club. Yet the nonnative speaker may not be aware that the semantic range of "hit" covers only one card game.

Semantic difficulties arise even with the most common words. Every American child in grade school knows that it is possible

to start a car, or *to begin a lesson.*

Yet the foreign student of English who has failed to learn the semantic limits of words may think it proper

to begin a car, or *to commence a motor.*

159

Students who makes errors of this sort may pronounce well and may use acceptable grammatical forms; yet this is not enough. They must also be able to select words that convey meaning accurately within a given context. One of the reasons behind the use of dialogs in the American Method is to present vocabulary in a natural situation so that the meaning is unequivocal both from the standpoint of word usage within the dialog sentences and social appropriateness within the cultural context that the dialog attempts to dramatize. To give the student complete confidence in what he is learning, some teachers use native speakers on tape, record, or sound film for the initial dialog presentation. As the student memorizes the dialog utterances, the teacher may explain the general meaning each word would have if translated literally. (Naturally, the student would be given only those equivalents relevant to the meaning of the utterance being learned.) On the other hand, teachers who incline toward the direct method would not approve of this use of English. In any case, modern methodology holds that it is more efficient to memorize a dozen connected, meaningful sentences each of which contains a word to be learned than to learn the same words in isolation with their matching English equivalents. It is felt that English equivalents given in the form of dictionary items tend to mislead the student into believing that a given item in the foreign language has the same range of meaning as the supposedly equivalent English word. On the other hand, the student who learns a new word in a specific context is less likely to push the new word beyond its semantic limits. By way of illustration we might take the French, German, and Spanish words *heure*, *Uhr*, and *hora* which can all be matched with the English equivalent "time," in the expression, "What time is it?" However, none of these words would be appropriate equivalents if one wanted to express many other meanings carried by the English word "time." Note below that completely different words are needed in French, German, and Spanish to cover the full semantic range of the English word "time."

English	French	German	Spanish
What time is it?	Quelle heure est-il?	Wieviel Uhr ist es?	¿Qué hora es?
This time, I'll go.	Cette fois-ci, j'irai.	Dieses Mal gehe ich.	Yo voy esta vez.
I don't have time.	Je n'ai pas le temps.	Ich habe keine Zeit.	No tengo tiempo.
I had a good time.	Je me suis bien amusé.	Ich habe mich gut amüsiert.	He pasado un rato agradable.

MOTIVATION AND THE FOREIGN LANGUAGE CLASSROOM

The question of how to motivate students to study foreign languages in American schools has been with us for a long time. In this century, educators have experimented with many different kinds of incentives (see Chapter 2). Despite all this, enrollments continue to drop in many schools and

160

colleges across the nation. Once again we hear charges from many quarters that foreign languages are basically irrelevant. An anthropologist named Paul Turner has even suggested that the situation is almost hopeless; and he cited research indicating that to learn a language properly one must identify positively with the people who speak it. For this reason, in his opinion, the language teaching profession is unlikely to prosper because: "Americans . . . are psychologically inhibited from identifying with other people because of our sensitiveness to our own immigrant past. To cover up our feelings of insecurity, we hold negative stereotyped images of foreigners that prevent us from identifying with them."[20] In Turner's view this means that there is little hope of improving student motivation by making changes within the profession itself. Instead he believes that efforts must be directed outside the profession toward changing attitudes of the general public in order to produce a better acceptance of second language learning. There are many who do not share Turner's pessimism regarding the inability of the profession to make a degree of progress by working directly with students in the classroom. They believe that young people of today and tomorrow will be increasingly receptive to foreign languages if only the professionals in the field can make certain basic modifications in the nature of foreign language instruction. Basically these modifications have much to do with the ways in which teachers attempt to motivate students.

Intrinsic Versus Extrinsic Motivation

For many centuries leading educators and psychologists have supported the idea that intrinsic student interest in the subject matter in question is essential to serious learning and to significant achievement. If we apply this concept to Turner's views mentioned above about the inability of Americans to become language learners, we have a basis for questioning his interpretation of the data. Turner based his theory of American second-language inferiority partly on a study by Lambert that indicated that Anglo students of French who wished to identify positively with the Canadian French culture and tradition proved to be superior learners of French when compared to those who looked on the French language as being merely instrumental to external aims such as earning money or otherwise succeeding in bilingual Canadian society.[21]

It could very well be that the favorable ethnic bias was *not* the key factor that influenced the results. A positive attitude toward the target culture is one secondary factor which *can* influence a student to become intrinsically motivated, but it is the intrinsic desire to learn the language that is basic. We know, in fact, that other factors can cause students to become intrinsically committed to the study of a second language. It may be a

[20] Paul R. Turner, "Why Johnny Doesn't Want to Learn a Foreign Language," *Modern Language Journal* 58 (April 1974), pp 191–196.
[21] Wallace E. Lambert, *A Study of the Roles of Attitudes and Motivation in Second Language Learning*, USOE Grant No. SAE–8817, Final Report, 1961.

mistake, therefore, to assume that one factor (favorable ethnic bias) is the sole determiner of optimum student performance.

The pedagogical question is, "How does the teacher in the typical classroom situation get students intrinsically motivated?" One can find hundreds of quotations to the effect that it should be done. Jerome Bruner for example, has stated that, "Ideally, interest in the material to be learned is the best stimulus to learning rather than such external goals as grades for later competitive advantage."[22] It may be that this art, this ability on the part of the teacher to get students "interested in the material," is the factor that has confounded a half century of empirical research efforts in the area of instructional methodology, especially those of the control-experimental group design. It has been documented that most of the large-scale studies have come out NSD—"No Significant Difference."[23] And for the few studies that favor the experimental strategy, there is usually a matching study somewhere that favors the older way of doing things. The end result is that the studies have told us virtually nothing. The same is true of research in foreign language education. The *Pennsylvania Study*, for example, shows that measures of student achievement do *not* correlate with measures of teacher proficiency in listening, speaking, reading, or writing in the language of instruction. Nor do they appear to relate to her/his knowledge of methodology, linguistics, or culture, as measured by standardized instruments. In fact, one of the researchers noted almost plaintively, that in some cases the highest student achievement was found in classes where teachers came out "substandard" on tests of language proficiency and knowledge of culture, methods, and linguistics.[24] The answer to such seemingly puzzling results may well be quite simple. It may lie in the fact that the key to good teaching involves inducing students themselves to want to learn. Hence pedagogical expertise and language proficiency, beyond a certain minimal level, may be basically irrelevant. Proficiency can even be a detriment as in the case of native-speaking teachers who show contempt for their American students and who, as a result, have unmotivated, low-achieving students. In large-scale studies, the ineffective native speaker can apparently neutralize statistically those highly effective native-speaking teachers who are sensitive to cultural differences and who learn to adapt successfully to the American school.

To define intrinsic motivation pedagogically on a very practical level one might say that it involves those techniques that induce the learner to want to do what he has to do in order to accomplish the task at hand. A classic example of this is found in Mark Twain's *Tom Sawyer* at the point in the story where the young hero convinces some neighborhood boys that his assigned task of painting the fence is, indeed, a pleasurable activity.

[22] Jerome S. Bruner, *The Process of Education*, New York, Random House, 1960, p. 14.
[23] J. M. Stephens, *The Process of Schooling*, New York, Holt, Rinehart & Winston, 1967.
[24] Phillip D. Smith and Helmut A. Baranyi, *A Comparison Study of the Effectiveness of the Traditional and Audiolingual Approaches to Foreign Language Instruction Utilizing Laboratory Equipment*, Washington, D.C., Office of Education, Bureau of Research (January 1968).

The result is that the boys end up doing Tom's work for him, and enjoying it. The act of painting in this instance meets the test of intrinsic motivation, which is "what a person does when external pressures to engage in the behavior are absent." However, the authors of that definition have noted

that not every worthwhile activity is intrinsically interesting. In their opinion many important and potentially interesting activities...may seem like drudgery until one has acquired a few basic skills. Thus extrinsic motivation is often needed to get people deeply enough involved in an area of learning for it to be profitably pursued.[25]

Therein lies a problem, particularly for teachers of foreign language. Extrinsic motivational devices such as report card grades, meeting of requirements, words of praise, pats on the head, and gold stars can function effectively as transitional or introductory devices. That is, extrinsic motives can get the students into an area of learning, which they might otherwise have missed, or they can serve to get students to a point of mastery where intrinsic satisfaction in the activity itself can begin to function. The problem is that we can extend extrinsic inducements to the point where they become educationally destructive. In this regard Greene and Lepper have noted that a person's intrinsic interest in an activity is decreased "by inducing him to engage in that activity as an explicit means to some extrinsic goal."[26] The implications of this are that, while we may well use as initial inducements such things as college preparatory needs, entrance and degree requirements, the grading system, and the promise of possible career applications, we had better use them sparingly and in a general way. For the misuse of extrinsic inducements is associated with high dropout rates, poor memory retention, and mediocre achievement. This suggests that teachers must, therefore, learn to use extrinsic motives only for the purpose of getting students exposed to language learning in the first place and to get them to engage in the essential but tedious kinds of language practice that are prerequisite to intrinsic satisfaction. It further suggests that for sustained learning to take place a satisfying emotional payoff must be built in as a regular part of the instructional sequence. However, the enjoyment must come as an integral part of the craftmanship that is inherent in the process of acquiring a second language. Enjoyment can also be used in such a way that it functions as an extrinsic inducement. However, when so used it presents the same dangers as do other extrinsic motives. Students can become so addicted to fun as an external reward that they will stop functioning effectively unless it is supplied. Hence we should be suspicious of fun-and-games activities that bear no functional relationship to the on-going course of study. When taken to extremes such techniques can lose the respect and support of students as effectively as the soul-deadening drudgery of the worst traditional classroom or the mindless, robotlike parroting of the misguided

[25] David Greene and Mark R. Lepper, "Intrinsic Motivation: How to Turn Play into Work," *Psychology Today* 8 (September 1974), p. 50.
[26] Ibid., p. 50.

audiolingual program. Thus the paradox of motivation is that work and play, effort and satisfaction, achievement and joy are interrelated and mutually dependent in such complex ways as to have defied adequate description over the years.

Ways of Motivating American Students

Not all motivational practices will be equally useful to everyone. There are teachers whose personality or school environments will so differ from that of the originator of a given technique as to render its application to other classrooms highly questionable. So, instead of presenting the reader with a "laundry list" of supposedly proven motivational techniques, it would perhaps be more productive to look at certain broad principles for motivating language students which have been developed over the centuries, and then relate selected practical examples to the various concepts. Because these principles reflect certain opinions and biases, I will refer to them as "assumptions."

Assumption Number One: Optimum Foreign Language Learning Takes Place in an Emotionally Supportive, Non-threatening Learning Environment.

There is evidence that stutterers are people who were emotionally threatened during the period of first-language acquisition. Thus it is reasonable to expect second-language performance that is characterized either by embarrassed stammering or mechanical recitation from students whose language instruction takes place in an emotionally repressive atmosphere. Adolescents and young adults are particularly vulnerable to sarcasm, public criticism, and ridicule. Many of them are desperately in need of supportive social interaction. There are many who believe that neither the standard teacher-dominated, whole-class approach nor the isolated learning required in certain kinds of individualized programs will adequately serve the motivational needs of young people. Although these learning modes may have their place, a third mode involving small groupings within the class can also be used to good advantage. By using such groupings, the teacher can make advantageous use of both cooperation and competition. One of the more promising trends in foreign language instruction today involves the combination of both of these social realities within the classroom. Competition can be destructive and demotivating when each individual is forced to measure his or her achievement against that of the entire class. Sometimes high achievers are even threatened by this process—for example, when a student is labeled as the "brain" who ruined the curve by scoring so high on the last test. At the other extreme the slower learner is devastated by being always at the bottom. However, by splitting the class into halves (or into smaller subgroups) for some activities, competition can be dealt with as a team effort. In fact, it might even be wise to establish a general rule that when pupils are put into public competition with one another it should be done by groups or teams rather than individually.

164

Assumption Number Two: Retention Is More Likely to Be Permanent When the Material to Be Learned Is in the Context of Active, Real-Life Experiences or Adequate Simulations Thereof

Considering the practical realities of the classroom, simulations will perhaps be of most use to most teachers. In the late 1900s the so-called "series system" developed by Francois Gouin became popular in foreign language instruction, especially in Germany. The class procedure followed these steps:

1 Using the students' native language the teacher explained the general content of the material to be learned.
2 The teacher enacted the events, describing at the same time in the target language what he was doing.
3 The single acts were divided into smaller ones and again enacted by teacher and pupils.
4 This was all done orally first, then in writing.

As a methodologist in the 1940s expressed it "The new element which he (Gouin) brought into language teaching was that the student is forced to be intensely active with his whole being while dramatizing the single sentences of a given selection, an advantage hard to overestimate."[27]

Historically, applications of the series system were reported to be extremely effective in teaching students to communicate orally. Modern applications of this approach to the development of listening comprehension skill have been made in recent years by James Asher.[28] Similar work was also done by Kalivoda, Morain, and Elkins at the University of Georgia.[29] The modern versions of the series system—which have become more sophisticated with the addition of audio-visual devices—are referred to as the *Audiomotor Approach* and *Total Physical Response*. Field trips to points of ethnic significance, dramatizations by students both live and on videotape or film, and travel or study abroad are other examples of activities that have had a favorable motivational impact on the language learner. Weekend excursions to a staged and simulated second-language environment, Saturday language folk fairs, and two-to-four-week language summer camps have also been highly successful in motivating students. However, not everyone can have access to such experiences. Therefore, it is part of the art of teaching to help students to project themselves into the role of a speaker of a second language by drawing on their potential for creative drama. According to Morain,

[27] Peter Hagboldt, *The Teaching of German*, New York, Heath, 1940, p. 13.
[28] James J. Asher, Jo Anne Kusudo, and Rita de La Torre, "Learning a Second Language Through Commands: The Second Field Test," *Modern Language Journal* 58 (January–February), 1974, pp. 1–2, 24–32.
[29] Theodore B. Kalivoda, Gennelle Morain, and Robert J. Elkins, "The Audio-Motor Unit: A Listening Comprehension Strategy That Works," *Foreign Language Annals* 4 (May 1971) pp. 392–400.

Experiments with the audiomotor unit have shown that physical action in accompaniment to verbal expression enhances the acquisition of language. The student actor must bring words, gesture, posture, movement, and facial expression into harmony. He is charged with the necessity of using all aspects of language congruently. To do otherwise is to fail to communicate the emotional content which is inextricably bound to language. [30]

Assumption Number Three: Optimum Learning Takes Place When the Learner Has a Degree of Meaningful Involvement in Determining Either What Is to be Learned or How It Is to Be Learned or Both

A dramatic example of favorable effects resulting from student involvement in determining, to some degree, the content of the curriculum is to be found in the Waukesha, Wisconsin high schools. Flying in the face of state and national trends, their advanced-course enrollments in French and Spanish increased sharply for several years after third-year minicourses were first introduced in 1972. The students at the second-year level were allowed to indicate their preference for a series of potential courses any of which were teachable and intellectually sound in the opinion of the teachers. The courses that received the highest student ratings were, indeed, the ones selected. This process of involving the students apparently had a positive feedback effect on the first two years of instruction. After implementation of the advanced-level minicourses, first- and second-year enrollments also began to rise significantly. The minicourses were taught in a variety of modes including whole-class instruction, small-group work, and individualized instruction. [31]

Many people feel that the minicourse approach is not practical during the first two years of instruction except when used occasionally to break the routine of elementary and intermediate instruction. This opinion is based on the belief that the first two years must be devoted to the acquisition of basics; and that, therefore, the student will have insufficient command of the language to work directly with interdisciplinary material. In this regard, there are teachers who have devised ways of capitalizing on the students' desire for originality during the beginning levels while at the same time overcoming most of the dangers of premature use of partially learned material. Basically this is usually an application of the idea that students should devise their own memory mediators.

A Spanish teacher in a flourishing high school program makes use of this principle by having students bring in or make their own pictures to represent utterances from current or past units of work. For example, the students at one time may be required to use imperatives, subjunctives,

[30] Gennelle Morain, "Humanism in the Classroom: A Dramatic Proposal," in Frank Grittner (ed.), *Careers, Communication and Culture*, Skokie, Ill., National Textbook Company, 1974, p. 6.

[31] Further information on various ways to involve students in the curricular process are available from the National Association of Secondary School Principals, Dulles International Airport, P.O. Box 17430, Washington, D.C., single copy 50 cents. Ask for the Curriculum Report entitled Robert LaFayette, *A Foreign Language Option: The Mini-Course* (October 1973).

166

present participles, or other appropriate forms. Students are encouraged to find or make humorous, ironic, sentimental, or other emotional connections between language and the visualization that it represents. The items are brought into class and discussed in Spanish. Examples of these student-made posters are also placed on display around the classroom and are later retired to a scrapbook so that the teacher can use the material for future reference with other classes. It is a simple, inexpensive technique for getting the grammar out of the book into a context that has meaning to the students. Part of the meaning comes from the fact that the students themselves are involved in supplying the curricular materials involving applied grammar. Another technique used by the same teacher involves the use of old greeting cards, valentines, and Christmas cards. The English captions or verses on the cards are covered over with thick white paper. The students then look at the pictorial material on the cards and supply original captions and verses in Spanish. This involves a somewhat more creative level of speech production, but within a very limited space. The verses are first written on a separate sheet of paper, are corrected by the teacher, and are then transferred to the card.

An even more elaborate example of this approach involves the use of film or videotaped productions in which the students prepare the scripts, do the scenery and staging, and actually produce a foreign language skit. At a simpler level there is the example of a German class that went on a field trip to the nearby *Oktoberfest.* Students took inexpensive cameras with them and they shot two-by-two slides of the various events. A German language narration was subsequently made of a selected series of slides as part of the class project. Projects of this type have been referred to as "culminating activities." That is, they are done only occasionally to give the students an opportunity to make an integrated application of the language skills they have acquired. However, the motivational value of a well-executed project or field trip can be enormous.

Assumption Number Four: Instruction Which Emphasizes Language Learning as a Creative, Holistic Process Will Achieve Better Long-Term Results Than Will Instruction Built upon Repetitive Drill Work and Atomistic Learning Increments

It has been suggested that the ability to perform well on isolated aspects of the foreign language is not the same as being able to use the language in any genuine way. Savignon has stated that teachers have been excessively concerned with the learning and testing of student performance on dialogs, choral drills, and patterned responses. The result has been that no time was left over "for that which only the human teacher can provide, communication." And she went on to suggest that "the human teacher knows, if you ask him, that communication is not the rapid-fire exchange of linguistically accurate complete sentences. It is the sometimes slow, sometime painful, sometimes non-verbal exchange of thoughts between human beings."[32]

[32] Sandra J. Savignon, *Communicative Competence: An Experiment in Foreign-Language Teaching,* Philadelphia, Center for Curriculum Development, 1972, p. 67.

167

A number of researchers in the area of communicative competence believe that the creative expression of one genuine whole idea or emotion, in resonably correct language, is to be valued over scores of mindlessly perfect drill responses. For the latter are seen only as a means to the former. It is thought that teachers have tended to value the instrument (the drill work) over the outcome (real communicative performance). All of this suggests that American teachers should aim at *quality* student performance on a much more limited number of linguistic elements. American curricula and textbooks contain so much material that teachers often become engaged in a frantic effort to finish the book by the end of the year. Several of the basic conditions for optimum motivation are destroyed in the process. As the year goes by teachers put on more and more pressure. Students become increasingly discouraged as it becomes apparent to them that the process leads nowhere except to increasingly difficult and seemingly unrelated masses of material to be drilled and memorized. Such programs become the fulfillment of Samuel Taylor Coleridge's lines:

Work without hope draws nectar in the sieve
And hope without an object cannot live.

There must be work, as every experienced foreign language learner knows. But the work must lead to satisfaction, which will, in turn, build hope in the recurrence of further satisfaction through the vehicle of language learning. All of this carries with it a certain view regarding the nature of language and language learning. In Diller's opinion, "Language . . . is not so much an arbitrary set of conventions to be used for communication as it is a means of thinking, of representing the world to oneself." This implies an active rather than a passive learning mode and the creation of a learning environment in which "the learner actively goes about trying to organize his perceptions of the world in terms of linguistic concepts."[33]

Assumption Number Five: Optimum Foreign Language Learning Is Most Likely to Occur in That Individual Whose Future Self-image Includes a Vision of Himself/ Herself Using the Language Successfully; the Teacher's Attitude Toward the Student's Achievement Potential Greatly Influences Subsequent Achievement
Goethe once said that, "If you treat an individual as he is, he will stay as he is, but if you treat him as if he were what he ought to be and could be, he will become what he ought to be and could be." In 1968 Rosenthal conducted a study which tended to support Goethe's statement.[34]

Rosenthal's method was to randomly assign fictitious test scores to a selected number of students from a population of young people of similar ability and socioeconomic background. The teachers of the selected

---

[33] Karl C. Diller, *Generative Grammar, Structural Linguistics, and Language Teaching,* Rowley, Mass., Newbury, 1971, p. 54.
[34] Robert Rosenthal and Lenore Jacobson, *Pygmalion in the Classroom: Teacher Expectation and Pupil's Intellectual Development,* New York, Holt, Rinehart & Winston, 1968.

children were then lead to believe that the test scores were valid predictors of academic potential. The result was higher achievement on the part of the youngsters who had been identified as "promising." Apparently, the teachers' belief in the abilities of the selected children was communicated to them in such a way as to improve their actual performance. In this regard, it is my general impression that teachers who are highly successful (that is, teachers who have high achievement and low attrition) are those who provide virtually all students with short-term, satisfying experiences of success in using the foreign language. They tend to radiate an attitude that says, in effect, "See, I knew you could do it."

Some applications of this principle, which this writer has seen in practice, are as follows: (1) In conversational situations, the teacher avoids public correction of student errors, allowing the conversation to flow freely, errors and all. However, he/she takes notes of the major patterns of mistakes and discusses them subsequently without identifying (and hence humiliating) any given student in front of the class. Subsequent practice is directed toward the main error categories. An effort is made to teach students how to monitor and correct their own errors and to help fellow students produce correct forms as part of the effort to communicate feelings and ideas to one another. (2) Where written work is concerned, the teacher avoids massive use of red ink and negative, judgmental remarks on the student's paper. Instead, comments are directed toward that which is correct. Remarks like, "Good, you used the preterite correctly in this paragraph," and "Fine progress on the use of the dative," should predominate. Again, errors are treated as a symptom of shortcomings in the instructional program rather than as a manifestation of student incompetence or laziness. With written work, the attitude can also be, "How can we help students to identify and correct these particular mistakes that many have been making?"

In addition to the five assumptions discussed above, I would add a sixth and seventh as follows:

Assumption Number Six: Optimum Language Learning Demands the Inclusion of Enjoyable Social Relationships in the Instructional Process.

Assumption Number Seven: Optimum Language Learning Is More Likely to Occur When the Evaluation System Is Positive and Rewarding Rather Than Negative and Punitive

Assumption six has been treated in a different context above. The same is true to a degree with assumption seven. However, with respect to testing, one must, perhaps, make certain concessions to competitive, judgmental approaches that are part of institutional policy, (for example, midterm and final exams). But this does not prevent the teacher from using the intermediate tests and quizzes as supportive learning tools rather than as a means of selecting out "the wheat from the chaff" or as threats "to do better next time, or else." Most tests can be given as diagnostic instruments to help the student. If optimum motivation is the goal, they should be so used. The following are a few selected examples of motivational techniques as applied by successful foreign language teachers. The examples are the inventions of teachers working in their own unique local situations and are, therefore, not always transplantable in toto to other contexts. However, the basic underlying ideas have wide applicability for the creative language teacher who is able to adapt them to the local instructional situation.

Motivation and applied grammar. Although certain New Key purists might frown at the practice, this writer observed one third-year Spanish class in which students in teams of five competed against their classmates in demonstrating their ability to conjugate irregular Spanish verbs in the preterite. The teacher used a stopwatch to declare the winner. Each error brought a penalty of one second. This is an example of the extrinsic use of games, the purpose of which is to get students to focus their attention upon particular points of grammar. However, the teacher also made good use of intrinsic motivation as evidenced by a subsequent observation of the same students interviewing an educator from South America. Speaking extemporaneously, the students asked him a wide variety of questions ranging from personal facts (occupation, place of residence, and so on) to opinions (what do you think of our foreign policy, of the Peace Corps, of American schools, and so on). From their responses and the questions they redirected to the speaker and to one another it was evident that the students were following what the native speaker was saying. It was also clear that the students had learned to be at ease in using the language freely in front of their peers. In fact, they were so secure that they could even criticize each other good naturedly in the presence of the visitor. Occasional remarks (in Spanish) such as, "You can't ask a question like that," did not appear to bother anyone. Such remarks came from fellow students, not from the teacher. The students made occasional mistakes in verb forms, number, and even gender, but they were fluent and clearly understandable. And the man from South America was obviously impressed and pleased by the exchange. There was certainly no evidence that the study of traditional grammar had in any way inhibited these students in their ability to communicate despite what critics of formal grammar instruction have said. This writer suspects that the inhibiting of student responses has more to do with the emotional tone that the teacher sets for the class than with the way in which he/she teaches grammar.

Motivation and student writing. Using various kinds of topics and stimuli, a German teacher had students in groups of 3 to 5 prepare short compositions to present to the rest of the fourth-year class for discussion and conversation. For example, one assignment involved the layout of a mansion in which a murder had taken place. The victim was the wealthy Herr Leich (Mr. Corpse). A list of suspicious characters was supplied along with a number of vocabulary items and useful expressions. Each group was to come up with their own correctly written version of "who done it," and to defend their decision. The murder took place in the study; the murder weapon was a knife. Was it the butler, the maid, the visiting ballet dancer, the count? Also involved in the exercise was a review of the passive voice, the use of conjunctions, and the use of relative pronouns. At

170

the end of the unit, students were asked to evaluate the procedures with an instrument entitled, "Clues About Classroom Life." In summary, we note that students were creatively involved in the group activity of preparing their own version of a murder mystery. There was friendly rivalry between the groups. And in the end the students had a further opportunity to feel that their views mattered. Not only had they been asked to create some of the instructional content for the fourth-year course, but they had also had the opportunity to evaluate the process of instruction from their own view-point.

Motivation and student conversation. One of the options selected by Waukesha (Wisconsin) Spanish students from among the list of more than 20 minicourses was the "Native Speaker Seminar." This involved listening to short presentations by native speakers and asking them questions. Some of the questions were of a general nature and were formulated in advance by the students. Other questions arose out of the presentation by and discussion with the native speaker. This brought the students somewhat closer to a free-response situation. Additional practice was provided through assignments that required students to interview one another and the various Spanish teachers in the building. Listening practice was also provided by means of taped material. Readings involving tran-scribed interviews of famous Spanish-speaking people were also used. (Dali, Cantinflas, and Franco were among the famous people represented here). Writing took the form of short, written summations of what the native speakers had said. The basic purpose of the seminar was to get the students to use the language functionally for receiving and communicating ideas. In this regard, the following directions for student participation were included in the instructional materials:

You will be expected to participate each day that guest speakers are invited to speak. You will do so by asking questions of the speaker or making comments on the subject of the day. *Do not be afraid to make mistakes.* (Your teachers do from time to time.) You are learning a *foreign* language. You need to practice. No one expects perfection. It's not just the natives that are good enough to speak the language. You are too.

The seemingly small successes that most students can achieve by means of this type of "Native Speaker Seminar" can have a dispropor-tionate effect (on the positive side) by helping the student build confidence in his ability to communicate with people from the target culture. It also helps to break down the stereotype of language learning as being dead subject matter contained in a book. Having a real live native speaker with whom to exchange ideas can be of immense value in this regard.

Motivation and vocabulary. Games to help motivate students to acquire foreign language vocabulary are far from new. Bingo, Scrabble, and a foreign language version of the old country-school spelldown have been used by teachers for many years. In one version of the latter, students are asked to sketch or cut out of magazines pictures relating to the vocabulary of past chapters. The pictures are placed in a large cardboard box. When

171

it is time for vocabulary review the class is formed into two teams. Members from each team take turns drawing pictures out of the box and asking appropriate questions (in the foreign language, of course). The question can be predesigned to review a particular aspect of the foreign language such as interrogatives, imperatives, or the use of complex syntactic patterns. For example:

What is this? (elementary level).
Tell me what I have here, please. (familiar or polite form)
Would you be so kind as to tell me what I have in my hand? (done with a feeling of exaggerated politeness)
Can you tell me what I have here?

The repetition of the selected expression by each student gives a limited degree of speaking and listening practice to everyone. However, the main purpose of the game is vocabulary review. Items that are missed are put back in the box after being correctly identified by the teacher. The game ends when all items have been correctly identified. The team with the highest score (that is, with the most right answers) wins. Also, teachers have adapted some of the popular TV quiz games by designing large boards with removable windows into which various parts of speech can be inserted for the purposes of the game.

WORDS OF CAUTION CONCERNING MOTIVATIONAL TECHNIQUES

There are a number of problems with the practice of listing specific instructional techniques that others have used. The first problem is that it is impossible to do justice to any given technique when it is described in writing. A second problem has to do with teacher self-image—that is, many teachers are unable to project themselves into the kinds of roles that some of the techniques would require. A third problem is that not all schools and communities are set up for such activities as field trips, audiovisual productions, or even small-group sessions within the classroom. (This author has found schools, for example, in which the student chairs are bolted to the floor, thus limiting flexibility in social groupings.) A fourth problem is the tendency within the profession to equate good education with a certain degree of plodding tedium and to regard enjoyment in learning as "soft pedagogy" and the lowering of instructional standards. In view of all this it would perhaps be appropriate to note that the techniques described above are from programs where student achievement in the traditional sense is not sacrificed. In each case, the motivational technique was designed not primarily to amuse students but to help them master some element of language better than they otherwise would have. In my own opinion, we still need the textbook, at least for the first two years, although we should be very selective about the items from the text which we choose. However, for any of the principles or suggested techniques

172

listed above to function, teachers will have to have a particular mind-set. What is needed is not a frantic compulsion to force a given number of verbs, concepts, or behavioral outputs on unwilling adolescent minds and to justify that behavior with the myth that students need the language for some external purpose such as college preparation, career advantage, tourism, international understanding or national defense. Instead, what is needed is the firm belief by the teacher that language learning is a worthwhile activity for anyone to engage in; that it develops potential within the human being that would otherwise remain dormant. More importantly, however, the teacher must demonstrate the truth of that belief by making the activity emotionally real to the students at their level of feeling and understanding. But it must go further than that. Motivation implies that the instructor should reach the student where he/she is. However, the term also implies "motivation toward some goal"; and that goal must involve both the integrity of the discipline and the further development of the individual. It is doing the student no favor to inspire him toward incompetence, which could well be the outcome if we were to submerge significant language content beneath a series of unfocused "fun" activities. On the other hand, our purpose must not be the "covering" of large doses of linguistic and cultural material in which students can perceive no relevance to contemporary realities or to future probabilities. Instead, this writer believes that we need to follow Genelle Morain's advice regarding the need to convert the language classroom into a place where the foreign language is used in a dramatic, emotionally laden way. Beginning with a quotation from Robert Benedetti, she expressed it as follows:

"Theatre is the most human of all the arts and we . . . can expand our humanity through our art in ways denied us by everyday life." We want our students to use language for real communication. We want them to express ideas and feelings. Drama permits emotional and linguistic involvement in the past, the present, and the future. It gives the classroom elastic horizons. Use it. You can expect dramatic results.[35]

SUMMARY

In the final analysis the degree to which the students themselves actually use the foreign language in the school environment (that is, classroom, laboratory, seminar rooms, and so forth) is the best measure of the psychological soundness of the language program. In a sense, it actually determines whether or not a given school has a foreign language program in the modern sense of the word. In some schools and colleges, teachers admit to spending as high as 75 percent of class time discussing grammar and other matters in English, while others report that students spend 60 percent of available

[35] Morain, op. cit., p. 11.

time translating into English and discussing literature in English.[36] In the interests of honest representation it would seem that such offerings should be labeled as "survey courses in grammar" or "seminars relating to foreign literature," rather than as courses in French, German, or Spanish. The problem of justifying the "foreign language" course designation increases in direct proportion to the use of English in the classroom. In fact, if English is the predominant vehicle of classroom communication, the very existence of foreign language as a separate subject area can be seriously questioned. Grammatical discussions could, for example, be rather easily formalized into a course or unit called "comparative linguistics," and literary assignments done in English might quite profitably be dealt with in a course called "world literature." It would seem that both types of activity could be transferred to the English department with no great loss to the humanistic educational values, either linguistic or literary. In fact, a great deal more ground could be covered in literature if the reading were done entirely in good English translation rather than the ludicrous, bumbling translations produced by novice students. Similarly, the anthropological and cultural aspects of language would fit logically into a modern social studies program. Direct communication in the language of the target culture is the unique anthropological experience which foreign language study has to offer; if this educational experience is lacking, then it is difficult to justify social studies content in the foreign language curriculum.

Thus, however important grammatical generalizations may prove to be in the instructional process, and however useful English may be for certain instructional purposes, their ultimate validity must relate to those objectives that are basic and unique to foreign language study (see Chapter 5 for detailed objectives). Accordingly, the teacher who subscribes to modern objectives must accept or reject given classroom practices on the basis of whether or not they promote direct, spontaneous communication in the target language. Apparently this acceptance is quite widespread. A 1963 survey of 23,537 high schools and 1,987 colleges and universities in 50 states indicates that, on the average, foreign language classes "spend about half of their time in the foreign language without using English" and that "grammar discussions in English" average well under twenty percent of class time.[37] Thus, if this sampling of tens of thousands of high school and college language teachers (French, German, Spanish, Russian, and Italian) is valid, we can conclude that a large segment of the active language teaching profession presently assigns to grammar and English an important but subordinate role in the language classroom. Although the field of psycholinguistics is far from an exact science, there does exist a body of knowledge relating to verbal learning and to the acquisition of skills from which certain tentative conclusions can be drawn. Clearly, more

---

[36] Scarvia B. Anderson, Lynn K. Gaines, and Rosemary Russell, *A Survey of Modern Foreign Language Instruction in High Schools and Colleges*, Princeton, N.J., Educational Testing Service, 1963, pp. 1–4.
[37] Ibid., pp. 4–15.

research needs to be done, and the existing hypotheses need to be further tested. However, until more exact information is available, the language teaching profession can act on the basis of evidence which now exists. The six principles listed below are drawn from psychological studies conducted over the past few decades:

1   The more meaningful (and personal) the material, the more likely it to be learned and retained. Fluency and automaticity are important in language learning, but these can be achieved parrot-fashion without the learner being fully cognizant of what he has learned. Genuine learning must include the ability to apply the target language to the world of reality in a personal way.

2   Drill work involving conscious choices between critical and contrasting elements is more effective than the same amount of drill work done in a repetitive manner and involving no contrasts. (However, introducing an excessive number of contrasts in a given drill can bewilder and discourage the learner).

3   Learning of basic language skills will be more efficient if the student is aware of the generalizations underlying the critical features on which he is being drilled. These critical features may either be learned inductively or may be pointed out by the teacher or text; it cannot be assumed that the student will perceive the important critical features by himself.

4   The more kinds of associations that are made, the better the learning will be. Thus, at the appropriate time, all possible sense modalities should be brought to bear on each item to be learned. Different ways of associating meaning in verbal learning include auditory (hearing), pictorial (visual conceptualization), motor performances (Gouin series), tactile (handling objects), and graphic (written symbolization).

5   The use of visuals in association with spoken and written symbols can greatly facilitate verbal learning. Approximately 80 percent of all human learning is done visually. Hence, sole reliance upon auditory stimuli at any stage of learning must be considered questionable for sighted learners.

6   In the learning of skills it is more efficient to distribute the drill into regular daily modules than to mass drill work into time segments several says apart from one another. Thus, in the beginning course (where drill work predominates) it is preferable to schedule classes in 30-minute daily modules for 5 consecutive days than to have 60-minute modules 3 times a week.

BIBLIOGRAPHY

Bigge, Morris L., *Learning Theories for Teachers,* New York, Harper & Row, 1964.
A clearly written explanation of various schools of psychology, including behaviorism and Gestalt-Field Psychology and their implications for the classroom teacher. See especially Chapters 3, 4, 7 and 8.

Grittner, Frank M., "Maintaining Foreign Language Skills for the Advanced-Course Dropout," *Foreign Language Annals* (December 1968), pp. 205–211.

This is also available as *Focus Report No. 1* from ACTFL, 62 Fifth Avenue, New York, N.Y. 10011. Article describes various interest-centered approaches to teaching foreign languages at the intermediate and advanced levels. The bibliography includes a list of sources for pen pals, tape pals, and slide exchanges along with summer-camp opportunities.

Grittner, Frank M. (ed.), *Student Motivation and the Foreign Language Teacher,* Skokie, Ill., National Textbook Company, 1973.

Ten foreign language educators examine the question of motivation from the theoretical and practical standpoint as it applies to foreign language teaching in the classroom.

Jarvis, Gilbert A. (ed.), *The Challenge of Communication,* ACTFL Review of Foreign Language Education, vol. 5, Skokie, Ill., National Textbook Company, 1975.

Maslow, A. H., *The Farther Reaches of Human Nature,* New York, Viking, 1971. A psychological model based on the development of human potential. Human self-actualization is seen as the ultimate goal of education.

Maslow, A. H., *Motivation and Personality,* New York, Harper & Row, 1970.

Nelson, Robert J., and Leon A. Jakobovits, (eds.), "Motivation and Foreign Language Learning ; Working Committee II," pp. 34–104 in Joseph A. Tursi (ed.), *Foreign Languages and the "New" Student,* Reports of the Working Committees of the Northeast Conference on the Teaching of Foreign Languages, New York, Modern Language Association Materials Center, 1970.

Rivers, Wilga M., *The Psychologist and the Foreign Language Teacher,* Chicago, University of Chicago Press, 1964.

Savignon, Sandra J., *Communicative Competence: An Experiment in Foreign-Language Teaching,* Philadelphia, Center for Curriculum Development, 1972.

7

■ *The whole process of becoming competent in any field must be divided into a very large number of very small steps, and reinforcement must be contingent upon the accomplishment of each step.* B. F. SKINNER ■ *The individual is right when he negates the mass production of souls and hearts and conceives of life as a creative design and not as a prefabricated pattern.* IGNAZIO SILONE

■Individualized instruction

It is a common belief in the foreign language teaching profession that student success in foreign language learning depends on the sequential, cumulative acquisition of complex skills and neuromuscular habits. These range from simple motor skills involving rapid manipulation of tongue, lips, and other speech organs to the highly cognitive aspects of language, including choice of correct word order, verb tense, vocabulary, and inflectional forms. It is also conceded that many students who elect to study foreign languages fail to acquire sufficient control of cultural information, phonology, morphology, syntax, and vocabulary to enable them to achieve success (according to local standards). In intensive language courses, such as those designed for military personnel, sophisticated prognostic devices have been used to select that minority of students having a good chance for success when instruction is confined within severe time limits. However, such a procedure is inimical to the success of the public school foreign language program, which is set up for the purpose of providing either general or college preparatory education. Generally, all students who wish to study a foreign language are allowed to do so at some stage in their progress through the secondary school. Consequently, the typical foreign language class in the public school program will contain students with wide differences in motivational drives and in the ability to acquire the requisite skills and areas of knowledge in the sequentially structured course of study. Yet the class work proceeds inexorably in a manner and at a pace to which *all* students are expected to conform; and all students are often expected to aspire to the same kind and level of achievement within the same time limits regardless of differences in motivation, aptitude, and socioeconomic background.

As work proceeds through the first year of study, many foreign language students seem unable to acquire and retain the necessary skill and knowledge for subsequent learning. Grades assigned at each marking period may well reflect students' inability to keep pace. Typically, the fast learners receive A's and B's, the slower learners receive C's and D's, and the slowest are failed or are given a "D minus." Often, the slower students are advised to drop the foreign language during the first year or not to continue such study during the next school year. It is assumed that this situation explains, at least in part, why over half the students enrolled in foreign language classes in American schools drop out between the first and second year.[1]

In view of all this, many educators feel that instruction should be individualized so that students are not forced to drop out of academic subjects such as foreign language. They feel that all, or nearly all, students can and should have significant educational experiences within all subject fields. The practice of eliminating low-achievers from the more challenging subject areas is considered immoral, if not illegal, by such educators. Periodically in American education, factors such as these have brought about demands for the schools to individualize instruction.

INDIVIDUALIZED INSTRUCTION: A HISTORICAL PERSPECTIVE

Two of the most prominent educational movements of the 1970s were labeled "individualization" and the "right to read." It is rather startling, therefore, to open the covers of the leading educational yearbook of 1925 and find that it consists of two sections: one on reading and the other on individualized instruction. In fact, 1925 represented the high-water mark of an era over a half century ago during which various plans of individualized instruction had been highly publicized and promoted.[2]

The ironic thing about all this is that just prior to the huge push for individualized instruction in the mid-1920s, Hall-Quest, a professor of education in Virginia, had commented that, "For centuries individual instruction was the common method of class management. Each pupil was called to the teacher's desk for the purpose of reciting. . . . The note-worthy efforts of Lancaster and Bell to improve this wasteful method had wholesome results." Hall-Quest went on to suggest the superiority of group instruction over what he called "individual instruction." In fact, he noted that "class instruction" had "proved an immense time-saver over the centuries-old individual instruction." The above quotations are taken from the first chapter of his book on *Supervised Study in the Secondary School*, in which he suggested that individual help should be administered to students in the social context of the regular classroom. This was the best learning environment, he said, to help students "learn how to learn,"

---

[1] Robert C. Lafayette, *The Foreign Language Dropout After Level I*. An unpublished research paper presented at Ohio State University, 8 May 1969.
[2] Guy M. Whipple (ed.), *Adapting Schools to Individual Differences: The Twenty-Fourth Yearbook of the Society for the Study of Education*, Bloomington, Ill., Public School Publishing Company, 1925.

178

which he saw as the main purpose of education. Also he viewed the role of the teacher not as a dispenser of knowledge but as a facilitator of learning.[3]

The supervised study movement, which Hall-Quest started, was quite durable. In fact, it was still the official policy in many high schools as late as the 1950s. Each teacher was expected to reserve a portion of each class period for supervised individual activities and to develop individualized study-guide materials accordingly. In the second half of the 19th century, the classification of pupils into grades became the accepted practice. This graded structure—which has persisted down to the present as the predominant form of school organization—was subjected to adverse criticism even in the 19th century. In the 1890s, several plans and systems intended to promote individualized instruction were implemented.

Attempts to individualize instruction through homogeneous groupings began to surface in pedagogical writings toward the turn of the century. At about that time Charles Eliot, President of Harvard, was saying that "uniformity is the curse of American schools. That any school or college has a uniform product should be regarded as a demonstration of inferiority—of incapacity to meet the legitimate demands of a social order whose fundamental principle is that every career should be opened to talent."[4] In a 1899 speech, Eliot also stated that "the process of instructing students in large groups is a quite sufficient school evil without clinging to its twin evil, an inflexible program of studies. Individual instruction is the new ideal."[5]

The only practicable way to individualize instruction, according to Eliot, was by offering a wide range of high-quality elective courses. To be sure, certain subjects would have to be required in the early years for the purpose of "exploring interests and talents," but in Eliot's opinion electives should be introduced at age 10 and should largely prevail from age 15 and beyond. Eliot's elective system was based on the highly optimistic view that virtually all students have some area of capability in which they can excel with joy. Thus, to Eliot, individualization was largely a matter of matching students to the subjects for which they were best fitted by allowing them to choose for themselves.

The movement toward structured curricular plans for individualizing instruction began to gain prominence in the years following World War I. Perhaps the most famous of all the various plans were those that became known as the Winnetka and Dalton plans named after the cities in which they were developed (namely, Winnetka, Illinois, and Dalton, Massachusetts). The Winnetka Plan was based on the ideas that F. L. Burk had put into practice in the training school at San Francisco State College

---

[3] Alfred Lawrence Hall-Quest, *Supervised Study in the Secondary School*, New York, Macmillan, 1916, pp. 14–24.
[4] Charles Eliot, "Shortening and Enriching the Grammar School Course," *Addresses and Proceedings*, National Education Association, 1892, p. 623.
[5] Charles Eliot, "Recent Changes in Secondary Education," *The Atlantic Monthly* 84 (October 1899), pp. 443–444.

during the years 1913 to 1924. One of his faculty members, Carlton Washburne, carried the work forward in the public schools of Winnetka, Illinois. Washburne, who became superintendent of schools in Winnetka, established a program in that city that endured from 1919 until the second World War. Despite Washburne's protests that he had no "plan," the program of individualized instruction, which he carried on, became known as the Winnetka Plan. Some elements of this plan had much in common with contemporary individualization movements. For example, Washburne stated as his first principle that the teacher should decide the exact amount of knowledge and skill to be mastered in the individualized subjects and should state this in terms of "goals of achievement." Washburne's "goals of achievement" are almost identical with the "behavioral objectives" of the 1970s. Except for the vintage language, his instructional goals could easily have come from a contemporary textbook on the writing of behavioral objectives.[6] Also, in advocating that "a test should be so devised that there is only one possible right word or number to be supplied," Washburne was anticipating one of the principles of programmed textbooks, which were to appear forty years later. Washburne also suggested the use of "assignment booklets," which have many of the characteristics of present-day "unipacs." He included explicit instruction for how to prepare a foreign language learning packet for individualizing Latin. Basically this involved supplementary materials to go with the textbook. These materials followed his general techniques of individualization, which included the following:

1   A determination of exactly what rules, vocabulary, and translation ability are to be required of the pupils.
2   A breaking up of these larger objectives into smaller work units.
3   A preparation of tests to cover each of these units.
4   A preparation of assignment sheets "by which the pupil can check the accuracy of his own prose composition or translation."[7]

In addition to the self-checking system, Washburne prepared an operational system for keeping each student's records of accomplishment up-to-date, a process that has not as yet been financially feasible in most schools, even with contemporary computer technology. Washburne also believed that the individualized program should permit students to progress through the assignment sheets at an individualized rate, each student being tested separately on each unit of work as soon as it was completed. As he put it, "Never allow a pupil (unless he is subnormal in mentality or health) to proceed with one unit until he has mastered the preceding one."[8] This was a fulfillment of the ideas expressed by contemporary advocates of "learning for mastery" (such as Bloom).

[6] Whipple, op. cit., p. 257.
[7] Ibid., p. 269.
[8] Ibid., p. 272.

The Dalton Plan was the other major attempt to structure individualization in the schools. This plan was first developed by Helen Parkhurst in 1919, in a school for crippled children, and, in 1920, in the Dalton, Massachusetts, High School. Parkhurst was quite emphatic in insisting that the plan was a vehicle for the curriculum rather than being a plan based on any specific curricular content. However, in the Dalton Plan, students were given a series of subjects to learn within a given block of time, typically twenty days. They were free to pace themselves through each of the subjects. They were also free to move about the school building at their own discretion to study in any one of the "laboratories" which were set up for each subject. When students completed the work on a given subject, they were not permitted to go on to the next level of work until they had completed a comparable level of work in all other subjects. From all of this, students were supposed to learn to budget their time, moving rapidly through their "good" subjects so that they could spend the time gained on their more difficult subjects. The students were also responsible for recording their own grades and for choosing the learning mode that they deemed most appropriate for themselves. As the originator of the plan, Helen Parkhurst, expressed it, "The Dalton Laboratory Plan is a sociological, rather than a curricular experiment. It aims to socialize the school and keep its life from becoming mechanical. It emphasizes a change in the conditions of life of the school instead of concentrating upon the curriculum as do most other educational experiments."[9] According to Parkhurst, the Dalton Plan was the most widely known form of individualized instruction. In 1925, she stated that her plan had been implemented in more than 1500 schools in England. It had also been designated as the official method in Holland and in Moscow; and the plan was gaining followers in Norway, Germany, Poland, Austria, and Spain in the mid-1920s. She further noted that 450 schools in Japan were operating under the Dalton Plan, as were 250 schools in China and 50 in India. Finally, she claimed to know definitely of 200 Dalton Plan schools in the United States. The fact that her book on individualizing instruction had been translated into 12 languages also attested to the popularity of the Dalton Plan around the world.[10]

Philosophically, Parkhurst was influenced both by Montessori and Dewey, as she acknowledged in her book. From these and other sources she evolved her own unique view on how the schools could build freedom, social responsibility, and personal dependability into the individual pupil. As Parkhurst, herself, expressed it:

Freedom is . . . the first principle of the Dalton Laboratory Plan. From the academic, or cultural, point of view, the pupil must be made free to continue without interruption his work upon any subject in which he is absorbed. Under the new plan there are no bells to tear him away at an appointed hour and chain him pedagogically to another subject and another teacher. Unless a pupil is permitted

9 Ibid., pp. 83–84.
10 Ibid., p. 83.

to absorb knowledge at his own rate of speed he will never learn anything thoroughly. Freedom is taking one's own time. To take someone else's is slavery.[11]

Parkhurst listed the second principle of the Dalton Laboratory Plan as cooperation or, as she preferred to call it, "the interaction of group life." To clarify her view on the matter, she quoted John Dewey's *Democracy and Education* regarding the purpose of a democratic education, which was seen as not merely to make an individual "an intelligent participator in the life of his immediate group" but also to bring the various groups into constant interaction so that "no individual, no economic group, could presume to live independently of others."[12]

Perhaps it was this emphasis on economic democracy that attracted educational leaders in the Lenin government of the new Soviet Union to the Dalton Plan. In 1928, a somewhat Dostoevskian account of student reactions to the Russian version of the Dalton Plan was published in English translation under the title, *The Diary of a Communist Schoolboy*. Some of the entries in this diary reveal problems similar to those experiences by contemporary implementers of individualized instruction in the United States. For example, there is skepticism at the outset about the validity of the whole procedure. A September 27 entry states: "The Dalton Plan is being introduced at our school. It's a system under which the teachers do nothing and the pupils have to find everything out for themseves."[13] Another entry mentions the lack of discipline in the labs (or materials centers), which made it hard for students to complete their tasks because of the noise.[14]

Then, as the staff began to impose more of their authority on the students, disenchantment with the Dalton Plan began to grow. The final culmination of this unrest was a student demonstration complete with anti-Dalton placards. The students even made an effigy of a "Lord Dalton" to whom they mistakenly attributed the plan. *The Diary* describes how the students hung the effigy in the school yard and set it on fire. The writer noted that the effigy flared up and "crackled delightfully," while the students stood around singing:

Bourgeois Dalton, here you burn ;
Go to hell, and don't return.[15]

The Stalinist government, which ultimately gained control, was not sympathetic to the Dalton Plan, and it was soon discontinued. It faded somewhat more slowly in other parts of the world, but the results were the same. The plan had disappeared rather completely by the mid-thirties. Yet many of the practices of the Dalton Plan closely resemble some of the

[11] Helen Parkhurst, *Education on the Dalton Plan*, London, Bell, 1922, p. 16.
[12] Ibid.
[13] N. Ognyov, *The Diary of a Communist Schoolboy*, New York, Payson and Clarke, 1928, p. 12.
[14] Ibid., p. 14.
[15] Ibid., p. 77.

contemporary attempts to individualize instruction. The use of the instructional materials center (IMC) in the 1960s is, in many ways, parallel to the use of the laboratories in the Dalton Plan. Then, too, the free movement of students about the building in some of the modern "flexibly scheduled" schools resembles the policies of student mobility in the Dalton Plan. Finally, there is something very contemporary about the way in which proponents of the Dalton Plan drew upon analogies with industrial production techniques. Some supporters of an educational systems approach today claim that it will make learning more efficient and systematic. In 1924, a university professor of education compared the Dalton Plan to a properly conducted scientific management system in which each worker becomes his own efficiency engineer.[16]

As for the area of foreign language instruction, references to individualization are rather scant in the early period. In 1916, Deihl reported on an individualized experiment in first- and second-year French and first-year German at the University of Wisconsin High School. Stent, an Englishman, provided "an interesting description of how French may be taught according to the Dalton Plan." (The article appeared in a London educational journal in 1924.) Mitchell, in 1918, and Handschin, in 1919, wrote articles on the individualization of instruction by means of supervised study. Beyond these few references, foreign languages received relatively little attention in the early years of individualization. For the most part, the writings dealt with other disciplines, particularly the "basic" subjects such as history, English, reading, and mathematics.

An off-shoot of the Dalton Plan, which appears to have outlived the plan itself, is the student contract. The contract grew out of the necessity for teachers to specify student "jobs" rather clearly. Some of the more refined versions of the contract approach were used for many years at the University of Wisconsin High School. Sample contracts for various subject areas were described by Harry Miller, the school's principal, in his book, *The Self-Directed School*, published in 1925. A lengthy discussion of how to use the contracts and of their dangers was also included. Basically, the contract, as it was used at Wisconsin High School, included the following procedures: (1) Each student would agree to complete a specified amount of work within the job period of twenty days. (2) There would be three or four levels of contract work for each job. Completion of the first level of the contract would guarantee the student a grade of D, the second level a grade of C, the third level a grade of B, and the fourth level a grade of A.

Miller was sensitive to the dangers of using student contracts. He was aware that it could easily deteriorate into a mechanical checkoff system. Therefore, he cautioned that the teaching process could not simply adopt industrial practices. In his view, the Dalton Plan tasks carried an unfortunate implication. "Piecework is suggested," he said, "But mastery cannot be secured in that way." That is, mastery of any subject

16 Whipple, op cit., p. 98.

area is not achieved "by gaining temporary skill in it and checking it off as a finished job."[17]

In conclusion, it might be said that the Dalton Plan aimed at individualization within the context of a heterogeneous social group by permitting the student to select his own learning pace and, in some versions of the plan, by allowing differentiated assignments through contracts agreed upon in advance. It was clearly student centered to the degree that the success of the plan depended upon the student's ability to motivate himself, to budget his own time, and to evaluate his own progress and performance.

A SUMMARY OF IMPLICATIONS DRAWN
FROM EARLIER INDIVIDUALIZED PROGRAMS

As publically financed, compulsory elementary and secondary education spread across the continent toward the end of the 19th century, school organization tended toward graded classes and lockstep group instruction. The country-school practices of individual recitation and peer teaching gradually gave way to the teacher-dominated classroom containing children or young people of approximately the same age. This approach turned out to be administratively manageable and economically feasible. The problem with the graded system has been that groups are never really homogeneous because of the many variables that exist among individuals.

Thus, for nearly a century educators have sought ways of modifying the lockstep approach to instruction so that the process could account for the inherent differences of the individuals involved. Unfortunately, the attempts at solving the problem have tended to be either simplistic or misapplied. Attempts to establish homogeneous groups on the basis of IQ and other scores is an example of the simplistic. Because grouping is often based on a single variable (and one of questionable validity), it had not succeeded either in individualizing instruction or in improving achievement. The elective system, properly implemented, took into account a larger number fo human variables. However, electives frequently became subject to a kind of "Gresham's Law of the curriculum" in which the bad courses drove out the good. Because of economic factors, the "good" courses often came to be defined as those that drew large numbers of students rather than those that had intellectual integrity. (This is a danger inherent in the present-day minicourse movement.)

The Dalton Plan is a classic case of misapplication from theory, to prototype, to practice. In the thousands of schools around the world in which the plan was transplanted, teachers tended to focus on the mechanics of the plan and to overlook its central purposes. Thus, instead of learning social cooperation, independence, and efficient budgeting of time, many students ended up racing through learning packets at the last minute in

[17] Harry L. Miller and Richard Hargreaves, *The Self-Directed School*, New York, Scribner, 1925, p. 94.

order to meet the deadline for the month. It may also be that the founder of the plan was naive with respect to students' ability to motivate themselves and keep their own achievement records in an adequate, honest, and systematic manner. Some individualized language programs in the 1970s are also beginning to fail for reasons similar to those outlined above—that is, schools have attempted to adopt the mechanics of various highly touted schemes without understanding the theoretical implications and practical limitations of them.

The Winnetka Plan worked well—in Winnetka, an affluent suburb north of Chicago. However, few other school districts were able to put the plan into operation. Similarly, in the present era, there is little evidence that the successful continuous-progress foreign language programs have proliferated to any significant degree. It may be that the reason for present and past failures lies in the fact that the process of implementing a plan is at least as important as the plan itself. The creators have an emotional investment in it; they have confronted the problems, found solutions, and made it work. Teachers in another school district lack both the experience and the feeling for someone else's plan to enable them to adopt it.

In conclusion, let me list in abbreviated form a few additional conclusions that are suggested by the history of individualization.

1   Not all students want to be "individualized."
2   Students do not develop self-discipline merely because a program based on it has been implemented.
3   Isolated task-completion, even with Skinnerian-type rewards, is demotivating to many students.
4   Most students appear to need social interaction as well as independent study.
5   There is some question about the wisdom of fragmenting the curriculum into separate, "cognitive" and "affective" components for the purposes of individualization.
6   Proof of performance on discrete linguistic objectives do not necessarily add up to mastery learning by the end of the school year, even if the items are tested and checked off individually.
7   Individualized programs tend to be prohibitively expensive.

If the past is any guide to the future, what can we expect next? We might note that the more mechanistic, behavioristic approaches to individualization in the late 1920s were soon supplanted by an emphasis on a student-centered, interest-based approach to curriculum. In the 1970s the call for humanized education and for alternative schooling may well be a harbinger of the next educational cycle.

MODELS FOR INDIVIDUALIZING INSTRUCTION ON THE CONTEMPORARY SCENE

In reading present-day educational journals and monographs, one comes away with the impression that all of the historical patterns of individualizing or personalizing instruction are reappearing simultaneously today. For purposes of clarity (and at the risk of oversimplification) this writer has categorized the various schools of individualization into three theoretical models that attempt to account for everything, ranging from the highly structured to the highly permissive approach to personalizing education. They are discussed below.

Permissiveness and Individualization

One individualization model, which has drawn enthusiastic advocates over the years, might be called the "Rousseauian model" in honor of the eighteenth-century French philosopher Jean Jacques Rousseau. In *Émile*, his classic book on education, Rousseau said that the educator "must always choose between educating the individual or training the citizen," and that "it is impossible to do both." Hence the good education is that which completely frees the student from the restraints of society. The student's natural self must be allowed to develop, free from the constraints of formal curricula, structured administrative procedures, and teacher-dominated instructional procedures. The role of the educator is to put students into situations in which the relevance of learning a particular thing is self-evdient. Students will then learn (according to this theory) because they recognize that personal benefits will result from their efforts. Conversely, no student should be expected to learn anything which he or she does not perceive to be relevant to his or her immediate concerns and interests.

In recent years, advocates of this model have been A. S. Neill in England with his *Summerhill* school and a number of Americans who support certain kinds of so-called alternative schools. Advocates of such schools have described our existing educational system with words like repressive, irrelevant, impersonal, destructive, joyless, obsolete, and authoritarian. There is the further charge that rather than being assisted and encouraged to develop their own individuality, public school students are locked into a regimented system that attempts to stamp them all into the same mold. As one critic put it, "The student is filled with facts and figures which only accidentally and infrequently have anything whatsoever to do with the problems and conflicts of modern life or his own inner concerns." The existing school system is seen to have been built on the "factory model"; and the factory school has as its purpose the mass production of a rather crude standardized educational product. Thus many of the current strategies for individualizing instruction are viewed as mere tinkering with a basically irrelevant institution.[18]

In summary, it can be said that the Rousseauian model of individualizing instruction implies the destruction of formal education as we know it

[18] Harold W. Sobel, "The Anachronistic Practices of American Education as Perpetrated by an Unenlightened Citizenry and Misguided Pedagogues Against the Inmates of the Public Schools," *Phi Delta Kappan* 51 (October 1969), pp. 94–97.

today. Its implementation would call for the abolition of the present structure of administrative, supervisory, and teaching roles. Each "educator" in a Rousseauian plan would serve as a sort of friendly consultant who would be at the service of the student when and if needed. The theory assumes that students know what is best for them educationally and that they will automatically seek and secure their own best education if left largely to their own devices. Opponents of Rousseauianism insist that the immature student's perception of his/her own educational needs should not be the *primary* determiner of curricular content and curricular method. In their opinion, students are not capable of judging what is best for themselves or of acquiring education for themselves. Applied in a more limited way, the Rousseauian model does introduce the idea of allowing the student a great deal of choice in the matter of what is to be learned and how it is to be acquired.

Other models of individualized instruction are based on the belief that the contemporary world is too complex and too distracting to allow students to muddle through completely on their own. An institution is needed to help students make sense out of a chaotic world by putting them in touch with the intellectual resources of the species. Therefore, other models of individualized instruction are concerned with making these educational resources more widely and easily accessible and more relevant to students regardless of socioeconomic background or other environmental factors.

Self-Pacing and Continuous Progress

At the other end of the spectrum from the Rousseauian model is the "self-pacing" model of individualized instruction, which, in its most extreme form, calls for having all students complete the identical curriculum, but allows them to do so within a self-determined period of time. The most prevalent self-pacing model today can be summarized as having the following characteristics: (1) It is based upon behavioral objectives—that is, upon a precise definition of how the student will be performing when he has achieved the course objectives. (2) The course is then divided into a series of sequential steps leading to these objectives. (3) The student is allowed to move through these steps at his own best rate. A fourth aspect of many self-pacing programs is quality control. This frequently includes a listing of the conditions under which the student must perform and the level of success that he must achieve on a given step before he is allowed to advance.

Although the above model, in somewhat more detailed form, is being promoted by educators in high places, it is by no means accepted throughout the profession. For example, Oettinger writing in the *Harvard Educational Review* states that, with this approach "the objective cannot be the cultivation of idiosyncracy. It is, rather, what an industrial engineer might call mass production to narrow specifications with rigid quality control. Each pupil is free to go more or less rapidly exactly where he is

187

told to go."[19] Oettinger goes on to say that educators' rhetoric tends to mask the fact that the techniques now being developed are only of value in training to very narrow and specific behavioral objectives but do not address themselves to the broader, more basic problems of education. In his words, "Training to minimal competence in well-defined skills is very important in a variety of military, industrial, and school settings. It is not, however, the whole of what the educational process should be."[20]

Glaser wrote a rebuttal to Oettinger's article in which he insisted that the rate of learning was a significant variable. Glaser suggested that learning rate could indicate a student's inductive capability, that it was related to the amount of *practice* a student requires to retain what he learns, and that it could suggest whether a student is impulsive or reflective. He added that "Rate also reflects aspects of motivation. Much research has shown that rate is a behavior which the instructional environment can significantly influence. Thus it is a good variable with which to begin attempts to individualize instruction."[21]

As a matter of fact, research has *not* tended to support the self-pacing model as it has been implemented in a number of public schools. For example, a study conducted with eighth-grade students in Pittsburgh in 1964 indicated that many students—including some who were bright and well-motivated—did very poorly under conditions of self-pacing. Some students were apparently overconscientious. They spent too much time on each given item. Others raced ahead too fast, covering a great deal of ground but retaining very little. The group of high achievers in the self-paced program were those—irrespective of IQ—who developed the knack of judging their own optimum learning rate. For them self-pacing was a good learning style.[22]

A great deal of individualization has also been done in the foreign language field. One psychologist, Gagné, has noted that foreign languages are of particular interest for individualization since they cover the full range of learning problems, including the psychomotor, the cognitive, and the affective domains.[23]

Over the past ten years there have been a number of attempts to individualize the learning of foreign languages using programmed materials. Attempts have been made to teach the various foreign languages either with or without the supervision of a live specialist language teacher. The results of such programs are not very impressive. Although a few highly motivated students of superior ability *have* been able to teach themselves the equivalent of one year's foreign language, the vast majority of students

[19] Anthony Oettinger and Sema Marks, "Educational Technology: New Myths and Old Realities," *Harvard Educational Review* 38 (Fall 1968), p. 701.
[20] Ibid.
[21] Robert Glaser, "Discussion of Educational Technology: New Myths and Old Realities," *Harvard Educational Review* 38 (Fall 1968), pp. 739–746.
[22] Gerard Kress and George Gropper, *Studies in Televised Instruction*, Research conducted under U.S. Office of Education Grant 7–48–0000–159, 1964.
[23] R. M. Gagné, *The Conditions of Learning*, New York, Holt, Rinehart & Winston, 1965.

who began the study of foreign languages by means of programmed instruction were unsuccessful. For the most part, the Skinnerian programs —which have predominated in the area of foreign languages—proved boring, tedious, and inefficient.[24]

Individualization and Learning Style

A third model for individualized instruction might best be called "the individualized learning style model." This model is based on the belief that each person has a unique way of learning and that, therefore, individualization of instruction should allow a maximum number of options in the *style* of acquiring knowledge. This model does not assume that all students can learn all things better through self-paced independent study. It concedes that many students may, in fact, learn some things better in large groups with externally imposed pacing or in small groups that operate in accordance with teacher-imposed guidelines.

There is another reason for putting the emphasis upon the style and process of learning rather than upon the pacing of students through a fixed body of content. In the opinion of some educators, the world is changing so fast and knowledge is expanding at such a rate, that the idea of teaching for specific, narrow objectives is outmoded, especially where general education is concerned. Such a system of prescribed training is said to be relevant only in a primitive or static society. According to the psychologist, Carl Rogers, the failure to comprehend this fact has led to our present problems in education. As he expresses it:

We are, in my view, faced with an entirely new situation in education. . . . The only man who is educated is the man who has learned how to learn; the man who has learned how to adapt and change; the man who has realized that no knowledge is secure, that only the process of *seeking* knowledge gives a basis for security. Changingness, a reliance on *process* rather than upon static knowledge is the only thing that makes any sense as a goal for education in the modern world.[25]

This kind of thinking has even appeared in higher education. One college president, for example, insists that the only role of the college professor is to help students find their own way of learning within the various fields of knowledge. As he expressed it, "This is going to be traumatizing to a lot of professors. Their major role is not to impart information. Their major role is to turn kids on—to help them plan a course of action. . . . Each individual student will have a curriculum and a course learning plan that is individual and unique for him. I think that's completely possible."[26]

---

[24] Susan Shulze, Jermaine Arendt, and Robert G. Rainey, *A Two Year Study of the Use of Programmed Materials for the Instruction of French in High School*, unpublished report prepared by the Minneapolis Public Schools, 1966.
[25] Carl R. Rogers, *The Interpersonal Relationship in the Facilitation of Learning*, Columbus, Ohio, Merrill, 1968.
[26] Leland Newcomer, "Charting a Unique Path for the Small Liberal Arts College," *College Management* 4 (September 1969), pp. 34–37.

189

Individualization by Means of the Systems Approach

The literature of the 1960s and 1970s contained many references to the "systems approach." There are many versions of this approach, some of which are described in the highly technical language of industrial planners. Clearly, a detailed analysis of such systems is not within the scope of this chapter. Yet inasmuch as some elements of the systems approach are being applied to present-day programs of individualized instruction in foreign languages, it would seem advisable to discuss some of the main features of this approach.

First, it can be stated that the systems approach is usually eclectic in nature—that is, any activities that lead toward fulfillment of the stated course objectives are acceptable so long as they work. In fact, a variety of learning activities can be deliberately manipulated in order to make learning more efficient. To some degree, the Trump Plan, which was developed in the late 1950s, anticipated this element of the systems approach. Trump advocated a type of high school plant that would contain cubicles for individual work. According to his plan, approximately 40 percent of a student's time would be devoted to purely individual work in these cubicles. In addition, the student would have access to a variety of resource centers and to such equipment as language laboratories and automated teaching devices. There would also be large-group sessions partly for the purpose of "buying" teacher time for individual and small-group contacts with students. Small "seminar" groups of about twelve students were also a part of the overall plan. According to Wilhelms, Trump was moving in the right direction. For, as Wilhelms expressed it, "In such a setting, it should be easier to evolve highly differentiated curriculum content and to develop individual study projects attuned to the student as a whole person, not merely to his level of intelligence or special ability."[27]

In practice, the Trump Plan can be rather rigid, particularly if it is implemented "from the top down." If the scheduling of instructional groups (for example, large-group, small-group and individual sessions) is arbitrarily set up in a rather inflexible weekly pattern, the results in terms of genuine individualization may be minimal. To correct this, systems analysts have built in a method of feedback evaluation to determine what is producing good results for the individual student and to change anything that is not. In a paper entitled "Learning for Mastery," Bloom rather clearly identifies the function of this second characteristic of the systems approach. As he sees it, one of the primary purposes of the feedback system is to determine the particular errors and difficulties that the majority of students are having in the regular large-group situations so that the instructional program can be modified to correct such difficulties. However, the feedback principle, according to Bloom, should go far beyond the mere overcoming of individual difficulties. More importantly, it should

---

[27] Fred T. Wilhelms, "The Curriculum and Individual Differences," *Individualizing Instruction: The Sixty-First Yearbook of the National Society for the Study of Education*, Chicago, University of Chicago Press, 1962, p. 72.

enable students to become more independent in their learning and it should help them to identify alternative ways by which they can comprehend new ideas. Ideally, the feedback system would be implemented in such a way as to overcome in the student feelings of defeatism and passivity about learning. In short, students should be made to feel that the system is aimed at finding the best possible way for them to learn and at supplying a great variety of instructional materials and procedures to enable them to do so. Teachers, too, according to Bloom, will be favorably influenced by the feedback principle; they will come to recognize "that it is the learning which is important and that instructional alternatives exist to enable all (or almost all) of the students to learn the subject to a high level."[28] According to Bloom and others, this high level of achievement means that 90 percent or more of any given group of students can learn any curricular material at the level of achievement that teachers have traditionally designated with the grade of "A" or "B." The only proviso is that they be given all the time they need and that the educational system be made flexible enough for them to do so. The feedback system would constantly inform students and teachers when any individual was failing to achieve the criterion level of achievement; and the instructional part of the system would designate ways to put him back on the track.

A third element of the systems approach as it is typically applied to individualized programs is the replacement of the time-oriented curriculum with a performance-oriented one. In practice, this means recycling of students who do not meet high levels of performance on their first or second try at meeting a given learning objective. In some school programs, the systems approach manifests itself in the shape of highly formalized packages of learning materials variously referred to as "unipacs," "learning activity packages" (LAPS), or "learning contracts," to name but a few of the more commonly used designations. There are many variations of such learning packages; however, nearly all of them contain the following eight components:

1   *The overall goal or purpose* of the learning package stated in the form of certain basic concepts. The purpose of this part of the package is to organize the various events, processes, and objects of the package into a small number of categories.

2   *Instructional objectives* (that is "behavioral objectives" or "performance objectives") are included, the intent of which is to tell pupils what they will have to be able to do when they are evaluated, the conditions under which they will have to perform, and the lower limit of acceptable performance.

3   *Learning materials* of all kinds (and of varying difficulty) are listed along with their availability and instruction for use. These include a variety of media involving the use of as many different senses as possible.

[28] Benjamin S. Bloom, *Learning for Mastery*, Los Angeles, UCLA, Research and Development Center, 1969, p. 9.

4   *Learning activities* provide alternative approaches for achieving the instructional objectives, and include such activities as large-group and small-group instruction, field trips, model building, drama productions, audiovisual productions, games, experiments, role playing, conferences with teachers and aides, personal contemplation, and the like.

5   *Pretests* are designed to assess the extent to which the student has already met the instructional objectives as a result of earlier formal or informal learning experiences. Pretesting is designed to allow students to concentrate their learning efforts on areas of weakness and to skip over material that they already know.

6   *Self-tests* are included for the purpose of helping students to determine for themselves their own progress toward the achievement of the instructional objectives. It also serves to give students an indication as to whether or not they are ready for the posttest. Also, if properly designed, self-testing results will indicate areas of weakness; areas that need additional work and, perhaps, a new attack on the learning of materials that have not yet been mastered. (This is, of course, related to the feedback principle discussed above.)

7   *Posttests* are used to assess the extent to which pupils have met the instructional objectives. If they meet the criterion performance level they are permitted to go on to the next unit of material. If not, the test results are used as feedback information to determine where students went wrong and to direct them to still additional learning activities that are likely to lead them closer to achieving the criterion level of performance.

8   *Quest activities* are often included (but are sometimes omitted). Quest activities are supposed to involve some kind of creative self-expression. That is, they are intended to originate with and lead beyond the learning package into pupil-initiated and self-directed learning activities of one kind or another.[29]

In conclusion, it might be noted that this version of the systems approach as it is applied to the instructional process (and which is representative of current individualization modes) is strongly oriented toward the self-pacing of students through a predetermined body of subject matter. Although there is some attempt to allow for individual learning style (see number 4 above) and although the "Quest" component may tend to promote divergent thinking, the main emphasis is on the fulfillment of clearly stated behavioral objectives. The heart of this and of other examples of the systems approach lies in the component that tells the student "what he will have to be able to do when he is evaluated" and what will be the "quality of performance expected of him."[30]

[29] For a more detailed discussion of this topic see Phillip G. Kapfer, "An Instructional Management Strategy for Individualized Learning," *Phi Delta Kappan* 49 (January 1968), pp. 260–263.
[30] Ibid.

CONSTRUCTING LEARNING PACKETS (UNIPACS) FOR THE FOREIGN LANGUAGE CLASS

A method for constructing unipacs, which has been widely used in various inservice projects, involves the procedures described below. Although individual teachers can use the procedures, better results are usually obtained through group efforts especially in the form of a sustained summer inservice or preservice activity (see also the section on "culture minicourses" in Chapter 9).

Step I: Identify the unit.
  A. Title of unipac
  B. Subject (which language, what cultural or grammatical topics, and so forth)
  C. Performance level (first-year, second-year, third-year, and so forth)
  D. Purpose (a brief statement of intent)

Step II: List the ideas, skills, or attitudes to be stressed.

Step III: Give learning objectives that are likely to result if students are successful. Include open-ended options to allow for "creative" applications.

Step IV: Make up a separate set of instructions and materials that are oriented to the teacher.

Step V: List student-oriented learning activities.

Step VI: Establish suggested learning experiences to match the goals and activities mentioned above. These will include:
  A. Large-group instruction
  B. Small-group projects
  C. Independent study
  D. Out-of-school trips

Step VII: Prepare formative evaluation instruments.
  A. Self-test devices
    1. pretest
    2. posttest
  B. Teacher learning checks
    1. pretest
    2. posttest
    3. observation of samples of individual student performance
    4. observation of team performance in game situation

Step VIII: Prepare feedback evaluation instruments of student reactions:
  A. What is good in unipacs?
  B. What is bad in unipacs?
  C. What would improve them?

Step IX: Make modifications in accordance with results of Step VIII.

Developing Listening Skill in Small Groups

Sample Lesson: "The Mission Impossible" Assignment

EQUIPMENT NEEDED: *A portable cassette playback machine with good fidelity. (A portable open-reel tape recorder will also work for the purpose of this exercise.)*
MATERIALS NEEDED: *A prerecorded tape by one or more native speakers that is slightly above the listening comprehension capabilities of the students in the*

193

exercise. Ideally, it should be five to ten minutes in length. The voices should be lively and natural. The material should be of high interest to the age group for which it is intended and there should be a definite beginning and end to the selection.

TECHNIQUE: *The class is broken into groups of three to five students. Each group must have access to the cassette player or tape player and must have an area where they can work effectively in a small-group situation. Each group elects a team leader for the "mission." Students know in advance that a prize will be awarded for the best fulfillment of the language mission. (The prize should be something humorous rather than something of great monetary value.) The teacher prepares an "assignment" tape in advance and makes enough copies for each group. The teacher's own voice is used for this purpose. The tape may be either in English or in the target language, depending on the language level of the students.*

SAMPLE TEXT: *Hello. This is your teacher. The mission for this grading period— should you choose to accept it—is to transcribe and interpret a message that has been intercepted from a foreign power. The message is in _____ (French, German, Latin, Spanish, or whatever the language being studied). Listen to the entire tape through to the end once or twice to get the general idea. After that, your team leader will play short segments, rewinding the tape as often as necessary, so that you can transcribe the message into writing. You may use a dictionary or other available resources. Each member of the group may wish to produce his or her own version of the message first. In the end, the purpose is to come up with a single text that represents the consensus of the group. The final part of the mission is to answer as accurately as possible the questions that are enclosed with the taped message.*

Should your team be captured by the building principal, I will disavow all knowledge of this assignment. The tape will not self-destruct in ten seconds; the school district cannot afford to burn up tapes in that manner. Furthermore, there is a school board regulation against smoking on school property. Good luck with your mission.

(End of Tape)

SAMPLE SITUATION ON THE "INTERCEPTED" TAPE: *A customer approaches a vendor in the market and asks the price of a rather ornate dueling saber, which he wishes to purchase for a young relative. The bargaining begins with ridiculous offers being made on both sides. After a period of bargaining they agree on a price somewhere in between and the purchase is made. The sample questions:*

1   *What is the nature of this incident?*
2   *Where does it take place?*
3   *What weapons are involved?*
4   *Please describe the weapons mentioned above.*
5   *How many people were involved in this episode?*
6   *What was the final outcome?*
7   *If any money changed hands, explain the purpose of the exchange and the amount of money involved.*
8   *Describe any behaviors here that you consider to be out of the ordinary in comparison to the way people behave in similar situations in your home town.*

RATIONALE FOR THIS EXERCISE:
1   *Drawing meaning from a foreign language through listening is an active, receptive process rather than a passive one.*

2   Problem solving and hypothesis testing are suitable procedures for
     developing listening skill for adolescents and young adults.
3   Group work, social interaction, and team competition greatly enhance
     student motivation.
4   Evaluation of student performance need not always be in the form of written
     tests and quizzes. In group situations, the teacher can move around the
     room and can observe the performance of the students in terms of such
     things as participation, cooperation, seriousness of purpose, and, of course,
     the quality of results produced by the group process.
5   Since language is communication, and communication involves social
     interaction, it is wise to provide for this reality by putting students into
     formal, amusing, and relaxed situations that require the use of one or more
     of the language skills.

A personalized discovery approach to culture and conversation. *Given this visual
evidence, what can we say about the society depicted.*

Procedures:

 I. First Day
    A. Form the class into small groups of 3 to 6 (can be determined by numbers
       drawn from a hat).
    B. Hand out realia, cultural data, or show a series of slides from the target
       culture (or all three).
    C. Ask each group to react separately to the data that they have examined.
       Have each student write a brief description of the culture based on the
       data presented.
    D. Ask the group to arrive at a series of hypotheses about the target culture
       based on the available data. (These are to be prepared for a large-group
       discussion on the second day.)
    E. Have each member take the responsibility for reporting on one or more of
       the hypotheses. (Differences from and similarities to American culture can
       be pointed out here.) Evidence must be cited to support each supposition.

Sample Material: Slide Series—All Saints Day in Boliva[31]

SLIDE 1. *(Entrance to a cemetery)* Narration: *(English for beginning levels;
Spanish at advanced levels.): "The celebration of All Saints' Day centers around
the cemetery. This one is in Sucre, Bolivia, and is a magnificent monument to the
wealth that once surrounded this city when it was in the center of one of the
richest silver mining areas in South America. The words at the entrance of the
cemetery say in Latin, "Today me, tomorrow you."*
SLIDE 2: *(An elaborate, ornate marble mausoleum)* Narration: *"This is an example
of a mausoleum of a wealthy family of the city of Sucre. A small altar is inside and
the tombs fill the walls and floor."*
SLIDE 3: *(Solid grave markers of a permanent nature in well-kept plots.)*
Narration: *"The middle-class section of the cemetery often finds members of
fraternal groups or labor syndicates buried in the same section."*
SLIDE 4: *(Poorly kept, run-down grave markers and plots)* Narration: *"This is the
poor section of the cemetery. The white crosses mark children's graves. In*

[31] Prepared by Michelle Smith, LaFollette High School, Madison, Wis., 1974.

195

underdeveloped countries the death of one or two children per family is not unusual."

SLIDE 5. *(Local people in procession)* Narration : *"On All Saints' Day the people of this Bolivian town near Cochabamba come in a small parade to the cemetery at the edge of the village."*

SLIDE 6. *(Graves amid barren landscape)* Narration : *"The cemetery is usually on the poorest land as the irrigated fertile land must be used for food cultivation."*

SLIDE 7. *(People putting flowers and wreaths on graves)* Narration : *"Each family who has had a death of a loved one in the last year decorates the grave with flowers and paper. The villagers come to pray for the recently departed. The village priest is seen here in the white hat."*

SLIDE 8. *(Graves with food and drink on top)* Narration : *"Bread and biscuits are baked in the shape of religious symbols and placed on top of the graves, along with fruits, candles and alcoholic beverages like chicha, a corn beer."*

SLIDE 9. *(People sharing food and drink in cemetery)* Narration : *"The villagers gather around each grave and say a few simple prayers for the soul of the dead person. After the prayers, the family members pass around the breads, biscuits, and chicha they have prepared."*

SLIDE 10. *(Child praying at graveside; others running in background)* Narration : *"For the children of the village this is not unlike trick or treat in the United States; they run from grave to grave saying the prayers as fast as they can so they can be rewarded with the treats."*

SLIDE 11. *(Women in black attire)* Narration : *"Women generally wear black clothing for the solemn occasion."*

SLIDE 12. *(Women socializing in cemetery)* Narration : *"All Saints' Day is also a social occasion and these women take time out to chat."*

II. *Second Day*
   Set up slides on carousel projector for reference (in case students wish to review the data or present it).
   A.   *Individuals from the various groups take turns reporting on their suppositions along with supporting evidence.*
   B.   *Teacher asks questions of each group to elicit information (not to correct or threaten).*
   C.   *Fellow students also are encouraged to question the presenters.*

III. *Third or Fourth Day, depending on time needed to complete preliminary presentations.*
   A.   *The teacher reshows the slides and asks questions (prepared in advance). The questions involve several of the levels of questioning outlined below.*
      1.   Memory questions : *The student is merely asked to recall an idea or fact presented earlier.*
      2.   Paraphrase questions. *The teacher presents information; the student must restate it in another way.*
      3.   Interpretation questions. *The student is asked to create an idea of his/ her own based on an idea supplied by the teacher.* Example : *"Which aspect of honoring the dead is, in your opinion, most different in Bolivia when compared to practices in the United States:*
         a.   *using grave markers*
         b.   *evidence of the previous social status of the dead*
         c.   *decorating graves with flowers*
         Explain your choice."
      4.   Application questions. *The students must show that he/she can use an*

idea (when the problem calls for it) even though he/she is not told specifically to do so. Example: "Your'group is to prepare a five-minute skit illustrating one significant aspect of All Saints' Day in Bolivia."

5. Analysis questions. *The student is asked to solve a problem with the conscious observance of the rules for good thinking of the type called for by the problem.* Example: "Make a constructive reaction to the following generalization: 'Bolivians have a disrespectful and flippant attitude toward the dead'." (The inductive process of thinking should be used to refute the assertion.)

6. Synthesis questions. *There is never one right answer to synthesis questions. Instead the student is asked to create something.* Examples:
   a. "Write a diary entry from the standpoint of a Bolivian boy or girl your age who has just returned from visiting the grave of a loved one on All Saints' Day."
   b. "Write a paragraph representing the feelings of the ghost of a recently departed person who could see and hear his/her loved ones visiting on All Saints' Day (but could not be seen or heard)."

7. Evaluation questions. *The student is asked to rate something as good or bad, right or wrong, beautiful or ugly, and so forth. Part of the answer should deal with the considerations that led the evaluator to make the judgement.* Examples:
   a. "What do you think of Group A's interpretation of All Saints' Day in Bolivia?"
   b. "What do you like and dislike about the Bolivian attitudes toward the dead? Explain and give examples."[32]

Further Followup
IV. First Day of Second Week
  A. The slides are reproduced into five sets of jumbo-sized prints (glossy photographs).
  B. Each small group is given the set of twelve pictures and told to classify them into three groups of four.
  C. Each group prepares (in the target language) a rationale for having chosen that sequence and selection of photos.
V. Second Day of Second Week
  A. Members of each group present their reasons for the picture groupings selected.
  B. The teacher referees a total group discussion.

PERSONAL STUDENT INVOLVEMENT IN CURRICULAR DECISIONS: THE MINICOURSE APPROACH

One method of determining what students like and dislike is to ask them. This may seem obvious, but the act of doing so can create problems. If the question of what to teach is left completely open, confusion will almost certainly result. Students usually expect and want a certain amount

[32] Norris Sanders, *Classroom Questions* New York, Harper & Row, 1966.

197

of guidance and direction. However, the opposite extreme in which the instructional staff makes all the major decisions, has led to student apathy, dropping out, and poor achievement. There is, however, a middle ground, which maintains the professional status of the teacher while at the same time permitting a degree of student decision making. A number of schools in the Midwest that have used this approach have reported enrollment increases, reduced dropout rates at the advanced levels, and improved student performance in the language. Basically the approach is as follows:

1   The instructional staff lists a number of courses that they feel competent to teach and that, in their judgment, have potential in terms of the integrity of the discipline.

2   A rating scale is set up to enable students to indicate their preferences. (In most cases this is done with second-year students during their second semester of study.)

3   The highest ranked courses are then offered as a series of miniunits for third-, fourth- and fifth-year students.

Surprisingly, even though the minicourse approach has not normally been applied to the first and second instructional levels, enrollments have tended to increase at those levels within a year or two after implementation of minicourses at the advanced levels. It may be that the very act of involving students—of taking their opinions seriously— has a favorable backlash effect on the beginning levels. Or, perhaps the significant variable is that the language program now offers some prospect other than additional years of drill work. Whatever the reason, the introduction of the advanced-level minicourse approach has had a favorable effect on the entire program. A few minicourses dealing with basic language skills or with interesting cultural topics can also be interspersed with regular class work during the beginning levels. This can help to break the standard routines or can be used to deal in-depth with a particularly troublesome aspect of the target language. Minicourses can also serve to move the student in the direction of more personalized, individualized instruction. The following steps have been used successfully in a number of junior and senior high schools in setting up the minicourse approach:

Step I. A general assessment of student preferences with regard to curricular content and learning style. The form given below has been used to good advantage.

Foreign Language Survey

Students: *Will you please answer the following questions as carefully and as honestly as you can. You need not put your name on this paper. The main purpose of this survey is to try to make language learning more enjoyable and worthwhile for all of you.*

1   *What did you enjoy most about your language class this year?*

198

2   What activities did you like least?

3   What would you like to spend more time doing in class next year?

4   Are you planning to continue your education after high school?
     _____ Yes   _____ No

5   What vocation do you want to enter after completing your education?
     First choice _____   Second choice _____

6   Are you planning to continue your language study next year?
     _____ Yes   _____ No
     If your answer is "No," please explain why.

7   Check any of the areas listed below that you would like to learn more about
     in your language class. Add any others that interest you.

     _____ 1. art   _____ 9. literature
     _____ 2. classical music   _____ 10. foods and cooking
            and composers   _____ 11. cars
     _____ 3. fashions   _____ 12. sports
     _____ 4. sports   _____ 13. folk music
     _____ 5. history   _____ 14. drama
     _____ 6. science   _____ 15. conversation
     _____ 7. travel   _____ 16. letter writing
     _____ 8. geography   _____ 17. news media
     Add others:

Step II. A listing of possible minicourse offerings (at least 20 for each
language), along with capsule descriptions of each.

*A rating system such as that given below is useful in determining the final ranking
of potential course offerings.*
*The Foreign Language Department of _____ High School would like to make
the study of languages as interesting and worthwile as possible to our students.
On this sheet you will find brief descriptions of some minicourses that may be
offered next year. These courses would be of varying length: two to nine weeks.
Students will sign up for a series of courses. A semester's work will give one-half
credit, a year's work will give one credit. These courses will be accepted for
graduation and college acceptance credit for language requirements.
You can help us by rating the courses according to how each appeals to you.
Please rate them carefully according to the following scale:*

5   I would very much like to enroll in it.
     _____

4   It sounds quite interesting to me.
     _____

3   It sounds good to me.
     _____

2   It sounds fair to me.
     _____

1   It has no interest for me.
     _____

199

_____ 1. Magazine and newspaper reading : *The student will learn what is going on in the Spanish-speaking world in regard to fashion, movies, theater, radio, television, and current events.*

_____ 2. Explorers and discoveries : *The course would include a study of such explorers as Colón, Balboa, Cortez, Pizarro, Ponce de León. Their explorations and the importance of each would be considered.*

_____ 3. Chicanos in society : *Students will study the Chicano movement in the U.S. and their problems as a minority group.*

B. FRENCH EXAMPLES:

_____ 1. Sports : *Discussion in French of various popular French sports. Studies accompanied by films on best-known sports.*

_____ 2. Fashion : *A study of the French fashion industry from its early years to the present. Included will be a study of the major fashion designers and current trends.*

_____ 3. Multimedia : *A course involving the study of and use of major means of communication in modern France. Reference books, periodicals, movies and television will be included.*

C. GERMAN EXAMPLES:

_____ 1. Marriage Partners by newspaper *(*Heiratspost*) : The student will learn to read the marriage want ads as selected from German newspapers. He or she will show an understanding of the origins and reasons for the existence of the* Heiratspost. *Using an assumed name and identity, each student will write an ad in the German manner to be published in a special edition of the* Heiratspost.

_____ 2. Driver education : *The student will learn to use the basic vocabulary related to driving a car and will describe, in German, the actions that he or she is performing, such as getting into the car, fastening the seat belt, starting the motor, shifting the gears, and so forth. A knowledge of basic driving regulations in West Germany will be included.*

_____ 3. Americans of German descent. *Contributions, great and small, to American civilization by German speaking immigrants are presented through readings and audiovisual presentations. Most of this is done in German. Each student gives a short German language report on an individual German American of his or her choice.*

Step III. Implementation

The courses receiving the highest student ratings are, indeed, offered. Best results are obtained if teachers can be employed during the summer to prepare some (if not all) of the unipac and other study guide materials. During the first year or two of implementation, it is also wise to seek extra funding. If local funds are unavailable, it would be advisable to check, well in advance, with the local school administration to see if federal funds (such as ESEA, Title IV) are available to purchase extra equipment, materials, and supplies.

Step IV. Evaluation and feedback

It is advisable to continue administering a feedback opinionnaire such as the one suggested above in Step I. It is also a good idea to commit in writing what the language staff plans to do in the way of evaluating the effectiveness of the

program. (This is particularly important if the staff is asking for additional money.)
At the very least, the plan to go to the minicourse approach might well contain a
statement such as the following:
A series of minicourses based on an assessment of student interests will be
offered to third-, fourth- and fifth-year students of French, German, and Spanish.
The courses will cover periods ranging from two to six weeks and will include
such varied topics as sports, travel plans, news media, discussion seminars with
native speakers, history, culture, music, art, reading for fun, and cooking native
foods. Criterion-referenced achievement tests, attitude surveys, and a measure of
the effect of the program on the dropout rate will be used to evaluate the
program.

A better approach, of course, is to develop in advance the actual evaluation techniques and devices, which are then appended to the entire proposed program.

Personalizing the Emotional Aspects of Communication

Dropouts from the foreign language program frequently claim that the course work was irrelevant (see Chapter 6). In many of these cases this simply means that the student has perceived the language learning process as a dull and sterile intellectual game. Those who stay with the language long enough to be able to study literature in the original do have an opportunity to experience emotions as expressed in lyric poetry and in the characters of plays, novels, and stories. Unfortunately, by that time, the foreign language program has lost well over 90 percent of the students. Therefore, a good case can be made for deliberately requiring students at all levels to express feelings that relate to them deeply and personally. The danger of this approach is that the teacher may inadvertently force the student to express emotions in a group situation that may prove psychologically harmful. Most teachers are not trained in group therapy and should, therefore, avoid inducing students to express feelings that they would rather keep to themselves. Thus, in dealing with the expression of emotions in a second language, the student should always be given an alternative course of action that permits him/her to gracefully opt out of a planned activity that may prove emotionally threatening.

Expressing likes and dislikes: the bag exercise. The purpose of this exercise is to get students to express feelings of liking and disliking that apply to them personally. The exercise would come at that point in the year after which students had been introduced to the verbs that express liking. The use of negatives with these forms would also be prerequisite to the exercise. (It happens that French, German, and Spanish all present definite learning problems with such verbs.) Also, additional vocabulary and idiomatic expressions of loving, hating, detesting, adoring, loathing, being joyful, and so on are introduced with an explanation of suitable contexts for use. A study sheet is prepared containing such information along with suggested review chapters as needed. Students are asked to provide their own plain grocery bag (or pasteboard box) on which pictures will be pasted.

201

The students are then instructed to go through old newspapers and magazines and to cut out pictures that represent items that they really like or dislike. Closure is achieved in this exercise after everyone has had the opportuntity to express his/her personalized views and has asked or answered at least one question relating to the exercise. The teacher reviews and, if necessary, provides some practice on points of grammar that have been causing problems. Finally, using the bag and its contents for reference, each student is asked to write a one-page summary entitled, "Some things about me as a person." Students are told in advance that this brief paper plus their participation in the group exercise will be the basis of evaluation.

They should seek out items that represent varying degrees of liking and disliking. The study guide can also instruct them to choose activities (for example, a picture of someone playing tennis) and contain pictures of singular and plural objects. The students are then to paste these pictures onto a large grocery bag or cardboard box with the negative items on one side and the positive items on the other. Small objects and additional pictures can be placed inside the bag or box. Also, if students have the grammatical sophisitication to deal with it, pictures of "What I would like to be" can be included in the container. Using both supervised study and out-of-class work, students have approximately a week to prepare for the group communications situation. The study guide informs them that they will have to be able to do the following:

1   Ask questions about other students' pictures.
2   Express like or dislike about single objects of their choice.
3   State that certain depicted activities bother them.
4   Express positive feeling toward activities that they like.
5   Express what they would like to be in the future.
6   Correctly pronounce the words and expressions relating to new and old vocabulary items.

On the final day, each person in the class brings in the bag or box. If possible, the class forms into a large circle. Using the foreign language, each student in turn presents several items that he/she likes or dislikes. After each presentation the teacher can ask different students if they agree or disagree with what was expressed. (Thus reinjecting, in a meaningful context, the question, "Are you in agreement?") Other questions can be "Are you surprised that Jane/John wants to be an airline pilot?" or "Do you also like to eat broiled octopus?" There are, of course, no right or wrong answers; students are free to like or dislike anything they wish and to express their feelings about it.

Other personalizing techniques. Other techniques, which can be targeted toward the learning of basic skills or particular linguistic phenomena, are given below. These are, of course, merely representative examples of devices that have proven successful in some classes. The possibilities for variation and innovation are unlimited.

202

Guessing games : *pairs of students*

First student: "How many people are there in your family ? More than three ? Less than ten ?" and so on. "When were you born ? Between August and December ?" "Before the tenth of October ?" and so on (once the month has been determined)
The roles are then reversed, and the second student asks the same questions of the first.

Newspaper reporter technique : *entire class*
Everyone prints his/her name on a slip of paper and places it in a box for subsequent drawing. Everyone draws one name (other than his/her own) The teacher hands out in random order a list of cards containing instructions and questions to be asked. The "reporter" has to get that information from the "subject" named on the slip of paper by the next day and report on it orally to the class. The subject of the report must verify the accuracy of the report (all in the foreign language, of course). The format would be as follows:
"The person I am reporting on is _____. Would _____ be so kind as to stand up ?"
(Subject stands)
Information obtained would include items such as:
1   *Ralph has one brother and two sisters. The brother is named Paul; the sisters are named Amalia and June.*
2   *Inga's mother has brown hair and blue eyes.*
3   *Tony's father is 43 years old. He works for the First National Bank.*
4   *Paul would rather go to the movies than stay home and watch television.*

After each brief report, the reporter asks of the standing subject, "Did I get that right ?" The student of the report answers with a "Yes," "No," or "Mostly." The reporter responds by saying "That's good," or "That's too bad." Then they both sit down.
(Next reporter)

Happiness exercise : *individuals to whole class*
The pupils are given a paper with the heading "Where do I feel happy ?" Under it are randomly listed places where one might be happy. The students are to individually rank order according to their preferences. The next day, the teacher asks students where they feel most *and* least *happy. They respond using the items listed* first *and* last *respectively. Sample expressions would be: at the movies, at home, in school, swimming, in the woods, and so on. Responses can be summarized into percentage figures to review or introduce expressions like: percent, the majority, a few, some people, no one, and so forth. For example: "Where do the majority of students in this class feel happy ?" or "Nobody feels happy in school ? Why is that ?"*

During the 1970s an increasing number of books and articles were directed toward the problem of making foreign language instruction personally relevant to students.[33] As a device for stimulating oral and written

[33] Edward Allen and Rebecca Valette, *Modern Language Techniques*, New York, Harcourt Brace Jovanovich, 1972, and Frank Grittner (ed.), *Student Motivation and the Foreign Language Teacher*, Skokie, Ill., National Textbook Company, 1974.

responses, Giannetti has developed a list of 110 "relevant topics" written in Spanish, many of which would be useful if translated into French, German, or any other modern language.[34] His topics include some items that call for simple narrations in various verb moods and tenses as well as others that require students to make value judgments. A large number of Giannetti's topics are in the form of sentences for completion and elaboration such as "My favorite television program is . . ." and "Last night I dreamed that. . . ." Others are simply questions or statements to be developed further by students such as "Is capital punishment justifiable?" or "The danger of a possible depression." Giannetti reports good student responses to this "relevant topic" approach. In his words, "There must be a decrease in time consuming lectures or force fed material and an increase in student oral expression based on well-liked topics."[35]

A simpler (but similar) personalizing technique—which also provides for vocabulary review—asks the student to prepare two lists from memory, one dealing with places where he/she is happy and the other with places where he/she feels sad. Students bring the lists to class and take turns presenting, in the foreign language, their first choice. Either a small-group or total-class instructional arrangement can be used here. Personal feelings can also be dealt with by having students fill out and discuss a values continuum prepared in the foreign language by the teacher. For example, in response to the question, "How are you?" students can place a check mark in the appropriate spot on a dittoed sheet prepared in the target language that contains information such as the following:

terrible   so-so   okay   fine   tremendous

```
┌──────┬───────┬──────┬──────────┐
│      │       │      │          │
└──────┴───────┴──────┴──────────┘
```

Sentence-completion exercises can be personalized by asking students to supply the names of real people to statements such as:

I work harder than _____.
I am older than _____.
I know more about astrology than _____.
I talk more than _____.
I eat less than _____.

The future tense (or a suitable substitute) can be naturally generated by having students answer a question such as "What will you do tomorrow after school?"

[34] George Giannetti, "Variety in the Advanced Spanish Class," in Frank Grittner (ed.), *Careers, Communication and Culture*, Skokie, Ill., National Textbook Company, 1974, pp. 100–109.
[35] Ibid., p. 106.

Another technique involves a list of questions that students repond to on a yes/no basis. They are encouraged to give reasons for their responses. Sample items translated from various languages are given below:

1   Would you move to another city?
2   Would you go to another school?
3   Would you join the army?
4   Would you go to a bullfight?
5   Would you marry someone of a different religion?

Students can also be asked to prepare their own questions or make up a values continuum of their own based on the types of material presented above.

German teachers can adapt the "lonely hearts" (*Heirastpost*) section of German language newspapers by having the class first learn to read and interpret ads in which people advertise for marriage partners. They further learn to deal with common abbreviations and to convert feet and inches into metric measures for a person's height. Then, using a blank such as those used for ads in Germany, each student prepares his/her own ad for a "mate," including typical personal data (which may be fictitious if the pupil prefers). The teacher than has the items typed onto ditto or mimeo masters and reproduces them for use in the various German classes. The students remain anonymous to everyone but the teacher, unless they choose to identify themselves. Similar techniques can also be used in other languages by adapting the personal want ads section of foreign language editions of popular newspapers.

SUMMARY

The number and kind of techniques for personalizing foreign language programs are virtually infinite. However, certain limits are often imposed by the nature of the student body, the attitudes of the local community, and the resources of the school. For example, in many communities a majority of parents and a substantial number of students want the educational program to be structured in a rather authoritarian manner. In such a situation, a teacher who wishes to develop autonomous, self-reliant language students would be well advised to begin with clearly defined group procedures keeping the class intact and moving students only gradually into small-group activities and independent study. Some teachers have been able to get students to express personal opinions about their feelings and attitudes toward a wide range of topics with no negative repercussions. On the other hand, teachers in nearby communities have found that the simplest open-ended questions have resulted in violent protests from parent groups. Thus teachers must be careful to avoid inadvertently structuring class procedures so as to pressure students into revealing inner feelings and emotions that they are not ready or willing to express. Certain topics are particularly sensitive—namely, those relating to religion, race, sex, and drugs. While such topics often must be dealt with in studying another culture, they are seldom usuable as content for personalizing the instructional program.

However, the existence of potential problems should not deter language teachers from seeking ways to personalize language content. In fact, the future of language instruction in American schools may well depend upon their success in doing so. There are, after all, no more than a handful of young people in any given community who can find satisfaction in the mere learning of linguistic forms and lexical items that are detached from their own perceptions of what is important. Most students, therefore, need to be shown ways of relating that language material to themselves as human beings. If the connection is not made, few students will continue to bother learning the language material. In this regard, a number of psychologists have noted that students must view curricular material as something worth having in their "life space" before any significant degree of learning can occur. Viewed from this perspective, the role of the teacher in individualizing instruction is *not* to establish or participate in some elaborate administrative scheme for more efficiently feeding linguistic data into the minds of passive students. Teaching is instead viewed as the very human process of getting young people to *want* to continue internalizing the linguistic data (by whatever means) so that they can convey and receive genuine messages from fellow human beings. The art of teaching demands that the instructional content be designed to meet the student at whatever developmental level he or she happens to be. The purpose of teaching demands that the student should progress from that point in some desirable direction by means of the discipline to which the teacher is dedicated. Hence, the ideal in personalized instruction is realized in those circumstances where the student perceives the learning activity as contributing to his/her personal intellectual, emotional, or aesthetic growth. Ordinarily the student will not express it in those terms, but the skillful teacher can read the signs given off by those who are experiencing positive growth through the given foreign language. Teachers must also develop a sensitivity to the opposite signals. For example, if students are being dehumanized at their own pace in a program that has been labled as "individualized," the people involved must quickly recognize that fact and act accordingly. There is ample historical precedent for terminating abortive individualized programs. It has, in fact, been the pattern.

BIBLIOGRAPHY

Altman, Howard B., and Robert L. Politzer, *Individualizing Foreign Language Instruction,* Rowley, Mass., Newbury, 1971.
Arendt, Jermaine D., and Percy Fearing, (eds), *The Extended Foreign Language Sequence: With Emphasis on New Courses for Levels IV and V.*

This booklet contains a great deal of pertinent information about individualizing foreign language instruction including a rationale for individualization, basic instructional objectives for individualized programs at various levels of instruction, a description of quarter and semester courses, a discussion of interdisciplinary courses, lists of printed and audiovisual materials suitable for use in individualized programs, a student-interest questionnaire, sample course descriptions, and suggestions for developing individualized units of instruction.

Born, Warren C., ed., *Toward Student-Centered Foreign Language Programs,* Middlebury, Vt., Northeast Conference, 1974.

Catalog of Mini Courses, Department of Foreign Language Education, University of Minnesota, Peik Hall, Minneapolis, Minn. 55455.

Request the annotated catalog of upper-level supplementary units for modern foreign languages from the above address and enclose 25¢.

Disick, Renee S., *Individualizing Language Instruction: Strategies and Methods,* New York, Harcourt Brace Jovanovich, 1975.

The theory and practice of individualizing instruction are dealt with here. The content ranges from a discussion of humanistic theories of motivation to the details of preparing instructional objectives.

Gougher, Ronald L., "Individualization of Foreign Language Learning: What is Being Done," pp. 221–245 in Dale L. Lange, (ed.), *Britannica Review of Foreign Language Education,* vol. 3, Chicago, Encyclopaedia Britannica, 1971.

Gougher, Ronald L., (ed.), *Individualization of Instruction in Foreign Languages: A Practical Guide.* Philadelphia, The Center for Curriculum Development, 1972.

Grittner, Frank M., and Fred H. LaLeike, *Individualized Foreign Language Instruction,* Skokie, Ill., National Textbook Company, 1973.

This book describes in great detail the techniques used in West Bend to individualize instruction by allowing students considerable freedom in the choice of learning pace and learning style. How to construct unipacs, suggestions for laboratory equipment, and evaluation systems are explained and illustrated. An extensive bibliography of books and articles is appended.

Lange, Dale L., (ed.), *ACTFL Review of Foreign Language Education,* vol. 2, Chicago, Encyclopaedia Britannica, 1970.

This 369-page volume contains 12 articles all related to the question of individualizing foreign language instruction. Included are: the rationale for individualization, individualizing the four skills, the use of media and the language lab, teacher certification, the classics, bilingual education, and enrollment trends. Britannica FL Reviews are sponsored by the American Council on the Teaching of Foreign Languages (ACTFL).

Logan, Gerald E., *Individualized Foreign Language Instruction: An Organic Process,* Rowley, Mass., Newbury, 1973.

Love, F. W., and L. J. Honig (eds.), *Options and Perspectives: A Sourcebook of Innovative FL Programs in Action, K–12.*

Contains detailed descriptions of more than 50 of the most innovative programs in foreign language teaching across the country—from "total immersion," study abroad, and individualized programs to minicourses, summer camps, FLES enrichment institutes, and many others. Order from ACTFL/MLA Publications Center, 62 Fifth Avenue, New York, N.Y. 10011. Cost is $3.50.

Neill, Alexander S., *Summerhill: A Radical Approach to Child Rearing.* New York : Hart, 1960.

Strasheim, Lorraine A., "A Rationale for the Individualization and Personalization of Foreign-Language Instruction," pp. 15–34 in Dale L. Lange, (ed.), *Britannica Review of Foreign Language Education,* vol. 2, Chicago, Encyclopaedia Britannica, 1970.

Valette, Rebecca M., and Renee S. Disick, *Modern Language Performance Objectives and Individualization,* New York, Harcourt Brace Jovanovich, 1972.

Valdman, Albert, "Programmed Instruction versus Guided Learning in Foreign Language Acquisition," *Die Unterrichtspraxis* 2 (1968), pp. 1–14.

8

■ Christ, What are patterns for? AMY LOWELL ■ Pattern practice is a means to an end. The end to be achieved is the ability to use the language freely. . . . Traditional exercises . . . are usually a test of whether or not the patterns have been learned, rather than a way of practicing the patterns. POLITZER AND STAUBACH

■The pattern drill

Of all the elements that constitute the new American Method, the pattern drill appears to be the most widely misunderstood. In the hands of a knowledgeable teacher, such drills are capable of producing an exhilarating classroom atmosphere with students sitting on the edge of their chairs listening intently for their cues and responding instantly when called upon. However, when used by a teacher who is not aware of the function and purpose of this type of drill, the results can be as stultifying as the choral chanting of verb conjugations and noun declensions. Visits to hundreds of foreign language classrooms and discussions with colleagues in other states have convinced the author that only a small percentage of language teachers are fully aware of the uses and limitations of pattern practice. Lack of knowledge in this area can greatly limit a teacher's effectiveness since a major portion of most of the newer texts and tapes consists of pattern drills. Furthermore, a number of publishers have produced drills that—although described as pattern drills in the advertisements—actually meet very few of the criteria established by linguists and foreign language educators. The following discussion will attempt to explain what pattern drills are and to describe ways in which they have been successfully used by teachers of foreign language.

WHAT PATTERN DRILLS ARE NOT

It is not uncommon to have a teacher react to a new technique by saying, "Oh, I've been doing that for years." In this statement lies the basis of a problem. For, if pattern drills are to be effective, it is necessary for teachers to desist from certain practices that have been associated with the teaching of languages in the past. Pattern drills have highly specialized purposes not easily furthered by some of the more traditional techniques of years past. It is true that pattern drills can be adapted to traditional purposes in much the same way that a boxcar can be taken off the tracks and converted into a dwelling. However, the boxcar in being converted becomes a substandard residence, while at the same time totally losing its value as a transport vehicle. Similarly, the misuse of a pattern drill usually results in the total negation of its value as a drill device. Thus, although the eight negative criteria listed below may—in their positive forms—have relevance for certain purposes, they are not compatible with the intent of the pattern drill. A teacher who fails on any of the eight criteria may, indeed, be engaged in a worthwhile teaching activity. That activity, however, will have very little in common with the intended application of pattern drills in the foreign language classroom.

Thus, in evaluating oral classroom drills, it can be stated that:

1   It is not pattern practice if the teacher takes the time to call on each student by name.
2   It is not pattern practice if the teacher allows students to reflect for 5 or more seconds prior to responding.
3   It is not pattern practice if the teacher engages in discussion midway through a drill.
4   It is not pattern practice if the students have their books open or if they in any way refer to printed words during the drill.
5   It is not pattern practice unless each successive response in a given drill is directed at a common structural problem.
6   It is not pattern practice if the drill material contains unfamiliar vocabulary.
7   It is not pattern practice unless nearly 100 percent of all student responses are complete, understandable, and fluent.
8   It is not pattern practice if more than 5 minutes are devoted to eliciting correct responses from 25 students using a 10-syllable pattern sentence.

It should be noted that the above criteria refer to a live teacher working with students in the usual classroom situation without a laboratory, electronic classroom, or tape recorder. Naturally, the criteria would be somewhat different in reference to using drills with electronic teaching aids.

Pattern practice does not involve the learning of new vocabulary. In fact, any groping for words on the part of the student tends to destroy the effect of the drill. Therefore, students should have learned all lexical items prior to beginning the drill. Quite often, this prelearning will be accomplished by mimic-memorization drills in which the student first listens to words and sentences modeled by the teacher or by an audiovisual device. The meaning of the individual words may be conveyed by pictures, by English equivalents, or by some of the other techniques discussed in Chapter 6. A commonly used technique during the acquisition of the basic vocabulary is to begin by having the entire class imitate the teacher and then progressively to work down to smaller and smaller group responses until each individual can produce the material with reasonable accuracy. Learning vocabulary in dialog form will often proceed as follows:

1   The entire class imitates the teacher.

2   Half the class recites one part of the dialog while the other half responds with the other part.

3   The roles are reversed and the dialog is recited again.

4   The same technique is used with one row of students designated by the teacher to recite to another row.

5   Finally, individual students recite across the room to one another or stand in front of the class to act out the dialog.

When all students can produce the basic sentences with an acceptable pronunciation, and when they understand the meaning of what they are saying, then the teacher proceeds with the pattern practice. Some teachers will launch directly into the drill without prior analysis of the structures that the students are to learn. Others will provide a grammatical explanation in advance so that the students know what it is they are learning. (See Chapter 6 for a more complete discussion of this matter.)

Phonology drills have been discussed at some length in Chapters 6 and 7. Although such drills often have the same format as the pattern drill, they lack several of the characteristics of pattern-drill exercises. In fact, under ideal conditions, students would have been thoroughly drilled on all the phonological problems that occur in the pattern-drill sentences before they engage in pattern practice. For pattern practice is directed toward the mastery of morphological and syntactical patterns in the target language. It is assumed, however, that the student will be using acceptable pronunciation throughout the structure drills both with respect to segmental and suprasegmental phonemes. In actual practice, the prelearning of phonology is often neglected. There is perhaps no more agonizing a supervisory task than the observation of students who are being systematically drilled upon structural features while simultaneously fixing habits of pronunciation that are unintelligible to the ear of the native speaker. To grasp the significance of this problem, imagine a group of Spanish-speaking youngsters who have learned to sing a song entitled, "Da Gude Sheep Lowly Pope." Only the music provides a cue to the meaning of the lyrics of the popular children's song, "The Good Ship Lollipop." Similarly, pattern practice in French, German, or Spanish that permits total anglicizing of the critical phonemes is of questionable value. Therefore, some form of prior phonology drill is called for, either in classroom or laboratory. The Spanish-speaking children, for example, could have profited by drill work that taught them first to discriminate the differences between the various English vowel sounds and then to produce these sounds.

To develop in students the ability to discriminate between basic phonemes, the teacher may say (or play a tape recording of) two sentences containing the problem phonemes. The drill might proceed as follows for Spanish-speaking students of English:

Teacher: You will now hear two sentences. If they are the same, say "same"; if they are different, say "different."

Tape: Bring me the wash. Bring me the wash.

Student: Same.
  Tape: Same.
  Tape: Wash the car while I'm gone. Watch the car while I'm gone.
Student: Same.
  Tape: Different.

Students learning English as a foreign language would go through a long series of such drills until they could distinguish the difficult sounds without error. Drill tapes ordinarily provide the correct response immediately after the space allowing the student time to react and respond. Thus, with properly designed materials, students can teach themselves if they have a tape recorder at their disposal. Normally they have achieved reasonable mastery when they can produce all the correct answers in the space provided before the taped master voice supplies the correct answer.

The drill above is based upon the principle of matching sounds of minimal contrast that exist in the target language. In addition to this use of minimal pairs, drills can be so structured as to require students to contrast their native language with the conflict sound in the target language.

Teacher: You will now hear two words. Tell which is the French word. If neither word is French say "neither." If both words are French, say "both."
  Tape: Number One A. rue. B. roo.
Student: A.
  Tape: A.
  Tape: Number Two A. rue. B. rue.
Student: Both.
  Tape: Both.

To do away with the necessity of having students give an overt response in English and, incidentally, to provide a running record of student progress, a printed sheet can be used for the student responses. Thus, instead of responding orally, the student would merely circle the one correct answer among the choices provided with each listening drill.

1   *A. both.*
     B. neither.

This would apply only for sound discrimination. The production of the correct sounds would, at the simplest level, involve the ability to imitate sounds that students had learned to identify aurally. At a more advanced stage, they would be required to produce the sounds in response to written stimuli.

In the early stages of learning the dialog utterances, something resembling pattern drill may take place. Most beginning students of foreign language are unable to retain even rather short utterances with sufficient accuracy to repeat them correctly after the teacher. Thus the teacher will build upon small blocks of partial sentences until the student is able to retain and repeat the complete utterance. Often, the learning proceeds as follows, until good control is achieved:

Teacher: Mr. Schmidt is a friend of mine. Now, repeat after me, Mr. Schmidt . . .
 Class: Mr. Schmidt . . .
Teacher: is a friend . . .
 Class: is a friend . . .
Teacher: Mr. Schmidt is a friend . . .
 Class: Mr. Schmidt is a friend . . .
Teacher: of mine.
 Class: of mine.
Teacher: Mr. Schmidt is a friend of mine.
 Class: Mr. Schmidt is a friend of mine.

Some teachers prefer the so-called "backward buildup" on the theory that the correct intonation is more easily preserved that way. The same mimic-memorization techniques would be used, but the sequence would now be:

> *of mine.*
> *a friend of mine.*
> *Schmidt is a friend of mine.*
> *Mr. Schmidt is a friend of mine.*

These and other techniques may form an important part of the language-learning process, but they do not constitute what is commonly understood as pattern drill.

WHAT IS A PATTERN DRILL?

The main function of the pattern drill is to make habituated responses out of those structures in the target language that present significant learning problems to the American student. Proponents of pattern practice see the technique as the link, which had heretofore been missing, in the chain of skill development that begins with dialog memorization and ends when students are able to apply language patterns spontaneously to express what they want to say in an unanticipated situation. To be fluent in a foreign language the student must have an immediate command of all the sounds, structures, and word-order sequences that are used commonly by native speakers. The drill is intended as a means of providing systematic practice on these elements so that the student has the *potential* for free conversation. Whether or not the students actually develop the ability to converse freely depends upon teacher and student followup (or lack of followup). The theoretical underpinnings of pattern practice are partly linguistic and partly psychological. The following are the basic principles on which this type of drill is based:

1 Learning the conflict points in the target language is the priority task in second-language learning.

2 In the initial stages of second-language learning, the listening and speaking skills must be acquired directly rather than being learned from the printed page.

3 Phonology, morphology, and syntax must be learned before the student begins to build a large passive vocabulary.

213

4   Foreign language material is best learned in complete meaningful contexts.
5   Language learning should proceed in small increments from the simple to the complex and from the known to the unknown.
6   Each stimulus should lead to one—and only one—correct response.
7   The student should always receive immediate confirmation of the correctness or incorrectness of a response he has given.
8   Automaticity of response does not develop of its own accord; the teacher must supply the necessary drill work in classroom or laboratory as the basis of fluency.

In a monostructural course, the pattern drill may be the heart of the program. In this case, the first lesson will aim at mastery of certain basic phonemes. Subsequent drills will become increasingly complex as the student gains control of additional sounds, grammatical structures, and vocabulary. Pattern drills are also used with traditional courses, usually in the form of oral drill work as a followup to the study of vocabulary, grammar, and reading selections. Ideally, only those structures and lexical items that lend themselves well to conversational work will be selected for pattern practice. However, in the texts that emphasize antiquated words and idioms, this is often difficult. The traditionally oriented text is designed to build a large recognitional vocabulary for the purpose of reading the "classics." As a result, the nonnative teacher may develop drill material that—to the ear of a native—sounds ridiculous. It is possible to have combinations in the foreign language as absurd as:

Behold yon stripling who driveth a hotrod !
Would'st care to indulge in a tankard of beer ?

In the polystructural course, the pattern sentences are drawn from the basic dialog, which typically consists of present-day conversational material. These "overlearned" dialog sentences provide the student with an ever-expanding supply of memorized lexical items. These items are continually reused throughout the course as the pattern drills focus on the mastery of increasingly complex structures. Some textbooks are liberally supplied with pattern drills that are available in the book and on tape. In other texts, pattern drills are unsuitable or are totally lacking. In any case, it is often necessary to supplement the commercially available drill material with exercises that meet the special demands of a given teaching situation. Thus, the language teacher may find it helpful to have some knowledge of the basic steps to be followed in constructing his/her own pattern drills.

CONSTRUCTING PATTERN DRILLS

The first step is to make a complete vocabulary inventory of all the words, phrases, and expressions contained in each chapter. These items should be listed by parts of speech for easy reference. Thus, if the teacher is designing a drill based upon the agreement of adjectives and nouns, it is a simple matter to leaf through the vocabulary inventories for all previous chapters and to select those nouns, verbs, and adjectives that go well together. The order of listing parts of speech is not of crucial importance, but it is best to follow a consistent pattern from one chapter to the next. A standard dittoed or mimeographed form can facilitate the systematic collection of word inventories. The following form has been used successfully:

TEXT TITLE _____   CHAPTER _____

Nouns   Pronouns   Verbs   Adjectives   Adverbs   Prepositions

Conjunctions   Interjections   Idioms   Grammar   Syntax

The second step is to identify grammatical topics in each chapter toward which the drills will be directed. Then, as vocabulary permits, each point should be covered thoroughly. Also, each drill should focus on one *new* language structure; never more than one. The number of student responses called for in each drill will be determined partly by the availability of vocabulary in the early chapters. Later in the year, the more difficult structure can be drilled again more thoroughly, as additional vocabulary is acquired. One must constantly bear in mind that genuine pattern drills must contain only vocabulary that is completely familiar to the student; and, except for the grammatical point around which the drill is built, the drill should contain only prelearned structure. This constant reentry through pattern practices of structures and vocabulary items can, in theory, gradually eliminate the interference that the native language habit system exerts on the acquisition of a second language.

The final step in producing a pattern-drill script for subsequent adaptation to the classroom or laboratory is the selection of the type of drill that best meets the demands of the structure to be learned. However, the type of drill that one selects will tend to reflect the drill writer's beliefs with regard to whether or not language learning is a cognitive process or a process of stimulus-response conditioning (see Chapter 6). Adherents of the conditioning school will tend to produce simple substitution drills that do not require the student to make any significant changes in the pattern sentence throughout the entire drill. The following is an example of a single-slot substitution drill:

Teacher's cue	*Student's response*
John is here.	*John is here.*
at home.	*John is at home.*
in school.	*John is in school.*
downstairs.	*John is downstairs.*
on the roof.	*John is on the roof.*

215

In this type of drill students are required only to remember the model sentence and to combine the new element with it. However, the new element is furnished by the teacher (or the tape), so that students are required only to imitate what they have just heard. Such a drill could be used in Spanish, for example, to teach the verb *estar*, which would be required in this sequence rather than the verb *ser*. As the students proceed through the drill, their attention is focused on the new elements (at home, in school, and so on.) According to the conditioning theorists, it is best to draw the students' attention away from the critical element in the drill (that is, away from the verb *estar*, in this case) because, by so doing, the structure becomes subconsciously implanted in the students' minds as a new language habit. Thus, when future situations require students to tell where something is, they will automatically use the verb *estar* rather than the conflict word *ser* because they will not have to stop and reflect on the matter. The conflict structure will have become a matter of habit rather than a matter of intellectual choice if enough of this sort of drill is provided. At least this is what the advocates of this type of drill claim.

However, there are others who feel that language learning is a more complex process than this, and that it does actually involve some form of extremely rapid cognition. This group tends to favor drills that require the student to make changes in the model sentence. The student's mental involvement may be simple and sharply focused, but it must be included throughout the pattern. The following is an example of a drill that requires the student to transform the cue given by the teacher:

Teacher's cue	Student's response
John did the work.	The work was done by John.
John set the table.	The table was set by John.
John started the car.	The car was started by John.
John ate the apple.	The apple was eaten by John.

In this case, all the vocabulary is still supplied in advance by the teacher. However, a greater degree of intellectual activity is involved here than in the substitution drill, because the student must be able to instantly transform the active voice to the passive and to make all necessary morphological and syntactical modifications.

THE FORMAT OF THE PATTERN DRILL

Drills that are recorded for laboratory use will usually follow the familiar programming format. At the very minimum they will contain the following:
1   Stimulus or cue.
2   Unrecorded space for the student to respond.
3   The reward in the form of the correct response.
1   A new stimulus.

216

This is the co-called three-phase drill. There are many who believe that this format is inadequate because it tends to frustrate students by compelling them to jump ahead to a new response before they have fully assimilated the old one. Thus some of the newer materials have included four- and five-phase drills, which include the following steps:

1 Stimulus.
2 Space for student response.
3 Reward in the form of correct response.
4 Space to repeat the correct response.
5 Repetition of the correct response.

The fourth step allows students to doubly reinforce a correct response by repeating it or to reshape an incorrect response if they have erred. The fifth step allows them a further opportunity to confirm the responses made in steps two and four.

In the classroom situation, the teacher can provide as many (or as few) reinforcements as the students appear to need. When a drill is being done en masse, the three-phase format is generally considered to be minimal. However, with individual responses, it may not always be necessary to confirm a correct answer. If a student answers correctly and clearly, the teacher may occasionally move on to another student. However, if a student falters or gives an indistinct response, it is considered good practice to supply the correct answer for him or her before proceeding to another student. Later the teacher will return to the student who responded incorrectly and elicit a correct response from him or her.

In either classroom or laboratory, it is important for the teacher or the tape to provide a clear explanation before the students undertake a given drill. In class, the teacher can have the students run through perhaps a half dozen responses chorally until the teacher is certain that they know how they are supposed to respond. If a commercially produced tape contains inadequate instructions, the teacher may record his/her own directions onto tape and splice the revised instructions into the laboratory lesson. Also, the laboratory drill is often best preceded by classroom drill on the identical material, perhaps a day or two ahead of time. The rapidity and accuracy of student response is the final determination of whether or not the students have been adequately prepared for a given drill.

However, assuming the student has been adequately prepared to manipulate all the vocabulary and structural elements contained in a drill, there is still a great need for overexplanation. Even the very bright student can misconstrue the intent of a drill. Those who are less well endowed mentally are almost certain to flounder unless the teacher takes extra precautions in introducing each new type of exercise. Misunderstood drill work leads to confusion, frustration, lack of classroom control, and loss of student respect for the teacher, the course, and the language itself. Thus, an extra minute or two spent on explaining the nature of the drill is generally time well spent. A rule of thumb would be, "Better to overexplain than to suffer the consequences of underexplaining." The following type of explanation is recommended for introducing all pattern drills, both in the classroom and in the laboratory.

Introductory Explanation

In the following exercises you will hear a question and you will reply by saying that you have not seen the person or object that is mentioned. To speak English, it is essential for you to learn to use the pronouns him, her, it, *and* them, *and to put them in the right place in the sentence. For speaking, you must be able to do this instantly, without taking a lot of time to figure things out. This drill will help you develop fluency with these important pronouns. Now, each time you hear the question, you can begin your response by saying, "I haven't seen . . ." Before you reach the end of the sentence, you must know which pronoun,* him, her, it, *or* them, *is the correct response. When you are able to supply all the correct pronouns in this drill without a moment's hesitation, then you have achieved good control of the material.*

Sample of Each Type of Response Expected

In this drill you will hear a question such as, "Where's mother?"
And you will answer by saying, "I haven't seen her.*"*

Then you may hear, "Where's my book?"
And you will answer, "I haven't seen it.*"*

Or you may hear, "Where are the chairs?"
And you will answer, "I haven't seen them.*"*

Or, finally, you may hear, "Where's John?"
And you will answer, "I haven't seen him.*"*

Modeling the Desired Reponse

This is done to "set" the pattern and to reexpose the student to the proper pronunciation and intonation of the utterance.

Now listen to the question and the answer, and repeat only the answer.

Stimulus provided by teacher or tape	Student response follows immediately	Reinforcement supplied immediately
Where's mother?		
I haven't seen her.	I haven't seen her.	I haven't seen her.
Where's my book?		
I haven't seen it.	I haven't seen it.	I haven't seen it.
Where are the chairs?		
I haven't seen them.	I haven't seen them.	I haven't seen them.
Where's John?		
I haven't seen him.	I haven't seen him.	I haven't seen him.

The Drill

From this point on the student must supply the response and listen for the reinforcement of the correct response.

218

Listen to the question and then supply the answer.

Stimulus	Response	Reward
Where's mother?	*I haven't seen her.*	*I haven't seen her.*
Where's my book?	*I haven't seen it.*	*I haven't seen it.*
Where are the boys?	*I haven't seen them.*	*I haven't seen them.*
Where are the girls?	*I haven't seen them.*	*I haven't seen them.*
Where is the chalk?	*I haven't seen it.*	*I haven't seen it.*
Where is my pencil?	*I haven't seen it.*	*I haven't seen it.*
Where is my brother?	*I haven't seen him.*	*I haven't seen him.*
Where are my books?	*I haven't seen them.*	*I haven't seen them.*

Similar procedures would be followed for the three commonly taught languages. Naturally, the explanations would be different because the structures are different in each language. However, there is just as much need for thoroughness of explanation in introducing French, German, and Spanish pronoun drills as there is in introducing English pronouns.

Below are samples of German, Spanish, and French pronoun drills based on the English drill presented above. They illustrate the unique learning problems encountered by the language student who speaks English natively. Note that both grammar and word order present significant learning problems in each language. Thus the drills, as they appear here, could only serve as the culminating exercise to determine whether mastery had been achieved. They would necessarily be preceded by exhaustive practice on the individual pronouns and on all the verb forms used in the drill. Only the stimulus and response are given in the examples below. Also, to highlight the position and form of the direct object pronouns, the repetitive sentence elements have been omitted in the response. In actual practice, of course, the drill would include reinforcement with the correct response and would contain only complete utterances.

German

Wo ist meine Mutter?	Ich habe sie nicht gesehen.
Wo ist mein Buch?	Ich habe es nicht gesehen.
Wo sind die Jungen?	sie
Wo sind die Mädchen?	sie
Wo ist die Kreide?	sie
Wo ist mein Bleistift?	ihn
Wo ist mein Bruder?	ihn
Wo sind meine Bücher?	sie

Spanish

¿Dónde está mi madre?	No la he visto.
¿Dónde está mi libro?	No lo he visto.
¿Dónde están los muchachos?	los
¿Dónde están las muchachas?	las
¿Dónde está la tiza?	la
¿Dónde está el lápiz?	lo
¿Dónde está mi hermano?	le (lo)
¿Dónde están mis libros?	los

Où est maman ?	Je ne l'ai pas vue.	
Où est mon livre ?	Je ne l'ai pas vu.	
Où sont les garçons ?	les	vus.
Où sont les filles ?	les	vues.
Où est la craie ?	l'	vue.
Où est mon crayon ?	l'	vu.
Où est mon frère ?	l'	vu.
Où sont mes livres ?	les	vus.

TYPES OF PATTERN DRILLS

Potentially there is no limit to the number of pattern-drill types. Human ingenuity can certainly discover an endless variety of ways to elicit the desired responses from students of language. Thus, the following list does not pretend to be definitive. It is hoped, however, that the list represents the main types of drills that have evolved during the relatively short history of pattern practice as a distinct teaching technique. Clearly, space does not permit a comprehensive matching of drill types for all conflict points in all three of the commonly taught languages. Indeed, to do this in any one language would be to write a book of considerable length. Thus, the drill formats will be given in English on the theory that the readers will be able to perceive for themselves how each format applies to various structural problems in the foreign language in which they have an interest. (In the following drills the stimulus is designated by " S," the student response by " R.")

Substitution drills

1. Simple substitution (possessive adjectives)

    MODEL:

That gets on my *nerves.*	*That gets on* my *nerves.*
That gets on his *nerves.*	*That gets on* his *nerves.*

S:		*R:*	
	her		*That gets on her nerves.*
	their		*That gets on their nerves.*
	our		*That gets on our nerves.*
	my		*That gets on my nerves.*
	his		*That gets on his nerves.*
	father's		*That gets on father's nerves.*
	mother's		*That gets on mother's nerves.*

2. Substitution with mutation (direct object pronoun)

    MODEL:

I lost my book.	*I lost* it.
I lost my girl.	*I lost* her.

S:		*R:*	
	I lost my pencil.		*I lost it.*
	I lost my book.		*I lost it.*

I lost my boy friend.	I lost him.
I lost my girl.	I lost her.
I lost my tomcat.	I lost him.
I lost my books.	I lost them.

(Note : It is clear that drill 2 would present different types of problems in each of the three languages. In French and Spanish, word order would be a serious conflict point. In German, the use of masculine and feminine pronouns to refer to inanimate objects would cause the most severe problems of interference.)

3. Substitution with choices (use of *some* or *any* in negative and affirmative sentences)

MODEL:

| Do you have some money? (Yes) | Yes, I have some. |
| Do you have some money? (No) | No, I don't have any. |

S:	Do you have some books? (Yes)	R:	Yes, I have some.
	Do you have some money? (No)		No, I don't have any.
	Do you have some examples? (No)		No, I don't have any.
	Do you have some cash? (Yes)		Yes, I have some.
	Do you have some money? (Yes)		Yes, I have some.

4. Substitution with pictorial cues (prepositions with objects)

Pictures are projected onto a screen or are drawn on large cards which the teacher can set in the chalk rail and point to rapidly.

MODEL:

| (Picture of a book in a box.) Where is it? | It's in the box. |

S:	(Picture of book under the box.) Where is it now?	R:	It's under the box.
	(Picture of book beside the box.) Where is it now?		It's beside the box.
	(Picture of book on top of the box.) Where is it now?		It's on top of the box.

5. Substitution with changing slot (ability to perceive various structural elements and to use them appropriately)

MODEL:

Bring him the book.
Bring her the book.
Bring us the book.

S:	Bring him the book.	R:	Bring him the book.
	_____ her _____.		Bring her the book.
	_____ us _____.		Bring us the book.

221

_____ table.	_Bring us the table._
_____ chair.	_Bring us the chair._
Sell _____ .	_Sell us the chair._
_____ car.	_Sell us the car._
_____ them _____ .	_Sell them the car._

6. Substitution through choice (infinitive with conditional)

MODEL:

Would you prefer to walk or ride ?	_I would prefer to ride._
Would you prefer to go or stay ?	_I would prefer to stay._
Would you prefer to read or write ?	_I would prefer to write._

S: _Would you prefer to walk or ride ?_	R: _I would prefer to ride._
Would you prefer to go or stay ?	_I would prefer to stay._
Would you prefer to read or write ?	_I would prefer to write._
Would you prefer to sing or listen ?	_I would prefer to listen._
Would you prefer to sit or stand ?	_I would prefer to stand._

Combination and Conversion Drills

1. Combination (adjective with noun)

MODEL:

There's a boy. He's smart.	_He's a_ smart _boy._
There's a girl. She's smart.	_She's a_ smart _girl._

S: _There's a man. He's clever._	R: _He's a clever man._
There's a girl. She's witty.	_She's a witty girl._
There's a student. He's shy.	_He's a shy student._
There's a building. It's tall.	_It's a tall building._

(Note : In Spanish and French this drill can be used for teaching either word order or adjective-noun agreement. In German, the drill is applicable to the teaching of adjective endings. Masculine, feminine, and (in German) neuter forms can first be drilled separately, then presented as mixed, random stimuli. When the students have achieved a high level of control over the singular noun-adjective combinations, then the plurals can be drilled in a similar manner. Finally, singulars and plurals can all be drilled as mixed random examples.)

2. Combination (word order in a dependent clause or, for those learning English as a foreign language, conversion from past emphatic to simple past tense)

MODEL:

What did _he_ say _? (I don't know.)_	_I don't know what he_ said.
Why did _he_ go _? (I don't know.)_	_I don't know why he_ went.

222

S: *When did he come ? (I don't*   R: *I don't know when he came.*
     know.)

   What did she see ? (I don't   *I don't know what she saw.*
     know.)

   How did they sing ? (I don't   *I don't know how they sang.*
     know.)

   What did they do ? (I don't   *I don't know what they did.*
     know.)

3. Combination (relative pronoun antecedent)
   MODEL:

   I have something. It's new.   *I have something that's new.*

   The student was here   *The student who was here*
    yesterday. He knows you.   *yesterday knows you.*

  S: *It was the older man. He*   R: *It was the older man who*
     bought the car.   *bought the car.*

    It was the blond waitress.   *It was the blond waitress who*
     She brought you the check.   *brought you the check.*

    I saw the boy. He took the   *I saw the boy who took the*
     money.   *money.*

4. Conversion (present emphatic to simple present)
   MODEL:

   Where does he live ? (in town) *He lives in town.*

   Where does he work ? (at the   *He works at the new factory.*
    new factory.)

  S: *Where does he stay ?*   R: *He stays with his folks.*
    (with his folks)

    Where does he eat ?   *He eats at home.*
    (at home)

    Where does she live ?   *She lives in the dorm.*
    (in the dorm)

    Where does she practice ?   *She practices in school.*
    (in school)

    Where does it start ? (at the   *It starts at the beginning.*
    beginning)

(Note : After the students have been drilled thoroughly on the third person
singular forms, "Where does he . . . ," "Where does she . . . ," and "Where does
it . . . ," then the drill is presented in the plural. Sentences such as, "Where do the
boys stay ?" and "Where do they eat ?" are used to elicit the plural verb forms.
Then a third drill introduces mixed singular and plural cues. When the students
are able to cope with both verb types without hesitation, then the first and second
person forms are introduced in separate drills. Final mastery of the pattern has
been achieved when the student can respond instantly and correctly to all persons
both singular and plural—"Why does he . . . ?" "Why does she . . . ?" "Why does
it . . . ?" "Why do they . . . ?" "Why do I . . . ?" "Why do you . . . ?" and so on).

5. Conversion (change of verb tense)
   MODEL:

   Mary is buying a new dress   *Mary bought a new dress*
    today.   *yesterday.*

   He's leaving early today.   *He left early yesterday.*

S: *He's having trouble today.*   R: *He had trouble yesterday.*
   She's singing today.   *She sang yesterday.*
   We're having beans today.   *We had beans yesterday.*
   The bookstore is closed today.   *The bookstore was closed*
                                  yesterday.

6. Conversion through substitution (person-number changes)

   MODEL:

      I am *in the library. (We)*   We are *in the library.*
      He is *in the library. (They)*   They are *in the library.*

   S: *We are in the library. (I)*   R: *I am in the library.*
      You   *You are in the library.*
      I   *I am in the library.*
      Howard   *Howard is in the library.*
      Howard and Mary   *Howard and Mary are in the*
                                   library.

      They   *They are in the library.*

(Note: This type of drill differs from the old chanting of conjugations in that the forms are drilled in random order.)

7. Conversion through addition (subjunctive drill in French and Spanish; use of conjunction *dass* in German)

   MODEL:

      I want to read the book.   *I want* you *to read the book.*
      I want to buy the book.   *I want* you *to buy the book.*

   S: *I want to see the book.*   R: *I want you to see the book.*
      I want to sell the book.   *I want you to sell the book.*
      I want to carry the book.   *I want you to carry the book.*
      I want to bring the book.   *I want you to bring the book.*
      I want to read the book.   *I want you to read the book.*

8. Conversion through substitution (position and form of direct object pronouns)

   MODEL:

      I gave him the book.   *I gave* it *to him.*
      I gave him the fork.   *I gave* it *to him.*
      I gave him the spoon.   *I gave* it *to him.*

   S: *I gave him the car.*   R: *I gave it to him.*
      I gave him the soap.   *I gave it to him.*
      I gave him the hat.   *I gave it to him.*
      I gave him the coat.   *I gave it to him.*
      I gave him the knife.   *I gave it to him.*
      I gave him the cars.   *I gave them to him.*
      I gave him the keys.   *I gave them to him.*

(Note: The above responses, which look so simple in English, present serious problems to the English-speaking student of French, German, or Spanish who is attempting to master the comparable structures in those languages. In German, for instance, the student has a difficult time accepting the fact that it can be a masculine or feminine form. French and Spanish present serious morphological and syntactical problems.)

9. Conversion (declarative to interrogative)

MODEL:

He lives *here.*	Does *he* live *here ?*
He works *here.*	Does *he* work *here ?*
We eat *here.*	Do *we* eat *here ?*

S: *He lives here.*	R: *Does he live here ?*
He works here.	*Does he work here ?*
We eat here.	*Do we eat here ?*
They live here.	*Do they live here ?*
She stays here.	*Does she stay here ?*
We stop here.	*Do we stop here ?*
It ends here.	*Does it end here ?*

10. Conversion through change of grammatical function (transitive versus intransitive)

MODEL:

The prices have risen.	*Yes, he* raised *them.*
The book has lain *there.*	*Yes, he* laid *it there.*

S: *The prices have risen.*	R: *Yes, he raised them.*
The book has lain there.	*Yes, he laid it there.*
The tree has fallen.	*Yes, he felled it.*
It has sat there.	*Yes, he set it there.*

(Note : This type of drill is particularly valuable for contrasting two structures that the student is likely to confuse. Thus it is appropriate for such problems as the difference between *ser* and *estar* in Spanish and the function of the dative and accusative in German. If the student learns to contrast the structures in a drill situation, he may have a better chance of producing the correct forms later than if he drilled on each form in isolation.) Note the following examples :

S : *¿ Es* Juan su amigo ?	R : Sí, pero ahora *está* en casa.
¿ Es Maria su amiga ?	Sí, pero ahora *está* en casa.
Jetzt geht er in *die* Stadt.	Jetzt ist er in *der* Stadt.
Jetzt geht er in *ins* Dorf.	Jetzt ist er *im* Dorf.

Chain Drills

1. One stimulus with two responses (comparative and superlative with the *-er* and *-st* endings)

MODEL:

Tom is tall.	*(Bill)*	*Bill is* taller *than Tom.*
	(John)	*John* is the *tallest in the class.*
Tom is smart.	*(Bill)*	*Bill is* smarter *than Tom.*
	(John)	*John* is the *smartest in the class.*

S_1:	*Tom is funny.*	*(Bill)*	R: *Bill is funnier than Tom.*
S_2:		*(John)*	R: *John is the funniest in the class.*
S_1:	*Tom is clever.*	*(Bill)*	R: *Bill is cleverer than Tom.*
S_2:		*(John)*	R: *John is the cleverest in the class.*
S_1:	*Tom is lazy.*	*(Bill)*	R: *Bill is lazier than Tom.*
S_2:		*(John)*	R: *John is the laziest in the class.*

(Comparative and superlative with the more-most structures)

S_1: Tom is intelligent. (Bill)   R: Bill is more intelligent.
S_2:   (John)   R: John is the most intelligent in the class.
S_1: Tom is incredible. (Bill)   R: Bill is more incredible than Tom.
S_2:   (John)   R: John is the most incredible in the class.

2. Initial stimulus by teacher; students supply additional stimuli

S_1: My name is Miss Smith;
what's your name?
(Teacher points to Paul Conner)

R: My name is Paul Conner;
(turning to designated student behind him)
what's your name?

S_2: (Teacher points to student across the row from Cathy)

R: My name is Cathy Brent;
(turning to designated student across the row)
what's your name?

S_3: (Teacher points to student two rows from Mary)

R: My name is Mary Calder;
(turning to designated student two rows away)
what's your name?

3. Directed dialog or restatement drill (interrogatives)

S: Mary, ask Frank where he is going.

R: Where are you going, Frank?

Frank, ask Mildred what she is doing.

What are you doing, Mildred?

Mildred, ask Henry why he is sleeping.

Why are you sleeping, Henry?

Henry, ask Paul when he is going to wake up.

When are you going to wake up, Paul?

4. Restatement drill (imperatives)

S: Mary, tell Frank to go home.   R: Frank, go home!

Frank, tell Mildred to pay attention.

Mildred, pay attention!

Mildred, tell Henry to wake up.

Henry, wake up!

Henry, tell Paul to hurry up.

Paul, hurry up!

Pyramid Drills

1. Cumulative substitution (word order of time and place)
MODEL:
I was born.   I was born.

S: I was born. (in Bonn)   R: I was born in Bonn.
(on the Rhine)   I was born in Bonn on the Rhine.
(June fifth)   I was born June fifth in Bonn on the Rhine.

(1938)   I was born June fifth, 1938, in Bonn on the Rhine.

2. Cumulative substitution (adjectives: position and endings)

MODEL:

I have a car.   *I have a car.*

S: *I have a car. (new)*   R: *I have a new car.*
  (red)   *I have a new red car.*
  (with spoked wheels) *I have a new red car with spoked*
            wheels.

  (wire)   *I have a new red car with wire*
            spoked wheels.

  (sports)   *I have a new red sports car with*
            wire spoked wheels.

  (chromium)   *I have a new red sports car with*
            chromium wire spoked wheels.

3. Expansion through replacement (syntax)

S: *She lives there.*   R: *She lives there.*
  in Boston   *She lives in Boston.*
  the city of   *She lives in the city of Boston.*
  my sister   *My sister lives in the city of Boston.*
  my older sister   *My older sister lives in the city of*
            Boston.

Translation Drills

Some language educators feel that English should never be used in drills of any kind. Others are of the opinion that English can be used to good advantage as stimuli for certain types of responses. One concern is that the English cue will create interference and will block fluency of response as the student struggles to find suitable equivalents from the native to the target language. The interference of English, however, can be strongly counteracted by using only a highly consistent pattern of responses in the foreign language. Also, if problem lexical items are avoided, the student can focus his attention exclusively upon the pattern which is being drilled. In this way, the English cues can lead regularly to fluent, accurate responses in the foreign language. They have the added advantage of impressing upon the student the nature of foreign language structures which do not exist in English. Thus, for example, the student translating the verb in drill 1 below, becomes acutely aware that the subjunctive is required to express meaning in Spanish whereas the indicative is called for in English.

1. Translation drill (subjunctive in adjective clause)

MODEL:

I'm looking for a man who Busco un hombre que coma
 eats a lot.   mucho.
I'm looking for a man who Busco un hombre que esté loco.
 is crazy.

S: *I'm looking for a man who* R: Busco un hombre que sea
 is intelligent.   inteligente.
 I'm looking for a man who Busco un hombre que tenga
 has money.   dinero.

227

I'm looking for a man who reads a lot.	Busco un hombre que lea mucho.
I'm looking for a man who writes.	Busco un hombre que escriba.
I'm looking for a man who sings.	Busco un hombre que cante.

2. Translation drill (personal pronouns in the dative)

MODEL:

How thoughtless of me.	Wie unüberlegt von mir.
How thoughtless of him.	Wie unüberlegt von ihm.

S: *How thoughtless of her.*	R : Wie unüberlegt von ihr.
How thoughtless of them.	Wie unüberlegt von ihnen.
How thoughtless of us.	Wie unüberlegt von uns.
How thoughtless of you. (familiar singular)	Wie unüberlegt von dir.
How thoughtless of you. (familiar plural)	Wie unüberlegt von euch.

USING PATTERN DRILLS IN THE CLASSROOM

Pattern practice is based on linguistic science and psychological theory But, however sound the underlying principles may be, the success or failure of pattern practice appears to relate as much to the skill and sensitivity of the teacher as to the pedagogical soundness of the drills themselves. The enthusiasm in the teacher's voice, the energetic way he/she moves around the room, the emotional bond the teacher has established between himself/ herself and the class; these, along with many other factors, determine to a significant (if unknown) degree the ultimate success of the drill work. Thus, since teaching appears to be as much an art as it is a science, no list of logically planned techniques is likely to solve all the problems of the foreign language instructor who supposes that good teaching results purely from following the steps in a cookbooklike manual. The apprentice teacher can perhaps gain some important insights from a list of practices that are often identified with successful teachers of foreign language. The following guidelines are based on classroom observation of such teachers.

Preparing the Class for Pattern Practice

1 Students are informed of what they are expected to do when they are called on to respond. Also, the purpose of the drill is made clear.
2 There are no tricks; students know exactly what types of morphological and syntactical changes will occur in the drill. They also know which part of the pattern sentence will remain unchanged during the entire drill. (Making one or two structural changes and pronouncing the sentence correctly at near-native speed is sufficient challenge in itself. Trick questions presented during oral drills tend to be demoralizing).

3 The students have been taught all the phonology that occurs in the drill.

4 The students have been taught the meaning of the structures that they are called on to manipulate so that they are not merely mouthing patterns of sounds that carry no message to the brain. (With some justification, critics have labeled noncognizant oral drills "pitter-patter practice.")

5 The teacher has selected a drill that covers all the important aspects of the structure toward which the drill is directed. (However, it is not necessary, for example, to have 30 different problems merely because there are 30 students in the class. Ten well-devised cues will often suffice. Each cue can be used over again several times.)

6 Several pattern sentences are done chorally to insure that students know how to respond.

7 The teacher checks to make sure that all books are closed and out of sight.

Executing the Drill

1 The teacher gives the cue *first*, then *points* suddenly to a student. (Using the student's name wastes time. Also, it is customary to start with a student who is likely to give a correct response. This gets the drill launched in the right direction and allows the slower students to develop confidence regarding the nature of the expected response.)

2 The teacher repeats the correct response, gives the next cue, and quickly points to another student.

3 The teacher moves rapidly about the room giving the cue and then pointing unexpectedly to the student who is to recite. (With most drills it is best to avoid going up one row and down the other calling on the students in sequence. Otherwise, the only student who is likely to be fully awake is the one who is due to recite.)

4 If a student fails to respond almost immediately, the teacher supplies the correct reponse and goes on to another student. Later, the teacher returns to the nonresponding student after the latter has heard a dozen or more correct responses from other students and from the teacher. (It is considered bad practice to stop and discuss a wrong response or to discuss grammatical principles in the middle of a drill session.)

5 The teacher demands universal attention. By moving constantly around the rows and delivering the cues in totally random order, the teacher can unexpectedly designate any student who shows the slightest inattention. (Some teachers develop special techniques that fit their unique personalities and that keep the students both amused and alert. For example, one teacher will look to the left and then point to a student on the right, or vice versa. Another teacher will begin raising the right hand, and then point suddenly with the left. If properly executed, techniques of this sort can gve youngsters great satisfaction in not being caught off guard. Psychologically, the purpose of such

229

theatrics is to get the students into the spirit of the drill so that they feel the need to be attentive and to react instantly and respond rapidly).

6   Because pattern practice requires intense concentration, teachers normally limit drill time to twenty minutes or less. In this amount of time, the competent teacher can provide rather thorough drill work on three or four basic language structures with all students in a class of (say) 25 responding several times on each structure being drilled.

7   If a majority of students are faltering, groping for words, giving wrong responses, and showing general unpreparedness, it is best to abandon that particular drill, at least temporarily. Assuming that the drill was properly designed, such failure indicates the need for reteaching the basic material.

PATTERN PRACTICE IN THE LANGUAGE LABORATORY

Many high schools are equipped with language laboratories or electronic classrooms that allow all the students in a class to hear the drill material from a central console. Minimal equipment usually includes a headset through which students hear the master program and a microphone that enables students to hear their responses. The same amplifier that makes the students' voice audible to their own ear also carries their utterances back to the console where the teacher can monitor them. In this situation the teacher's role changes drastically where pattern practice is concerned. For, in the laboratory, students do not have to wait to be called on; they are all responding at the same time. Both the stimulus and the reward are supplied by the tape, with a pause for student response. The main function of the teacher is to determine whether the students' responses are generally satisfactory, and to make note of students who are having difficulty with the drill material. If only a few students are unable to perform acceptably, the teacher can prescribe remedial drill work for later laboratory sessions. If most of the students are having difficulties, then it is usually advisable to stop and spend additional time on the structures that are causing the difficulties.

If each student position is equipped with a dual-channel tape recorder, then a more sophisticated set of procedures is possible. In fact, total individualization is possible because, theoretically at least, each student can be working on a different tape and can be learning at his/her own rate with that tape. In practice, however, few teachers have found it possible to cope with more than two or three levels of progress at one time. Many high school teachers are even bewildered by the thought of having any students engage in work that is separate from the lock-step activities of the total class. Thus, even in situations where each student position is equipped with a tape recorder, the following procedures are most often followed:

1   The students record the cue, their own responses, and the reward onto the student track of the tape in the booth recorder.

2   At the end of the drill they rewind the tape and listen to their own responses as compared to the master cues and responses.

3   The teacher monitors the students throughout both of these steps in much the same manner as she/he does in a laboratory that has no tape recorders.

The value of the student playback-compare activities is often questioned. Those who are against the practice contend that students merely tend to reinforce errors and that, for the most part, adolescents are not able to hear their own mistakes sufficiently well to make the playback feature worthwhile. Those who favor student tape recorders insist that students will learn best if they are able to hear themselves on tape with their own voice placed in juxtaposition to a native speaker's voice articulating the same material. The question is largely academic at present. For various reasons, high schools have tended to install the electronic classroom or the laboratory without booths. Thus, the new teacher of foreign languages is most likely to encounter the listen-respond type of equipment if, indeed, the school has a language laboratory at all.

Either type of laboratory can serve as a library installation to which students come before school, after school, or during free hours. Because of their self-correcting feature, pattern drills are excellent for such self-study work. Students who have not mastered a given language structure can request a specific tape from the laboratory assistant or from the teacher who is on duty in the laboratory. The student can then continue going through the drill until he/she is able to provide a correct response to every stimulus within the space allowed on the tape. If the laboratory is equipped with student recorders, the students have the advantage of being able to stop and start the tape and to play difficult passages over and over. In the electronic classroom, the tape is played at the console, and students have no control over its progress. Thus they must listen to it through to the end and request a replay of the entire drill if they wish to hear certain difficult parts over a second time.

EVALUATING COMMERCIALLY PRODUCED PATTERN-DRILL TAPES

Many publishers of modern language textbooks include mention of tapes in their promotional materials. In some cases these "tape programs" are nothing but a recorded version of the contents of the book, which has been read into a microphone by an uninspirational native speaker. In other cases, the tapes follow a programming format, but are deficient in psychological and linguistic sophistication. Therefore, it is seldom advisable to purchase tapes without having examined a representative sampling of the contents of the tape program. As a general practice, foreign language teachers might do well to refuse consideration of any text series that, by policy, does not permit prior examination of the tape program (or at least of a broad sampling of that program). The criteria listed in Table 7 are suggested for evaluating any recorded material which is represented as "pattern drill" or "structural exercises."

231

■7

PATTERN DRILL EVALUATION SHEET

Name of Tape Producer—————————————————————
Accompanying Text (if any) ———— *Language* ———— *Level* ——————

I. Instructions on Tape

    A. Language Used—Instructions Are—
        1. In English   (   )
        2. In foreign language   (   )
        3. In both   (   )
    B. Clarity of Instructions
        1. Purpose made clear   (   )
        2. Purpose not clear   (   )
        3. Highly confusing   (   )
    C. Examples Used to Set the Pattern
        1. 0–3 examples   (   )
        2. 3–5 examples   (   )
        3. More than 5   (   )

II. Quality of Voice

    A. Overall Impression
        1. Good   (   )
        2. Fair   (   )
        3. Poor   (   )
    B. Specific Qualities
        1. Monotonous   (   )   or lively   (   )
        2. Stilted   (   )   or natural   (   )
        3. Too slow   (   )   or normal rate   (   )
        4. Hesitant   (   )   or smooth   (   )
        5. Reading intonation   (   )   or speaking intonation   (   )

III. Quality of Recording

    A. Overall Impression
        1. Good   (   )
        2. Fair   (   )
        3. Poor   (   )
    B. Specific Flaws
        1. Background noise   (   )
        2. Hum   (   )
        3. Volume varies   (   )
        4. Hiss   (   )

IV. Type of Drill

    A. Format
        1. Two-phase (cue-pause-next cue)   (   )   (Not acceptable for laboratory use.)
        2. Three-phase (cue-pause-correct response-next cue)   (   )
        3. Four-phase (cue-phase-correct response-pause-next cue)   (   )
        4. Other   (   )   ——————————————————
    B. Pauses
        1. Too long   (   )
        2. Too short   (   )
        3. Appropriate for near-normal response   (   )

   C. *Content and Structure*
     1. *There is—*
       a. *Sufficient drill on the grammatical point* ( )
       b. *Insufficient drill to fix the pattern* ( )
       c. *Excessive number of problems* ( )
     2. *Length of master utterance is—*
       a. *Short enough to retain* ( )
       b. *Too long to retain* ( )
     3. *The response required by the cue is—*
       a. *Unmistakable* ( )
       b. *Ambiguous* ( )
       c. *Usually clear* ( )
     4. *How many changes must the student make in each cue?*
       a. *One* ( )
       b. *Two* ( )
       c. *More than two* ( )

_____   _____
   (Name of Evaluator)   *(School or Department)*

READING, WRITING, AND PATTERN PRACTICE

In the early years of the post-World War II language-reform movement, it was believed that introduction of the written word should be postponed for weeks or even for months in the high school foreign language course. This belief was apparently based on the fact that some of the more successful intensive programs involving military personnel and adult civilians had required language students to spend 200 hours or more in prereading instruction. The reason for withholding the written word for such long periods in the initial stages of instruction was to thoroughly ingrain habits of pronunciation and intonation, which were supposedly "contamination proof" when the student was subsequently exposed to the written word. Proper prereading instruction did apparently minimize the number of phonological monstrosities, such as the previously mentioned pronunciations of "sheep" for "ship" and "lowly pope" for "lollipop." (The literate person who speaks Spanish will almost invariably equate the written letter *i* in "ship" with the *ee*-sound of his native language and the *o*'s in "lollipop" with the Spanish vowel *o*.)

However, the long prereading period of the intensive programs does not appear to be valid in the regular junior or senior high school program. The intensive courses typically operated from dawn to dark, and therefore a 200-hour prereading period actually represented no more than a few weeks on the calendar. In the high school program, however, 200 hours constitute more than an entire nine-month school year. Yet experience indicates that even the most competent high school teacher can seldom sustain a prereading period of more than a few weeks. (This problem is discussed further in Chapter 9.)

233

There is reason to believe that the graphic symbols, properly introduced, need not be a hindrance, and can actually be a great help in the learning process. The key to the problem may well be the timing and manner of their introduction rather than the length of postponement. Thus, if students have demonstrated the ability to produce a given series of phonemest there is no proven reason why they should not immediately learn to articulate those phonemes in association with appropriate graphic symbols. Nor is there any proof that they should be restrained from writing the symbols in response to auditory, graphic, or pictorial stimuli. Thus, once students have demonstrated good oral control over the phonological elements of a given pattern drill, they may then profitably use the written forms to reinforce their audiolingual learning.

Reading pattern drills aloud can provide oral homework activity that would be unavailable in a purely audiolingual course. Students can be taught to cover the answers while responding orally to the cues on a printed drill sheet. If they then carefully check each oral response immediately, the students will be reproducing some of the learning conditions associated with programmed instruction. When work with phonology has proceeded far enough, the oral reading practice can be sandwiched between purely oral drill sessions on the identical material. It appears that many students cannot distinguish such basic spoken morphological elements as noun, verb, and adjective endings until they have seen them in written form. And it is axiomatic that the ability to distinguish critical sounds is a prerequisite for producing them. Hence, for many "visually dependent" students, the availability of the written word may be an absolute necessity for full success with pattern practice and with other oral-aural aspects of language learning.

Procedures similar to those described above can be used effectively in the area of writing. That is, students can be instructed to write certain sentences contained in the pattern drills in response to the printed cues, while again using the correct response for immediate reinforcement. With all such homework, the teacher must do a good job of selling the students on the need for responding and then immediately reinforcing their own responses until complete accuracy is achieved. Unless they see the value of this procedure, many students will rely on merely copying the answer directly from the text. A few check tests early in the year can serve to convince the copyists of the usefulness of the stimulus-response-reward technique.

Written responses can also be elicited in reponse to oral stimuli, although here it is more ecomonical to select only a few responses from the pattern rather than to have students reproduce the entire drill. Also, short dictations involving recombinations of structures and lexical items from several drills can be useful for teaching spelling and for demonstrating the interchangeability of sentence elements. At the more advanced levels, students can be asked to create their own pattern drills based on rearrangements of prelearned material. To get the students started, the teacher can supply some of the cues and some of the responses and ask the students to complete the pattern. The following is a sample of an assignment that could follow after ten or more verbs had been introduced in the past tense:

234

S: I lose my books.	R: I lost my books.
S: I find everything.	R: I found everything.
S: I see him today.	R:
S:	R: I hated that story.
S:	R: I spent a lot of money.
S: I have a good time.	R:
S:	R:
S:	R:
S:	R:

Gradually, students can be encouraged to create their own entire drills as part of their written work. Those who produce acceptable drills can be allowed to try them out on the class. Students will tend to produce extremely complex and ambiguous drills if left to their own devices. They must be constantly reminded that the rules for constructing pattern drills are: (1) Use only vocabulary that is contained in earlier chapters, and (2) use only those structures that have been presented previously (or use different forms of hose structures.)

THE LIMITATIONS OF PATTERN PRACTICE

As with any other teaching tool, the pattern drill is subject to the danger of being viewed as a panacea for all the problems related to language instruction. Overenthusiastic proponents of the drill have tended to use it to the exclusion of other techniques that are needed to produce free responses in the new language. The next step after pattern practice is to take students from the point where they are able to make minimal changes in cues supplied by the teacher and move them to a point where they are able to use the responses to the cues for generating their own utterances both orally and in writing. Thus the teacher must insist that the students engage in followup work involving the creation of sentences that apply to them personally. In the early stages, it is a great challenge to students to express things they would like to say while limiting themselves to the narrow range of structures they have learned. Pattern-drill work has conditioned them to produce, within a specific pattern, the one right response that the stimulus allows, while the world of reality demands that they produce both the pattern and vocabulary that a new and unpredictable stituation calls for. For example, students may have learned various patterned responses such as: "I haven't seen it," "I haven't seen them," and so on, and they may have been drilled on the structure, "Have you been to class?" "Have you been to the play?" "Have you been there yet?" and so on. Yet students are victims of arrested language development if the method of instruction has left them unable to combine the interrogative structure of the second pattern with the transitive verb and the direct object forms contained in the first pattern. (Thus, if someone mentions that a certain play has been running for several weeks, they should be able to ask, "Have you seen it yet?") Clearly a major function of the teacher, if he/she is to be anything but a warm-blooded

235

drill device, would seem to lie in the direction of developing in students this ability to produce new combinations of the structural elements and lexical items that have been mastered during the drill sessions.

THE STEP BEYOND DRILL PRACTICE

When the students have reached the stage where they are able to read aloud with reasonable accuracy of pronunciation, they can be trusted to produce their own drill responses by referring to the written pattern drills of current and past lessons. Ultimately, the student must become involved in the process of recombining sentence elements that are capable of recombination and of avoiding combinations that are not interchangeable. One way to approach this goal is to require the student to produce a certain number of original utterances in writing, which the teacher then checks for accuracy of form, and meaning. The utterances must be based on structures already learned ; and the vocabulary must be largely that which is contained in the earlier lessons. However, sometimes a few new content words are needed to make the utterances fully adequate. These, too, must be carefully checked by the teacher. The student finally has to present his/her sentences orally, either as a solo performance or in conjunction with another student. Students working in pairs or in small groups can often produce better results than can be achieved singly. In some cases the teacher will appoint a good student to be the chairman of such a study group, which usually consists of no more than 3 or 4 students. The competent student chairman can help minimize the number of errors produced in the written form of the pattern recombinations and can help correct pronunciation errors during the oral stages. During the work periods, the teacher becomes a roving consultant who is available to help when the chairman and his study group get into difficulties. Also, the teacher must be skillful in keeping the students working at the assigned task. Students must not be permitted to engage in social chatter ; nor can loud, disruptive behavior be tolerated. The author has seen such groups working smoothly, quietly, and efficiently. Some room noise is inevitable during the oral practice sessions, but it can be kept at a reasonable level. The teacher can learn to distinguish between purposeful oral activity in the foreign language and nonproductive noise.

Simple visuals can also be used to elicit free application of prelearned structures and vocabulary from an assembled class. The teacher must naturally select the content of the pictorial material very carefully. Simple line drawings depicting situations and actions within the range of vocabulary and structural knowledge of the student are generally better than pictures cluttered with a wide range of items. Also, the skill that the teacher exhibits in drawing out questions and comments from the students is a major determiner of how well the students learn to reapply the structures upon which they have drilled. Some teachers have a special aptitude for stimulating free conversation. The author can recall visiting a class of adult students enrolled in a Spanish conversation course. The teacher entered the room and wrote three words on the chalk board, which in Spanish meant "The Great Society." Then he asked the students to express their opinions in Spanish about the significance of the three words. This simple device was enough to keep everyone talking for the rest of the class period. The teacher's main problem was to restrain some of the more opinionated and vocal students so that the meeker members of the class would have a chance to participate. The Spanish was not always perfect, but the students were motivated to dig deeply into their repertoire of words and structures so that they could express their views on the validity of The Great Society slogan and so that they could react to some of the outspoken opinions of other members of the class. In this situation the step beyond pattern practice had been taken to the fullest. The students were now concentrating on a message they wished to express rather than on the structure of the language per se. Also, the teacher had relinquished his role as chief performer and had assumed a role comparable to that of an orchestra leader. That is, he was indicating who should perform at any given moment, but was not insisting that all conversational exchanges be directed by him.

Naturally, the complexity of material that the students are able to discuss freely will be limited according to how far they have proceeded through the course of study. Consequently, they will be expected to produce utterances that may seem quite childish during the early lessons. Therefore, the teacher must constantly explain to the students the importance of finding ways, however simple, to apply the patterns they have learned to the world of reality; pattern practice in itself is not reality. In most cases such drills are merely a representative sampling of an infinitely expandable pattern. Learning the specific content of the drill is a first small step. Learning to apply the pattern is the important step.

BIBLIOGRAPHY

Delattre, Pierre, "French Prepositional Pattern in Linking a Verb to an Infinitive Object," *Modern Language Journal* 48 (January 1964), pp. 29–35.
Hok, Ruth, "Oral Exercises: Their Type and Form," *Modern Language Journal* 48 (April 1964), pp. 222–226.
Lado, Robert, *Language Teaching,* New York, McGraw-Hill, 1964, pp. 103–113.
Mathieu, Gustav, "Pitfalls of Pattern Practice," *Modern Language Journal* 48 (January 1964), pp. 20–24.
Politzer, Robert L., "Some Reflections on Pattern Practice," *Modern Language Journal* 48 (January 1964), pp. 24–28.
Stack, Edward M., *The Language Laboratory and Modern Language Teaching,* New York, Oxford University Press, 1960, pp. 7–47.

■ *WESTERN REPORTER: "Mr. Ghandi, what do you think of western civilization." GHANDI: "I think it would be a good idea."* ■ *Reading maketh a full man; conference a ready man; and writing an exact man. . . .* ■ *. . . some books are to be read only in parts; others to be read, but cursorily, and some few to be read wholly, and with diligence and attention.* FRANCIS BACON ■ *To translate is to betray.* ITALIAN PROVERB

■Learning the four skills in a cultural context

The specific objectives of a foreign language program with regard to the four skills of listening, speaking, reading, and writing have been stated earlier in considerable detail (Chapter 5, Tables 3 through 6). However, because of the decades of misunderstanding regarding the function of English in relation to the foreign language it might be well to mention a fifth skill at this point—the skill of translation. Many European countries have entire educational institutions or university departments devoted to teaching this skill. In fact, it is a recognized profession in some countries. If one examines the nature of this profession in detail, one will discover that there are various levels of specialization. Some, for example, will become specialists in translating the written material of certain specified professional or business occupations. Often, the specialization will go even further; it may be found, for example, that a given specialist will limit his/her focus to (1) written material, (2) in the medical field, and (3) from English to French only (not the reverse). The same is true of interpreters. The people who transform oral rather than written material from one language to the other tend to be skilled only in one direction. Thus it is perfectly ordinary for an interpreter to be able to understand everything that is said in a Spanish conference and to be able to give instant American English equivalents for the comments of each speaker, and yet not be able to interpret back the other way without making errors which may offend or puzzle the Spanish-speaking audience. It is because of the near impossibility of finding persons skilled in two-way translation that most important conferences involving worldwide political decisions are staffed with specialists who can translate in one direction for each language involved. Despite all precautions, serious mistranslations occur at the highest levels. Former Premier Khrushchev's allusion to his belief that communism would outlast capitalism was sensationalized into headline news when his comment was rendered into English as, "We will bury you." The activist American mentality apparently interpreted this statement as meaning, "We will bulldoze you under." The Russian expression carried a more tranquil connotation. It conjured up the image of people standing around the grave of the deceased; of burying someone who was dead.

The purpose of this discussion is to point out the complete futility of expecting novice language students in the secondary school to translate from one language to the other. Even the professionals, after long years of rigorous training, make serious blunders. The process of rendering an equivalent form of expression from one language to another is so perilous, so exacting, and so tied to the semantics of the native language that its validity as an instructional objective must be seriously challenged by secondary school teachers of foreign language. By its very nature, active translation from one language to another introduces a great deal of error, confusion, and misunderstanding into the learning process. Thus, if any work is done at all with this skill, it would seem logical to introduce it only after the student has achieved a high degree of competency in the direct use of the four basic skills. All this does not exclude the discriminate use of English in the teaching process as described in Chapter 6. Instead, we refer here to the *active* skill in which the student is expected to translate on daily exercises and on tests and examinations. Each use of translation—either from target language to English or the other way around—is a step away from the development of direct communication skill. In a real sense it is a short-circuiting of the objectives of the American Method, which call for direct use of the four language skills.

LISTENING COMPREHENSION

The necessity for speed in comprehending auditory signals distinguishes this skill from the other three. In a large number of language situations there is no opportunity for slowing down the flow of speech reaching the ear. For example, in listening to a play, a lecture, a movie, a television program, or a radio broadcast, the listener has but one chance to hear what is spoken, and has no control over the rate of delivery. Even in a face-to-face conversation, communication is badly disrupted if the nonnative speaker is forever asking the native to repeat what he has just said. Therefore, the full development of listening skill demands massive exposure to a wide variety of native speakers discussing familiar topics and using a normal conversational delivery. During the beginning stages of learning a new language, tapes, records, films, and live visitors from foreign countries can be used to present such listening exercises. By using rearrangements of familiar lexical items, the teacher can expose students to listening experiences of increasing complexity. Any unfamiliar items that appear in such presentations must be taught in advance so that the student's attention is not drawn toward puzzling new vocabulary items and away from the message carried by the exericse. Students tend to become discouraged if they are constantly stopping to ponder the meaning of new words or the function of totally unfamiliar structures. However, new vocabulary items that appear in listening exercises need not be taught for active use. Prior to playing a tape or showing a film, a few minutes will often suffice to develop aural recognition of the half dozen new words that appear on the tape or sound track. Any other aspects of the filmed or recorded material that tend to confuse the student should also be explained in advance. It is considered good practice to follow each listening exercise with a short quiz to determine whether or not the students have actually understood what was said (see Chapter 11).

In the other "passive" skill (reading), considerable effort has been expended to produce a wide variety of high-interest reading selections of graded difficulty. Unfortunately, the producers of commercial tapes and records have not devoted equal time to the development of interesting material for listening. All too often the listening exercises consist of nothing more than a taped version of the identical material that the students are learning to say or that they must subsequently write. Such activities are a necessary part of language learning, but they are no substitute for practice in listening directly to an aural message that one has not previously heard. Ideally, such listening material would consist of highly interesting stories, plays, and poems that are graded in difficulty. Thus, at the early levels, transcriptions from foreign radio programs and foreign films intended for native audiences are of little value. The density of new words, slang expressions, and unfamiliar structures is too high to permit even minimal comprehension. The teacher must either adapt existing materials or must produce his or her own.

SPEAKING ABILITY

Speaking is a productive skill that requires the learner to retrieve almost instantaneously the precise sounds, grammatical forms, word-order arrangements, and content vocabulary that will express what he/she wants to say in an unanticipated situation. Nonnatives can be allowed an extra second or two to react to an auditory stimulus and can articulate their sentences more slowly and deliberately than a native speaker without serious loss in communication. However, excessively slow delivery will usually make the native speaker uncomfortable. The resultant emotional tension soon causes the conversation to bog down entirely as the oversolicitous native speaker begins to finish sentences for the nonnative and to correct errors. All too often, conversation between an American and a foreign acquaintance terminates when the latter diplomatically shifts from his native language into English. Each time this happens, another black mark is chalked up against the American foreign language community, and the stereotype of the American as a monolingual simpleton is further reinforced. The trend toward dialog memorization and pattern drill has done much to accelerate the number of syllables a student can articulate in a given number of seconds and has, perhaps, improved pronunciation, intonation, and speed of reaction to specific stimuli. However, unless the teacher deliberately involves the students in the spontaneous creation of utterances that express their own ideas, the newer techniques appear to produce results that show little improvement over older techniques. In short, it appears that one learns to express oneself only by being induced to practice self-expression during each step of the learning process. The teacher cannot wait for free conversation to "jell" as an automatic product of years of drill work or rule memorization. The attitude that language is a way to communicate the student's own ideas can be established during the first few days of the course. In developing free oral expression, the teacher must allow a wide tolerance for student errors even though the teacher may secretly note errors for the purpose of assigning subsequent remedial drill. The teacher must resist the tendency to break in and correct publicly each student attempt at self-expression. Overcorrection of young children who are learning their first language can produce stuttering. Overcorrection of adolescents who are learning a second language will produce silence.

Ultimately the student must be able to respond intelligently to what someone else has said in the foreign language, if speaking is one of the objectives of the course. Some critics claim that students in audiolingual programs are no better off in this respect than those who are trained traditionally. Wilga Rivers speaks of "students who perform very well in a pattern drill session, and can repeat memorized phrases perfectly in directed dialogue, but are at a loss to find correct ways of expressing their thoughts in a spontaneous conversation."[1] Such students have only learned to produce a specific response to a specific cue (see p. 132). In free conversation, however, the student "must select a response that will convey his meaning, not one that will fit the situation in an automatic sequence."[2] Apparently, free use of the language does not happen accidentally; the teacher must arrange it. The grammarian requires students to memorize "rules of correctness," which they are then supposed to apply as they speak. The direct-method teacher advocates a sink-or-swim approach in which only the foreign language is used in class; the student must speak to survive academically. The audiolingual teacher tries to teach control of structure in advance through pattern practice. Then students are supposed to apply the patterns to the real world—that is, to use the patterns flexibly to express what they want to say as the situation demands. The following points reflect the reactions of veteran language teachers to the problems associated with teaching free expression.

The Classroom Environment and Free Expression

Most students (teenage and older) are somewhat hesitant in speaking *English* in front of a class. It is unrealistic, therefore, to expect flawless, free expression in the foreign language. Overexpectation on the part of the teacher can kill students' desire to express their own thoughts. Yet students

[1] Wilga M. Rivers, *The Psychologist and the Foreign Language Teacher*, Chicago, University of Chicago Press, 1964, p. 68.
[2] Ibid.

241

must learn to recombine what they have learned in a way that is appropriate to a new and unexpected situation. They must be able to do this with each new grammatical structure but within the limits of their active vocabulary. Under present circumstances it seems that this phase of learning must be carried out in the classroom if it is to be done at all. Some of the dangers of teaching free expression are the following:

1   The tendency to jump in and correct student errors is almost certain to lead to embarrassment, stammering, timidity, and silence. The principle of immediate correction does not apply here. Errors are bound to be numerous; they can be noted secretly for subsequent drill.

2   The free-expression period should be identified in the students' mind as a time when they are trying to express their thoughts in the language rather than being preoccupied with the mechanics of language. This calls for a relaxed, nonpressured atmosphere. Laughter is inevitable as students produce nonstandard French, German, or Spanish utterances. Teacher and students must accept these blunders as an unavoidable part of the trial and error process. (We must remember that in learning English, children often say things like "I goes" or "He brung it" or "He disappeared it.")

3   Students do not learn free conversation by hearing the teacher; they learn by conversing freely *themselves*. (Some teachers do most of the talking themselves, and then wonder why the students are not more fluent. It is an occupational hazard.)

Sample Techniques for Teaching Free Expression

1   It may be that the main value of visuals is not to teach culture or to present new vocabulary but rather to elicit free conversational responses from students. One teacher was observed using slides of the local community to draw Spanish conversation from her students. The following types of responses were elicited by allowing students to respond to a picture of the local drugstore:

I have a coke there after school.
Mr. Knight is the owner of the drogueria.
That's not the right word.
Why not?
You can't get a coke in a drogueria.
That's right; they only sell . . . .
Who knows the word for "drugs"?

Such comments are not always rapid-fire; there are many long pauses. But once a few comments have been made, other related remarks tend to build on them as the students discover that the foreign sounds can actually be related to the real world as they know it.

2   Map work can be used in a fashion similar to the foregoing. In both cases, however, one must guard against excessive and unnatural question-and-answer techniques.

242

Where is Spain? Spain is east of Portugal.
Where is France? France is east of Spain.
Where is Germany? Germany is east of France.
Where is Poland? Poland is east of Germany.
(and so on for Russia, Alaska, Canada, Greenland)

This is a chain-type pattern drill; it bears little resemblance to normal conversation.

3   Summer camps and trips abroad can be effective if they are properly managed (see p. 265).

INTRODUCING THE SOUNDS OF LANGUAGE
BEFORE THE GRAPHIC SYMBOLS

According to proponents of the American Method, prereading instruction is essential to developing sound language habits. It is felt that, if reading is to reinforce the audiolingual skills rather than contaminate them, then thorough drill on phonology must always precede reading. This does not mean that the entire phonological system must be mastered before the student is allowed to read or write. Indeed, the transition from speaking to reading has been carried off successfully by skilled language teachers with a delay of only a day or two in the introduction of the written word. Yet the prereading phase, however short, is important because of a simple fact of learning psychology, namely, that it is easier to form a new habit directly than to form the same habit by undoing a wrong one. To introduce students to French, German, and Spanish through the writing system is to guarantee the formation of bad habits. Because the alphabets of these languages are almost identical to that of English, the unwitting student quite naturally assumes that the letters represent English sounds. Thus, for example, students of German will pronounce *Buch* as [buk] and students of Spanish will say something like [pearō] for both *perro* and *pero* unless their prereading training has taught them to cope with these critical phonemes. The result would be garbled communication in both languages. The German native would hear *Bug* (ship's prow) instead of the intended word referring to "book" and the speaker of Spanish would hear a rather unintelligible sound which is neither the word for "dog" nor the conjunction "but."

According to this line of thought, the language student should first learn to produce such troublesome sounds as the French, German, or Spanish *r* without ever hearing these sounds referred to as "*r*-sounds" and without seeing the graphic representations (namely, *R*, *r*, *rr*, and so on). Linguistically, the teacher is putting the cart before the horse when he/she teaches students to pronounce letters. (In learning to read the native language it is always the other way around; the student learns to associate letters with sounds he has long known how to produce.) However, this in itself is not the chief reason for beginning with speech rather than with writing. Perhaps the main reason for the rejection of the writing-first approach is the abundant evidence that this system has produced generations

243

of language students with almost irremedially bad pronunciation in various foreign languages. Apparently the initial introduction of foreign language material has a lasting influence on the learner's pronunciation. Thus, the negative results of allowing beginning students to associate foreign language graphemes with phonemes that they have not mastered orally encourages excessive interference from the native language habit system. It may be that the association is so strong in many learners that the mere sight of a letter of the alphabet triggers the nervous system in such a way that the tongue is prevented from assuming the necessary positions for foreign language articulation. On the other hand, if students are asked to place their tongue in certain unfamiliar positions without reference to any familiar letters of the alphabet, they may well learn to articulate the problem sounds and to drill them to the point where they become well habituated. At that point, reading the foreign language graphemes aloud becomes not "a funny way to pronounce English letters" but rather a logical representation for newly acquired sounds.

There are other reasons given for preceding the reading phase with oral drill. One reason stems from the belief that even rapid silent reading is accompanied by subvocalization of the sounds for which the graphemes stand. Thus the development of direct foreign language reading (as opposed to translation back to English) would best be done in association with genuine foreign language sounds. A second reason has to do with the meaning of words. As students read they must draw meaning from the lexical items that come into view as they scan each line of the page. If they have drilled on the basic words in meaningful contexts, they will not have to rely for meaning on English equivalents (which, as we have seen, are never really "equivalent").

WITHHOLDING THE WRITTEN WORD FOR EXCESSIVE PERIODS OF TIME

Children beyond the primary grades are perfectly well aware that French, German, and Spanish appear in written form. By the age of ten, if not earlier, they have already become quite dependent upon the English writing system as a standard memory aid and as a useful learning tool. Therefore, it appears unrealistic to expect students to adjust readily to an approach that forces them to rely solely upon listening and speaking for lessons done in class. For homework, the purely audiolingual assignment becomes an even more questionable practice. In fact, great enthusiasm for the "prolonged period of prereading instruction" appears to have had no substantial body of research to justify it as far as foreign language instruction in the conventional secondary school environment is concerned. There is even evidence to indicate that the length of the time lag between the learning the auditory symbol and the introduction of the written symbol is not of major significance as long as the teacher exercises care in the way that the written symbol is

244

introduced.[3] Furthermore, any advantages realized from an excessively long prereading period may be more than neutralized by the tendency of youngsters to surreptitiously invent their own orthography based on English spelling. Students who secretly devise their own writing system are not only bypassing the entire intent of the prereading period, they are also developing unacceptable spelling habits that will have to be subsequently unlearned. Thus, the ideal system would seem to be one that capitalizes on the students' acquired taste for the written forms of language while minimizing the negative transfer caused by the premature introduction of those forms. One way to accomplish this balance is to introduce only as many of the problem phonemes as the teacher is capable of dealing with. Thus the students can begin seeing the written forms of French, German, or Spanish during the very first lesson if the teacher introduces only words containing letters that present no serious pronunciation problems. For example, the French *n*, the German initial *d*, and the Spanish *ch* can be introduced early in certain contexts without serious danger if the student has learned them audiolingually a day or two earlier. The same cannot be said of the French *r*, the German *ch*, and the Spanish *d*. These require thorough oral drill and careful introduction of the graphic symbols to be certain that the student is not reverting to the strongly ingrained sound-to-letter association of the English language. The teacher can find ways to select only a few of the "pitfall" phonemes for reading presentations in each of the early lessons. The other part of the reading task in the early lessons is to learn new orthographic representations for sounds that are similar (if not quite identical) to sounds that exist in the English language. With a little ingenuity, a large number of meaningful utterances can be created using only "nondangerous" letters along with those critical phonemes that have been mastered in earlier lessons. Naturally, with the passage of time and with constant reintroduction of drill upon the critical phonemes, the number of "safe" letters will grow. When most students have mastered the main problem phonemes in association with the appropriate graphemes, then the writing system can become an extremely useful tool to be used in support of the listening-speaking skills. For, at that point, students can begin to rely on written stimuli for oral reading and for listening to other students read aloud. ·

READING ABILITY

True reading means the direct communication of meaning from the printed page to the reader's mind. Rapidity of reading comprehension is not so crucial as is the case with listening. However, word by word plodding through a page is not reading, nor is it truly reading if students must stop several times on each line to look up English equivalents for new words. Students are reading when they are engaged in the process of drawing

---

[3] Ibid., pp. 111–113.

meaning directly from the black marks that (in the common European languages) run from left to right across the page. As with the other skills, the student's knowledge of English can be both a help and a hindrance in the development of reading skill.

The advantages of having already learned to read English are: (1) Students have already gone through the difficult process of learning to associate graphic symbols with sounds and their meanings in English; in learning the English alphabet, they have mastered most of the alphabetic symbols used to represent French, German, and Spanish in writing. (2) The habit of scanning sentences from left to right is so well established that they assume it is the normal way to read a language. (These same habits can have a negative effect upon the learning of languages that are nonalphabetic or that are not read from left to right across the page.)

The disadvantages of having already learned to read English are: (1) The students' English pronunciation habits strongly influence their articulation of foreign language phonemes when they read aloud; it is quite likely also that students tend to subvocalize with an English accent. (2) Students are inclined to think that foreign language words are symbols that stand for English words and that the semantic range of any given vocabulary item is roughly identical with an "equivalent" that is given in a bilingual dictionary. Worse yet, they may draw completely false cultural inferences from translated items or from words that look deceptively like English words. This tendency can be counteracted in advance by using visuals and cultural notes to explain, for example, that bread in France is a nourishing, unsliced loaf that forms a more significant part of the Frenchman's diet than the sliced white fluff that the American purchases in a wax or plastic wrapper. Similarly, the German student can be taught that a *Gymnasium* is neither a sports quadrangle nor a comprehensive high school in the American sense. With more difficulty, the American student of Spanish can be taught that the word *corrida* refers neither to "bull" nor to "fight" and that few Spaniards or Latin Americans view the contest as a slaughter of helpless animals. One of the most challenging tasks in the teaching of reading (as well as the other skills) is the establishment of genuine cultural referents. Temporarily, the problem can be sidestepped by having the students use the foreign language to refer only to their own environment. However, if this process is carried too far, the students may never become involved in learning the genuine foreign culture referents. Until these are introduced, the students are merely learning a sort of secret code in which strange sounds and written symbols are used to refer to American realities.

Because the student comes to the high school class with the ability to read English, the teacher of foreign languages need not repeat the process of requiring students to read infantile sentences such as, "Look Jane, look!" "See Spot run." "Run Spot, run!" In fact, adolescent students are almost certain to rebel against any content that they associate with a period of development tracing back to their early childhood. Conversely, they will tend to reject material that is written too specifically for the college-age student. Thus, if students are to be induced to stay in the foreign language program and to develop direct-reading ability, they must pass through an inter-mediate reading stage during which they are exposed to a great deal of material that is sufficiently simplified to fit their reading ability but is also tailored to their level of intellectual sophistication. In short, if they do not find both challenge and pleasure in reading directly in the foreign language, they will either abandon the venture entirely or else they will resort to prac-tices that completely short circuit the entire reading process. Perhaps one of the greatest travesties of foreign language education has resulted from the premature reading of literature. Evidence of the absurdity of this practice can be found in any college or university bookstore. One needs only to examine the shelves containing used literature books in any foreign lan-guage and note the vocabulary sections blackened and ragged from over use along with the text sections in which students have scribbled an English equivalent above every third or fourth word. The grinding drudgery of look-ing up several dozen words per page may be dear to the tradition of the "grim" humanist; but the process bears little resemblance to anything that, in the native language, might be called reading. If genuine reading is to take place, students must take full advantage of the skill they bring to the lan-guage class from their native English. Yet, at the same time, they must be insulated against the interference caused by that language.

The Primer Stage of Reading-Skill Development

The American Method calls for an early phase of skill development in which reading is based entirely upon *material that the student has learned to say and comprehend aurally*. During the period that typically encompasses the first two years of high school foreign language study, a series of carefully sequenced steps are supposed to lead to direct-reading ability within the limited vocabulary range of this early level. It is assumed that all elements of phonology, morphology, and syntax that are included in subsequent read-ing exercises have been thoroughly learned through oral drill work. The very first reading on any given lesson will involve material drawn from the oral drills. Students will first see the identical written representation of utterances that they have mastered audiolingually. During this process of learning to read, the following procedures seem advisable:

1   With books closed, the students hear the teacher read a group of utterances containing the target graphemes. (The teacher checks to make certain that the class understands the meaning of all utterances.)

2   With books open, the students follow each utterance as the teacher reads aloud. (Students do not read aloud.)

3   With books open, students read chorally trying to imitate the oral delivery of the teacher (or tape.)

4   The teacher spot-checks student performance by calling upon indi-viduals to read aloud. (Again, going up one row and down the other is considered bad practice. The teacher is likely to get better participation by designating students in random order and by taking the sentences out of sequence. Thus, the individual reading might begin by having

several students in different parts of the room take turns reading sentence three. Next, three students might be designated in turn to read sentence one, four students sentence two, and so on. Then the teacher would move unpredictably about the room having each sentence read three or four times by different students until all sentences have been covered and until all students have participated.) From the oral reading, the teacher can get a general impression of how well students are able to associate the difficult graphic symbols with the sounds for which they stand.

5   Throughout steps 3 and 4, the teacher follows each student response by reading the utterance correctly.

After the students have demonstrated their ability to read prelearned material in an acceptable manner, the next step is to learn to read the problem graphemes in *unfamiliar contexts*. The following procedures seem advisable at this juncture:

1   Familiar structures and known lexical items are reorganized to convey an unfamiliar message.
2   Sheets containing the new sentences are passed out to the students or are projected on a screen.
3   Students are allowed reasonable time to read the new passages, after which the steps of choral and individual oral reading described above are repeated.

The other essential ingredient in the "primer phase" of reading development is evaluation. At various points, students are tested on their ability to read aloud the target graphemes understandably and to draw meaning from recombinations of the vocabulary and grammatical forms that have been presented earlier (see p. 345).

One of the chief objectives of the primer stage of reading development is the unequivocal establishment in the student's mind of the relationship between the sounds of the foreign language and the graphic symbols used to represent those sounds. Such matters are difficult to prove, but there is considerable circumstantial evidence to the effect that effective reading (even silently) requires a strong base of listening and speaking. It appears that reading is actually a slowed-down form of listening, in which readers first receive visual messages through the eyes. Following this step, they convert the graphic symbols to subaudio symbols, which they then decode through the same channels of thought as those that lead from the ear to the brain. Thus, any ambiguity in interpretation of the sound represented by the written symbol may slow the process of drawing meaning from the printed page. To illustrate this we can show what would happen in reading English if the reader suddenly encountered the sentence. "The *fough* is a rare bird living in the *Treaux* region of Africa." The reader is greatly slowed by the two unknown words, not because there is any doubt about their meaning, but because he/she is unsure of how to pronounce them. Does the first word rhyme with "cow?" Or perhaps it has the same sound as "too" or "tow" or "fluff.' What is the vowel sound of the second word? Is the x silent? All of these questions can be pondered in a second or two and the reader can decide to settle for a "foo bird" and a "Trucks region" without being concerned about the accuracy of his/her pronunciation. He/she is not likely to encounter either word again, and the few seconds of lost time are not significant.

However, in reading a foreign language, every sound can be as difficult as *fough* or *Treaux* if reading is introduced before phonology has been mastered. In this situation readers have two alternatives: they can assign English sound values to each syllable or they can stop and look up the phonetic representation of each word (assuming that they have a dictionary with phonetic spellings and that they know how to use it). From the standpoint of modern learning goals, neither alternative is satisfactory. The first encourages unacceptable habits of pronunciation, and the second makes genuine reading an impossibility. Thus the reasons for heavy emphasis upon listening and speaking drill in the American Method go beyond the mere importance attached to these skills as valid learning objectives. Of equal importance is the belief that an audiolingual command of the language is the indispensable underpinning of reading and writing skills.

The Intermediate State of Reading-Skill Development

Up to this point, the high school student will often have an active vocabulary of less than 1000 words. His passive, or recognitional, vocabulary may be several hundred words higher, but it is unlikely to exceed 2000 items. However, we know that, if reading ability is to proceed beyond a type of material containing only slight variations of the topics contained in the beginning lessons, then a large recognitional vocabulary will be needed. It has been mentioned earlier that there are between 5,000 and 10,000 high-frequency lexical items that recur constantly when communication takes place in European languages. In the area of reading, the meanings of these high-frequency words must be learned in their most common contexts if the student is ever to be liberated from dependence on a bilingual dictionary. Low-frequency words (and unusual meanings of common words) can be guessed at or can be looked up in a dictionary. However, research indicates that the density of new items cannot exceed one per thirty-five words of text, if genuine reading by direct association is to take place.[4] Thus the key question is, how does the language student acquire the large recognitional vocabulary necessary for such "liberated" reading? The intermediate stage of reading development (a period covering roughly the third—and much of the fourth—year of high school) is devoted to this expansion of vocabulary. Most of the third year is also devoted to the further mastery of basic language structures. However, long after morphological problems have ceased

[4] George Scherer and Michael Wertheimer, *A Psycholinguistic Experiment in Foreign Language Teaching*, New York, McGraw-Hill, 1964, pp. 93–94.

to trouble the would-be reader, vocabulary deficiencies continue to plague him/her.

During the last half of the 1960s, a number of proposed solutions to the vocabulary-building problem had already been incorporated into the texts and readers in common use. Implicit in each of these solutions is the total rejection of the practice of memorizing word lists in which a precise English meaning is ascribed to each "matching" word in the target language. The tremendous inefficiency of word-pair memorization had long been recognized, but many teachers had continued to employ this technique simply for lack of a suitable alternative. Also, the perpetuation of the grammar-translation method in colleges and universities may often cause the high school teacher to continue the use of translation as a means of testing reading ability and to continue with word-list memorization as the method for learning vocabulary. The fear among secondary school teachers that their students will not do well when they go on to college is often given as a reason for adhering to traditional methods. Nonetheless, a considerable number of teachers at both college and university levels have persevered in their attempts to develop direct-reading ability (as opposed to decoding the foreign language into English). Chief among the techniques used to build a vocabulary sufficient for the development of this ability are the use of inference, the use of programming techniques, the use of graded readers, the use of vocabulary-building exercises in the target language, and the use of visuals. A few texts have incorporated nearly all of these techniques into their overall format. Others, perhaps unfortunately, have relied heavily upon only one or two of the possible approaches. However, there is nothing to prevent the teacher from going beyond the text and utilizing techniques compatible with the ultimate goals of the instructional program. The following is a discussion of the more commonly used techniques related to the building of vocabulary.

Inference: the sensible guess. For purposes of illustration, let us concentrate for a moment upon the third word in the following sentence:

Suddenly the flangel *swooped out of the sky and snatched an unsuspecting spider monkey from the midst of his chattering companions.*

Assuming that the reader knows the meaning of the other twenty words, is there any doubt about the meaning of the word *flangel*? From the contextual clues one can immediately infer that a *flangel* is a very large predatory bird living in the jungles of Central or South America. It might aid retention to see a picture of a bird with a pointed beak, sharp talons, and colored plumage or to read a marginal note describing the bird either in English or the target language. However, it is questionable whether such obvious items ought ever to be glossed. Not only is it expensive for the publisher to produce the extra references but also their inclusion deprives students of the opportunity to cultivate the art of sensible guessing in the target language; an ability which they have developed to a high degree in their native English. It is a simple fact that growth in vocabulary accompanies Americans throughout their lifetime. Yet only a tiny portion of this repertoire of words can be accounted for through systematic word study or through reference to a dictionary. Occasionally they make wrong guesses (the author has heard a school janitor state that "smoking is strictly *verbatim* here"), but, by and large, normal Americans learn to use, with remarkable accuracy tens of thousands of words they have never consciously studied.

Naturally, there are greater problems with guessing meaning for young adults learning a second language than for those same persons when they are working with their native tongue. Their most obvious problem is vocabulary. Guessing the meaning of *flangel* is no great task when the other words are known. However, let us change a few of the content words and see what happens to the meaning:

Suddenly the flangel gleeped *out of the* simmel *and snatched an unsuspecting* brill *from the midst of his* fribbeling *companions.*

Now, with the number of unknown words increased from one to five, the ability to infer the meaning of the 21-word sentence is almost nil. Yet this sort of nonsense unit is precisely what confronts the student who is prematurely thrust into the reading of literary selections. Thus, essential as the skill may be, inference cannot thrive in a situation where the key content words are unknown. Clearly then, the density of unknowns must be reduced to the point where the practice of sensible guessing can begin to operate. (This assumes that students already have good control over the morphology and syntax of the language they are about to read so that they are not misled by the grammatical forms and word-order sequences of the target language.)

Vocabulary building exercises. Many veteran teachers have long used techniques for reducing the number of unknown lexical items to the point where the student can read the next day's assignment without major difficulty. Those texts, both traditional and modern, which supply a cumulative listing of high-frequency vocabulary items, are of particular value in helping the teacher to select items in a reader to which the student has not yet been exposed. Some of the newer readers have gone even further; they have supplied the actual exercises for building vocabulary. The vocabulary exercises consist of items that have not appeared earlier or have not been reentered frequently. Some of the techniques for presenting these items are as follows:

An example of visualization:

The student sees a picture of a medieval street. Under the picture is a caption that states, "The street is narrow." Immediately following is another picture of a slender boy. The caption states that "The boy is thin." With this as a takeoff point, the students develop concepts regarding the thinness of people, paper, pencils, and other applicable items in contrast with the narrowness of streets, buildings, hallways, and the like.

An example of paraphrase:

The word signature refers to writing one's name on a paper.

An example of restatement:

I always put my signature at the end of a letter.

251

An example of an action followup to the above activities (done completely in the target language):

This is my signature. (The teacher writes his signature on the chalkboard.)
Now, write your signature on a piece of paper and hold it up. (The students sign a sheet of paper and hold it up. Those who have not previously caught on will now understand by following the example of their classmates. The teacher quickly moves up and down the rows to see that all students have correctly followed directions.)

Examples of other ways to convey meaning entirely in the target language, by placing the new word in a context where its meaning is fairly obvious:

building—The Empire State building is the largest building in the world.
forest—A forest is made up of many trees.
went—Went is the past tense of the verb go.
stupid—The word stupid is the opposite of the word intelligent.
songs—Songs are what people sing. We sing songs in music class.
was—Washington was our first president. Kennedy was president until 1963.
discovered—The archeologist discovered King Tut's tomb.

Note: The number of devices for clarifying meaning is limited only by the imagination of the teacher and the knowledge of the students. On the latter score, the teacher must not assume too much. For example, Napoleon's name might be used in association with the word emperor. Nero or Alexander the Great might be less well known to contemporary high school students. What is considered to be general knowledge for one generation may be highly esoteric information for a later one.

An example of expanding vocabulary through word families. Fill in the blank with the correct item from the list following these sentences:

A school is a place in which we gain knowledge.
A man with great knowledge is a _____.
A _____ piece of work is one into which much study and effort has been put.
Students with good _____ ability should go on to college.
Students who do excellent work in high school often receive a _____ for attending college.
scholastic
scholarship
scholar
scholarly.

In working with root words and the prefixes and suffixes that may be attached to them, it is often necessary to point out the identical elements that exist throughout the list. Many students are incredibly timid about guessing word meanings. In Spanish, for example, even such an obvious cognate as nación will often stop a student. For this reason, some reading texts will mark true cognates with an asterisk or other mark of identification. Then, once the student has gained confidence in his ability to perceive the meaning of the basic word, the door is opened for instant recognition of related words when they appear. A few examples relating to nación are:
nacional*
nacionalidad*

nacionalismo*
nacionalista*
nacionalización*
Naciones Unidas*
internacional*

Once the student has developed the knack of perceiving cognates (that is words similar in spelling and meaning to English words) and derived words from within the target language, then he has automatically increased his reading vocabulary by hundreds or even thousands of words, depending upon what language he is learning, and how far he has proceeded in the acquisition of vocabulary.

Graded reading materials. A graded reader is a book separate from the regular text, which, if used properly, will be given to their students at that point in their study of the language when they are able to read it directly and pleasurably. Further, the graded reader should be so scaled in difficulty that the completion of the first selection develops in the student the ability to cope with the second selection which, in turn, prepares the ground for progress through the slightly more sophisticated third selection, and so on until the end of the book. Ideally, the graded reader would be built upon the specific course content that preceded its introduction—that is, the reader would utilize largely vocabulary and grammatical structures that had been previously introduced. The potential number of lexical items can be increased by utilizing cognates, derived words, and infrequent footnotes or marginal glosses. Indeed, by the latter half of the 1960s, a number of texts of this type had been produced to be used in conjunction with 4-level programs (see bibliography at the end of this chapter).

Unfortunately, not all materials labeled as "graded readers" meet the criteria suggested above. Some are based upon such a minimal word count that they are necessarily repetitious and devoid of content that young people can read with pleasure. Others, at the other extreme, are little more than emasculated summaries of literary selections assembled according to apparent order of difficulty and bound together under one cover. If unimaginative editing has not robbed such readers of their style, their content may be interesting enough to justify the time a teacher might devote to the development of special vocabulary-building exercises aimed at reducing the density of unknown lexical items. However, this often becomes a hopeless task; the teacher soon finds that these edited selectiens contain too many "surprises" in the form of idiomatic expressions and complex grammatical forms. As a result, vocabulary building begins to consume a disproportionate amount of class time. In such cases, the limited pleasure derived from the subsequent reading hardly seems to justify the effort. Thus, all so-called "graded readers" might well be subjected to a thorough analysis before they are purchased in large numbers. Among the suggested criteria for judging such readers are:

1   Level of interest—This aspect can be tested with a cross section of second-year students who are then asked to fill out an interest-inventory sheet.

253

2   Length and complexity of sentences—Beginning selections might contain an average of 10 words per sentence for early intermediate reading. This could increase to a 100 words per sentence at the advanced levels.[5]
3   Abstract content is best avoided—Simple story lines and interesting informational discussions referring to concrete, easily grasped situations are best at the intermediate stage. There should be a minimum of elaborate figures of speech and of esoteric allusions. The teen-age mind is more receptive to heavy-handed humor, for example, than to subtle repartees or satyrical discourses.

At this stage, the goal is to develop skill in reading in such a way that students have an opportunity to develop confidence in their ability to derive pleasure and satisfaction from the pursuit of that skill. They are at this point,, somewhat comparable to the second- or third-grade elementary school pupils who have just discovered that they can read simple material on their own. The right kind of graded books and periodicals can build upon the satisfaction that students derives from this realization. Conversely, the motivational spark that is ignited by independent reading can be permanently extinguished if the wrong kind of reading material is introduced at this point. The most common blunder committed by well-meaning teachers is the introduction of literary material that is beyond the interest and intellectual grasp of the adolescent youngster. Almost no one at that age is ready for the likes of Kleist, Camus, or Calderón in the original. To expect secondary school youngsters to read such authors is as sensible as expecting the toddler, who has just learned to walk from the couch to the coffee table, to immediately thereafter compete in the 100-yard dash at the Olympic Games. For most high school students, the analogy is no exaggeration. Generations of nonreading students who have been prematurely thrust into a foreign language "lit" class attest to the fact that the intermediate student is not ready for undiluted literature. And who would presume to dilute it?

Programmed readers. To a certain extent, every good graded reader is programmed. That is, the material is logically sequenced to lead to the desired skill development, the new lexical items are presented in minimal steps, and the students are provided with the opportunity to check the rightness or wrongness of their reading ability at each appropriate phase in the development of their reading skill. However, graded readers are not programmed in the full sense of the word (see discussion of programmed material in Chapter 7). This distinction would not be significant if it were not for the fact that programmed reading materials have been produced and are presently in use in a number of classrooms. Thus, we use the word "programmed" here to refer to materials that are not only logically sequenced into minimal learning increments, but that also contain most of the other characteristics of programmed instruction such as immediate reward

[5] For more precise measures of readability see William Bottiglia, *Language Learning*, Ann Arbor, Mich., University Microfilms, 1963.

capability for total self-instruction, minimization of error, and eliciting of overt responses from the reader.

The simplest form of programmed reader is the interlineary book in which English equivalents for the unknown words are supplied between the lines of the text. A plastic shield with evenly spaced strips of clear and transparent material fits over each page of the reader in such a manner that the English words cannot be seen. Thus, students can read an entire page without ever referring to the English section of the text. On each sentence they can attempt to guess the meaning of each new word using contextual clues. At all times they can check the accuracy of their inference by sliding the shield a quarter of an inch downward to reveal the English equivalent. If the materials are carefully graded, the interlinear texts can supply most of the characteristics of programmed instruction without resorting to the standard programming format. One advantage of such texts is that the interlinear vocabulary items stick out clearly on each page, which makes it a simple matter to count them to determine whether or not the density of new lexical items exceeds the suggested minimum of one new word per thirty-five words of running text. Another variation of the interlinear text is to supply the English equivalents in microscopic print so that they are legible only when the reader places a magnifying glass over the needed word. This obviates the need for the plastic shield, which can be easily lost, but replaces it with the more expensive magnifying glass, which can be either lost or broken.

Those who are inclined toward the direct method object to this system of programming on the grounds that it tends to perpetuate the myth that English equivalents are the source of meaning for foreign words. Clearly, there is the danger inherent in the interlinear system that students will be tempted to refer constantly to the English word between the lines, thereby destroying their will to read the foreign language for direct meaning. If this happens, then the programming device has negated the entire intent of the programmed reader.

Completely programmed texts on the Skinnerian format do exist.[6] One problem with those that aim specifically at developing reading ability at the intermediate level is the impossibility of knowing which structures and vocabulary items the student does or does not know. Consequently, the programmer has no alternative but to program everything. Thus, a student who has proceeded far enough through the regular classroom work to have control over the essential phonological problems will find a large part of the program tedious and repetitive. To compensate for this fact, the student must develop the art of varying his speed of progression through the frames of the programmed reading course. One advantage to having fully programmed readers is that they can provide a rapid review of vocabulary and structure for the student whose retention has been good, while at the same

[6] Alfred Fiks, "Foreign Language Programmed Materials: 1966," *Modern Language Journal* 51 (January 1967), pp. 7–14.

time offering a carefully sequenced course of study for the student whose retention has been less than minimal. A second advantage is that each student can move at his own/her own pace toward the liberating level of vocabulary acquisition provided only that the steps leading to the desired terminal behavior have been adequately programmed and that the budget of the local school district is adequate to purchase the massive supply of programmed texts needed to carry the student to the desired goal. In reality, programmed texts for the nonoral reading skills appear to stand the best chance of becoming economically feasible in the near future, for they can be used by the student without requiring expensive tapes and equipment. Moreover, since the overt response can be a silent reaction, the use of programmed readers is not physically restricted to a special laboratory room. The readers can be used anywhere—in the library, study hall, or at home. It is somewhat of a paradox, in view of this, that the majority of the early materials were designed to develop the listening-speaking skills. The scant supply of programmed reading materials is also paradoxical when one considers that, of all the language skills, reading is the one that is most individualized and that draws most heavily on the process of convergent thinking, two of the alleged strong points of programmed learning. For, once it is printed, the content of a book is static ; and the communication bond that is subsequently established is between the fixed graphic symbols and the lone reader. Using the powers of his/her intellect and imagination, each reader draws a uniquely individual interpretation from the little black marks on the page. The well-devised programmed course will teach the student to infer the meaning of those ink marks and will follow with an immediate confirmation of each inference, thus—in theory at least—building confidence through success. Much research remains to be done to determine whether or not skillfully designed programmed materials can bridge the chasm existing between the primer stage of reading and liberated reading (that is, reading of unedited, contemporary, adult material without recourse to a bilingual dictionary). It appears that no exhaustive study has ever been conducted to determine whether or not any American graduates from the foreign language reading program ever pick up a foreign language book or magazine after completion of their high school or college "lit" course. However, from the paucity of foreign language novels, plays, periodicals, and other non-English reading matter available in the nonuniversity bookstores and libraries, it appears that almost no one ever reads a complete work in the foreign language after having completed the foreign language "requirement" in school or college. This apparent reluctance of nonimmigrant Americans to read anything but English could be interpreted as an indictment of foreign language instruction for the past half century, particularly when one considers that the only ostensible purpose of that instruction was to develop "reading ability." Again, the ultimate goal of the American Method in the area of reading is to develop a form of coordinate bilingualism of the single-residence variety (see Chapter 5), which will enable the student to read, with enjoyment, materials from the foreign culture that are comparable to the items he reads in his native English.

256

The Advanced Stage: Liberated Reading

Readers are partially liberated when they can read with relative ease (and with a speed only slightly less than their English reading rate) genuine but especially selected materials from the foreign culture. The content of such materials is chosen on the basis of proven appeal to adolescent readers. These reading materials will also contain a dictionary section along with special notes to enable students to cope with difficult passages without having to refer to a regular dictionary. By this level, it is hoped that students have learned to program their own vocabulary development. That is, they will begin to note new words that recur often and will make a special effort to learn these words by themselves, thereby progressively reducing the density of unknowns that will confront them in future reading. Ideally, they will begin to make a self-study notebook of recurrent lexical items. The act of writing helps to fix the word in the students' mind, and the existence of the word list provides a convenient memory jogger. In making such a list, students should be encouraged to adopt the best possible techniques for vocabulary building, such as those mentioned earlier in this chapter. If they avoid using English equivalents wherever possible, they will be reinforcing positive attitudes toward developing coordinate bilingual abilities. Also, the programming technique can be used by having the new word appear on the left of the page with the definition appearing on the right. In this way, students can create their own programmed study of vocabulary by placing a shield over the simpler meaning of the new word and checking their attempts to define it. The following example in English could be adapted to any European language.

Example of new vocabulary presentation

Defeat was inevitable	*could not be avoided; unavoidable*
A look of consternation	*an expression of fear and amazement*
A valid reason	*a reason with a good basis; well-justified*
He clung to the edge	*He held on tightly (cling, has clung)*
A penurious landlord	*the opposite of generous with money; very stingy*
They have three children.	*One child plus one child equals two children.*

Naturally, students should not stop repeatedly on each page to make entries in their vocabulary notebook. This practice would destroy any attempts at genuine reading. Instead, they should simply underline any item that has recurred several times (if it is their own book) or jot the item down on a sheet of note paper. Then, when they have finished their intended reading at a fairly normal pace, they are ready to concentrate on the new lexical items. After they have studied them, they should reread the troublesome passages at a speed that is fairly close to their rate of reading English. The teacher and the students should be satisfied if the students can grasp the essential aspects of the plot, can distinguish the main personality traits of the characters, and are aware of the more obvious facts about the setting of the story. Discussions about the story can be simple and factual and can be for the most part, in the target language. Attempts at literary criticism may have a highly negative effect on students who are trying earnestly to develop direct-association reading.

Fully liberated reading in a foreign language—a common phenomenon in Europe—has seldom been achieved in American secondary education. The author has visited hundreds of high schools whose bookstores sell English-language paperbacks of best-sellers and significant works of literature. Yet, even though the high school may show four or five foreign languages on its course offerings, paperbacks printed in these languages almost never appear on the stands. The reason for this lack of foreign books is probably that they could not be read by enough students to warrant their purchase; although students who have achieved the goal of fully liberated reading would be able to take any book of moderate difficulty and read it pleasurably and with direct association of meaning. We are not suggesting books by avant-garde or esoteric writers, but short stories, novels, plays, and poems that are read enjoyably by people now living in the target culture. These might well include the popular fad books as well as the classics-for-young-people. If any great number of liberated readers are to be produced within the framework of the American comprehensive high school, then this diversity of reading materials is a clear necessity. The same wide spectrum of reading tastes that exists among American students in their English-language reading is likely to appear where foreign-language reading is concerned. This implies the need for a vastly expanded selection of readers available either in the regular school library or in a departmental library. To expect a single anthology—however good—to carry the entire reading load for the fourth-level course is no more realistic in the foreign language course than it is in the English class. Once students have proceeded beyond the intermediate level in reading skill, the key to further progress (either in English or in a foreign language) is to put into their hands books that they will read because they enjoy reading them. The reasons most commonly given to justify this lock-step progression through a given reading selection are:

1   It is necessary for the purpose of assigning grades on a competitive basis.
2   It is necessary for the class to have some common knowledge for the purpose of discussion.
3   It is not possible to keep track of student progress when they are all reading different material.

The first of these arguments is easily countered. If competitive grading is a necessity, then individualized reading will produce a greater disparity of progress among students, thus adding the factor of quantity of reading accomplishment to that of quality. The second argument has little real validity; there are plenty of other matters that can serve as a common ground for classroom discussion. Furthermore, the assignment of extensive reading does not preclude the use of common reading assignments for classroom discussion. As is the case with reading in the English class, most of the reading in the liberated phase will take place outside of the regular classroom. The third objection is perhaps most valid of all. It is not uncommon for secondary school teachers to meet between 100 and 150 students daily. Clearly, the establishment of individualized instruction for this number of youngsters would be a Herculean task. However, the potential for liberated reading is seldom realized before the third or fourth year of instruction. And, at this level, classes generally consist of a small number of well-motivated, self-directed students. With proper safeguards, such students can be allowed to engage in self-study activities that will facilitate evaluation by the teacher. In the area of reading, for example, they can be asked to submit a weekly progress report including the number of pages read and a brief summary of the plot development during the week's reading. With this sort of assignment, it is a distinct advantage to have no two students reading the same book at the same time. With the lock-step reading program there is always the danger that only a few of the best readers in the class are getting the necessary reading practice on each chapter. The other students rely on oral summaries of the story supplied in English by the class "brains." A further safeguard against such shortcuts is to convince the students that the chief measure of their reading progress will be the periodic exams that evaluate general achievement in reading rather than knowledge about specific facts (see Chapter 11).

The common practice of having all students read the same book at the same pace, chapter by chapter, is an excellent way to arrest the reading development of all students with potentially superior reading ability. The prevalence of this practice in American schools and colleges may to some degree explain why it is almost impossible to find a graduate of an American foreign language program who does further reading in the foreign language.[7]

WRITING ABILITY

At the simplest level, writing in the foreign language involves spelling and word order. Thus, the very first exercises aimed at developing writing skill might logically include such activities as copying, short dictations, sentence transformations, and reordering of scrambled sentences. Naturally, the more complex syntactical exercises will have to be withheld until the various word-order problems have been sufficiently drilled through the other three skills. However, the simpler written exercises can be started in the very early lessons as a followup activity to the work that has been done on the listening, speaking, and reading skills. At all stages, writing—properly used—can reinforce these skills. As is the case with reading, there is no proof that the written symbol should be withheld for excessive periods with adolescents and young adults. And there is every reason to capitalize on the universal

[7] Although the evidence is limited, there is one study that suggests that teaching of foreign language reading may be quite ineffective. See, Sam Rosenzweig et al., "Operation Babel: A Survey of the Effectiveness of Foreign Language Requirements for the Ph.D. Degree in Psychology." *American Psychologist* 17 (May 1962), 237–243.

human desire for self-expression by allowing rudimentary writing involving those utterances the student has learned to understand, say, and read. The very first writing will involve material that has been learned via the other three skills several days in advance of the actual act of writing. As the student moves through the course, writing can relate backward to material learned in previous chapters. In a more limited way, it can involve the drill material of the most recent unit of language work. In all cases, the important consideration is the degree of mastery of the critical phonemes. Writing, like reading, must not (according to modern thinking) be allowed to cause a deterioration in the speaking and listening skills. In fact, if the teacher knows how to capitalize on the body of material that the student has memorized orally, this prelearned knowledge can greatly accelerate the development of writing skill. To illustrate the steps through which one would proceed in developing direct-writing ability, we have used the lyrics of the "Star Spangled Banner." This was chosen in the belief that it is the one set of utterances that American readers are likely to have overlearned to the degree required of students in the contemporary modern foreign language class. (In other respects the example is unsuitable since the words are sung, not spoken, and because they are not in dialog form. However, they are adequate for the limited purpose of demonstrating the learning technique).

Step One : First writing

The students have already learned to hear, say, and read the material they are about to write. The first writing of this material is done in class with the teacher carefully checking to be certain that each line has been written correctly. All accent marks, punctuation marks, and other orthographic features of the material are double checked.

Step Two : Memory writing

The students are told to prepare for a dictation on the material by teaching themselves through a modification of the programming technique. They are taught to place a shield over the dialog utterances and then to write them one at a time from memory after which they carefully check the spelling of each word in each sentence.
EXAMPLE:
Students write from memory, "Oh, say can you see, by the dawn's early light," (Students move shield down the page to check their written response. They correct all errors.)
Students write next line, "What so proudly we hailed at the twilight's last gleaming." (Students reveal correct response and once more correct their errors.) In this manner students continue through the dialog material until they can write the entire passage flawlessly from memory.

Step Three : Spelling

To this point students have copied the material directly from the page and have "copied" from memory with immediate reinforcement from the printed page. Next they learn to spell certain key words by hearing them read in a dictation either from the teacher or from a tape. Students work with a dittoed or mimeographed sheet from which the key words have been deleted and replaced by a dash. The

teacher reads the passage through twice at a reasonably normal rate of delivery.
The students fill in the blanks.
EXAMPLE:
Oh, say can you _____ by the _____ early light,
What so proudly we _____ at the _____ last gleaming?
_____ broad stripes and bright stars, through the _____ fight,
O'er the _____ we watched, were so_____ streaming.
Some teachers make a practice of having students make a carbon copy of the
dictation. (Only the answers come through onto a blank sheet of paper.) The
carbon copy is then signed and handed in immediately after the dictation. Each
student then corrects his/her own paper (for purposes of immediate
reinforcement) as the teacher reveals answers written on the chalkboard or
projected on a screen from an overhead transparency. The entire process can take
less than ten minutes of class time. In some cases, the teacher collects the
dictations after having instructed the students to make all corrections and to
circle those items that are wrong.

Step Four: Limited self-expression

Once students have established control over the sound-to-letter correspondence
by means of copying and dictation exercises, they can begin to move into those
types of exercises that allow them a limited degree of self-expression. As with the
other productive skill—speaking—they must learn to keep their urge for written
self-expression within the limits of the structures and vocabulary items they have
learned to manipulate in earlier lessons. The following are but a few examples of
the type of exercises suitable to this stage of development. (These sentences
would appear only in the target language; English would not be used in any way.)

Completion exercises. In completion exercises the rules are that the student must
use only that vocabulary and those grammatical forms that have been thoroughly
drilled in the previous chapters.
In summer I like to _____.
You didn't tell me that _____.
Why did you _____.
He says that the teacher _____.
In no case should students attempt to look up equivalents of words and
expressions that exist in American English. This practice almost invariably leads
to disaster because of the different semantic range of words between one
language and the other. For example, if they try to complete the first sentence by
saying, "In summer I like to have a good time," they will almost certainly go
wrong if they have not mastered the expression that conveys the idea of "enjoying
oneself." In French, German, and Spanish, this idea is generally expressed without
using either the common equivalents for have or for time. Thus, the main purpose
of the completion drill is to induce students to produce written recombinations of
structures and vocabulary items that they do know how to manipulate and to be
as creative as possible within these bounds.

Recombination exercises. Students are instructed to produce complete, sensible
sentences by modifying and rearranging a series of words.
to work/the city/every day
As is the case with completion exercises, students have some leeway here
regarding the sentence they produce. However, the same limitations of

vocabulary and structure apply. Thus, the following variety of sentences might appear:

He goes to work in the city every day.
I work in the city every day.
We want to work in the city every day.
They have to work for the city every day.

If much of this type of exercise is done in a supervised study situation, students are likely to come up with a wide variety of sentence types. The bright student may produce some unexpectedly elaborate sentences without deviating from the rules of the game. Some excessively ambitious youngsters, on the other hand, may produce elaborate but faulty sentences. Both types of written responses should be checked and handed back as soon as possible with congratulations to the successful student and redirection to the one who has gone astray. For the busy teacher, it is better to assign frequent, regular, short written exercises than to ask for long written assignments that cannot be corrected quickly and handed back immediately. If students are to be encouraged to engage in divergent thinking, they need to be informed that they are on the right track whenever they strike off on their own. For, as we have seen, the cultivation of the ability to do divergent thinking is the one area of language instruction in which the human teacher is demonstrably superior to the machine.

Step Five : Paragraph writing

During the elementary stages of writing, the drill work will have focused principally upon developing sound-to-letter correspondence and upon producing genuine but isolated sentences. The intermediate stage has arrived when the student has acquired sufficient vocabulary and knowledge of structure to write coherent paragraphs. As with the other stages of learning, this skill must be developed carefully and systemically. Some techniques of long standing include:

Conversion exercises. *Students are given a short paragraph that is complete and correctly written. They are instructed to convert it in some way. For example, they might be expected to change all the conjugated verbs to the present tense, or past tense, or to some other appropriate form. Or perhaps the paragraph is so written that all nouns and pronouns can be changed from singular to plural without changing the essential meaning of the paragraph in other respects. In some languages it might be useful to have the students change a series of direct quotations into indirect discourse. Similarly, a student might take a third-person narration and rewrite it in the first person.*

Cued narration
    Example :

MY BEST FRIEND

What is his/her name ? Age ? Lives where ? How long have you known him/her ? Things you have done together since then. (Note previous lessons: go skiing, swimming, skating, dancing, to movies, to basketball game, to football game; also play chess, cards, tennis, basketball; also, listen to music, records, the radio or watch television.) What do you both want to do after you graduate from high school. (Get a job ? Go to college ?)
A paragraph written from a series of cues need not utilize all the cues. Moreover, it is perfectly all right for students to utilize additional structures over which they have control. Thus, a student who has studied English as a foreign language for

several years might produce the following paragraph based on the cues given above:

MY BEST FRIEND

My best friend's name is Paul Smith. He is 17 years old. For the past eight years he has lived next door to me on Lincoln Avenue. During this time we have often gone swimming together. In winter we have also attended basketball games, gone to movies, and played chess at home. When we graduate from high school next year, we both hope to attend the state university.

Summarization exercises. *Students hear a short, simple story read aloud twice. Then, without reference to any resource material whatever, they rewrite the narration in their own words. Similarly, a story can be assigned for outside reading with the explanation that it will have to be summarized in writing later in the week. To facilitate accuracy, the student can be given a series of questions that contain the necessary vocabulary for summarizing the story. The answers to these questions will provide the minimal acceptable summarization of the story and the questions themselves will contain most of the vocabulary needed to write the paragraphs.*

Original dialog production. *Using the vocabulary and grammar at their command, students are instructed to adapt a dialog to their own personal experience. For the less imaginative students, some direction in the form of suggested topics may be needed.*
Mother (or father) may I _____?
Well, maybe, but first _____.
But mother, (father), I _____.
I have heard that story before. If you expect to _____, then you will have to

_____.
All right, I'll _____ _____. Then may I _____?

Free composition. *Many students will arrive at the end of a four-year high school language course without being able to produce spontaneously written compositions in the foreign language. That is, many will still be somewhere in the intermediate stages of composition where they are able to transform narrative material, but are not able to create a coherent series of related paragraphs on a chosen topic. This should surprise no one. A rather large proportion of incoming freshmen at any college or university campus are unable to produce mature narrations even in English. Writing in any language is a complex art. It consists of much more than the rendering of talk onto paper. Anyone who has attempted to read the transcript of a semiformal conference, which has been copied directly from tape to typewriter, can attest to this fact. In speech there is a high tolerance for redundancy, for repetition of the same type and length of sentence, and for simple everyday vocabulary. Remarks that seemed lucid and witty over the conference table, appear as a string of inanities when they are reproduced in print. In any language, good writing calls for conciseness, precision, and variety of sentence structure. However, in learning to write a second language additional problems are introduced. There are certain conventions, levels of style, rules of punctuation, and other aspects that differ sharply from the writing standards of English. These must be acquired along with the acquisition of other more basic aspects of the writing skill. Thus, free composition in written expression is only for those students who have gained excellent control over all the basic language* structures and whose vocabulary has reached the stage where they are able to engage in liberated reading. From this background students can begin to utilize models of good contemporary prose to express what they want to say at something above a primary school level. The steps toward something that resembles free composition in the foreign language might be as follows:

1   Using a model of a personal letter to learn form and style, students write a personal letter to someone they know. Hopefully, it will be someone who reads the particular foreign language. An ideal outlet for such compositions is a pen pal in the foreign culture. With a cooperative young person in the target culture, the student can write letters in which the first part is in the foreign language, the second part in English. The pen pal follows the same procedure with his letters. Then each student in each country makes corrections in the foreign language section and mails back the corrected copy. In this way both correspondents profit from writing experience and both have a native tutor available via air mail. (A similar procedure can be followed in developing speaking skill if both correspondents have a tape recorder.)

2   A number of models of business correspondence can be used in a similar manner to teach students to write more formally. Again, the student will use the model letters only as a guide. The content of the letters produced by the students will have to be different. Possible topics are:

a.   Writing to a fictional hotel requesting room reservations for a given period of time.

b.   Writing to a bookstore to inquire whether they have certain specific books, what the prices are, if they have cloth-bound volumes as well as paperbacks, and so on. (New vocabulary items might be supplied by the teacher in advance.)

c.   Write a letter of invitation to another student in the class. (The teacher must exercise great care and tact to see that all students both write and receive an invitation.) Then, each student is required to reply, affirmatively or negatively, to the invitation. (Again, model forms are needed.)

3   Well-motivated and gifted students may be encouraged to attempt a more creative type of composition. Light verse, simple short stories, short skits, and critical essays have been written by high school students in a foreign language. Some schools have a monthly student newspaper mimeographed in a foreign language and distributed to all students who are enrolled in the language beyond the first year. Some schools produce a literary magazine that includes a foreign language section. Any such positive recognition for achievement is to be encouraged. Also, written work can carry over into the audiolingual areas. For example, the secretary of the language club might read the minutes of the last meeting in the foreign language. For example, the skits that the advanced students have written can be presented before all the students who are enrolled in that language, perhaps in the school's little theater. Also, brief reports of current news events can be read aloud in class or over the public address system with the switches turned only to those classes in which the appropriate languages are taught. The author has seen a hilarious version of a current news report done in German by an advanced language class. The students had written their own reports using current German newspapers for resource materials. The same sort of activity can be done in the other commonly taught languages.

FOREIGN STUDY PROGRAMS

There is some evidence to indicate that travel to a foreign country and immersion in the foreign language environment of that country can greatly enhance the skills acquired in the academic school program.[8] However, the mere act of traveling abroad will not necessarily produce this result. A striking example of human potential for learning almost nothing from travel and residence abroad is the case of American military personnel and their dependents who frequently spend several years on foreign soil without having developed any significant skill in the language of the host country. This is partly explained by the fact that these individuals never really leave home, but reside in an American ghetto surrounded by fellow Americans and by American institutions such as public schools, supermarkets, liquor stores, and the like. However, a further explanation is the lack of initial contact with the foreign language and culture. Apparently, the most value is received from foreign travel if the traveler has first completed the equivalent of two levels of foreign language instruction as outlined in Chapter 5.[9] Of the dozens of widely publicized overseas study programs that have sprung up in recent years, many have no prerequisites with regard to prior foreign language study. Thus, students may spend over a thousand dollars to travel to Europe in the hope of becoming fluent in their chosen language only to find that very little learning resulted from the time and expense occasioned by the trip. This becomes doubly unfortunate when one considers that the same amount of time and effort could have produced excellent results with a properly designed, properly timed foreign study program. It is for this reason that the National Council of State Supervisors of Foreign Language in 1966 enlisted the services of a nationally recognized authority on foreign study programs, Professor Stephen Freeman of Middlebury College, to set up criteria for evaluating such programs. These published criteria are now available through the State Foreign Language Consultant or Supervisor in the Department of Public Instruction of each state. The criteria are published under the title: *Criteria for Evaluating Foreign Study Programs for Secondary School Students.*

TEACHING THE FOUR SKILLS
IN A CULTURAL CONTEXT

Throughout the history of foreign language teaching in America there have been recurrent claims that one of the chief outcomes of foreign language instruction was a "better understanding of the foreign culture." However, there is reason to believe that, in practice, the teaching of culture in the

[8] John B. Carroll, "Research on Teaching Foreign Languages," *Handbook of Research on Teaching*, New York, Materials Center, Modern Language Association, 1964, p. 1085.
[9] Ibid.

average foreign language classroom has been something less than ideal. Some teachers have assumed that the learning of the sounds and patterns of a second language constituted a significant cultural experience in and of itself. For such people, the fact that the student is learning to manipulate new sounds, new grammatical patterns, and new word order arrangements is adequate evidence that he has broken through the barriers of mono-lingualism and monoculturalism that are so characteristic of the mind-set of many Americans. There are others who contend that this is not enough; that it is, indeed, possible to develop a rather high degree of proficiency in manipulating the elements of a second language without ever penetrating into the "soul" of that language. That is, many American students may merely be using a second system of oral and written symbols to express Anglo-American "realities."[10]

To a certain degree that result is inevitable for the majority of young people who will never experience direct contact with the target culture. To expect students to emerge from a school program fully bicultural is to insure disillusionment. Both the shortness of time and the artificial nature of the school environment militate against the achievement of such a goal. From the standpoint of vocabulary alone, the foreign language teacher faces an enormous problem with respect to the teaching of culture. It is clearly not possible to teach all the nuances of meaning and all the emotional overtones carried by each lexical item. Yet if foreign language learning is to be anything more than a troublesome secret code used to express what students already know, then they must come away from the experience of foreign language learning with the firm conviction that foreign words express a version of reality different from the English "equivalents." They must further come to realize that few real equivalents exist across cultures; and they must be con-stantly alert to the fact that the semantic range of words from one culture to another is vastly different. In some cases, the differences in the cultural function of seemingly simple objects is so enormous as to defy all efforts at translation. For example, there is an Ashanti word that is translated as "stool." In the Ashanti way of life, a stool has great significance for every individual. What North Americans would consider a simple piece of furniture is to the Ashanti a mark of social standing, a vehicle for recording the im-portant events of their life, and, after their death, it becomes a public record of their mortal existence. Stools of a given tribe are stored in a central location where professional "stool readers" can have access to them for recounting events of the past. This example helps to dramatize the enormous degree of miseducation that can result when a teacher of foreign languages attempts to convey meaning by merely matching English words or sentences with the alleged cross-cultural equivalent.

A further aspect of vocabulary lies in those areas for which no equiva-lent forms exist. In Spanish there is no word comparable to the English word

[10] H. Ned Seelye, *Teaching Culture: Strategies for Foreign Language Education*, Skokie, Ill., National Textbook Company, 1974, p. 18.

for "pet." On the other hand, Spanish is much more concerned with differentiating the parts of an animal body from that of the human body. Thus, for example, while English differentiates between the animal paw and the human hand, Spanish goes further to differentiate in its vocabulary between an animal neck and the human neck, an animal leg, and the human leg, and so on.

The illustrations above are based largely on vocabulary items. Of course, language is much more than a collection of lexical items. For example, there are morphological and syntactical patterns in many languages that reflect a structuring of reality markedly different from that of English. This version of reality is imposed upon children in any culture as an an automatic part of their inculturation into the patterns of their native environment. The language must relate to those patterns. If they remain monolingual (or if they learn other languages while keeping their ethnocentric biases intact) they tend to accept the native language and the version of reality that it symbolizes as the norm. All other languages are seen as queer ways of expressing their own "correct" version of reality. For example, unlike the speaker of English, the native speaker of Spanish is not the agent in forgetting such things as theater tickets or in missing a train. Instead, Spanish idiom shifts the blame to the object. In effect, Spanish expresses the idea that "the tickets forgot themselves on me," or "the train took off and left me." Also, while a North American clock or wristwatch "runs," the Spanish timepiece merely "walks" (with the verb *andar*.) In German the syntactical patterns "the dog bit the man" and "the man bit the dog" can both be used to express the same essential idea. The accusative ending on the definite article will indicate—in either word-order sequence—that it was the man who was bitten rather than the dog. The lack of case endings in English mandates the syntactic pattern in which the direct object follows the verb.

The foregoing examples were given to illustrate both the complexities and potentialities of integrating the teaching of language skills with the teaching of culture. It is also important to cite the dangers inherent in this approach. From the standpoint of a language teacher, one danger is that instruction might be reduced to little more than a long series of "fascinating" anecdotes about the "peculiarities" of the target culture, thereby reinforcing negative stereotypes about the foreign culture and confirming the student's suspicions that "those people are really pretty funny and they do everything backwards." Also, there is the danger that the teacher and the students may overgeneralize from limited data. For example, to refer back to an example given above, students might tend to assume that the Spanish language with its "walking clocks" gives evidence of lackadaisical behavior among speakers of Spanish. I have personally heard persons use similar linguistic evidence to explain why "Germans are precise" and "Frenchmen are emotional." In this regard, scholars are highly skeptical of attempts to draw specific relationships between language and culture. As Edward Sapir expressed it, ". . . we shall do well to hold the drifts of language and of culture to be noncomparable and unrelated processes. From this it follows that all attempts to connect particular types of linguistic morphology with certain correlated stages of cultural development are vain. Rightly understood, such correlations are rubbish."[11]

The point here is not to discourage students and teachers from exploring the intricacies of language and culture, but to caution them against drawing spurious conclusions. This does not prevent the learner from examining samples of patterned behavior, linguistic or otherwise, and presenting evidence in a descriptive manner. Nor does it prevent him from making cross-cultural comparisons of language and cultural patterns. In fact, in this area the foreign language teacher could profit greatly from the experience and practice of the social scientist. The foreign language community has sometimes neglected its responsibility for helping students to look objectively at patterns of linguistic and cultural behavior. Elsewhere we mentioned the Spanish textbook that informed the students that "Spanish does it backwards." This was in reference to the Spanish placement of object pronouns before the conjugated verb. From the standpoint of teaching cross-cultural understanding, this is clearly an abomination, for it tells the student that the syntax of English is correct and that any departures from that pattern are strange and deviant. If students are taught to be biased about syntax, the implication is almost inevitable that cultural patterns of behavior that differ from their own are also deviant and strange. Perhaps a better approach would have been to present the two patterns as being of equal validity. Another approach is to encourage students to make their own value judgments about the relative superiority of one pattern over the other (leaving the outcome open-ended with no final "one right answer" ever being supplied by an authority figure).

A final danger related to the teaching of culture has been succinctly expressed by Valdman. Speaking to a large group of foreign language educators he stated that "we must overcome the temptation to wander into areas that are marginal to our field. The goals of language teaching are to form incipient bilinguals and biculturals, not apprentice linguists or bargain basement cultural anthropologists."[12] The basic message here is that the language teacher must avoid converting his/her classroom into a thinly disguised area studies program taught mostly in English. This means that cultural instructions must bear a functional relationship to the basic communications goals of the local language program. In this regard, the teacher might well ask whether or not his cultural assignments meet one or more of the following criteria:

1   Does the activity help the student to understand the cultural referents that underlie target language utterances?

2   Does the activity help the student to use more effectively one or more of the basic linguistic patterns or idiomatic expressions of the target language?

[11] Edward Sapir, *Language*, New York, Harcourt Brace Jovanovich, 1921, pp. 218–219.
[12] Albert Valdman, "Grammar and the American Foreign Language Teacher," pp. 66–80, in Frank Grittner (ed.), *Student Motivation and the Foreign Language Teacher*, Skokie, Ill., National Textbook Company, 1974, p. 79.

3   Does the activity help the student to understand better one or more of the social, political, economic, or educational patterns of the target culture?

4   Does the activity largely involve the student in using the target language for either receiving or communicating messages or does the lesson culminate in an activity that requires the use of the target language?

One of the reasons for teaching culture is to give the student something worth listening to, talking about, reading about, or writing about. Any cultural content that fulfills this purpose (and which is also accurate) would, therefore, seem to be justifiable.

The language teacher would do well to heed Seelye's advice not to make culture "a series of disconnected footnotes to literature" and to avoid teaching "trivial" information in a noncreative way. Nevertheless, the principle still holds that even the most insignificant items will take on great importance if the student can take them seriously enough to use them in a communications situation.[13] In this regard, Nostrand states that "activities in which the student feels emotionally involved—in which he feels impelled to exchange meaningful utterances—are better than those that engage only the intellect."[14] Nostrand has also described in some detail eleven "experimental techniques" and nine "cognitive techniques" for helping the student to gain varying degrees of direct experience of the target culture and knowledge of its patterns.[15] In addition to knowing *how* to teach cultural material, it is also advisable to have a basis for knowing *what* to teach, what to select from the mountains of cultural material available in categories ranging from table setting to the history of the opera. There have been many attempts over the years to delimit cultural content (see cultural section of the bibliography for this chapter). Some of these have been rather lengthy, elaborate, and technical and hence of little direct practical value to the classroom teacher. Perhaps a somewhat shorter list of basic organizing principles would be of more use. This writer suggests therefore, that teachers at the local level settle on a short list of concepts (such as those given below) which would be used as a guide in developing and selecting units of work to be integrated into the foreign language program from the beginning through to the advanced levels.

Sample Organizing Principles

1   Attitudes toward the proper social and economic roles of men, women, children, and adolescents differ across cultures.

---

[13] Seelye, op. cit., pp. 15 and 121.

[14] Howard Nostrand, "Empathy for a Second Culture: Motivations and Techniques," in Gilbert Jarvis (ed.), *Responding to New Realities*, Skokie, Ill., National Textbook Company, 1974, p. 281.

[15] Ibid., pp. 281–307,

2   Attitudes toward social class and place of residence differ across cultures.
3   Virtually all words in the target language evoke feelings and images in the native speaker that differ sharply from those evoked by similar words in the learner's language.
4   The "world view" of people in the target culture differs in many ways from that of people in the learner's culture.
5   Social mores and popular everyday customs differ across cultures.

PERSONAL STUDENT INVOLVEMENT IN A CULTURAL TOPIC

To illustrate how the first topic in the list of principles above was applied to the classroom situation, let us cite the example of the role of women in a Spanish-speaking culture as contrasted with the role of women in a particular local community in the United States. The procedures used were as follows: First, eight questionnaire items were taken from a poll that had recently been administered to young men and women in Mexico. This poll had to do with perceptions of young Mexicans relative to the characteristics and roles of women in their society. Second, the poll was administered to all students of Spanish in the school district and to local teachers. (Students and teachers were not allowed to see the responses given by the young Mexicans until after all questionnaires had been returned.) Third, the results were used in advanced Spanish classes of the school district to discuss, in Spanish, the attitudes revealed by the various patterns of reponses in the two cultures.

In order for the reader to get some feeling for how this kind of activity can give the student a feeling of involvement, a modified form of the actual poll is given below. Instead of collecting the actual data and computing the percentages, the reader can guess at what percent of Mexican young men and women would respond with "yes," "no," or "don't know" on each of the four questions. The same procedure can then be followed for each of the categories for American young people of both sexes and for American teachers of both sexes. That is, the reader is invited to guess what percentage of the sample population of American young people would have responded with "yes," "no," or "don't know" on each of the questions. After having guessed at how each of the three groups of both sexes had responded, the reader can then check his/her own responses against the Results of the Poll in Appendix 1 at the end of this chapter.

An alternative procedure (for those who are working with American students of Spanish) is to prepare a poll including only the four questions plus a place to indicate "male" or "female" and "student" or "teacher." The responses can then be tabulated, the percentages computed, and the results compared with the responses given by the Mexicans. If not enough teachers can be found who are willing to participate, the comparisons can be made between only the two groups of young people.

270

THE ROLE OF WOMEN IN SOCIETY

Guess how people would respond in both cultures. Indicate one percentage for each blank. Reading horizontally, each group of three blanks should total 100 percent.

	Men			Women		
	Yes %	No %	Don't know %	Yes %	No %	Don't know %
1. Is the place of women in the home?						
Mexican young people	___	___	___	___	___	___
American young people	___	___	___	___	___	___
American teachers	___	___	___	___	___	___
2. Are men more intelligent than women?						
Mexican young people	___	___	___	___	___	___
American young people	___	___	___	___	___	___
American teachers	___	___	___	___	___	___
3. Do you think the majority of married men have mistresses?						
Mexican young people	___	___	___	___	___	___
American young people	___	___	___	___	___	___
American teachers	___	___	___	___	___	___
4. Do you think it is proper for a girl to go out alone with her boy friend?						
Mexican young people	___	___	___	___	___	___
American young people	___	___	___	___	___	___
American teachers	___	___	___	___	___	___

A similar approach has been used in French classes by adapting opinion polls from *L'Express* dealing with the following topics: "Money in Your Life," September 4–10, 1972; "Love," March 6–12, 1972; "Women's Liberation," May 8–14, 1972; and other topics from subsequent issues. The results of comparing their own attitudes with those of French young people were remarkable in terms of the high level of animated student discussion (in French), that these topics produced. Below are sample results translated from French:

THE VALUE OF MONEY: SAMPLE RESULTS

	French youth %	American youth %
1. What does money represent for you?		
Pleasures: buying what you want	56	34
Security	22	43
And so on		
2. Choice of career: what is the most important factor?		
Interesting work	57	52
Job security	23	3
High pay	9	32
And so on		
3. With more money, what would you buy first?		
Car	22	21
Put in savings account	19	44
And so on		

Another poll item, which achieved good results in terms of student response and personal involvement in the cultural topic, could be directed toward differences in "world view" between American and French women. The poll can be conducted quite easily by handing out slips of paper and asking the students first to indicate whether they are male or female. The girls are then asked, if they could have one (and only one) wish fulfilled, which of the three would they select.

1   to be more beautiful
2   to be richer
3   to be more intelligent.

The boys are asked to select the answer that they think the girls would choose. The reader can guess at the results by filling in all the blanks given in the table below. What percent of each group responded in favor of each of the three categories. (The totals for each column should be 100 percent.)

If I could have one of the following wishes fulfilled I would choose:	What percent of French women responded to each of the three questions?	What percent of American women responded to each of the three questions?	What percent of American men indicated desirable female responses for each of the three questions?
1. to be more beautiful	_____	_____	_____
2. to be richer	_____	_____	_____
3. to be more intelligent	_____	_____	_____
Total responses	100%	100%	100%

After you have completed your estimates check your results with those in Appendix 2 at the end of the chapter. Then consider the following questions: (1) What do the results suggest about the value systems of French and American people? (2) To what degree do the results support the stereotype of French women as presented in movies and folklore?

Culture Assimilators

A number of foreign language educators have developed a technique for the out-of-class study of cultural contrasts, which is commonly referred to as "the culture assimilator." This approach usually involves a series of episodes in programmed format relating to a critical incident of cross-cultural interaction. Typically the episode involves a situation in which an American has erred in interpreting a situation that confronted him/her within the target culture. The student reads the episode and is then asked to choose one of four interpretations of what went wrong. Each choice is keyed to a different page in a "scrambled" textbook. Only one of the choices is correct. If the student chooses the wrong answer he/she is referred back either to the assimilator itself or to earlier material that contains the information needed to solve the problem of the cultural conflict. For example, the young American living as a guest in a German family finds that the host's reactions to his leisurely daily shower has progressed from disapproving frowns, to broad hints of displeasure, to an outright suggestion that fewer showers should be taken. The student of German is then asked which of a list of alternatives best describes the reason for the behavior described in the episode. For example:

A   Germans have not caught up with American standards of sanitation and cleanliness. (See page _____.)

B   The host is a miserly fellow who is worried about the few pennies it costs to heat the water. (See page _____.)

C   Hot water is generally very expensive in Germany; hence daily showers are prohibitively expensive. (See page _____.)

D   The host felt that the American was deliberately and ostentatiously belittling German behavior patterns. Hence the German is trying to "put the guest in his place" by telling him what to do. (See page _____.)

The responses scattered through the text would respond to each of the above in somewhat the following manner:

You chose A. The earlier readings on laundry and house cleaning should have told you that this answer was false. (Remember "The Case of the Boiled Laundry," in which the elastic was boiled out of several pairs of men's socks?) Reread that earlier selection once more along with the present episode, and make another choice.

You chose B. You have no basis in the information given for making this generalization about the host.

Read the episode once more and make another choice.

You chose C. Good work! You selected the only answer that is justifiable on the basis of our cultural studies to this point. The other choices are either not consistent with German attitudes toward personal hygiene or else they are based on nothing more than idiosyncratic traits. You may have drawn your conclusions from our previous readings relating to the fact that fuel of all kinds is expensive in Germany and that, therefore, the constant use of hot water would be a financial burden to the German household. (One group of students computed the cost of following the American bathing pattern for a family of five in a German city. The costs came to nearly $80 per month increase for daily baths and showers!)

Incidents relating to cleaning and bathing customs do occur regularly. Sometimes Germans are thought to be "too clean" as when they ruin synthetic fabrics because of the practice of boiling the laundry. At other times German bathing habits are equated with lack of cleanliness. The real basis of the problem is economic. Bath water like gasoline is very expensive—hence smaller cars and fewer showers.

You chose D. This is possible. Putdowns occur now and then, particularly if the American is interpreted as having been condescending. However, the assimilator does not deal with isolated incidents.

Reread the episode and make another choice.

273

Culture Capsules

A culture capsule is designed to present one phenomenon from the target culture that contrasts sharply with a comparable phenomenon in American culture. Each capsule is supposed to take up no more than ten or fifteen minutes of class time. Over a period of years, the student is to be exposed to a number of such capsules drawn from those representative aspects of the target culture that one must know in order to begin to understand why the people act as they do. H. D. Taylor, the originator of the capsule idea, suggests that the capsules should be selected so as to deal with eight categories, which, if properly covered, should lead "to both understanding and to sympathetic appreciation" of the target group.[16] Examples of pedagogically useful categories are summarized here in simplified form as follows:

1   *Subcultural category:* biological characteristics, natural resources, geographical factors, historical periods
2   *Technological category:* food, shelter, clothing, tools, and transportation
3   *Economic organization category:* family versus industrial or company bosses, rural versus urban, main types of employment, attitudes toward work
4   *Social organization category:* kinship, family, marriage, race, ethnicity, loyalty units, social class, church versus state, clubs, prestige neighborhoods
5   *Political organization category:* legal system, government and party systems, military power, labor power, industry power, graft versus "pull," family influence in politics
6   *World view category:* God and the supernatural, honor and dishonor, male versus female, striving versus relaxation, nationalism and heroes, law and order
7   *Aesthetics category:* celebrations, music, dancing, humor, sports, games, art, literature, theater
8   *Education category:* schools, instructional methods, pupil behavior, universities, mass education, literacy verus illiteracy.

The capsules are not to be taught as generalizations, however, but rather as specific items related to people's behavior, beliefs, or view of life. For example, capsules might deal with differences relating to the dietary importance of bread in France and the United States, German versus American passenger trains, the bullfight versus American football, or any one of thousands of other specifics. Slides, news items, and realia from the target culture are used as learning devices and as stimuli to elicit questions about the cultural item under discussion (see the following section on "culture clusters" for specific examples).

There is some disagreement as to the proper format and use of culture capsules. For example, there are some who say that the capsules should be

[16] H. Darrel Tayler and John L. Sorensen, "Culture Capsules," *Modern Language Journal* 45 (December 1961), p. 351.

prepared by the students as a part of an active research project. Others say that the classroom teacher should prepare the capsules to insure accuracy and conformity to the local curricular plan. Still others suggest that capsules should be prepared only by experts in consultation with natives from the target cultures. (In the latter category, J. D. Miller and associates have prepared a rather sizeable collection of culture capsules relating to French-speaking, German-speaking, and Spanish-speaking countries, among others.)[17] Another question relates to whether the native or target language should be used with culture capsules. H. D. Taylor advocates the use of the target language. Roger Pillet, on the other hand, has made a case in favor of presenting cultural material in the native language of the learner.[18]

Alternate approaches have been to create foreign language capsules for the less complex cultural concepts while using the native language for describing cultural items that would be too sophisticated to present in the language of the novice learner. Still another practice has been to write the capsules mostly in English giving foreign language illustrations. There is no simple way to resolve such questions. Teachers who choose to make use of culture capsules will tend to base their decisions on the available skills of the local instructional staff and in the local community, on the availability of funds for supplementary cultural materials, and on the values that local staff members hold regarding the use of the native language or the target language in the instructional process.

Culture Clusters

Culture clusters are built upon a series of culture capsules aimed toward a culminating dramatic activity in the classroom, which, ideally, would involve most if not all of the students. According to their originators, culture clusters are best taught in the following way:

1 Different aspects of the broad topic are presented in the form of ten 20-minute culture capsules on three or four successive days.
2 Each capsule in the series contributes insights into the more complex pattern of culture represented by the entire cluster.
3 Thirty minutes are allowed in the last day to stage the teacher-directed skit, which reviews and draws together the concepts presented earlier in the week in each of the culture capsules.[19]

A Sample Culture Cluster

Title: *Social Rules in Middle-Class French Culture.*
Format: *Four separate culture capsules that lead to a simulation based on the total cluster.*

[17] Materials are available from the Culture Contrasts Company, 2550 East 3370 South, Salt Lake City, Utah, 84109.
[18] R. A. Pillet, *Foreign-Language Study: Perspective and Prospect*, Chicago, The University of Chicago Press, 1974.
[19] Betsy Meade and Genelle Morain, "The Culture Cluster," *Foreign Language Annals* (March 1973), pp. 331–338.

275

Time : *Fifteen minutes per day for four days; fifty minutes on the fifth day.*
Level : *First or second year if done in English. Third or fourth year if done in French.*

Cultural concepts illustrated :

1   *Middle-class manners and rules of social intercourse are definite and are not to be violated by people who wish to be socially accepted.*
2   *Entertaining in the home is less common than in the United States. However, when this is done, certain procedures will be followed.*
3   *Attending a social event in a friend's home (in this case a dinner party) calls for attention to details that differ in many ways from practices in the United States. Sample areas include bringing presents to the hostess, shaking hands, introductions, giving compliments, and excusing oneself.*

Goals :

1   *Students playing the role of a parent will be able to express opinions of disapproval of unacceptable behavior using the appropriate French terms.*
2   *In a simulated social situation students will be able to correctly introduce and address people of the same and opposite sex and of different age groups. Students will shake hands in the French manner.*
3   *Students will learn to excuse themselves in a variety of simulated social situations using the various appropriate expressions.*
4   *Students will learn to give and accept compliments using appropriate forms and reacting to compliments in an appropriate way.*

In realizing the objectives listed above, the teacher allots five days to presenting material relating to the objectives and to leading students through the various activities described in the capsules. If class size permits, students should act out the various parts, using the correct language, gestures, handshaking technique, and so on. By the fifth day, students should be able to simulate the social events at a dinner party up to the point where the hostess declares that "dinner is served." On that fifth and culminating day, the teacher will orchestrate the events in such a manner as to involve all of the students in one or more of the illustrative cultural activities. In the four preparatory days the teacher would use slides, lectures, film clips, short written selections, and so on, to prepare students for the culminating experience of the fifth day. The following illustrative content for a culture cluster is drawn from The Relationships and Rules of Social Life in France *by Madeleine Cottenet Hage.*

First Day : General Rules

The French are said to be very formal. To put it another way, they are very conscious about form as opposed to content; things have to be done with a certain style. One might argue that formality is perhaps not exclusively French, but shared by other European nations, when compared with the United States. Also one must be very clear: the formality of the French is, in reality, the formality of a fraction of the population, the middle class and the upper class. In the lower middle class and the working class, one has no time for form and style, one meets every day as it comes. The content of a meal is more important than the tablecloth on which it is served, and the content of a friendship more important than its delicacies.

This emphasis on form in the middle and upper classes creates a gulf between them and the other social groups, with the result that a child raised in a working-class background will be considerably hampered if he moves up the

276

social ladder. Language, manners, as well as attitudes, are class indicators of which most members of the middle and upper classes are very much aware. Rarely does money compensate for what upbringing and culture have failed to produce.

Two very typical phrases are used with children, in these social groups, to forbid them from doing something: ça ne se fait pas, and c'est vulgaire. In France, the realm of "vulgarity" is clearly delineated: There is a vulgar way of eating, of sneezing, of speaking, of dressing, and of wearing a hairstyle. One may deplore the fact that, in some circles, one can be more squeamish about vulgarity than about dishonesty, for instance, but inbred attitudes are very hard to eradicate.

Second Day: Entertaining in the Home

ENTERTAINING AT HOME

In comparison with most Americans, French people entertain less at home. For many Frenchmen, entertaining at home becomes toute une affaire, which requires formal scheduling and lengthy preparations. Throwing a party at the last minute for someone who happens to be in town is unheard of, and inviting someone for a meal au pied levé is reserved for close friends. Otherwise, when you are being invited à la fortune du pot, you will probably discover that le pot is quite elaborate indeed.

Note: What the French do not have is the American custom of inviting for brunch.

BRINGING A PRESENT

The hostess is always touched if a guest brings her a small present, such as flowers, candies; these are sometimes replaced by a toy for the children. It is not generally assumed by her that if you do so, you will not be in a position to reciprocate or rendre l'invitation, as it is interpreted in America.

When bringing flowers, many people tend to choose roses or tulips that are sold by the piece. In this case, they will often bring an uneven number, seven rather than six, eleven rather than ten. Strange as it may seem, it is supposedly a way of showing that you are not mincing expenses by calculating it close. A more acceptable explanation, however, is that uneven numbers make for lovelier arrangements. In any case, flowers are presented wrapped in their paper, unlike in Germany where the custom is to take the paper off.

THE DINNER PARTY

When guests arrive—ten to fifteen minutes after the time mentioned to them—they are taken to the "salon" or living room, according to the case, and served apéritifs. These are generally sweet wines like porto, sherry, Cinzano; if you hear Martini, don't jump to the conclusion that you will be served your favorite American drink, for it will certainly be the European drink, another sweet wine. Whisky has now been introduced into French homes and Americanomania has popularized mixed drinks in circles that are "ofay."

Drinking apéritifs however, is not prolonged much beyond the arrival of the last guests. It is merely a way of bridging over the time until dinner, and the prelude to the main part of the evening.

"Le dîner est servi." The guests and their hosts repair to the dining room.

Third Day: Making Personal Contact

INTRODUCTIONS

Monsieur and Madame Lomond have invited several friends for a dinner party, none of whom know each other. So, as they arrive, she takes them to the

277

other guests and introduces them saying "Permettez-moi de vous présenter Monsieur X." *Then she names the second person Madame Y. Madame Y holds out her hand and they shake hands; you will often hear people say* enchanté, *but books on etiquette point out that this custom is totally inappropriate. The man's name will be said first or, in the case of differences in age and rank, the younger or lower-ranking guest will be named first.*

In large parties, where it may not be possible to introduce everyone, a man may very well introduce himself to other guests, with a simple "Jean Banon." A woman does not. What do guests reply ?:

A man to a woman :	"Mes hommages, Madame."
A man to a young girl :	"Mes respects, Mademoiselle."
A woman to another woman :	"Madame."
A woman to a young girl :	"Mademoiselle."
A woman to a man :	"Monsieur."

HANDSHAKING

There is a great deal of handshaking in France. Not only do people shake hands when they are introduced to each other, but each time they meet after an interval that may only be 24 hours. Colleagues at work, friends coming to a party will shake hands. Acquaintances may cross a street in order to shake hands, but only if they feel particularly warm and friendly to this person and want to chat for a while. Conversely, your not doing it for someone you know well might be taken as a sign of coldness and aloofness. But more and more, among the younger generations, the tendency is to greet another person verbally, quite often with a slight arm gesture, the arm being raised halfway to the side at shoulder level and the hand wavered slightly. Hands are shaken slightly differently in France. Generally, two people grasp each other's hands fully and shake only once downward. Shaking hands several times would indicate unusual pleasure—for instance, at meeting once again after a long absence—or warm congratulations. People are often quite sensitive to the way in which others shake hands. For instance, a strong, firm grip is supposed to be very manly and an indication of strength of character. On the contrary, a loose handgrip is interpreted as a sign of "mollesse," weakness, lack of interest.

Who holds out the hand ? In most cases it is the woman or the older and higher-ranking person. Now, sometimes it is difficult to decide who should start. So you may see four hands trying to shake at the same time and crossing each other in a vain attempt to reach another one. This is considered a sign of bad luck and the four hands will very quickly withdraw and prepare for a successive approach. Ladies first.

Fourth Day : Giving Compliments and Excusing Oneself

COMPLIMENTS

In France, people do not acknowledge a compliment with a "thank you." This American manner either delights because of its frankness, or shocks. But in either case, no one is used to it. If, for instance you compliment your hostess on her dress, she will most probably acknowledge it by saying, "Oh, c'est une petite robe que j'ai fait faire, il y a trois ans, pour la première communion de notre fille." *Or, if you compliment her on her dinner, she is likely to reply* "Oh, c'était bien simple. J'aurais bien aimé mieux vous recevoir mais. . . ." *In other words, though*

French people like compliments as much as anyone, they act with sincere or feigned embarrassment when compliments are paid to them, and they will immediately point to a defect in the object of the compliment, as a way of humbling themselves. By doing so, they do not at all wish to imply that you, the compliment-giver, have shown bad taste or are being insincere. However, you may feel compelled to reiterate your compliment so as to reassure your friend about your sincerity. You might say: "Ah mais, je vous assure, elle est vraiment très jolie, cette robe" or "On ne dirait pas que vous l'avez déjà portée."

"EXCUSEZ-MOI", "OH, EXCUSEZ-MOI."

One of the many signs of the French formality in social relationships might well be the frequency with which they use excusez-moi. These two words will be used in two different sets of circumstances. First, whenever a Frenchman asks for permission to do something or for a favor to be done to him, such as: "Excusez-moi, puis-je prendre cette chaise ?" (that has been left vacant at the neighboring café table), or "Excusez-moi" if you must step in front of someone to get off the metro car at the next station, or "Excusez-moi, pourriez-vous me passer le sel ?" In short, any time you are likely to disturb anyone for any reason.

You will use the same formula to apologize for minor offenses. "Excusez-moi d'être si en retard mais . . ." and then a Frenchman will proceed to explain why he is late. Not infrequently, when the apology comes immediately after awareness of the "fault" (like stepping on somebody's toe), it will be proceeded by an emotional "Oh, excusez-moi," especially if the offender is a woman. Excusez-moi may be replaced by Je suis désolé. If the offense is perceived as serious, a Frenchman may say "Je suis navré," such as "Je suis navré de ne pouvoir rien faire pour vous."

In both sets of circumstances, the other person may reply with a gracious "Je vous en prie" and he will add, to an apology, "Ce n'est rien" or "Il n'y a pas de quoi," even if inside he feels surges of anger.

Note: You will hear many people say "Je m'excuse." This form is denounced as incorrect by all grammarians who point out that one cannot excuse oneself, one can only ask to be excused. Actually, the more polite turn of phrase is "Je vous prie de m'excuser," and is the one which is used in letters.

Culture Minicourses

The culture minicourse tends to be somewhat longer and more elaborate than any of the techniques above. Typically, instructional time devoted to them will range from two to four weeks. (It would, perhaps, be more accurate to refer to them as "cultural units" rather than "minicourses" since they are frequently used in aggregate to make up semester or year-long courses, particularly at the third- and fourth-year levels of instruction.) Minicourses are also used to break the routine of regular textbook instruction during the first- and second-year levels of instruction, while, at the same time, teaching elemental skills. With regard to format, they are often set up according to the unipac formula discussed in Chapter 7. However, for some purposes, that format may be too restrictive. Hence, teachers should feel free to improvise and to adopt whatever approach best meets local needs.

A sample cultural instructional unit. During the early 1970s, a number of colleges and universities held summer workshops for experienced

279

classroom teachers, the purpose of which was to produce classroom-ready materials which could be used in toto or be adapted in part by other teachers. Some of these units were targeted toward the teaching of grammatical structures or literary material. However, a considerable number of them were aimed at teaching culture. The most extensive work in this area was done at the University of Minnesota under the direction of Emma Birkmaier and Dale Lange. They have made their units widely available to teachers around the nation, a commendable example of idea sharing that has all too seldom taken place. Workshops have also been conducted at the University of Wisconsin from which cultural instructional units were produced. The material outlined below is drawn from a cultural unit that has been used successfully by teachers in Wisconsin and elsewhere.[20]

An Instructional Unit on the Bullfight

Title: ¡ Corrida !
Subject: *Spanish Language and Culture, Social Studies (Area Study Approach).*
Performance level: *This unit is designed for students completing first-year high school Spanish or its equivalent.*
Purpose: *Its purpose is to familiarize the student with the bullfight as an art form and a sport in the Hispanic culture.*

I. *Pretest: What do I know about the bullfight?*
II. *Statement of Idea*
   A. *Major Concept: The* corrida *is an art form as well as a sport, and only through examining its procedural, historical, and aesthetic aspects can the student view it as such.*
   B. *Component Ideas:*
     1 North American and Northern European misconceptions of the bullfight need to be clarified.
     2 Such clarification can be brought about by analysis of the procedures and progression of the bullfight.
     3 A look at the historical evolution will allow the student to understand the bullfight as an integral facet of Hispanic culture.
     4 Aesthetic appreciation of the bullfight will be aided by vicariously experiencing the mood and feeling associated with the corrida *through the media used in this unit.*
III. *Instructions to the Teacher*
   A. *An instructional aid, "¡ Corrida !", is a culture unit concerned with the procedural, historical, and aesthetic facets of the bullfight. In offering materials and suggestions it does not determine what skills will be emphasized, what activities will be used, or what methods of evaluation will be employed. Rather, this is left to the teacher so that he/she may adapt the materials according to each individual teaching situation.*

[20] Kathy Bauman, Solveig Bergh, Jim Hendrickson, and Donna Sukawaty were the teachers who did the basic work on this project under the direction of F. Grittner. Lucia Garner, University of Wisconsin, Department of Spanish and Portuguese, did valuable editing and supplied the native voice on the taped materials. The unit was done during the summer of 1972.

280

B. *Equipment Needed: A slide projector, overhead projector, tape recorder, and projection screen.*

C. *Materials Needed:*
    1 Eighty slides in carousel tray illustrating in sequence typical bullfight scenes.
    2 English-Spanish, Spanish-English dictionary.
    3 Prerecorded tape entitled "¡ Corrida !". Contains narration for 80 slides with background music typical of the kind heard at bullfights.

IV. *Suggested Activities*

  A. *Class Activities:*
    1 Reading of background articles (in English) before the slide presentation.
    2 Practice in using appropriate bullfight vocabulary with the use of slides and transparencies.
    3 Dialog work (choral and individual) using "La Corrida de Toros" *found in the transparency section.*
    4 Word association and idiomatic expression exercises (example: matar—matador ; banderillero—banderilla).
    5 Reading of Spanish background article "La Corrida de Toros" *(in Spanish).*
    6 Writing in English or Spanish (using the vocabulary presented in the unit) the student's view on bullfighting.
    7 Writing of a short, first-person narrative on an afternoon at the bullfight from the point of view of the bull.

  B. *Creative Activities:*
    1 Researching and giving a demonstration of the pases *before the class.*
    2 Making of a capote, *a* muleta, *a bullring model, a* montera, *a* banderilla, *and so on.*
    3 Playing on own instruments the pasodoble *(music of the* paseillo).
    4 Debating the humanity–inhumanity of the bullfight.
    5 Researching the superstitions connected with the corrida.
    6 Researching the famous bullfighters, male and female.
    7 Tracing the historical development of the bullfight.
    8 Writing a creative story as though one were an assistant or a friend of a famous bullfighter.
    9 Reading and presenting a report on one of the novels mentioned in the "Extra Readings" section.
    10 Researching and presenting orally or in written form the opera Carmen, *including musical selections.*
    11 Making a word puzzle on "¡Corrida !" vocabulary.

V. *Posttest: What have I learned about the bullfight ?*

VI. *Components*

  A. *Introduction: (One page, double spaced, in English) An indication of the complexity of the bullfight, and how it differs from other art forms and sports.*

  B. *The Heritage: (Three pages, double spaced, in English plus introduction of Spanish technical terms) Tracing the development of bullfighting from prehistory, through Roman times and through the Arab period down to the present time.*

  C. *The Brave Bull: (One page, double spaced, in English) Specifications for bulls, including how they are raised, selected, tested, and transported to the area at the age of three or four years.*

281

D. *The Bullfight: (Two pages, double spaced, in English with 24 technical terms in Spanish)* The events and characteristics of the day of the bullfight are summarized here. The drawing of lots, the prayers of the matador, the sights and sounds of the bullring, the three acts of the bullfight, the dragging away of the dead bull, the special recognition for exemplary performance.

E. *Ferdinand the Bull versus El Toro Bravo: (One page, double spaced, in English)* A contrast in cultural attitudes between Mexicans and North Americans with respect to the bullfight.

F. *La Corrida de Toros : (Three pages, double spaced, in Spanish)* An explanatory essay on the bullfight, which does not merely duplicate but expands on the material presented earlier in English. *(Reading comprehension is the goal here.)*

G. *Text for Accompanying Slides: (Four pages, double spaced, in Spanish)* Short, simple, but correct Spanish utterances interspersed with pasadobles *background music. Sights and sounds and historical material about bullfighting. Slides in color with a few black-and-white photos that illustrate the major aspects of the bullfight. Bullfighters winning (mostly) and losing (sometimes); killing the bull and being thrown and gored. (The written text is for teacher reference as well as for student use. The tape develops listening skill via high-interest subject matter.)*

H. *Glossary: (Spanish to English)* One hundred and five terms used in the unit ranging from aficianado *to* volapié.

I. *References: (One page, single spaced)* Books and records for reference and further reading.

J. *Pre- and Posttest measures are used here to show the* students *how much they have learned rather than to grade them.*

CULTURE, ETHNICITY, AND HUMAN RELATIONS

An area of culture that had been somewhat neglected in the past but that began to receive increasing attention in the 1970s is the ethnic heritage of the United States. Michael Novak has pointed out that only about 30 percent of all Americans are of English-speaking ancestry.[21] Evidence of the rich non-English heritage of America is available in many forms. Foreign language records; available in archives of state historical societies; annual celebrations, which maintain many of the characteristics of the ethnic heritage; preserved or restored buildings, which have been converted into museums or places of business; and active ethnic clubs are but a few of the resources that the foreign language teacher can draw upon for relevant materials. An outstanding example of what can be done to exploit this rich heritage is to be found in the state of Minnesota. Under the leadership of Percy Fearing, State Consultant in Foreign Languages, the State Department of Education published Human Relations Minicourses in French, German, and Spanish. Using material from French-, German-, or Spanish-speaking

[21] This comment was made in a speech delivered April 5, 1975, at the Central States Conference in St. Louis, Missouri.

groups of the past or present, committees of language teachers developed informative minicourse materials, which can be easily reproduced and adapted for use within the foreign language classroom. The German minicourse emphasized various German-speaking religious minority groups such as the Amish and the Mennonites who are still active in Minnesota. The French and Spanish units have a somewhat different focus, in that they emphasize historical and political aspects of the Franco-American and Hispano-American groups rather than the religious. However, they too, are designed to provide accurate information about the heritage of the target ethnic groups and, thereby, to help students to understand these groups as they presently exist and as they have existed in the past.

LIMITATIONS OF CULTURAL MATERIALS

Culture capsules, cultural assimilators, culture clusters, and culture minicourses, have been used successfully by experienced classroom teachers. However, there are certain dangers inherent in the use of such techniques. Perhaps the most serious limitation is the tendency to oversimplify and overgeneralize about the behavior of people in the target cultures. This is particularly true of those items that purport to be describing, "how people live and behave today." A given description of contemporary behavior in any present-day culture will probably, at best, be accurate for only a slight majority of the people in one particular social class of the national or linguistic group in question. For example, the opinion polls presented elsewhere in this chapter show a *distribution* of opinions rather than a *stereotyped pattern* of responses among people from the target culture. This tendency can also be seen in the data that Gordon presents in his book on culture.[22] This, in turn, raises the deeper question of the degree to which foreign language teachers can become involved in the use of sociological and anthropological data without running the risk of teaching misconceptions. Most language teachers, after all, are amateurs in these areas. The social scientist may, after years of careful research and data collection, hazard a tentative and highly qualified generalization about observable behaviors within a culture or subculture. The amateur, not having gone through the entire process of research, may tend to look upon each generalization as some kind of revealed universal truth. To counteract this tendency, it would be well to try to bring students to the realization that specific cultural data are inevitably colored by the biases and perceptions of those who collect them. Students might also be led to realize that, within any culture, there is a great diversity of behavior and opinion. Finally, they must always bear in mind that other cultures—like their own—are changing constantly, even though the nature and direction of change may be somewhat different from that which is taking place in the United States.

[22] Raymond Gordon, *Living in Latin America*, Skokie, Ill., National Textbook Company 1975.

Another problem with the kinds of cultural materials discussed above has to do with how they are prepared and by whom. Commercially prepared materials relating to contemporary culture tend to become dated by the time they reach the classroom. In fact, when one considers the time lines that exist between original field research, preparation of manuscripts, and processing of the final publication, one could almost regard such materials as historical items rather than contemporary sociological or anthropological works. Similarly, teacher-prepared materials will be limited by the recency and depth of the teacher' experience in the foreign culture. Materials prepared by the students themsleves will naturally be limited by the resources (or travel money) available, as well as by the skill and perceptiveness of the students themselves in selecting the most relevant information from those sources at their disposal. However, despite these limitations, there is much to be said for the practice of involving both the students and the teachers in the search for cultural material and in the generation of cultural hypotheses.[23] The specific cultural facts may be transitory and applicable only to a limited group of people within the target culture. The *process* of examining cultural data, on the other hand, will be much more durable than the information itself. Engaging in the investigatory process will often lead students to the formation of new attitudes. This outcome is less likely to occur, however, if the cultural component of the language program consists of nothing more than a compendium of facts to be learned and recited on a test. Hence it might be well, in dealing with cultural material, to keep most questions and exercises open-ended—that is, questions such as the following might well predominate:

1   What does this information *seem* to say about the target culture?
2   What else could this data mean?
3   What else do we have to know before we can begin to formulate hypotheses?

In guiding student investigations of cultural topics, the teacher would have in mind certain organizing principles or generalizations, such as those discussed earlier or those suggested by Howard Nostrand and H. D. Tayler.

THE STUDY OF LITERATURE
IN THE FOREIGN LANGUAGE PROGRAM[24]

The study of literature is often introduced into the foreign language program in the fourth or fifth year. By that time, the basic structures of the language have been drilled, reinforced, and often deductively reviewed in oral and written forms. Many teachers and students look upon application of those

[23] Frederick L. Jenks, "Conducting Socio-Cultural Research in the Foreign Language Class," in H. Altman and V. Hanzeli (eds.), *Essays on the Teaching of Culture*, Detroit, Advancement Press, 1974.
[24] This section was written by Constance K. Knop, Professor of French and Education, University of Wisconsin, Madison.

284

skills to the study of literature as a reward for years of language study. Others see studying literature as a means of continuing to learn about the target culture. This view is based on the belief that, through literature, one may discover points of views and attitudes that are particular to the people who speak a given language. At the same time, the study of literature is said to bring out universal qualities that are common to all people, transcending the limits of language, time, culture, space, and sex lines. For example, the humor of Molière still makes us laugh, three centuries later. We can see the universality of human foibles, attitudes, actions, and needs in his characters and works.

Another justification for the study of literature in the foreign language program is to train students to understand different genres ; to perceive how a play differs in style, techniques, restrictions, and achievements from a poem, novel, or short story. By reading several examples within each genre and by summarizing characteristics common to each of them, students may be helped to analyze the unique qualities of the various genres. They may then approach a given genre equipped with guiding principles that are likely to contribute to a fuller appreciation of each.

The study of literature need not be done in isolation from language learning per se. In fact, vocabulary study and analysis of grammar are legitimate activities that can enhance the understanding and appreciation of the literary work under consideration. Also, the use of word families, context clues, and inferencing can serve the goals of literary appreciation while, at the same time, being used to review and expand students' guessing ability and knowledge of the language. Discussing a literary work, in oral and written form, can concurrently serve the purpose of developing students' skills in self-expression and communication.

The study of literature will hopefully lead to personal interaction between the student and the work. This is probably the most difficult, but the most important, goal ro teach. After years of structured practice in the language, students look for "right" or "wrong" answers in the classroom. To be asked for their opinions and personal reactions with respect to a character, event, or stylistic effect is, on occasion, a surprising or even frightening experience for students. Yet the study of literature is likely to be a dry, sterile activity unless this kind of personal response is elicited from students.

Determining Goals

The first problem facing the teacher of literature is that of determining goals that are viable in a given language program for the particular groups of students involved. Some teachers may choose to develop detailed performance objectives for the entire year's work or for a given unit.[25] Others may prefer general objectives such as increasing ability in reading speed and comprehension, developing literary appreciation, learning to recognize different genres, or discovering universality in the human experience. Whether they

---

[25] For a detailed description of such objectives, see Florence Steiner, "Teaching Literature by Performance Objectives," *Foreign Language Annals* 5 (March 1972).

285

are very detailed or general, goals must be established to give purpose, direction, and justification to the study of literature and, thus, to motivate and guide students in their work.

Selecting Specific Works to Study

Several criteria should be considered before selecting the literature to include in the program. The following are suggested as basic considerations:

The linguistic ability of the students. Students can be alienated from literature if they begin reading works that are too difficult for them linguistically, intellectually, or stylistically. Teachers should compare the level of their students' ability with the difficulty of the text in such areas as range of vocabulary, complexity of sentence structure, difficulty of grammatical structures, and use of dialect. Giving students a sample paragraph from the work and checking their general comprehension of it can give an indication of the compatability of the linguistic level of the students with that of the work (see cloze procedures in chapter 11).

The level of the students' intellectual development and of their literary appreciation. If a work is likely to be too complex for them in English (for example, Descartes or Goethe), it is highly unlikely that they will understand it in the target language. On the other hand, some works that could lend themselves to complex philosophical and intellectual discussions (for example, Camus' *The Stranger* or Twain's *Huckleberry Finn*) may be read and enjoyed at a much more simplistic, straight-narrative level. Discussion with the school's English teachers regarding the content and experiences in those classes would give one a concrete idea of the literary background, training, and appreciation of the students in a given school.

Areas of interest to students. Contemporary literature most often appeals to students because of their interest in the content and their identification with the characters and events. Generally, the vocabulary and grammar are close to items studied in class (as contrasted to sixteenth- or seventeenth-century usage). Choice of specific works might be organized around themes that interest and concern students (for example, antiwar attitudes, friendship, sports). Again, it is important to ask the students about their interests and needs in reading literature. An interest survey can be set up at the start of the year to determine students' preferences and past reading habits.

Difficulties inherent in each genre. The short story seems to be the least difficult genre stylistically and, thus, is useful as a beginning literary experience. Each short story usually has only one focus dealing with development of a character, of a plot, of a mood, or of a theme (whereas other genres bring several or all of these together into one work). Students can concentrate on techniques used to develop one of these areas and thus become prepared to study a more complex work in which all of these elements are interrelated. The teacher would be well advised to include a variety of stories that do, in fact, involve these different elements. Literary study should ultimately deal with all the various genres so that students gain a balanced view of the literary achievements of the target culture.

286

Novels by nature of their length often cause students to become bored if study drags on for weeks on just one work. A short novel or novella can be a satisfactory compromise in this area. Another possibility is to do in-class study on the first third to half of a longer novel, helping students get used to the author's style and getting them into the plot and character development. Then, the rest of the novel can be assigned for independent reading outside of class, with periodic checks on students' progress and comprehension.

Plays cause problems because they are meant to be seen and heard, not read silently. It is important to help students visualize the setting, characters, physical positions, and interactions on the stage. Films, audio recordings, pictures of the characters in costume, and acting out scenes in class are all useful techniques for developing understanding and appreciation of the work. In addition, students should be encouraged to read all stage directions to have a clear idea of what is happening physically on stage.

Poetry tends to be loaded with metaphorical expressions difficult for students to understand. It can almost be taken for granted that they will need training in discovering, understanding, and appreciating poetic techniques. In this regard a careful *explication de texte* of poems can train students and give them confidence in reading a poem. D'Alelio and Dufau offer a type of programmed self-instruction in this area. One poem is presented with specific questions for the five steps of *explication de texte* (*situation, forme, sujet, analyse, conclusion*). Students work out answers to the questions on their own and then turn to a detailed *explication,* following the questions, to self-check their analysis. After several of such training sessions, students read poems with just the guide questions and so go on to do their own *explication.* Finally, they study just the poems alone, with no guide, and thus eventually work out an *explication de texte* completely on their own.[26]

On the other hand, a positive experience with poetry can be offered by *not* thoroughly analyzing a poem. Listening to a recording of an interpretative reading of a poem, discussing the mood or feelings it evokes, and guessing what the subject of the poem might be are techniques that can demonstrate to students the importance of sound in a poem without belaboring interpretation of the work.

Initial poetic experience might well be directed toward highly narrative and humorous poems to help students with more concrete vocabulary and to overcome prejudices and fears they might have developed from having studied overly emotional and very abstract poetry in the past.

All genres might well be included in the fourth- and fifth-year curriculum. At this instructional level, the development of knowledge about the styles of different genres is a realistic goal. The teacher should, however, anticipate difficulties that each genre entails and should plan learning activities accordingly.

[26] D'Alelio, Ellen and Micheline Dufau, *Découverte du poème,* New York, Harcourt Brace Jovanovich, 1967.

Student editions. It will ease the difficulties in teaching literature, helping both teacher and student, if a student edition of the work is available. Student editions normally include background information on the author and work, vocabulary and grammar explanations, guide questions, footnotes to explain obscure or unclear references, and pictures of the characters and settings. All of these aids clarify and reinforce the meaning of the work. However, student editions that consist of rewritten literature should usually be avoided. Abridged or excerpted versions are preferable. Such editions may omit portions of the work, giving summaries of those parts that are left out. By and large, editors should not tamper with the actual language of the author. Developing literary appreciation requires exposure to the vocabulary, style, and content of literary masterpieces, not watered down, simplified versions of them.

Literary history. In high school, students need not study the chronological development of the literature of a country. Works should be selected for their interest and appeal to students, not because they represent a literary movement or an important literary event. Choosing and organizing literature is much more effectively done by genres or by recurring themes, depending once again on the overall goals for the course.

Developing and Checking Comprehension of the Work

Another problem facing the teacher of literature is developing and checking students' comprehension of the work. Before beginning the study of literature, teachers must help students learn to read on their own for general comprehension. Students need training in learning to guess at new vocabulary. Exercises in inferencing, using context clues, and looking for word families are useful for building guessing ability. Metz[27] and Santoni[28] suggest doing vocabulary exercises that use actual items from the work to be studied *before* beginning the reading. By working on vocabulary in isolated sentences, students can focus in on guessing at the meaning of new words without being overwhelmed by long, complex passages. By familiarizing themselves with vocabulary items beforehand, students can then look at the entire context of the sentence or paragraph. Thus, they will be reading for general comprehension rather than word by word, which will be conducive to developing in students a broader understanding and appreciation of the work.

Another way of helping students learn to read for general comprehension is to assign very specific questions based on each section of the work. In this way, students are guided in seeking out important factual information contained in the reading. The teacher can use these questions to check students' overall understanding of the work. Before attempting to discuss style, literary appreciation, or personal student reactions, the teacher should

[27] Mary Metz, "An Audio-Lingual Methodology for Teaching Reading," *Foreign Language Annals* 6 (March 1973).
[28] Georges V. Santoni, "Methods of Teaching Literature," *Foreign Language Annals* 5 (May 1972).

first be sure that the students understand the basic information contained in the reading selection.

What Language to Use in Discussing Literature

As Janet King has pointed out, it seems useless to spend three to four years (or college semesters) developing a linguistic skill and then to abandon it when working on literature.[29] At the same time, one cannot expect that using the target language is an automatic given. The teacher must find ways of facilitating and insuring the use of the target language in class.

Students usually lack vocabulary for discussing literaure in the target language. At the start of their study, they need a list of terms along with definitions and examples in the target language (for example, terms for stylistic devices such as foreshadowing or metaphors; vocabulary such as "plot," "characters").

Guide discussion questions should be assigned the day before so that students look for and think out their answers. The automatic responses expected in beginning language classes are not appropriate for questions that require information, evaluation, analysis, appreciation, and personal reactions. If the teacher is presenting a brief lecture (for example, on the author or background information to the work), writing an outline of the main points on the board can be helpful. Better yet, a handout of that information might be given out on the preceding day, with subsequent class discussion of the important points. Some teachers may prefer to limit use of the target language to factual, informational discussions with the use of English permitted to elicit personal interpretations, class discussions and in-depth analysis of the work. Otherwise, students need vocabulary and guidance on the literary terms, questions, and discussion items if they are to be expected to communicate in the target language.

The Organization of Time in a Unit on Literature

It may be effective in some instances to persue the study of a given work every day for several weeks. Another possibility is to plan the study of literature for alternate days of the week (for example, Monday–Wednesday–Friday). With the latter approach, students may be assigned longer segments of the work and may enjoy a break from the usual routine by studying culture or grammar on Tuesdays and Thursdays or by having those days to do supervised study or in-class work on their literature assignment. The day-after-day study may be more appropriate to a shorter literary work, such as a poem or short story (where the assignment can be completed after one or two weeks). The alternate-day approach would be more appropriate for longer works.

Different in-class grouping can also be set up to enable some groups to work together on culture, others on history, still others on literature.[30]

[29] Janet King, "The Use of Audiolingual Techniques in the Third- and Fourth-Year College Classroom," *Foreign Language Annals* 2 (December 1968).

[30] Florence Steiner, "Teaching Literature in the Secondary Schools," *Modern Language Journal* 56 (May 1972), p. 283.

After working on instructional units in their separate groups, the students can then come together to share with each other their progress, learning, and insights.

Activities with a Piece of Literature

Introductory activities are important to give students background information that helps them understand and appreciate the work. *Brief* remarks might be made to relate the author and work to important historical events or to place the work in the development of literary movements or genres. Biographical details about the author that are relevant to the work might be included. General characteristics of the author's style, themes, and techniques can be discussed. Some long-range questions might be set up, such as, "How does this author create comedy and humor?" Such questions can provide a theme for recurring discussion and can be used for reviewing the entire work.

Daily activities ordinarily begin with some review work in which students are asked to summarize the reading up to that day's assignment. This approach encourages students to review the material already studied and helps them perceive a particular day's assignment in terms of the whole work. Their résumé of that day's reading also provides a check on their comprehension.

Résumés may be elicited in response to specific questions assigned the day before or asked in class. The answers form a summary of the important points in the reading. Also useful is the chain technique in which one student begins the résumé, and each student adds one sentence to it, building upon the previous student's contribution. This chain process can be facilitated through the use of visual aids, drawing of key scenes and events, or verb cues written on the board and arranged in proper order. The sentences elicited by such stimuli would be designed to form a summary of the assigned literary material.

Résumé work in class is important training in helping students learn to synthesize the material read into a coherent summary of the important points of the work. As their study continues, students may be asked to write out their own résumé at home with guidelines being provided as to how many sentences or main points to include in the summary. Several of these résumés are later read in class. Overall comprehension of the day's reading might also be checked by true-false or multiple choice questions in oral or written form. Varied ways of eliciting the résumé (or of questioning) should be used from day to day, but every class period should ordinarily begin with a check on the students' general comprehension of the assignment.

Careful study of key passages is a useful daily activity for checking students' comprehension and for training them in reading literature. Analyzing a passage may begin with a study of the linguistic elements: What tenses are used in this passage and for what purpose? Why are impersonal expressions used and what is their effect? Are there changes in the normal syntactic patterns and why? Why is this word used instead of a similar, almost synonymous one; and what is the effect of using one word over the

290

other? In this way, study of the language choices made by the author leads directly into a discussion of the style and the effects it has on the reader.

That particular passage and its stylistic devices can then be fitted into the structure of the work. Students may be asked what event occurred before, which occasioned the events or tone of the passage in question; or what does this passage suggest, happens afterwards. Does this passage create foreshadowing? Is there a change in vocabulary or grammar usage from the preceding passages, and what does that imply? By dealing with questions of this nature, students can begin to judge the significance and importance of a given passage in the context of the entire work.

Finally, students may be asked to relate the passage or the effects of the style to themselves. Their reactions and their identification (or lack of it) with the characters, events, and emotions generated by the passage are dealt with here. When eliciting personal reactions and evaluations, it is important to ask students for references in the text to back up, elucidate, and justify their statements. This will avoid interpretations that are farfetched and based more on personal whimsy than upon literary appreciation. Dunning points out that "having students offer a *because* or having them deal with *why* is the first step in developing their literary taste. . . . This implies moving from generalities to specifics." He stresses that the role of the teacher is to involve students in issues of taste. In getting students involved, "teachers must use such questions as 'WHY do you think that?' and 'WHERE in the story do you find evidence?' and 'IN WHAT WAY does that seem to you good?' These are taste-building questions."[31] Through in-depth study of given passages, students may be trained to understand, analyze, and appreciate literature and to relate it to their own lives.

Other daily activities may include reading passages aloud and role playing, especially with plays and poetry or passages where tone of voice and emotional connotation are crucial. Daily small-group activities might include groups of two or three students making up questions on the reading or answering teacher-made questions, preparing a brief *explication de texte*, making up a dictation to give the class, or preparing a dialog based on a passage. The groups then share their work with the entire class.

In the daily study of a literary work, the teacher may find it effective to begin the next day's assignment with the total group, reading aloud and explaining the vocabulary of the first part of the next assigned passage. In this way, students gain confidence because they understand the beginning of the new material and are motivated because the assignment is already underway. Having daily guide questions for the next day's work helps students focus in on the most important elements of the plot and prepares them for that day's discussion.

Daily activities should be planned—first, to check students' overall comprehension of the reading assignment; then, to work on one or two key passages in depth, for comprehension, analysis, and appreciation; and,

[31] Stephen Dunning, *Teaching Literature to Adolescents: Short Stories*, Glenview, Ill., Scott, Foresman, 1968, pp. 29–36.

finally, to discuss students' personal reactions to the work. Study and use of a variety of skills (oral, reading, writing and vocabulary development) should be involved so that linguistic practice and growth are insured.

Finalizing activities with a piece of literature can be the most interesting and rewarding ones conducted with the work, both for the students and the teacher. These activities serve many purposes. They help the students to view the work as an artistic whole, rather than as a collection of disparate parts. An overview and insight into the plot and character developments can be gained, along with an awareness of the development and interaction of subplots. Students can go back through the work, studying different kinds of stylistic devices and approaches used by the author, analyzing their intent and effect, and comparing and contrasting specific examples of each of those devices (for example, foreshadowing, visual images, metaphors, irony, creation of suspense, and satire). Characteristics of a particular genre can be discussed in general and then with specific reference to how they were carried out in that particular work. Personal reactions to the piece of literature can be encouraged and developed with emphasis on analyzing *why* each student reacted in the way he/she did. Students will be working on self-expression in the language but also on creating their own personal literary appreciation.[32]

The following examples are offered as suggestions for finalizing activities with different genres. In many cases, the suggestions can be worked out in genres different from the specific one in which they are here listed. The activities can be carried out as oral or written assignments, as individual presentations, group projects, class discussions, or debates.

Short Stories

1   Discuss the elements and characteristics of a short story. (This can also be done as an introductory activity and then returned to at the completion of the work.)

2   Identify the event around which the story is constructed and the situation in which the characters find themselves vis-à-vis that event. Describe the characters involved, and discuss or project their reactions to the situation.

3   Select a trait you think a character possesses. Analyze who or what reveals this trait (author's comments or vocabulary? character's actions or his words? testimony of other characters?) For example, note in Flaubert's *A Simple Heart* how Felicity's selflessness is revealed. Discuss your reactions to these traits.

4   Choose 10 to 12 verbs that you feel can reconstruct the story. Class discussion of the verbs and sentences follows with the alternative of the class as a whole writing a résumé of the story using those verbs or each one writing his own.

---

[32] For a more detailed description of such activities, see Constance K. Knop, "Terminal Activities in Teaching Literature," *Bulletin of the Wisconsin Association of Foreign Language Teachers* (Spring 1972).

5   Select what you consider the turning point or pivotal moment of the story. Defend your choice.

6   Rewrite the ending as you would have liked it.

Novels

1   Identify with a character and his/her responses. For example, write a letter as one character would (Dr. Rieux writing to Mme Rieux to express his reactions to the plague in Camus' *The Plague* or Mathilde in Maupassant's "The Necklace" writing a diary entry after losing the necklace); or pretend to be a character and express his/her reactions to an important situation in the novel (for example, Emma Bovary after the ball, or Julien Sorel after riding in the procession for the priest in Stendhal's *The Red and the Black*.)

2   Investigate the character at the start and end of the novel. Reread the first and last appearances of that character in the novel (for example, in *Mme Bovary*) to see how the character is different; discuss how and why he/she has changed; analyze the interplay of the situations and the character development.

3   Form a panel of "experts." Each may be a character from the novel and answer others' questions regarding his/her activities and motivation. Or each may be responsible for discussing a particular situation in the novel; for example, defending the consistency or inconsistency of the author in portraying scenes and characters.

4   Have a trial in which one of the characters is tried (by the students or by the students portraying other characters in the novel). For example, Meursault's trial in Camus' *The Stranger* could be redone with the outcome to be decided by the students; regarding a short story, Hauchecorne's version versus that of Malandin's tale in Maupassant's "A Piece of String" could be presented to a jury.

5   Choose the character you liked or admired most or least and discuss why.

6   Draw pictures of the characters and accompany them with a verbal description. Each student presents his/her picture and others try to guess who that character is; or the verbal description may be given first for them to guess about, followed by viewing the pictures. Similarly, pictures of important scenes can be drawn and used as stimuli for discussion, description, or résumé work.

Plays

1   Note stage movements and directions, sound effects, objects, pauses' entrances, and gestures suggested throughout by the author; and try to visualize each scene. A recording or film of the work can be used before and/or after this study.

2   Act out and tape record the most important scenes as a visualization and summary of the play. Bring in props. (This is a good chance to motivate lower-level classes by presenting the play to them.)

3   Discuss the style. Is it comic or tragic? How is each one created? By words? Actions? Interplay of characters? Visual effects?

4   Go back and study the first presentation of the main character. Prepare an anaylsis of him/her based on that passage. Then pick out moments of vacillation, hesitation, and choice throughout and how he/she changes (or does not change) at these points. Do these important moments affect changes in the other characters?

Poetry

1   Analyze the selection of sounds, assonance, and alliteration in the poem and their effect in creating a mood or feeling (for example, "Chanson d'automne" lends itself well to this type of analysis as do other Verlaine poems).
2   Draw a picture, or pictures, suggested to you by the poem.
3   With narrative poems such as those of LaFontaine—which make a good introductory activity with poetry because they can be more easily understood than more abstract ones—the teacher may use a filmstrip or a picture to help students realize that one line of verse may evoke an entire picture. Or ask them to retell the story line in their own words and then analyze the differences in word choices between their rendition and the poem.
4   Paraphrase the mood of the poem in prose or poetry—for example, describe a situation in which you felt the same way as suggested by the mood or emotions of the poem.
5   The teacher can have students work on a project to integrate the arts (or other teachers in the school can take part). For example, after reading "Clair de lune" by Verlaine, listen to Debussy's composition and view paintings of the impressionists (for example, Monet). Ask students to analyze the effects each one creates.

Asking students for suggestions for terminal activities motivates them to take part in the activities and adds to the choices available to future students.

Finalizing activities call for personal reactions from students and personal interaction with the piece of literature. Such activities help students see literature not as a daily piece of linguistic drudgery to be worked out but rather as an integrated whole, a complete work of art that they can relate to their own lives.

BIBLIOGRAPHY

General

Allen, Edward A., and Rebecca M. Valette, *Modern Language Classroom Techniques,* New York, Harcourt Brace Jovanovich, 1972.
Brooks, Nelson, *Language and Language Learning: Theory and Practice,* New York, Harcourt Brace Jovanovich, 1964.
Chastain, Kenneth, *The Development of Modern Language Skills: Theory to Practice,* Philadelphia, Center for Curriculum Development, 1971.
Dacanay, F. R., *Techniques and Procedures in Second Language Teaching,* Quezon City, Philippines, Phoenix Press, 1963.

Order from : Alemar's, P.O. Box 2119, Manila, Philippines.

Rivers, Wilga M., et al., *A Practical Guide to the teaching of French. A Practical Guide to the Teaching of German. A Practical Guide to the Teaching of Spanish,* New York, Oxford University Press, 1975.
Three separate books examine foreign language teaching methodology in the light of research into various schools of psychology and linguistics. The following aspects of language learning are discussed : oral communication, pronunciation, grammar instruction, listening comprehension, reading comprehension, and writing.

Rivers, Wilga M., *Teaching Foreign Language Skills,* Chicago, University of Chicago Press, 1968.

Culture

Altman, Howard B., and Victor E. Hanzeli (eds.), *Essays on the Teaching of Culture,* Detroit, Advancement Press of America, 1974.
American Express. Social situations and travel needs in French, German, Italian and Spanish.
Cassettes, readers, and illustrated booklets. Minicourses could be built around these materials quite easily. American Express Language Centers, Publications Department, 2125 South Street, N.W., Washington, D.C. 20008.

Bourque, Jane, *The French Teenager,* Detroit, Advancement Press of America, 1973.
EMC Corporation. Everyday life in France, Germany, and Spanish-speaking nations.
Filmstrips, cassettes, books which are up to date. EMC Corporation, 180 East Sixth Street, Saint Paul, Minnesota 55101.

Gorden Raymond L., *Living in Latin America,* Skokie, Ill., National Textbook Company, 1974.
A series of case studies based on misunderstandings that have arisen between North Americans and their Colombian hosts. The emphasis is on aspect of everyday life including such things as the use of rooms in the home, dating, giving gifts, family relationships, being a proper guest in a Latin American home, and similar topics.

Lafayette, Robert C. (ed.), *The Cultural Revolution in Foreign Language Teaching,* Skokie, Ill., National Textbook Company, 1975.
A central states report covering a wide range of culture-oriented topics including ethnic heritage, black English, sexism, study abroad, and evaluation.

Miller, Dale, *100 French Culture Capsules, 100 German Culture Capsules,* and *100 Spanish Culture Capsules.*
According to the author, these one-page culture capsules were developed "to fill a need (on the part of teachers) to have available a usable fund of cultural material for classroom presentation." Write to J. Dale Miller, Box 7149 University Station, Provo, Utah 84602.

Programmed Language Instruction. General Culture (French, German, Spanish, and Italian).

295

Programmed Language Instruction, Inc., 42-05 48th Avenue, Woodside, N.Y. 11377. Cooking, French holidays, modern French housing, meals, market, average family, and so on.

Seelye, H. Ned, *Teaching Culture: Strategies for Foreign Language Educators,* Skokie, Ill., National Textbook Company, 1974.
A very practical book that attemps to delimit the topic to a manageable number of cogent concepts pertaining to the study of culture in the language class. Includes guidelines for asking questions, preparing test items, using culture assimilators, culture capsules, culture clusters. Excellent bibliography.

Summer Camps and Summer Programs

Durette, Roland, "Language Institute for Students," *Modern Language Journal* 49 (February 1965), pp. 106–107.
This article described a six-week summer program conducted entirely in French and including games, sports, field trips, films from France, use of visiting speakers, and many other activities.

Mauritsen, Vernon P., Language Camps, Concordia College, Moorhead, Minnesota 56560.
Request information about French, German, Spanish or Russian language camps.

Correspondence: Letter, Tape, and Slide

Letters Abroad, 209 East 56th Street, New York, New York 10022.
Affiliated with Fédération Internationale des Organisations des Correspondances et d'Échanges Scholaires.

Office of Private Cooperation, U.S. Information Agency, 1776 Pennsylvania Avenue, Washington, D.C. 20025.
World Pen Pals, University of Minnesota, 2001 Riverside Avenue, Minneapolis, Minn. 55404.
World Tapes for Education, Box 15703, Dallas, Tex. 75215.
Membership includes a newsletter and an updated list of members around the world.

Literature

Bird, T. E. (ed.), *Foreign Languages: Reading, Literature and Requirements,* Middlebury, V., Northeast Conference, 1967.
Chatham, James R., and Enrique Ruiz-Fornells, "American Doctoral Research on the Teaching of Literature," *Modern Language Journal* 56 (May 1972), pp. 323–325.
Chatham, James R., and Enrique Ruiz-Fornells, "American Doctoral Research on the Teaching of Literature, Part 2," *Modern Language Journal* 56 (December 1972), pp. 495–503.
Dunning, Stephen, *Teaching Literature to Adolescents: Poetry,* Glenview, Ill., Scott, Foresman, 1966.
Dunning, Stephen, *Teaching Literature to Adolescents: Short Stories,* Glenview, Ill., Scott, Foresman, 1968.
Hankins, Olan, "Literary Analysis at the Intermediate Level: A Proposed Model," *Modern Language Journal* 56 (May 1972), pp. 291–296.

Hester, Ralph M., "From Reading to the Reading of Literature," *Modern Language Journal* 56 (May 1972), pp. 284–291.

Howes, Alan B., *Teaching Literature to Adolescents: Novels,* Glenview, Ill., Scott, Foresman, 1972.

Howes, Alan B., *Teaching Literature to Adolescents: Plays,* Glenview, Ill., Scott, Foresman, 1968.

Lohnes, Walter F. W., "Teaching the Foreign Literature" in Emma M. Birkmaier (ed.), *Foreign Language Education: An Overview,* Skokie, Ill., National Textbook Company, 1972.

Wainer, Howard, and William Berg, "The Dimensions of de Maupassant: A Multi-dimensional Analysis of Students' Perception of Literature," *American Education Research Journal* 9 (Fall 1972), pp. 485–491.

APPENDIX 1 ROLE OF WOMEN IN SOCIETY: RESULTS OF THE POLL

Among the ideas drawn out from the students were: (1) Not all Mexicans agree on all topics—that is, there is no single stereotyped Mexican attitude toward women with regard to these particular categories. (2) In some cases, there is more divergence of opinion across generations than across cultures—that is, a large percentage of young people in both cultures are in closer agreement with each other on certain issues than they are with the American teachers. (3) On certain issues, there are strong differences across cultures. Below are four sample items on which these stronger differences of opinion occurred:

	Men			Women		
	Yes	No	Don't know	Yes	No	Don't know
	%	%	%	%	%	-%
1. Is the place of women in the home?						
Mexican young people	91	6	3	90	7	3
American young people	31	45	24	27	54	19
American teachers	66	17	17	32	64	4
2. Are men more intelligent than women?						
Mexican young people	44	44	12	23	60	17
American young people	17	57	26	6	79	15
American teachers	4	79	17	4	96	0
3. Do you think the majority of married men have mistresses?						
Mexican young people	51	33	16	63	17	20
American young people	26	52	22	10	57	33
American teachers	0	83	17	0	82	18
4. Do you think it is proper for a girl to go out alone with her boy friend?						
Mexican young people	35	56	9	34	55	11
American young people	74	17	9	85	8	7
American teachers	66	34	0	91	9	0

APPENDIX 2 FRENCH WOMEN'S ATTITUDES: RESULTS OF THE POLL

Among the ideas drawn out from the students were: (1) The distribution of attitudes across cultures and across sex lines—that is some French women did want to be richer or more beautiful even though the majority opinion favored being more intelligent while the reverse pattern was obtained in the American sample. (2) The poll results seem to fly in the face of the stereotype of sexy French womanhood.

If I could have one of the following wishes fulfilled I would choose:	What percent of French women responded to each of the three questions?	What percent of American Women responded to each of the three questions?	What percent of American men indicated desirable female responses for each of the three questions?
1. to be more beautiful	4	77	67
2. to be richer	30	14	33
3. to be more intelligent	62	9	0
Total responses*	100%	100%	100%

* There were four percent "don't know" answers from the French Respondents.

10

■ *Anyone who* can *be replaced by a machine* should *be.*

■The language laboratory and other electronic media

EVOLUTION OF THE HIGH SCHOOL LANGUAGE LABORATORY

The history of the language laboratory began at Louisiana State University in 1947 with the installation of 100 cubicles equipped with disc players, headsets, and microphones.[1] During the following ten years, the number of college and university installations grew to 240 while the public and private high schools were installing less than 70 laboratories nationwide.[2] The enactment of the National Defense Education Act in 1958 changed this ratio quickly and irreversibly. With the availability of federal funds to match local moneys, public high schools began to expand their facilities by thousands of installations each year. Private and parochial secondary schools found their own sources of funding, and they too joined the language laboratory movement. An unpublished report from the United States Office of Education in 1965 showed a nationwide total of more than 6000 language laboratories at the secondary level. Based upon previous rates of growth, there is good reason to assume that the number of installations in existence by 1967 was over 8000 at the secondary school level alone. Thus, within two decades, the concept of the language laboratory, which had begun on a rather modest basis at the university level, became accepted almost unquestioningly by secondary school leaders throughout the nation. In fact, the image of the language laboratory as an essential part of secondary education became so firmly established that school architects often included as a matter of course a room designated as the "language laboratory" in their preliminary floor plans for a proposed high school building. However, there is evidence to indicate that the predominance of the university during the first decade of language labora-

[1] Joseph C. Hutchinson, *Modern Foreign Languages in High School: The Language Laboratory*, Washington, D.C., U.S. Office of Education, Bulletin No. 23, 1961, p. 1.
[2] Ibid., p. 2.

tory development created a stereotype in equipment design which was not fully adaptable to foreign language programs as they exist at the secondary level. It was only natural that the secondary school people should have turned to the only existing models during the early years of the language laboratory. Thus, a number of college and university figures became prominent in the early 1960s as consultants for laboratory installations. It was quite understandable that these people gave advice based upon their experiences with college-level students. In this process, however, several basic differences between college and secondary education tended to be overlooked. Among the differences most pertinent to this discussion are the following.

The Schedule

College-level courses may meet two, three, or four times weekly. When students are not in class they are free to go wherever they wish. Thus, the college or university student has dozens of open hours each week. In contrast, high school students are usually scheduled into academic courses on a five-days-per-week basis. Also, they are typically under adult supervision from the time the tardy bell rings in the morning until the dismissal bell sounds in the afternoon. As a result, the high school schedule affords little opportunity for open-hour lab work.

Responsibility for Learning

College students are on their own to a much greater degree than is the case with their high school counterparts. Thus they can be told, for example, that they will be tested on their ability to perform in certain aspects of the spoken language and that tapes are provided in the language laboratory that will help them to develop the required skills in some other way. If they fail to achieve what is expected, that is their problem. At the high school level, a much larger share of the responsibility for learning is on the shoulders of the teacher. In most states, students are required by law to be in school well into the late teens. Because of this, they cannot simply be "flunked out" as they are in higher education. There is no place for them to go. The influence of compulsory attendance carries over to all high school course work, including such elective subjects as foreign language. The teacher of a foreign language may insist that one or two of his/her students are not capable of continuing after the first few weeks of school. But the percentage cannot go very high, simply because teachers in other subject areas have no desire to have their subjects serve as a dumping ground for rejects from the foreign language program. Thus, the secondary school foreign language teacher is generally charged with the responsibility of moving a hundred or more students through the language program for an entire school year. The students within this group represent an extremely wide range of academic abilities and motivational drives. A substantial number of students will often be from homes where there is no strong incentive for academic achievement. Thus, the high school teacher is

300

charged not only with the responsibility to teach but also with the responsibility for motivating reluctant learners. If a large number of youngsters fail to respond, that is the teacher's problem; and the students know it.

Staffing

The college concept of language laboratory utilization was based to a large extent on open-hour use of the equipment. This implies the need for laboratory technicians, laboratory assistants, and a director of language laboratories who is available on a full-time basis to supervise the complex operation of procuring and cataloging tapes in each language, to produce correlation charts relating each tape to each appropriate chapter in the various texts, to set up a yearly laboratory budget, to arrange for preventive maintenance and for replacement of worn parts, and to perform a thousand other services necessary for the proper functioning of the laboratory facilities. By contrast, the staffing changes permissible in the high school budget will typically consist of giving one teacher one extra free period per day to serve as director of the language laboratory. In many cases, the local school budget does not even permit this much of a concession to the staffing needs that the college-type of language laboratory creates. Thus it is that, even though high school installations outnumber installations in higher education by many thousands, the newly organized National Association of Language Laboratory Directors (NALLD) was able to enroll only a handful of members below the college level.[3]

In view of all this, it should not seem surprising that the college-oriented concept of language laboratory utilization caused many problems when it was first introduced into the secondary school program. The first laboratories simply were not designed for the secondary school curriculum. In the larger high schools, scheduling was a problem from the outset. Lacking the open-hour flexibility of the college schedule, teachers had to take students out of the regularly scheduled classroom sessions and march them down the hall to the laboratory room. Because there were several sections of various modern languages meeting each period of the day, each language teacher might be assigned only one period per week in the language laboratory. This created a situation in which laboratory attendance was dictated by the complexities of the schedule, without regard for whether or not the students were at a point where they could profit from laboratory drill work. This fact, coupled with other problems such as lack of teacher familiarity with equipment, a shortage of suitable tapes, and the disruption of class activity occasioned by having to shuttle energetic adolescents back and forth down the hallway, often led to total demoralization of both the teacher and the class. The resultant negative attitudes sometimes led to vandalism as students vented their frustrations against the electronic equipment. Despite these and other problems, many teachers found ways to make the equipment achieve positive results in terms of

[3] T. R. Goldsworthy, "Status Report: National Association of Language Laboratory Directors," Madison, Wis. (December 1966).

better student performance in the audiolingual skills.[4] However, while some were learning to adapt to the language laboratory as it had developed in the colleges, others were experimenting with equipment that more closely reflected the realities of the secondary school foreign language program. One result of this experimentation was the development of an electronic teaching system that was contained within the conventional classroom. Through the late 1960s, both the laboratory and the so-called "electronic classroom" were in use; and a different pattern of utilization began to emerge for each type. The utilization of the language laboratory became more closely identified with the Instructional Materials Center Concept (IMC Concept), while the electronic classroom became a device for providing supplementary drill within the regular classroom period. The following discussion will deal with the advantages and limitations of both approaches to the use of electronic teaching systems.

FUNCTIONS AVAILABLE TO THE STUDENT IN VARIOUS TYPES OF ELECTRONIC INSTALLATIONS

Before proceeding into the more technical aspects of electronic teaching systems, it might be well for the reader to review the principal functions that existing installations provide for the student. Item 2 below describes the function of the student position as it is found in most electronic class-rooms. Most language laboratories contain at least a few student positions of the type described in item 3. Items 4 and 5 represent more recent approaches to providing one or more of the functions described in the first three items.

1   An *audiopassive* (listen only) installation is one in which students simply listen to materials recorded by the teacher or by a native speaker. If students' respond during pauses on the recording, they neither hear themselves through their headphones nor record their responses. Their own voices are partially muffled, producing an effect of semideafness.

2   In an *audioactive* (listen-respond) installation, students hear themselves as they respond to questions posed on the master tape. This is done by a system of interconnected microphone, amplifier, and headphone.

3   The *audioactive-compare* (listen-respond-record) laboratory allows students not only to listen to the master tape and hear their own responses over the headphones but also to record both questions and answers on tape by means of a tape recorder installed in their booths or, in the case of a remote-control laboratory, a nearby cabinet. Students can also play back their own responses which they then compare with the correct responses recorded on a different track of the same tape.

[4] Sarah W. Lorge, "Language Laboratory Research Studies in New York City High Schools: A Discussion of the Program and the Findings," *Modern Language Journal* 47 (November 1964), pp. 409–419.

4   *Remote-access* (dial-access) systems enable students to select the program they need by means of a dial or push button. A central tape library provides many lesson sources in a remote location. These are available without tape handling. Remote-access systems programs can be audiopassive, audioactive, or audioactive-compare.

5   *Wireless systems* can broadcast one or more programs to any number of students. Battery-powered receivers provide portability and are instantly expandable simply through the purchase of additional units. Remote monitoring and intercommunication are not possible with most systems.

THE ELECTRONIC CLASSROOM AND THE LANGUAGE LABORATORY—A COMPARISON

There are several ways in which the electronic classroom differs from the language laboratory. Physically, the electronic classroom is a dual-purpose room serving both as a regular language classroom and also as a device for electronically broadcasting language drill work to an entire class or to individuals or groups within the class. The electronic classroom has no booths to provide physical and acoustic isolation of the student. By contrast, the language laboratory is equipped with acoustically treated student cubicles located in a room separate from the regular language classroom. Both the electronic classroom and the language laboratory include a teacher console from which several programs can be simultaneously transmitted to individual students or to small groups of students within the class. In both systems, the teacher is able to communicate with students and to listen to them individually via the monitor panel. The language laboratory may or may not provide a record-and-playback mechanism in the student booth. The electronic classroom ordinarily has no provision for students to record and playback their own voice or even to record a program that is broadcast from the console. When a school chooses the electronic-classroom concept, the trend is to put in several installations one in each room where a modern foreign language is scheduled throughout the day. This is considered neither feasible nor desirable where the language laboratory is concerned.

Because of the many problems mentioned earlier (that is, budget deficiencies, scheduling problems, lack of staff, vandalism of equipment, and so on), many schools have elected to install electronic classrooms rather than the more expensive language laboratory. If the concept is fully implemented, each teacher with a full teaching load will have an electronic classroom contained within his/her room. Thus the problems associated with scheduling and class-to-lab movement are eliminated. The students can shift from classroom work to laboratory drill in seconds without moving outside the room. Moreover, the students can engage in drill work whenever the teacher feels they are ready for it, and the teacher can cut the drill work short whenever he/she judges that it has reached the point of diminishing returns. The students are never scheduled capriciously into unwanted laboratory attendance. As a result, there are fewer frustrating situations that might cause the students to vent their dissatisfaction against the equipment. Also, unlike the situation that occurs with the booth-type language laboratory, youngsters do not vanish behind cubical walls. (By definition, the electronic classroom has no booths.) The opportunities for student misbehavior are thereby greatly reduced.

There are other pedagogical reasons for selection of the electronic classroom over any type of equipment that tends toward infrequent, unsupervised utilization. Studies over the past half century have indicated that, where skill development is concerned, it is better to distribute drill work into a large number of short practice sessions rather than to mass the drill work into one long practice session. Twenty minutes of concentrated drill work daily is considered the optimum "dosage" by many practitioners of electronic-assisted instruction. This can be provided easily in a school that has been equipped with a sufficient number of electronic classrooms. Conversely, daily utilization by all students is seldom possible in those schools that have only the one centralized language laboratory. It is true that, in relatively small schools, it is often possible for teachers to approach this optimum daily utilization by having one language class use the laboratory during the first half of a class period, while another class moves in during the second half. However, a great deal of precious class and laboratory time can be lost in the process of moving students from one place to another and of getting them to settle back down once they arrive.

Another pedagogical consideration with teenage youngsters involves their need for professional, adult supervision. While it is true that a paraprofessional aide can hand students tapes and tell them which cubicle to occupy, many teachers would question whether this is enough. Will students be attentive while they are listening to the tape if the teacher is not directing the drill session? Or, even if they are attentive, will they be perceptive enough to detect the differences between the sounds that they are producing and the sounds that are coming from the master tape? There is evidence to show that superior achievement *is* possible where students have an opportunity to hear a recording of their own voice in juxtaposition to the correct response, provided this type of exercise is performed daily. Summarizing the results of her study of student performance with various types of equipment (as compared to. control groups who had no access to a laboratory), Lorge states:

The recording-playback group generally achieved better results than the audio-active group in the same time pattern, more consistently in the daily time pattern. Recording-playback may have greater effect because a variety of activities is more interesting than a single activity and brings various kinds of involvement with the language, or because greater concentration is needed to compare the model speech with the imitation, or because the student finds it particularly interesting to hear his own voice and listens more attentively.[5]

[5] Lorge, op. cit., p. 418.

The implications of Lorge's study are that each student should have the opportunity for *daily* practice with well-designed master tapes. This indicated the superiority of the language laboratory system which permits students to record their own voice and to play it back in comparison with the master program. However, the simple economics of public school financing makes it clear that this situation will almost never be feasible if historical budget limitations persist. When one considers that the cost of a teaching station plus the cost of a 30-position language laboratory represents a total expenditure of between $40,000 and $60,000, then it is not difficult to imagine why school boards are reluctant to approve the installation of more than one fully equipped laboratory per high school. And, for a number of reasons discussed earlier, the single, centralized laboratory tends to be utilized less than the optimum five-time weekly per class. Thus the factor of time appears to be much more significant than the presence or absence of recording facilities. Indeed, Lorge found that using the laboratory only once a week produced learning results that were actually inferior to results achieved by the control group, which used no electronic equipment whatever.[6] Another study involving more than 5000 students in 21 school districts of New York State gave strong evidence to support Lorge's suggestion that one laboratory drill session per week may be worse than none.[7] This study reports that most students "spent only one classroom period per week in the laboratory" and that "significant differences that favored the no-laboratory group predominated and appeared in connection with each language skill tested."[8] (Unfortunately this report is of limited value because it dealt only with students who were scheduled once-per-week in the laboratory, a pattern of utilization that has subsequently been discredited.)

Thus, it seems that the school systems are often compelled to choose between optimum equipment design and optimum equipment availability. In view of the foregoing discussion, it would appear that the best choice will generally be the one that provides maximum availability of equipment for student practice.

ADVANTAGES OF ELECTRONIC TEACHING SYSTEMS

There are certain functions that the electronic classroom or the language laboratory can perform better than the unaided teacher. Perhaps no one has defined these more simply and lucidly than Alfred S. Hayes, one of the earliest pioneers in language laboratory installations. Therefore, we have

---

[6] Ibid.
[7] Raymond F. Keating, *A Study of the Effectiveness of Language Laboratories*, New York, Institute of Administrative Research, 1963, p. 13.
[8] Ibid., pp. 38–39.

produced the list below in exactly the form in which Hayes presented it in a U.S. Office of Education publication.[9]

1   In a language laboratory all students present can practice aloud simultaneously, yet individually. In a class of 30 students, 29 are not idle while one is busy.

2   The teacher is free to focus his attention on the individual student's performance without interrupting the work of the group.

3   Certain language laboratory facilities can provide for differences in learning rates.

4   The language laboratory provides authentic, consistent, untiring, models of speech for imitation and drill.

5   The use of headphones gives a sense of isolation, intimate contact with the language, equal clarity of sound to all students, and facilitates complete concentration.

6   Recordings provide many native voices. Without such variety it is common for students to be able to understand only the teacher.

7   The language laboratory facilitates testing of each student for listening comprehension. It has generally been impracticable for the unaided teacher to test this skill.

8   The language laboratory facilitates testing of the speaking ability of each student in a class. It has generally been impracticable for the unaided teacher to test this skill.

9   Some teachers, for reasons beyond their control, do not themselves have sufficient preparation in understanding and speaking the foreign language. The language laboratory provides these teachers with an opportunity to improve their own proficiency.

10   The language laboratory makes it possible to divide the class into teacher-directed and machine-directed groups.

11   Certain language laboratory facilities can enhance the student's potential for evaluating his own performance.

12   Given specially designed instructional materials, the language laboratory can provide technical facilities for efficient self-instruction.

ADMINISTERING THE LABORATORY AS AN INSTRUCTIONAL MATERIALS CENTER

In theory, the language laboratory equipped with private cubicles and student tape recorders seems to provide answers to many of the problems associated with foreign language instruction. In the early years of the language laboratory movement, idealistic language educators pictured a type of utilization in which equipment would overcome many of the short-comings of the lock-step classroom progression. It was not difficult to

[9] Alfred S. Hayes, *Language Laboratory Facilities: Technical Guide for the Selection, Purchase, Use, and Maintenance*, Washington, D.C., 1963, GPO, Bulletin no. 37, pp. 16–17.

conjure up visions of the language teacher diagnosing student difficulties with pronunciation and structure, and then immediately—before bad habits could form—programming the student into drill work especially tailored to meet his/her specific, individual problem. By the mid-1960s, the equipment people had developed hardware that improved somewhat on this vision, they introduced remote-access equipment to the school market. With a special arrangement of switches and remotely located tape-playback mechanisms, the students can simply dial a number assigned to them by the teacher and, as if by magic, receive the exact drill they need to cope with the learning problems their teacher has identified. Again, in theory, the equipment allows the teacher to become a true professional who, like a doctor, diagnoses ills and prescribes treatment. The preventive medicines for the language learner are all contained in neat, easily retrievable audiovisual packets located in the Instructional Material Center Laboratory. At least, that is the vision in the mind of audiovisual enthusiasts and venders of language laboratory equipment. Unfortunately, this dream is seldom realized in full and is often not realized even in part, despite the expenditure of many thousands of dollars for equipment and materials. There are many prerequisites for the proper functioning of a language laboratory. The failure of any one aspect in the chain of laboratory administration can lead to ineffective utilization of the equipment. The minimal circumstances that exist in any successfully operating IMC Laboratory follow:

Availability of Program Materials

A vast number of carefully selected tapes and other materials are necessary if any IMC concept is to function properly. Despite this seemingly obvious fact, the author has found laboratories costing thousands of dollars for which little or no program materials had been provided. A projector without films and a laboratory without tapes are equally useless pieces of hardware.

Accessibility of Program Materials

Even where tapes have been purchased in abundance, they are often rendered useless simply because they have been locked in a storage cabinet or are otherwise not accessible to the student. There may be an aura of magic about the remote-access system or the less elaborate audio-active compare laboratory, but that magic can only be conjured up in those circumstances where it has been preceded by hundreds of hours of drudgery. Among the types of work essential to the proper functioning of any IMC installation are the following:

1   Purchasing of tapes for each day's work in each level of each language.
2   Labeling, cataloging, and storing each of these master tapes so that they can be easily located.
3   Dubbing student copies of the master tapes and labeling, cataloging, and storing these.

4   Producing printed correlation charts for each tape in each level of each language so that they are identifiable according to unit of work, grammatical or phonological topic, chapter of text, and so on. If the laboratory is a remote-access system, then there is the additional problem of assigning a number to each tape and to placing each tape on the remote recorder during the period of time when it will be in demand.

5   Having an efficient way of delivering a taped program to the student, either through a broadcast-and-student-record system or by means of a tape check-out system.

Scheduling Feasibility

If the IMC laboratory concept is to work, the teacher must be able to assign each student a certain number of out-of-class laboratory periods. If conditions permit (such as in a school system on a flexible schedule), the student may have some choice in the matter. In the more traditional schedule the laboratory may be made available during every period of every day so that students may sign up for the laboratory during their free periods instead of going to the library or study hall. Students can also be permitted to engage in laboratory work before and after school. In any case, once the schedule is set, the student has the responsibility to attend and to do the assigned work. This work is assigned in addition to the regular classroom sessions in the traditionally scheduled school. It is regarded by the teacher as homework comparable to reading assignments in English or drill exercises in mathematics.

Staffing

All of the foregoing implies that someone will be available to supervise laboratory sessions. Clearly, a full-time librarian-technician is needed to perform the functions listed above. Further, persons are needed to see that the equipment is kept in proper working order, and that sufficient copies of each taped lesson are available when needed. The person in charge of an IMC-type of installation must also be knowledgeable enough to serve as a liaison person between the various members of the language staff. The taped program received by a student when he/she enters the laboratory must be precisely the program that the teacher has assigned and that the student recognizes as the one he/she needs and is able to use. The Instructional Materials Center librarian must be a highly skilled individual.

As we have seen, few schools below the college level have found it possible to staff, equip, and service IMC laboratories for instruction in foreign languages. In staffing, for example, we note that, despite the existence of an estimated 8000 high school language laboratories, only 134 directors of secondary school laboratories could be identified throughout the nation in 1966.[10]

The lack of a fully equipped language laboratory does not necessarily completely rule out the IMC concept of utilization. Many high school

[10] Goldsworthy, op. cit.

308

teachers who perceive the value of out-of-class oral drill have found ways to adapt the electronic classroom to this purpose. Thus, intsead of having the student take a tape into a booth (or otherwise receive the program for use on an individual tape player), the teacher or a laboratory assistant may broadcast the tape from the console to where the student receives it via an audioactive (listen-respond) unit. Lacking student recorders, the electronic classroom permits the school to minimize both the initial investment in equipment and the continuing maintenance costs for that equipment. However, the opportunity for individual pacing is lost in the process. Students cannot stop, pause, or rewind their tape. They can only listen and respond to the program as it plays inexorably from the console.

SPECIFICATIONS FOR ELECTRONIC EQUIPMENT

Experience with electronic equipment used in teaching modern foreign languages clearly indicates that their effectiveness is in direct proportion to the quality of sound they are capable of producing. Whether it is from tape, disk, or film sound track, the signal that comes through to the students' ear must be of sufficient quality to enable them to hear the sounds of the new language distinctly. A signal that is weak, distorted, or obscured by noise can negate the value of audiovisual materials which are pedagogically sound in every other way. Clearly, it would be ideal if all language teaching devices had the fidelity characteristics of the best custom-made high-fi sets. Similarly, it would be well if all films, records, and tapes used in the foreign language classroom were properly amplified and broadcast through full-range speaker systems. However, despite the desirability of such equipment, the high cost of supplying it to every language classroom has necessitated a more realistic approach. Experience has shown that a satisfactory compromise can be reached with medium-fidelity, moderately priced equipment. Studies of student's ability to distinguish minimal differences between two foreign language sounds conducted at the Massachusetts Institute of Technology indicated that "system frequency response of less than 7300 cps, and especially below 5000 cps, prevented a substantial number of American boys and girls from perceiving phonemic contrasts in German and French."[11] Studies conducted at the University of Wisconsin revealed that sound energy registered by a French speaker is very strong, up to 8000 cps and beyond.

It may be concluded from all this that the first essential characteristic of electronic equipment used in the teaching of modern languages must be an adequate frequency response. For student headsets and microphones—the weakest links in the component chain—this may be defined as 80 to 8000 cps, plus or minus 3 db. It should be noted here, that the

[11] M. Buka, M. Z. Freeman, and W. N. Locke, *International Journal of American Linguistics* 28 (January 1962), p. 70.

listed frequency response of a component is meaningless unless the db (decibel) tolerance is also given. (The smaller the db tolerance, the better the fidelity.) Also, because of various factors relating to the nature of electronic systems, it is always better to purchase components that exceed the minimum standards. It is usually good practice to have a qualified technical consultant review the various bids submitted, for the purpose of determining which bidder is supplying the most for the money. Such scrutiny of components will often reveal that one of the higher bids offers sufficiently more in equipment fidelity and durability as to warrant the additional cost. The consultant who makes such judgments should be a disinterested third party; one cannot, for example, expect sales representatives for language laboratory equipment companies to supply objective data in such matters.

EFFECTIVENESS OF AUDIOVISUAL MATERIALS IN RELATION TO THE LOCAL CURRICULUM

Questions about the efficacy of equipment and materials must first be directed toward solving problems relating to curricular content and instructional techniques. One must begin with those elements of the foreign language curriculum that the local foreign language staff considers worth teaching. It is also necessary to consider the *manner* in which, in their view, that content ought to be learned. When these two considerations have been dealt with, the next step is to seek out or to produce materials that teachers can accept or, better still, enthusiastically endorse. That is, teachers must be firmly convinced that equipment and materials do actually contribute to student learning and that they do so in an aesthetically satisfying and pedagogically defensible way. Even this is not sufficient. In addition to teacher acceptance it is also essential to have indications from the *students* as to whether or not the audiovisual programs are valuable adjuncts to the usual classroom work. It is not difficult to conduct brief periodic surveys of student opinion regarding, for example, which exercises were most helpful, most enjoyable, most easily understandable or conversely, which were least helpful, most boring, most confusing. This kind of feedback research should then be followed by scrupulous editing of existing software programs. This, in turn, may result in such actions as the replacement of an unsuccessful commercially produced drill with a locally produced one or in the addition of more intelligible explanations to introduce those exercises that have been universally misunderstood. Or the teacher may decide to reduce the number of oral memorization exercises in favor of listening comprehension. These are only a few of the possibilities for program improvement. Pioneers in the language laboratory field have long recognized the need for improved software in developing effective utilization of that particular kind of audio-

310

visual equipment. In this regard we have the statement of Alfred Hayes, one of the world's first laboratory directors, that

... the most glaring mistake we have made was to underestimate the magnitude of the problem of developing the necessary teaching materials, for the tape recorder remains inert, mute, ugly when it has nothing to say, or when what it says is ill-considered, ill-planned and unrelated to some self-consistent view of the teaching process which it can so effectively extend, or, in certain respects, even make possible for the first time, such as ... intensive listening practice. ...[12]

Belasco[13] has also emphasized the importance of listening comprehension and Valette[14] has given a number of practical suggestions for teaching listening, reading, writing, and literature by means of the language laboratory or electronic classroom. Reinert has noted the lack of variety and humor in existing tapes and has given specific examples of how high school laboratory programs have been improved in this respect through the use of poems, anecdotes, and adaptations of children's literature.[15] Folk songs and popular tunes can be used to apparent advantage in the high school laboratory, not only as a respite from tedious drill material but also to teach basic structure and vocabulary. Some songs are marvelously repetitious. The same verb structure that evokes dispirited responses when presented as a memorization drill will often be articulated with enthusiasm if it occurs in lyric form to the accompaniment of teenage music. The teacher must select the songs with great care, of course, and must not overdo this kind of laboratory activity. One purpose of such programming is to add some excitement, spice, and variety to the learning experience. Studies of the characteristic of successful foreign language teachers have indicated that nonpredictability, variety, and creative supplementation of the basic curriculum are teacher characteristics that are related to student success in the foreign language classroom.[16] It seems reasonable to suggest that lessons taught with the aid of audiovisual media need also to conform to the characteristics of the successful language classroom.

As was noted above, a large number of language laboratories were installed in public and nonpublic high schools and colleges around the nation during the 1960s. In those years, laboratory instruction tended to be focused entirely upon the audiolingual aspects of communication, with little provision for the use of visuals. Furthermore, a large number of

[12] Alfred S. Hayes, "New Directions in Foreign Language Teaching," *Modern Language Journal* 49 (May 1965), pp. 281–293.
[13] Simon Belasco, "Nucleation and the Audio-Lingual Approach," *Modern Language Journal* 49 (December 1965), pp. 482–491.
[14] Rebecca M. Valette, "The Use of the Language Laboratory in Intermediate and Advanced Classes," *NALLD Newsletter* 11 (May 1968), pp. 4–9.
[15] Harry Reinert, "Creative Lab Usage," *NALLD Journal* 4 (October 1969), pp. 57–63.
[16] Robert L. Politzer and Louis Weiss, *Characteristics and Behaviors of the Successful Foreign Language Teacher*, Technical Report No. 5, Stanford University School of Education, USOE Grant OEC–6–10–078, April, 1969.

311

the secondary school installations had no provision for students to record and listen to their own voice or, indeed, even to use the student position independently. As a result, the predominant mode of utilization in a large number of high schools involved having the teacher play a tape from the console to an entire classroom full of students, all of whom received the same directions, the same content, and the same form of practice simultaneously. Seldom was the laboratory used to provide for individual learning styles or learning rates. In short, the high school language laboratory often functioned as a very expensive tape recorder–amplifier system. Some teachers claimed that there was an advantage in being able to monitor students from the console and to intercommunicate with them when they needed help. Other teachers insisted that they could do this just as effectively with a good tape recorder and two large speakers located so as to make the language material clearly audible in all parts of the room. With this system the teacher simply walks around the room listening to student responses and, if necessary, talking to them directly. Other advantages of this simpler system are that the high service costs for language laboratories are eliminated, as are many other problems such as student discipline, vandalism to the equipment, and loss of time in moving from the classroom to the laboratory. There are many people who have come to believe that the only justifiable form of high school language laboratory is one that allows students to study independently, at their own rate, using a cassette or tape that enables them to stop, reverse, and redo material that they have not comprehended. There is also reason to believe that students should be able to terminate the learning activity of their own volition as soon as they have fulfilled the purpose for being in the laboratory in the first place. There should be a specific purpose for going to the laboratory; the students should know what that purpose is and they should have a basis for evaluating whether or not the work in the laboratory has fulfilled that purpose. In practical terms this means that each tape ought to be accompanied with a study guide indicating the learning outcomes, the procedures to be followed in the lab in reaching these outcomes, and a simple device for helping students to evaluate whether or not they have achieved what they set out to do. Perhaps because of the profession's romance with the language laboratory and other expensive hardware, other more practical and less costly media have been neglected. It is no secret that the results achieved by laboratories have not measured up to the promises of their promoters. It may also be that too large a portion of the available resources for learning devices was directed toward media that demanded a high degree of passivity on the part of the learner. In retrospect, it also appears that much more time, effort, and money went into perfecting the hardware than into developing software that was both interesting to the learner and designed to involve him/her, at some point, in the active use of the foreign language. Too much of the work with electronic media appears to have involved either rote repetition or manipulation of language structures that had no personal meaning to the language learner.

AUDIOVISUAL DEVICES AND STUDENT CREATIVITY

Many people agree that a great deal of listening practice must precede (or at least accompany) the learning of the more active, productive skills, such as speaking and writing. However, if this listening practice is to be anything more than a series of noises that cause the learner's eardrums to vibrate, then the student must somehow be involved in actively receiving meaning through the foreign sound system at something approaching the native rate of delivery. For the most part, this means that students should *want* to understand the message that is being relayed to them by means of electronic media. It follows, therefore, that the message should be something that is worth relaying, and that the student is likely to perceive it as such. Thus, the questions dealt with earlier under the headings of motivation and individualized instruction cannot be separated from the topic of using audiovisual media. If the medium is, in fact, the message, then the message is to be found in the quality of the software and in the pedagogical techniques, not in the hardware. If there is anything to be learned from the decade of the sixties, it is that people can be bored to death as readily with technological devices as with live human presentations. It would appear, therefore, that greater attention needs to be paid to the following areas: (1) Helping students to improve their ability to listen receptively to foreign language material at their level of understanding, and (2) Helping students to use the target language with the degree of creativity that enables them to express their own ideas in the target language.

THE OVERHEAD PROJECTOR

The overhead projector is perhaps the most widely available projection device in schools and colleges today. Many educational institutions have made this equipment available in every classroom. The most common use of this device involves the teacher delivering a lecture based on written, pictorial, or graphic material, which was either produced locally or was supplied by a commercial publisher. This type of utilization tends to involve the students in a rather passive process of listening to the teacher and reading what is projected on a screen. The learning check that follows is often in the form of a traditional test. There are, in fact, many learning goals for which this approach is quite appropriate. However, to limit use of the equipment to this single format is to risk neutralizing it's ultimate effectiveness as a learning tool.

The overhead projector can also be used to elicit productive responses in the areas of speaking and writing. One technique is to produce one's own line drawings (if the requisite artistic skills are available) or to find suitable drawings in books and magazines that can be copied and made into transparencies. The material can then be projected on a screen; and the students can be asked to respond to it orally or in writing within a

313

given period of time. The work can be done either individually or in small groups. The following are examples of techniques that have been used successfully by classroom teachers:

1   A map of the downtown area of a European city is projected on the screen. An X is placed at the "International Hotel," which is in the left hand corner of the screen. Town landmarks such as churches, restaurants (with suitable foreign names), and other appropriate buildings and places are indicated on the map. Each student is given ten minutes to write a set of directions for telling another person how to get from the International Hotel to the railroad depot. A dictionary and other references may be used in preparing the directions.

2   Alternate or follow-up procedure: Students form pairs (classroom conditions permitting) and take turns giving each other directions as per above instructions. The teacher then draws two names out of a hat at random. The first student whose name is drawn moves the X on the overhead projector to any position he or she desires. The first student then asks the second student (in the target language, of course), "How do I get from the opera house to the art gallery?" The second student must try to explain it, using a pointer to indicate where the student must go straight, turn left, how many blocks to go, and so on. The first student moves the X along the map diagram in accordance with the instructions. Students are awarded points for correctly giving and receiving instructions. The student who is following instructions is, of course, not penalized for ending up in the wrong place, provided he/she has followed instructions correctly.

3   A series of cartoon situations (without captions) can be made into transparencies and projected on the screen. Depending upon their degree of language proficiency, students can be asked to write a short description of their version of what is happening in the cartoon frames. The students can then break into groups of four in which they are given fifteen minutes to prepare a group consensus. After the small-group sessions, students from each group take turns explaining one of the frames to the total class. At the end of the session, the teacher gives a "creativity award" for the best production.

Direct Student Use of the Overhead Projector

With proper planning and direction, students can make direct use of the overhead projector in connection with the instructional process. Students with artistic ability, for example, can make simple line drawings relating to the material in the textbook. If the school has a supply of durable transparencies, an erasable kind of pen can be used for this purpose. When the lesson is over, the transparency figures can simply be erased with a moistened kleenex or cloth. If a more permanent type of transparency is desired, students can draw their cartoon figures on regular paper, using a fine-point, felt-tipped pen. Copy material produced in this way can be readily converted into transparencies. At the beginning levels it is best to

314

focus on very simple items that are currently being studied. Students can produce or locate simple line drawings that relate in a creative or amusing way to the grammatical structure at hand. For example, in one Spanish class a first-year student drew a picture of a man in pajamas with an obvious hangover. The figure looked despondent with disheveled hair and sloppy attire. The caption under the picture said, in Spanish, "How handsome!" At the more advanced levels, students were doing line drawings representing tricky idioms from the textbook and the use of the subjunctive, among other things. One picture showed a student surrounded by thousands of dollar bills. The caption here said, "If I were rich I would buy a new car." The purpose of this kind of technique is to establish a meaningful connection between oral symbol or written symbol and to involve the learner directly in creating the connection. The theory behind this is that, before the language learner can establish a connection between target language symbols and the target culture, he/she must first internalize the forms in terms of his/her own cultural background. This carries with it the further belief that it does learners no harm to learn to communicate first in the target language using as referents phenomena within their own culture. Those who believe that all semantic referents must be to the target culture, will probably disagree with this technique. It might be pointed out, however, that to hold strictly to target language cultural referents is to eliminate from consideration a technique that has proven very effective in many classrooms. It should also be noted that if students do get the opportunity to travel to other countries, they will frequently be asked questions about their own culture. Thus, a good case could be made for learning how to talk about one's own culture first and then later learning to contrast phenomena in one's own culture with phenomena of the second culture.

The overhead projector can also be used to good advantage to teach the syntax of the target language. First the teacher prepares transparencies made up of a variety of selected linguistic items that can be combined into meaningful utterances. The words and letters are then cut up and shuffled in random order. Students are asked to come to the overhead projector and produce sense-making utterances by properly arranging the words, verb endings, and so on, on the overhead projector. The actual procedure allows for considerable flexibility. For example, the student who puts the material on the projector can ask a fellow student in the class to read what is there. A second approach would be for the teacher to ask, "Is that a complete sentence?" Depending on their level of skill development, students can be asked either to paraphrase what has been projected or to supply an approximation in English. The teacher, using the foreign language, should ask students, "Is that correct or incorrect?" Students should be required to answer in a complete utterance. Students who can see that the effort of a fellow student was incorrect, should then be asked to go to the projector and make it correct.

The items given below were used successfully in a junior high school Spanish class. The lesson was carried out in the manner described above.

Nearly half the students participated in the exercise in a ten-minute period. The class was carried on completely in Spanish.

Recombination items, each on a separate piece of transparency.

le	a Juan	a las chicas
te	a ellas	la corbata
nos	a Josefa	aprieta
les	a la maestra y a mi	no

Audiovisual Production by Students

A further technique is to have a series of line drawings on transparencies or slides, which are then projected on a screen. Students are asked to select from words available a proper caption to go with the visual. Once again, students are actively involved in creating the learning mediators. They are asked to supply much of this material, either by producing original drawings or by tracing them out of books and magazines in a form that can be reproduced with the equipment available in the local school. At the more advanced levels, students can be asked, as a project, to produce brief cartoon stories that they narrate orally. For example, using various books on the bullfight, students can prepare transparencies or slides showing in sequence the various elements of the bullfight and the various *pases* which expert matadors are capable of performing. Other cultural topics that have been presented this way in the target language are a series of maps and pictures showing the routes followed by French explorers in America as well as depicting some of the events relating to French exploration. A presentation in German involved graphic pictorial and statistical items relating to the immigration of Germans to this country in various periods of time. To avoid projects of this type from getting out of hand, it is well to follow the procedures outlined below:

1 Delineate the topic clearly and sharply so that it is focused upon a limited number of items that are capable of visual presentation.
2 Establish a time limit for the delivery of the presentation. (Usually the topic should be presented in no more than five minutes.)
3 Insist that the students do a creative restructuring of their research material rather than merely reading something from an original source.
4 Make sure that the technical details, such as using the right kind of ink and the right kind of paper to insure optimum reproduction of the transparency, are taken care of. (The same principle of technical quality applies to projects done with slides, videotape, or motion picture.)
5 Have the students prepare a tentative script in advance, and have them consult with the teacher beforehand so as to minimize grammatical errors and other kinds of inaccuracies.
6 Direct the students, insofar as possible, toward a review of those prerequisite grammatical forms that they have already studied. A bit of guidance in the way of grammatical review will also help to minimize errors in the final student production.

7   Ordinarily it is best not to interrupt students during their actual presentation. The point of this kind of exercise is to get students to communicate actively with respect to a topic that they have put together. Interruptions tend to inhibit the fluency of the student who is performing and of all others who will subsequently be asked to perform. The teacher might well make unobtrusive notes of student errors for use later in designing practice material. It is not wise to identify the student after the presentation with the errors that were made. The student should be evaluated solely on the basis of the quality of the content of the presentation and on his or her ability to communicate that which was intended. A few minutes can also be allowed after the presentation for questions from the class. These, too, should be in the foreign language.

Quizzes, Tests, and Games on the Overhead Projector

The overhead projector can also be used efficiently in connection with certain kinds of quizzes, tests, and games, especially in those cases where simple, predictable responses are called for. For example, the scrambled sentence, when unscrambled, usually has only one or two possible word-order patterns. Thus, a transparency containing the correct answers can be prepared by the teacher in advance. After the test or exercise has been given to the students, the correct answers can be projected on the screen and students can either exchange papers or be asked to correct their own, depending on the situation. Similarly, the solutions to certain puzzles or games can be projected after the students have engaged in the appropriate learning activity. This enables the teacher to move around the classroom answering personal questions as the students refer to the screen in the correction process. Where it is desirable to take test items one at a time, the teacher can simply place a sheet of paper over the transparency and move it down one item at a time thereby progressively revealing each answer in sequence.

SLIDES, FILMSTRIPS, AND MOTION PICTURES

A number of the activities described above can be done as well or better by means of slides, filmstrips, videotapes, or super 8- or 16-millimeter motion pictures. One gains color and/or motion with these media. However, costs are generally much higher and the logistics of producing or presenting a good finished product are often formidable in comparison to materials prepared or projected on the overhead projector. On the other hand, good professionally prepared materials are available on slides, filmstrips, and 16-millimeter color film. With properly designed instructional approaches, such materials can be used effectively to teach certain aspects of culture and language skills while providing a welcome change of pace in the instructional process. With commercially available motion pictures it is usually advisable to teach the new vocabulary items from the sound track in advance and to alert the students to the features in the film toward which their attention should be directed. The students should not, of course, be told everything in advance or they will have little interest in viewing the film later. The preparatory study should bring them to the point where they can view the film with understanding and pleasure. It is also advisable to provide follow-up activities that assess the students' comprehension of what happened in the film or other audiovisual presentation. A formal test or quizz is not always the best follow-up to an enjoyable film experience. Knowing they will be formally tested can inhibit students' appreciation and comprehension. Less obtrusive evaluative procedures can often be used instead of quizzes. Small-group discussions can be employed to see which "team" can come up with the best summary of what happened. An opinion poll can be distributed and subsequently discussed to determine students' reaction to the film. One purpose of such a poll can be "to determine whether this film is suitable for use with future classes." In connection with the poll, students can be asked questions about the plot, characters, setting, and value system revealed by the filmed episode. The degree to which students can answer such questions will provide an index to the group's understanding of the film's content. Results obtained in this way should not, of course, be used in connection with the grading process. The purpose of the unobtrusive measure is to determine the extent to which students are learning as a result of intrinsic interest in the material itself. To covertly assign grades on the basis of an open request for opinions would be to undermine the entire effort.

Increasingly, local school audiovisual departments are equipped with facilities for producing color slides, videotapes, and motion pictures with soundtracks. With proper planning and budgeting, the foreign language teacher can exploit these media to good advantage. Cultural material from a variety of sources can be drawn together and shot on color slides for efficient teacher presentation. There are many other ways that the teacher's presentations can be enhanced by having materials prepared for class use. However, the teacher's preparation time is, after all, quite severely limited. Thus a further use of media is to involve the students themselves in some kind of culminating activity in which they are the producers, writers, directors, actors, technicians, and presenters. This is not the kind of activity that one plans for every week of every semester; one or two a semester is usually more than enough. Even one during an entire school year can have excellent results in terms of increased student motivation. The following are examples of how teachers have used various media to obtain creative student involvement in the use of the target language.

1   *Videotape.* Students (in groups of three) prepared original skits based on a novel that was being read in class. They used the characters and the basic situation of the novel, but were free to modify the plot. The skit was written by the students, checked by the teacher, and then scheduled for production on video cassette. Skits could run from eight to ten minutes. To be acceptable, the skits had to be prepared cor-

rectly, following the model of modern Spanish drama. Reading, writing, speaking, and listening skills were involved. Tapes were played back, discussed, and evaluated by fellow students. A few students were given the option of preparing and presenting parodies of commercials for viewing between skits.

2 *Super 8.* A third-year German class dramatized *The Music Man* (*Der Musikmann*) and prepared a taped narration to accompany the color motion picture sequence. Appropriate music from the musical was in the background. Once again, listening, speaking, reading, and writing skills were involved.

3 *Slide and filmstrip.* A visit to the nearby annual *Oktoberfest* produced a large number of slides of German-related activities. The third-year German students used inexpensive cameras to document the visit. A descriptive narration was written in German to accompany a selected sequence of slides. The slides were later converted to a filmstrip. All language skills were again involved.

4 *Slides.* Third- and fourth-year French students collected cartoons from French-language periodicals. These were photographed and made into color slides. The captions were discussed in French with relation to the content of the cartoon. Students had to pay close attention because later they are expected to be able to describe the cartoon and explain it from memory with no greater stimulus than the caption. Listening, speaking, and writing skills were emphasized along with vocabulary development. Also, forty famous French foods were presented in color by photographing recipe cards as follows: (1) the picture of the food with a written description, (2) the same card without the caption. Students had to first learn to read all the caption correctly and rapidly from a tray of slides. Then, without the captions, they had to be able to identify each of the foods correctly, using as a stimulus only the appetizing picture. Vocabulary building, pronunciation and a degree of culture were involved here.

5 *Sixteen-millimeter films.* A visitor from Mexico along with local staff members dramatized the use of gestures, physical contact, critical speaking distance, and other nonverbal as well as verbal factors relating to communication. This culture capsule on film was made available throughout the large school district.

RADIO BROADCASTING AND FOREIGN LANGUAGE LEARNING

Radio has perhaps been the most neglected of all the commonly available electronic media. In May of 1953, the *French Review* contained an article on "The Adaptation of Radio to Foreign Language Teaching"; and in May of 1961, the same journal included a second article by the same author, William N. Felt, entitled "Radio and the Foreign Language Laboratory." A few other articles and research reports appeared during the 1960s and 1970s, but, by and large, their number has constituted a small trickle in comparison to the flood of articles, books, and commercial materials relating to foreign language instruction with such media as television, videotapes, audiotapes, films, and filmstrips. There are both technical and pedagogical reasons for this situation. On the technical side, there is the difficulty of receiving the desired programs in the appropriate target languages at the various locations of schools across the country. For those with technical expertise, this may not seem to be too much of a task. However, the problem of receiving and amplifying a radio signal in a form that is comprehensible (and hence usable) in the classroom or laboratory can be formidable indeed to the busy foreign language teacher.

The pedagogical aspects of using radio are also challenging. The instructional approaches of the 1960s and 1970s have tended toward a high degree of content specificity in advance—that is, the teacher has been expected to plan for certain specific student outcomes. Obviously live radiobroadcasts are not readily adaptable to this kind of preplanning. There is a way to overcome this difficulty to some degree and to provide useful listening material even for beginning and intermediate levels. It involves the taping of short segments of high-interest, currently relevant broadcasts from the target culture, focusing on topics such as international incidents involving American celebrities, visits of the American President to other countries, major news reports, an editorial on America or about Americans, a discussion of the generation gap in the target culture, and so on. After a segment of such material has been successfully dubbed "off the air," it can be made pedagogically more useful through the following steps:

1   Playing the entire segment of several minutes duration.
2   Following with the same material, adding one-minute pauses in which the student "rests" and mentally integrates the material. (No overt responses).
3   Repeating the taped broadcast several times in the above manner.
4   Administering a listening comprehension check at the end of the exercise (see the last section of Chapter 11).

The theoretical and practical justification for this approach has been discussed in an article by Belasco.[17] and in Nelson's extremely useful "Focus Report."[18]

However, as Nelson points out, while the technique discussed above is a useful and highly recommended adaptation of radio, it does not, in fact, exploit the full potential of that medium. Once the radio signal has been captured on tape, it is no longer radio. For radio is "free, evanescent voice communication" rather than a replayable recorded message.[19]

[17] op. cit.
[18] Robert J. Nelson, *Using Radio to Develop and Maintain Competence in a Foreign Language*, Eric Focus Report No. 11, New York, ACTFL Materials Center, 1969.
[19] Ibid., p. 5.

320

In a very real sense, the ability to comprehend the varied and unpredictable messages contained in live radiobroadcasts is a measure of one's listening competence. Radio involves one-shot oral messages of presumed interest to listeners in the target culture. For this reason it is an ideal medium for maintaining and refining students' listening comprehension skills at the intermediate and advanced levels. In Nelson's opinion, foreign language news broadcasts are the most useful in this regard because they provide a means of self-testing for the student.[20] Students can be instructed to check the accuracy of their understanding of the foreign language broadcast against oral or written news reports in English.

Radio Equipment Needs

It would seem, then, that a high-quality multi-band shortwave receiver should be standard equipment for any foreign language program with a sequence of three years or more. Where foreign language broadcasts can be picked up via AM-FM radio, appropriate receivers would, of course, also be recommened. Furthermore, some schools are in a position to staff and fund two-way shortwave equipment, thus allowing for conversational exchanges with ham radio enthusiasts around the world. The possibility of establishing this kind of facility should also be explored, even though the costs are higher and even though the licensing procedures present certain difficulties. The cost of sending equipment is naturally much higher than that of receiving equipment. Receivers of adequate quality can be purchased for a few hundred dollars. Public schools will in some cases be able to use federal money (for example, ESEA Title IV funds) to acquire this and other types of equipment for use in foreign language teaching.

In summary, it should be noted that during the 1970s the pedagogical climate in foreign language education tended to shift away from an emphasis on rote drill work and toward activities that would involve students in meaningful direct communication of thoughts, feelings, and ideas. Such a climate would seem to favor strongly the increased use of radio as an instructional medium.

SUMMARY

It seems safe to say that audiovisual devices are valuable when they succeed in putting the student into profitable sustained contact with the foreign language. We have evidence that students are capable of acquiring a significant portion of their language learning with the aid of such devices. However, there appear to be certain minimum prerequisites for their effective utilization. Effective use of audiovisuals is related to factors

[20] Ibid., p. 5.

which are summarized below in the form of questions that must be satisfactorily answered if optimum utilization is to be expected:

1   What evidence exists regarding the quality and proper functioning of electronic and mechanical components as they pertain to foreign language instruction?

2   What evidence exists regarding the availability and effectiveness of the materials (software) and the acceptance of these materials by the students and teachers who must use them?

3   Does an analysis of instructional programs indicate the presence of such characteristics as variety of content, novelty of approach, the use of humor, and so forth, or is the programming monolithic, repetitive, and dull?

4   What evidence is there to show that the software is appropriate for use with existing hardware?

5   To what degree does the process of testing and evaluation reflect the activities performed by the students in using the equipment and materials?

6   What provision has been made to facilitate transfer of learning from the instructional situation to the world of reality as the students perceive it?

7   Do audiovisual activities frequently involve the students in creating at least some part of the message in an active, personal way?

BIBLIOGRAPHY

Adelaide, Sister Ruth, S.C., "A Unique Use of Media: 'Twinned Classroom' Approach to the Teaching of French," *Audiovisual Instruction* 13, (May 1968), pp. 468–470.
This article describes the use of tape-slide exchanges between matched elementary classrooms in France and America. The techniques are adaptable to the MOS program.

Arendt, Jermaine D., (ed.), "The Overhead Projector in Foreign Language Teaching," *Audiovisual Instruction* 12 (May 1968), pp. 463–467.
This article provides a concise yet remarkably complete set of guidelines for the use of the overhead projector for foreign language instruction. It includes instruction on how to prepare transparencies along with specific examples in French, German, and Spanish.

Nelson, Robert J., *Using Radio to Develop and Maintain Competence in a Foreign Language,* New York, ACTFL Materials Center, 1969.
Oettinger, Anthony G., and Sema Marks, *Run Computer Run: The Mythology of Educational Innovation,* New York, Collier Books, 1969.
Reinert, Harry, "Creative Lab Usage," *NALLD Journal* 4 (October 1969), pp. 57–63.
Richardson G., "The Use of Visual Aids in the Teaching of Modern Languages," *Advances in the Teaching of Modern Languages,* vol. 1, edited by B. Libbish, New York, Macmillan, 1964.
Slides from Flat Copy, Ectagraphic Visual Maker ($120), Kodak Company.

322

A kit contained in a briefcase; can be used on flat surfaces to produce color slides or black-and-white slides almost without fail. Instamatic camera is used with two camera stands, each of which has built-in close-up lense. Flash cubes required.

Valette, Rebecca M., "The Use of the Language Laboratory in Intermediate and Advanced Classes," *NALLD Newsletter* 2 (May 1968), pp. 4–9.

Sources of Information and Materials by Language

French. FACSEA, Society for French American Cultural Services and Educational Aid, 972 Fifth Avenue, New York, N.Y. 10021.

German. TAP Guide, National Carl Schurz Association, Inc., 339 Walnut Street, Philadelphia, Penn. 19106.

Latin. American Classical League, Miami University, Oxford, Ohio 45055.

Russian. The Russian Studies Center for Secondary Schools, The Andrew Mellon Library, The Choate School, Wallingford, Conn. 06492.

Spanish. Spanish American Service and Educational Aids Society, Cultural Relations Office, Embassy of Spain, 1477 Girard Street, N.W., Washington, D.C. 20009.

11

■ *O wad some Power the giftie gie us*
To see oursels as ithers see us !
It wad frae mony a blunder free us,
An' foolish notion.... ROBERT BURNS

■Evaluation of the foreign language program

Among the many ways of evaluating the success of a contemporary foreign language program we have chosen three for discussion in this section. The first of these involves a tabulation of characteristics relevant to foreign language instruction. With this approach, evaluators look at such things as the quality of the staff, the availability of audiovisual equipment and materials, the breadth and depth of foreign language offerings, and similar evidence. From this it is assumed that a given school has a quality program if, for example, it has four years or more of course offerings in several languages ; it has a high percentage of teachers with Masters degrees ; and if students have available an adequate supply of books, tapes, and electronic equipment. The limitation of this method of evaluation is that it reveals only that the program is potentially good or bad. There is no guarantee that the potential will be realized. For example, the teacher with the Masters degree may be performing badly in the classroom, the language laboratory may go unused day after day, and the audiolingual texts with last year's copyright may be used in a manner reminiscent of the nineteenth century. Clearly, by itself, the listing of external program characteristics does not provide sufficient data for program evaluation.

A second approach to evaluation of the foreign language program involves a careful analysis of teacher and student activities to determine whether or not these activities are consistent with stated course objectives. If listening, speaking, reading, and writing are listed as course objectives, then a major portion of class and laboratory time must involve active student use of the language in the pursuit of these skills. Evaluators will thus make a study of all classroom activities showing how much time the teacher spends talking in English versus the time spent talking in the target language. A similar count will be taken of student use of the native and target languages. A further breakdown of student-teacher interaction will reveal how much of the use of the target language involves mere rote imitation and how much involves more creative use of the language. After

324

a broad sampling of classroom activities has been taken, it might be found, for example, that 30 percent of class time is devoted to teacher talk in English, 30 percent to teacher talk in the target language, 10 percent to rote student responses in the target language, 15 percent to student discussions in English, and 15 percent to nonlearning activities such as silence, confusion, moving back and forth to the chalkboard, and so on. It may be discovered through further analysis that the students are largely passive listeners who are seldom given the opportunity to recombine expressions that they have been asked to memorize and who are almost never asked to create utterances of their own in the target language either orally or in writing. This type of evaluation can indicate the activities that will need to be changed if classroom work is to be made consistent with course objectives. One of the major difficulties of this means of evaluation is the establishment of evaluative criteria upon which all teacher and supervisory personnel can agree. The staff must agree that a causal relationship exists between student-teacher interaction and the stated course objectives. Also, the evaluator must be a trained observer with a fairly good command of the languages used by those teachers he/she is called upon to evaluate. Perhaps the best solution to the latter problem is to train each language teacher to evaluate tape recordings of his/her own teaching behavior.

Ideally, evaluation would also involve a third approach: the direct measurement of student achievement. The ultimate question is, after all, "Are the language students actually learning to comprehend, speak, read, and write the new language?" To answer this question some high schools use standardized proficiency tests for each level of progress throught the language program. The norms that are provided with such tests give some indication as to whether or not the local youngsters are progressing as well as the average language student in the nationwide sample upon which the test was standardized. Another approach is to develop local achievement tests based upon the actual course objectives set by the local staff. Assuming that local objectives have been stated in a form that is of use to the test maker and that the achievement test is then well designed, this type of testing would seem to offer the most advantages. Students who have conscientiously done their assignments throughout the year will encounter on this test the same type of material with which they have been working during the year. Standardized proficiency tests, on the other hand, will often contain vocabulary items and language structures to which students have not yet been exposed, while omitting many of the things they have mastered. Yet, proficiency tests of proven reliability offer some advantages seldom available in locally devised testing programs. They permit a broader perspective of student achievement, they are printed in a high-quality, professional manner, and they provide native voices on tape along with other aids such as machine-scored answer sheets, directions for administering and scoring, and many other conveniences that are difficult to provide locally. In view of all this, it may be advisable for schools to combine achievement testing with proficiency testing for a comprehensive evaluation of student performance.

EVALUATIVE CRITERIA FOR THE FOREIGN LANGUAGE PROGRAM

One evaluative technique commonly used by educational agencies at the local, state, and regional levels involves the presentation of a series of questions to members of the school staff. Questions that are answered affirmatively will indicate areas in which the program is strong; questions receiving negative responses reveal areas in which improvement is needed. Theoretically, great benefit will be derived from the very act of having the foreign language staff discuss such a list of criteria for the purpose of assessing the extent to which the local program measures up to the standards implicit in the questions. In some instances, the self-evaluation is followed by a team of language specialists from outside the school district who observe classroom teaching and who examine other aspects of the language program. After the visit, the evaluators may write a report indicating the degree to which their observations coincide with the self-evaluation responses. The following criteria are samples of the types of items often used by state and regional evaluators during the 1960s to evaluate public and non–public school foreign language programs in many parts of the United States.

Criteria Pertaining to the Foreign Language Staff

1   How many modern language teachers have taken the MLA Proficiency Test for Teachers and Advanced Students?
2   If any language skills fall below the 50 percentile, are teachers engaged in further education to upgrade their basic language skills?
3   Do all members of the foreign language staff meet the minimum state foreign language certification requirements?
4   How many staff members have 30 semester hours or more in the foreign language they are teaching?
5   How many Staff members have a Masters degree in the language they are teaching?
6   How many staff members have studied or traveled in a country where the language they are teaching is spoken?
7   How many staff members have attended foreign language workshops?
8   Does the local school have any standard screening process to assure that all language teachers are competent to teach the foreign language course as defined by the local curriculum guide?
9   How many foreign language teachers have had a regular credit course in foreign language teaching methods within the last five years?
10   How many staff members have attended at least one foreign language workshop, meeting, or conference (other than department meetings) during the current school year?
11   How many foreign language teachers have engaged in interclass visits within the school or have traveled to other schools in or out of the district to observe foreign language instruction?

12 Does the staff include paraprofessional personnel with nonlanguage backgrounds to perform the more routine noninstructional tasks?

13 Does the staff include paraprofessional personnel who are native speakers of the foreign language to perform certain routine instructional tasks under the direction of the certified teacher?

Criteria Pertaining to the Organization of the Program

1 Is a four-year sequence of study offered in at least one foreign language at the senior high school level?

2 Does the minimum justification for offering an advanced course exceed eight students?

3 Does the program offer only as many different languages as the school can support as evidenced by the number of third- or fourth-year courses?

4 Is a reasonable portion of the total school population enrolled in foreign language study? (Approximately 35 percent of all ninth-through twelfth-grade students are currently enrolled in one or more foreign language courses.)

5 Is there evidence of a strong program, good guidance procedures, and flexible scheduling practices in the form of sustained enrollments?

Level I FL course: 50 percent of all eligible youngsters.
Level II FL course: 35 percent of all eligible youngsters.
Level III FL course: 25 percent of all eligible youngsters.
Level IV FL course: 15 percent of all eligible youngsters.

6 Is the school's foreign language department organized with one person responsible for the effective working of the department regardless of the number of buildings in which foreign language instruction is carried on?

7 Is foreign language instruction offered below grade 9?

8 Is instruction in grades 7 and 8 offered five times weekly for not less than 30 minutes per class meeting?

9 Are students who successfully complete Level I course work in grades 7 and 8 offered a suitable Level II course in grade 9?

10 Are continuing foreign language students from the junior high school kept separate from beginning students of foreign language when they enter senior high school?

11 In schools with two or more teachers in the same language, is the possibility of team teaching or back-to-back scheduling being explored?

12 Does each teacher's schedule of classes and other duties include a reasonable amount of preparation time?

13 Is the district foreign language program, elementary through senior high school, coordinated by one person?

14 Do all language teachers of the district meet at least monthly to plan the effective articulation of the language program?

15 Is the language program designed to meet the needs of all students rather than being designed only for the college-bound?

16 Are usable curriculum guides available in each language?

Criteria Pertaining to Methods of Instruction

1 In the introductory courses is the primary emphasis upon the learning of new speech habits rather than upon the memorization of formal rules of grammar?

2 Is the use of grammatical generalizations subordinated to functional use of language structures for direct communication?

3 Is the introduction of reading and writing skills not unduly prolonged?

4 Are the reading and writing skills given proper attention along with the listening and speaking skills?

5 Are students required to learn vocabulary in complete meaningful contexts rather than as isolated lists of words?

6 Is at least 50 percent of class time devoted to student use of the foreign language as opposed to discussions about the language carried on in English?

7 Does the study of each foreign language include the development of understanding about the customs, beliefs, and traditions of the people who speak the foreign language?

8 Do the advanced courses include the broad cultural view rather than emphasizing American stereotypes of the foreign cultures?

9 Do the advanced courses provide for the maintenance of skills acquired in the beginning courses?

Criteria Pertaining to Physical Facilities and Their Utilization

1 Does each modern foreign language classroom contain a tape recorder, overhead projector, record player, and other necessary equipment for use at all times?

2 Is other instructional equipment readily available as needed?

3 Is adequate storage space provided for tapes, books, filmstrips, slides, and supplies?

4 Is it possible to provide near total darkness in all language classrooms?

5 Is adequate chalkboard space available?

6 Are there as many positions in each language laboratory and electronic classroom as there are foreign language students in the largest foreign language class?

7 Was there adequate preservice and/or inservice training for all foreign language staff members with regard to the utilization of electronic teaching devices?

8 Are the materials used in the laboratory or electronic classroom an integral part of the regular classroom work?

9 Do first- and second-year students use the language laboratory or electronic classroom at least four times weekly?

10 How many language laboratories have been installed in the district's schools? (Language laboratory refers to equipment with booths.)

11 How many electronic classrooms have been installed in the district's schools? (Electronic classroom refers to boothless equipment installed in a classroom that has conventional seating. Students have a headset and microphone, and the equipment has provisions for the teacher to monitor and intercommunicate with all students.)

12 Is there sufficient laboratory or electronic classroom equipment to enable all foreign language students to engage in daily oral drill for 20 minutes or more?

13 Are self-instructional materials used to allow gifted students to proceed at a rate commensurate with their ability?

14 Are self-instructional materials used to allow the academically deprived students to proceed at a rate commensurate with their ability?

15 Do third- and fourth-year students have regular access to the laboratory equipment?

16 Is a skilled paraprofessional available in the language laboratory to relieve teachers of routine duties?

17 Are skilled technical personnel available to perform routine maintenance and repair duties?

18 Are native-born paraprofessionals used to perform routine functions under the direction of a certified instructor?

19 Are special language tables available in the cafeteria so that students in each language can practice using the foreign language during the noon hour?

Criteria Pertaining to the Materials of Instruction

1 Do all students have the necessary course materials?

2 Are the course materials consistent with the instructional goals listed in the curriculum guide?

3 Are course materials readily adaptable to a varied presentation of lessons?

4 Does the library contain a wide selection of books in each foreign language taught which are appropriate for the various levels of instruction?

5 Does the library have an extensive selection of books in English dealing with the countries where the languages are spoken?

6 Are other reading materials available, such as newspapers and magazines in the foreign language?

7 Do the foreign language classrooms have large foreign language text maps?

8 Do the language laboratories contain an extensive library of tapes and records that are systematically cataloged and correlated with the other instructional materials?

9 Are appropriate professional journals available for each language taught?

EVALUATING THE INSTRUCTIONAL PROCESS
THROUGH INTERACTION ANALYSIS

One point upon which most foreign language supervisors appear to agree is that classroom teachers of foreign languages have a badly distorted view of what they are actually accomplishing with their classroom activities. The author has visited many schools where the staff proudly claimed to have a modern audiolingual course of study. However, after visiting all teachers at all levels of instruction it was revealed that 80 percent of the classroom work involved teacher talk, most of which was in English, and that, on those rare occasions when the students were allowed to speak, their responses were either repetitions of what the teacher had said or were responses elicited with reference to written material. It is not unusual to find that all functional communication between students and teacher is carried on in English. Teachers are often astonished when a tape recording of their classroom procedures is played back and systematically analyzed, to find that their use of the target language was both minimal and uncreative and that actual student use of the language was almost nil. It should be obvious to the teacher that the complex sets of skills, which are listed as objectives in the local curriculum guide, cannot possibly be developed unless the students have an opportunity to engage actively in the acquisition of those skills. Yet in all too many cases, the teacher continues to be the active performer, the students the passive listeners. Because of this lack of consistency between goal and method, a number of foreign language educators have developed a system of interaction analysis aimed at allowing teachers to study their own behavior and that of their students in a systematic and objective manner. The insights gained by this analysis can serve as a guide to changing teacher behavior. The system of interaction analysis described here is an adaptation of the process developed by Ned Flanders.[1]

The Flanders System of Interaction Analysis

The Flanders system of interaction analysis is particularly appropriate for the foreign language field because it is concerned primarily with verbal behavior. The assumption is that the verbal behavior of individuals, both in English and in the target language, provides a relevant sample of their total behavior vis-à-vis the foreign language instructional process. The various patterns of observable verbal behavior are broken down into categories. The first major division is between talk by the teacher and talk by the students. Each of these divisions can then be divided further on the basis of whether the talk involves the native or the target language. Finally, the quality of the talk can be described both with regard to the oral behavior of the teacher and of the students. Through the systematic observation of dozens of different foreign language teachers, Nearhoof

---

[1] N. A. Flanders and E. J. Amidon, "The Role of the Teacher in the Classroom," Philadelphia, Temple University, January, 1962.

330

has devised ten interaction categories that include all the major verbal activities commonly occurring in the foreign language classroom.[2]

Interaction Categories for Classroom Observation

With these ten categories clearly in mind, the trained observer is then able to provide a quantitative evaluation of the teaching process by assigning a number to every 3 seconds of elapsed classroom time. At the end of the observation period, these numbers can then be tabulated to determine what proportion of class time has been devoted to each category of verbal behavior. In the Nearhoof project, each teacher in the study had volunteered to record all classroom activities onto audiotape. These actual classroom activities then served as the basis for establishing and refining the interaction categories. However, this same use of audiotape recordings (or better still, videotape recordings) can permit teachers to evaluate with a high degree of objectivity their own classroom performance.

For the teacher or supervisor who wishes to make use of this inter-action-analysis technique, the first step is the memorization of the ten categories in association with the appropriate number. Time simply does not permit the observer to refer back to the categories while he/she is engaged in the process of observing and recording his/her observations. The categories are as follows:

1   Teacher use of the foreign language for *communication*.

FL used by teacher to give directions which then elicit desired pupil action.

FL used by teacher to discuss ideas relating to cultural contrasts, geography, history, literature, and so on.

FL used by teacher to explain problems of structure, of sound system, of written system, or other pertinent concepts.

FL used by teacher to answer pupil questions.

2   Teacher use of the foreign language for *reinforcement*.

FL used by teacher to correct pupil errors (provides correct response or causes correct response to be elicited).

FL used by teacher to let students know immediately that their response has been successful.

FL used by teacher to shape new responses or to reshape unsuccessful responses (that is, response is broken into smaller parts, the smaller parts are drilled, and then the full response is attempted); FL also used to give hints (that is, paraphrase, restatement, and so on), to help pupils produce new response.

FL used by teacher to provide model for drills.

FL used by teacher to elicit rote response in pattern practice.

[2] Orrin Nearhoof, "Teacher-Pupil Interaction in the Foreign Language Classroom: A Technique for Self-Evaluation," from an unpublished research paper, Iowa City, 1965.

3   Teacher uses English to *clarify meaning* or provide a cue. (A few words of English used quickly and briefly by the teacher.)
4   Teacher uses English as the *functional classroom language*. (This includes the use of English by the teacher for the items of communication and reinforcement described in 1 and 2 above.)
5   Students use foreign language for *rote response*.
     FL used by students in mimicry-memorization drill and pattern practice.
     FL used by one student to elicit rote response from another student.
     FL used by students in any type of repetitive drill exercises (that is, class repetition of a dialog, sentence, conjugation, and so on).
     FL used by students to read from text, chalkboard, and so on.
     FL used by students for any type of exercise that requires only an automatic response.
6   Students use foreign language *to recombine* prelearned material.
     FL used by students to answer questions.
     FL used by students in which they are required to recall and recombine structures (oral or written) to form an acceptable reply.
7   Students use the foreign language *to ask a question* that they themselves have originated.
8   Students use the foreign language *spontaneously*.
     FL used by students to discuss a topic of common interest (not rote recitation of prelearned material).
     FL used by students to react freely to pictorial or other situational presentation.
9   Students use *English* for classroom communication.
10   *Noninteraction* activities (for example, silence, confusion, organization, other language activities such as language laboratory, singing, silent reading, and so on). For specialized language-related activities that are not easily categorized, these symbols are used to identify the time interval of the activities:
     0–S—singing
     0–R—reading (silent)
     0–W—writing
     0–L—laboratory

Procedure for Categorizing Teacher-Pupil Interaction

Best results are obtained when the observers spend several minutes orienting themselves to the situation before they actually begin to categorize. They will thus develop a feeling for the total atmosphere of teacher-pupil interaction.

The observer records a category number every 3 seconds or with each change of activity. However, often during rapid question-answer sessions or when the teacher interrupts a pupil's response to correct or shape the correct response, more than one notation is required during the 3-second period. This follows the above statement regarding change of activity.

Teacher: Tiene Ud. un libro rojo ? (2)
  Pupil: No tiene ...   (5)
Teacher: Tengo.   (2)
  Pupil: No tengo un libro rojo. (5)

Thus, if more than one category occurs during the 3-second interval, then all categories used in that interval are recorded. Conversely, each change in category is recorded. If no change occurs within 3 seconds, repeat the category number.

However, if a silence is long enough for a breack in the interaction to be discernible, and if it occurs at a 3-second recording time, it is recorded as 0. If no change occurs within 3 seconds, repeat that category number. See description of categories for other uses of 0.

These numbers are recorded in sequence in a column, and at the end of the observation period the observer will have several long columns of numbers. It is important to keep the tempo as steady as possible, but it is even more important to be accurate. The observer may also wish to write down marginal notes from time to time which can be used to explain what has been happening in the classroom.

The observer stops classifying whenever the classroom activity is changed so that observing is inappropriate as, for instance, when there are various groups working on a written assignment or doing silent reading. He/she will usually draw a line under the recorded number, make a note of the new activity, and resume categorizing when teacher-pupil interaction continues. At all times the observer notes the kind of class activity he/she is observing. A shift to a new activity should also be noted.

Aids for Categorizing

1   Always begin and end each observation by recording a 0.
2   If a teacher calls on a pupil for a desired response, and if this action plus an ensuing silence constitute a 3-second interval, this should be recorded as 0.
3   As stated before, during an interval when interaction observation is inappropriate (when the group is reading silently or singing in the foreign language), the observer should draw a line under the last recorded category number and indicate the time. When positive interaction recommences, again indicate the time and begin with 0. Thus, by using 20 numbers per minute, it is possible to include all classroom activity for the observation period.
4   If the teacher intermingles English and the foreign language, this should be recorded as 4.

Teacher: Take out your books and open them *à la page deux cents trois.*

5   Drill and practice on a group basis falls in category 5, and when the drill is on an individual teacher-pupil basis, categories 2 and 5 are also used.

Teacher: *J'ai deux frères.* (2)
  Class: *J'ai deux frères.* (5)
Teacher: *trois frères.* (2)
 Pupil 1: *J'ai trois frères.* (5)
Teacher: *Nous* (2)
  Pupil 2: *Nous avons trois frères.* (5)
Teacher: *voitures.* (2)
 Pupil 3: *Nous avons trois voitures.* (5)

Recording Data in a Matrix

There is a method of recording the sequence of events in the classroom in such a way that certain facts become readily apparent. This method consists of entering the sequence of numbers into a 10-row by 10-column table that is called a *matrix* (see Table 8). The generalized sequence of the teacher-

■8

SAMPLE INTERACTION MATRIX

	1	2	3	4	5	6	7	8	9	0	
1											0
2		I			IIII	III					8
3											0
4				IIII						I	5
5		III								I	4
6		II		I							3
7											0
8											0
9											0
0		II									2
Total	0	8	0	5	4	3	0	0	0	2	22

pupil interaction can be examined readily in this matrix. The following example shows how an observer would classify what happens in the classroom and how the observations are recorded in the matrix. The observer has been sitting in the classroom for several minutes and has begun to get some idea of the general climate before beginning to record. The teacher begins, *"Alors, Pierre, comment allez-vous aujourd'hui?"*

(Observer classifies this as a 2.) Pierre responds, *"Très bien, merci. Et vous?"* (Observer records a 6.) Teacher, *"Très bien, merci. . . . . . . Jacques, quel temps fait-il?"* (Observer records a sequence of two 2's.) Pupil, *"Il fait beau."* (6). Teacher, *"Marie, faites-vous du russe?"* (2). Pupil, *"Non, je fais du français."* (6). Teacher, "Today we are going to complete our examination of the irregular verb *faire.* In our various structure drills and dialogues we have used only two basic sound forms of *faire: fais (fait,* same sound) and *faites.* Using our basic frame, *je fais du français,* we shall develop this important verb." (Observer records a series of five 4's followed by a 0 because of a period of silence during which the teacher picks up several 3 by 5 cards for the drill session.)

Teacher: *Répétez, Je fais du francais.*   (2)
  Pupils: *Je fais du francais.*   (5)
Teacher: *Vous faites du français.*   (2)
  Pupils: *Vous faites du français.*   (5)
Teacher: *Tu fais du français.*   (2)
  Pupils: *Tu fais du français.*   (5)
Teacher: *Ils font du français.*   (2)
  Pupils: *Ils font du français.*   (5)

(Observer records the sequence of 2, 5 followed by a final 0.)
    The observer has now classified the following sequence of numbers in this fashion:

0
2
6
2
2
6
2
6
4   *in matrix sequence*
4   *(0,2) (2,6) (6,2) (2,2) (2,6) (6,2) (2,6)*
4   *(6,4) (4,4) (4,4) (4,4) (4,4) (4,0) (0,2)*
4   *(2,5) (5,2) (2,5) (5,2) (2,5) (5,2) (2,5) (5,0)*
4   *(The rapid recording of the sequence 2 and 5 results from the change of*
0   *activity occurring in the 3- second-interval.)*
2
5
2
5
2
5
2
5
0

335

SAMPLE MATRIX SUMMARY

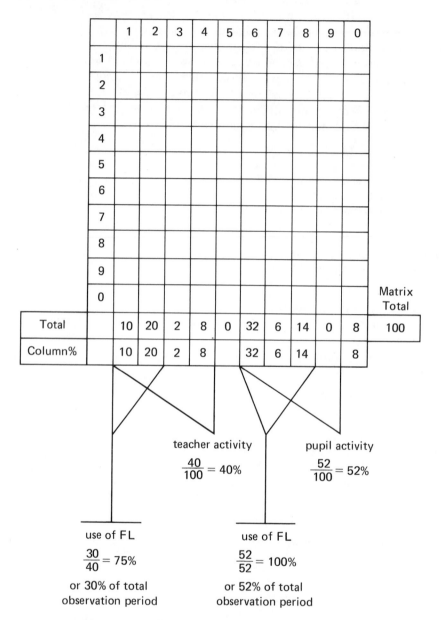

teacher activity
$$\frac{40}{100} = 40\%$$

pupil activity
$$\frac{52}{100} = 52\%$$

use of FL
$$\frac{30}{40} = 75\%$$
or 30% of total
observation period

use of FL
$$\frac{52}{52} = 100\%$$
or 52% of total
observation period

Techniques for Tabulating Matrix Data

Tabulations are now made in the matrix to represent pairs of numbers. Notice in the listing of matrix sequence that the numbers have been marked off in pairs. This first pair is 0,2; the second pair is 2,6, and so on. The particular cell (see Table 8) in which the tabulation of the pair of numbers is

SPANISH I MATRIX SUMMARY (30 MINUTES)

	1	2	3	4	5	6	7	8	9	0	
1	0	0	0	0	0	0	0	0	1	1	
2	0	9	0	3	6	29	0	15	00	14	
3	0	0	0	0	0	0	0	0	1	1	
4	1	2	0	11	1	9	0	2	13	11	
5	1	2	0	7	219	0	0	0	0	3	
6	0	35	1	6	3	12	0	1	0	8	
7	0	0	0	0	0	0	0	0	0	0	
8	0	9	0	0	0	0	0	33	0	2	
9	0	4	0	12	0	0	0	0	0	3	
0	0	15	1	11	3	6	0	3	4	46	Matrix Total
Total	2	76	2	50	237	66	0	54	19	89	590
Column %	0.3	12.9	0.3	8.5	39.3	11.2	0	9.2	3.2	15.1	

teacher activity
$$\frac{130}{590} = 22.3\%$$

pupil activity
$$\frac{139}{590} = 23.5\%$$

use of FL
$$\frac{78}{130} = 60\%$$
or 13.3% of total observation period

use of FL
$$\frac{120}{139} = 86.3\%$$
or 20.4% of total observation period

made is determined by using the first number in the pair to indicate the *row*, and the second number in the pair for the *column.* Thus, 0,2 would be shown by a tally in the cell formed by row 0 and column 2. The second pair, 2,6, would be shown in the cell formed by row 2 and column 6, and so on. Notice that each pair of numbers overlaps with the previous pair, and each number, except the first and the last, is used twice. It is for this reason that a 0 is entered as the first number and the last number in the record. Zero was chosen because it is convenient to assume that each record begins and ends with silence. This procedure also permits the total of each column to equal the total of the corresponding row.

It is convenient to check the tabulations in the matrix for accuracy by noting that there should be one less tally in the matrix than there were numbers entered in the original observation record.

In the example, we have 23 numbers and the total number of tallies in the matrix is 22. This is shown in Table 8.

Using the Matrix to Determine General Aspects of Classroom Interaction

After observers tabulate a matrix, they then have the job of developing a description of the classroom interaction. They have several ways of describing the interaction but begin by reporting the different kinds of statements in terms of percentages. The first step is computing the percentage of tallies in each of the columns. This is done by dividing each of the column totals, 1 through 0, by the total number of tallies in the matrix. This computation gives each category as a proportion of the total interaction in the observed classroom situation. A similar procedure is used to determine the percentage of teacher activity, teacher use of FL, pupil activity, and pupil use of FL. To determine the percentage of teacher activity, divide the total of categories 1 through 4 by the matrix total. For example, in Table 9, teacher activity (columns 1–4) totals 40. Then 40 is divided by the matrix total, 100; and we find that the amount of teacher activity is 40 percent of the total amount of classroom activity. To calculate the percentage of teacher use of the FL in relation to the percentage of teacher activity, divide the total of columns 1 and 2 by the total of columns 1–4. In Table 9, teacher use of FL is 30; and by dividing 30 by the total teacher activity, 40, we find the percentage of teacher use of the FL is 75 percent. In short, teacher activity constituted 40 percent of the observation period, and the teacher used the FL 75 percent of the time he/she was in direct interaction.

The same procedure is employed to determine total pupil activity and pupil use of the FL. Pupil activity is recorded in columns 6 through 9, with pupil use of the FL located in columns 6, 7, and 8.

Table 10 is an analysis of a Spanish I class. The observation period was 30 minutes.

An examination of the matrix summary reveals the following information:

Total teacher activity	*22.3% of observation period*
Teacher use of FL	*60.0% of teacher activity*
Teacher use of FL	*13.3% of observation period*
Total pupil activity	*23.5% of observation period*
Pupil use of FL	*86.3% of pupil activity*
Pupil use of FL	*20.4% of observation period*
Drill and practice sessions	*39.3% of observation period*
Interaction recorded in category 0	*15.1% of observation period*

338

■11

SAMPLE INTERACTION FORM[a]

Date _____   Teacher _____
Class _____   Observer _____
School _____   Other notes _____
                                       _____
                                       _____

0	8	4																
2	8	5																
2	2	5																
0	8	5																
0	8	5																
6	8	5																
6	8	5																
2	2	5																
6	8	5																
2	8	5																
2	2	5																
2	6	5																
6	8	5																
6	8	5																
1	8	5																
1	0	5																
1	0	0																
1	4																	
8	4																	
8	4																	
8	4																	

[a] The actual length of the form is much longer. It usually provides space for 40 category numbers per column.

Two activities constituted the major portion of interaction recorded in category 0: (1) pupils preparing themselves for language laboratory session and (2) distribution of some printed materials to the class.

Table 11 is a sample interaction form.

EVALUATING STUDENT ACHIEVEMENT
IN THE FOREIGN LANGUAGE CLASSROOM

The first step in determining how to measure language skill is, of course, to decide what it means to have achieved that skill. Once this has been determined, testing becomes a matter of taking representative samples of student performance. A good test will consist of items that selectively sample all the significant aspects of the skill being tested. At the same time, a good test will avoid those items that require students to draw upon unrelated skills or to draw upon knowledge they may not possess. For example, many American youngsters read English very well but would have difficulty in explaining to an Englishman how baseball differs from cricket. Americans, not knowing the English game, would be at a loss to supply satisfactory answers simply because they lack the knowledge needed to translate facts about the American sport into terms that have meaning to the British cricket fan. It would be absurd, of course, to judge the Americans' English-reading ability upon how successfully they were able to compare the game of cricket with the game of baseball. Yet, to varying degrees, this is somewhat comparable to the process that often passes for testing in the foreign language classroom. When we ask students questions involving literary interpretations, we are testing something other than their skill in using the language. When we ask them to translate from the target language into English, we have—in addition to the situations that are nonequivalent from one culture to the other—vocabulary items, grammatical forms, and word-order sequences that differ in the target language. Translation is the process of decoding linguistic graphic symbols from one language into the nearest cultural equivalents in the other. It can be a fascinating activity, but it is also a very complex process. Because of this, it includes much that has nothing to do with the four basic language skills. And this makes it a very poor device for testing direct student control of those skills. Modern evaluation methods call for testing procedures that measure each skill directly and as a separate entity. Thus, for example, no reading should be involved in the listening test and no writing should be required in the speaking test. In actual practice, such total separation of skills is not always feasible. However, according to modern testing authorities, a high degree of "purity" can be achieved if the persons who construct the tests are constantly aware of the importance of testing each skill separately.

Achievement Testing and
Proficiency Testing

It should also be made clear at this point that we are discussing *achievement* testing rather than *proficiency* testing. Proficiency tests can be administered without regard to a specific course of study. Achievement tests, as the term is used here, refer to measurements of student achievement in relation to a given course of study. Achievement tests should directly utilize the vocabulary, grammatical structures, and content of the texts and materials that have been used prior to testing. (Standardized proficiency tests aimed at students in fifty different states clearly cannot do this.) As was mentioned earlier, proficiency tests can be useful tools in overall program evaluation. There is also a need for periodic measurement of student achievement; and this, ordinarily, must be done by local staff members. The following is a discussion of the types of tests which might reasonably be devised and constructed by the foreign language teacher. Table 12 provides a checklist of items that pertain to the contruction of achievement tests.

■12

A CHECKLIST OF BASIC PRINCIPLES FOR CONSTRUCTING
ACHIEVEMENT TESTS

---

1. *Test that which has been taught. Normally tests can involve:*
    a. *Simple recall of prelearned material.*
    b. *Rearrangement of prelearned material.*
2. *In presenting test items it is considered good practice to:*
    a. *Begin with the simplest items.*
    b. *Proceed to the more difficult items.*
3. *In selecting test items remember to:*
    a. *Choose problem sounds, structures, and word-order sequences.*
    b. *Avoid tongue twisters and absurdities.*
4. *In setting up multiple-choice items it is common practice to:*
    a. *Include at least one "distractor."*
    b. *Include plausible but incorrect items as distractors.*
    c. *Include only one unambiguous item that correctly answers the question.*
5. *Directions on the test should be in English. However, the questions (multiple-choice items) should be mostly in the target language.*

Sources of Material for Teacher-Made Tests

A final but very practical question is: How does a teacher with (say) five classes, a study hall, and lunchroom duty manage to create tests of the type described in this chapter? Some of the newer texts answer this question, at least in part, by providing tests for evaluating each unit of work. Even when such tests are not fully appropriate, they can be adapted to fit the local approach to teaching. Where such tests do not exist, it is advisable to borrow ideas from those who have made a special study of the matter. That is, teachers can model their own tests after the proficiency tests that are commercially available. It is possible to use the format of these professionally produced tests as models, while adapting the structures and vocabulary from the local curriculum. Where not forbidden by copyright, the visuals in the test booklets can be used directly by making a transparency to be used with the overhead projector. All students can then see the visual without having to have the booklet in their hands. Also, there are other sources of transparency masters that can easily be adapted to testing. The value of visuals is in direct proportion to the teacher's ingenuity in creating suitable test questions to accompany them.[3]

TESTING ACHIEVEMENT IN LISTENING COMPREHENSION

In Table 3, Chapter 5, the various aspects of the specified goals for the achievement of listening skill were categorized as follows:

Phonology: The ability to hear all the meaningful sound contrasts of the foreign language when it is spoken at a normal rate in complete utterances.

Morphology: The ability to hear all the changes of meaning caused by modifications of word forms when the language is spoken at a normal rate in complete utterances.

Syntax: The ability to hear the foreign language without being confused by syntactical arrangements.

Vocabulary: The ability to hear and understand words in normal conversational contexts.

Culture: The ability to detect nuances of meaning relating to social position, family relationships, customs, national traditions, literary classics, and so on.

The ultimate outcome of an ideal program in the area of listening skill was also designated as, "The ability to comprehend aurally new arrangements of familiar material when spoken at normal tempo and with normal intonation and rhythm."

A *proficiency* test would aim at assessing the degree to which this latter objective had been realized. However, there are many intermediate stages in the learning process that require the teacher to judge the extent of progress toward that ultimate goal. For such measurements of *achievement* it is convenient to focus rather sharply upon the five elements listed above. When this is done, it is then possible to determine with a high degree of accuracy whether or not the student is actually acquiring the potential for comprehending normal native speech. Thus, for example, phonological discrimination can be tested by requiring the student to choose between a series of minimal pairs.

---

[3] The bibliography at the end of this chapter lists sources of tests and visuals that can be used in proficiency testing or which can serve as models for constructing achievement tests.

Examples

The student *sees* this:

and he *hears* the following: It's a clock. It's a cloak.
Or he *sees* this:

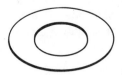

And he *hears:* It's a ditch. It's a dish.

These are rather "pure" achievement-test items involving listening skill (assuming the student has been duly exposed to all the vocabulary items). Each of these examples requires students to discriminate between two basic phonemes by correctly associating that which they hear with an unequivocal visual. Written material is not used in listening-test items because, if students are asked to read or write, then their errors may be due to deficiencies in these skills with the result that the purity of measurement is destroyed.

Morphology and Listening Tests

Control of morphology can be tested by compelling the student to select utterances that are appropriate to a given situation. For example, the past tense of certain irregular verbs can be tested as follows:

Step One: The student *hears* (in the foreign language)

Ralph was at a party. Only a few of his friends were there at the beginning. After they left, Ralph found that the other guests ignored him completely. What did Ralph do?

Step Two: Next the student *hears* (in English):

You will now hear four answers only one of which uses a fully appropriate verb tense. These are labeled A, B, C, and D. Circle the letter (A, B, C, or D) on your answer sheet according to which best fits the situation.

Step Three: Finally the student *hears* (in the foreign language):

A. *Ralph goes home.*
B. *Ralph is going home.*
C. *Ralph went home.*
D. *Ralph has gone home.*

Notice, in the above example, that all choices are potentially correct for *some* situation. However, only the simple past tense (item C) fits the given situation. Note also that all the items in steps one and three are in the simple past. There are no tricks or traps or extraneous details. The item is a straight-forward test of the students' ability to recognize the verb tense to which they have been exposed. The danger of this kind of item is that it may become too long and involved so that students are tested on their ability to recall trivial facts rather than upon their ability to distinguish morphological changes. Thus, a large number of short, clear items, using all three steps given above, will serve better than a single lengthy dialog in step one followed by a series of questions in step three. In a similar fashion, items involving syntax, vocabulary, and culture can serve as the focal point of oral choice questions. A simple but effective technique for oral testing is to project on a screen a transparency containing four situational pictures each of which has one common element and one different element. Then students are asked to match a series of statements with each picture.

Step One: The students see:

Step Two: The students are instructed to circle the correct response on the answer sheet, which can be set up as follows:

```
1    A   B   C   D
2    A   B   C   D
3    A   B   C   D
4    A   B   C   D
```

Step Three: A number of statements are spoken by the teacher, or, better still, are played from a tape recorded by native speakers. Each is spoken twice only, with a normal speaking intonation. (A few samples are given below along with an indication of what each item is testing.)

1   This airplane is inside. (Vocabulary test, item C, the word inside.)
2   This plane will soon be in the air. (Test on future tense—two planes are in the air; only the one in item D is about to take off.)
3   This plane is the most modern. (Test of superlative—item A.)
4   This is the oldest airplane of all. (Test of superlative.)

TESTING ACHIEVEMENT IN READING

Drawing upon objectives listed earlier (see Chapter 5), we can identify five elements that relate to reading skill. They are:

Phonology: The ability to associate the appropriate graphic symbols with the sounds for which they stand.

Morphology: The ability to draw meaning directly from the printed page through recognition of changes in meaning caused by modifications in structure.

Syntax: The ability to read directly in the foreign language without being confused by syntactical arrangements.

Vocabulary: The ability to recognize in context a wide range of vocabulary items with sensitivity to the differences between spoken and written vocabulary and between contemporary and older literary forms, words, and expressions.

Culture: The ability to read everything from newspapers to works of literature. This implies a basic knowledge of the history, literature, current world position, and so on, of countries in which the target language is spoken.

Obviously, the last category represents the ideal achievement. It will ordinarily be realized only by some of the better students who stay with the language for a period of four years or more. At all levels of instruction we are involved to a certain degree with the first four; phonology, morphology, syntax, and vocabulary. If we teach these elements systematically throughout the learning process, we have established a basis for sampling. We can further refine the sampling technique by concentrating upon the most serious points of difference between English and the target language. It is axiomatic in modern linguistics that learning the problem sounds and structures is the priority task in second-language acquisition. For example, in testing reading skill with regard to German syntax, the sentence, *Er ist schon hier,* would have little relevance. The transfer from the English word pattern, "He is already here," is so direct, that no learning problem (with regard to word order) is presented. On the other hand, the same sentence when it becomes a subordinate clause does present a problem. For example, the sentence, *Ich weiss, dass er schon hier ist* (literally, "I know that he already here *is*"), will inhibit the unskilled students of German when they try to read aloud, and will slow them down when they read silently. Therefore, this is an area that demands extra attention in the teaching process, and that, as a matter of course, must be tested to see if the student has gained sufficient control of the structure.

345

Oral Versus Silent Reading

In the testing of reading skill we are compelled to identify two areas: (1) reading aloud and (2) reading silently. Reading aloud requires active manipulation of the speech organs and a measurement of the accuracy of the sounds produced; therefore it relates largely to phonology. Silent reading involves a more passive assimilation of meaning directly from the printed page; therefore it relates mostly to the other four elements mentioned previously (that is, morphology, syntax, vocabulary, and culture). Testing oral reading carries the implication that students have been thoroughly drilled on every sound they are expected to reproduce from the printed page. Testing silent reading (particularly at the early levels) presumes that students have been exposed to all structural and syntactical elements and to most of the vocabulary.

Reading and Phonology

Many literate people do not read well aloud, even in their native language, particularly when standing in front of an audience. Therefore, it is unrealistic to expect self-conscious youngsters to stand before their classmates and produce perfectly intoned foreign language utterances from the printed page. In the early stages of second-language acquisition, reading aloud is largely a process of using graphic symbols as cues for the production of auditory symbols. Because many of the French, German, and Spanish graphemes are identical to those used to represent English sounds, interference from English is extremely great during oral reading. The student must constantly suppress the inclination to produce the English phonemes associated with the little black marks rather than the sounds of the foreign language. Therefore, during the first few years of instruction, it is a considerable accomplishment if students can read, deliberately and accurately, short sentences containing the segmental phonemes that they have previously mastered in a different context. To expose students to the problem graphemes before they have learned the phonemes for which they stand is to guarantee that they will mispronounce them. Thus we can predict with near certainty that American students of Spanish will read *carro* and *caro* the same way (and will read them both unintelligibly) if they have not been thoroughly drilled on the contrasting intervocalic Spanish *r* and *rr* sounds. Lacking such drill, they will naturally revert to their native retroflex *r* and will produce, to the ear of the native speaker of Spanish, a sound somewhat like *cado,* a nonword.

Testing Oral Reading Ability

The most basic aspect of oral reading seems to be an awareness on the part of the student that graphic symbols are merely visual cues used to activate the organs of speech. A written sentence is a series of graphic cues which students must scan and reinterpret in terms of those tongue, lip, and lung actions needed to produce the appropriate sequence of sounds. If students

346

dwell too long on the graphemes, they may well produce atypical utterances, even in their native language. Therefore, long before the actual testing is done, students should have had considerable practice in reading complete sentences aloud, with minimal attention to the pronunciation of individual words. This practice would necessarily include all normal liaisons or pauses characteristic of the target language. To summarize the main aspects of reading aloud it might be said that students should:

1   Avoid hesitant, word-by-word delivery.
2   Produce all liaisons where appropriate and avoid them where not.
3   Approximate the stress and intonation patterns nearly enough so that the intended meaning of the sentence is not distorted.

The following techniques would serve to measure the extent to which acceptable oral reading has been achieved:

Work samples. Students are required to read one at a time in the classroom or through the intercommunication panel of the language laboratory.

1   One method is to have students read aloud dialog material that has been memorized as part of the regular lesson. Each word in a sentence can first be read from back to front to prove that students are not merely reciting from memory. Then the sentence can be reread in the normal way. The backward reading proves whether or not students can recognize the individual lexical items. The forward reading shows their control of the suprasegmental phonemes (that is, intonation, stress, juncture, and so on.)
2   Another approach calls for the reading aloud of sentences that contain rearrangements of familiar lexical items. This tells more about real reading ability than the reading of memorized dialog material. However, with both of these techniques the teacher's judgment is necessarily rather subjective and arbitrary when work samples are taken under normal classroom conditions. Thus a rather generalized grading notation seems advisable. Below is a rough sample:

Good: Fluent delivery with good pronunciation and intonation.
Satisfactory: Comprehensible delivery with several mistakes in the above.
Unsatisfactory: Hesitant delivery with many mispronounced segmental phonemes and no sense of stress and intonation patterns.

Work samples can serve for a large part of the evaluation of oral reading on each unit or lesson. However, a more formalized testing is called for, perhaps two or three times each semester. Given adequate personnel, testing would be done more regularly to enable the staff to determine the effectiveness of the instructional program and to diagnose student difficulties. Ideally, the program would be modified in accordance with test results.

A formal test. Oral reading ability is tested by having all students read the same material.

347

1 Provide two or three simple sentences containing the phonological problems to be tested; use familiar but rearranged vocabulary items. (Preferably these should be on a ditto or mimeo sheet rather than copied from the board. Students may copy incorrectly, thus invalidating the test.)

2 Project the sentences on a screen and let everyone practice reading orally for a few minutes. (The test is whether the student can—under any circumstances—produce the problem phonemes in response to a printed stimulus. Thus the element of surprise has no relevance here.)

3 Turn off the projector and have the students come to the tape recorders and record the sentences, along with their names. (In some laboratories this can be done en masse, in others, in small groups. It can be done in the classroom with one tape recorder if the teacher has good control of the class. With a teacher aide or intern, students can be tested separately in an adjoining office. Another possibility is to record from booth to console recorder.)

4 Just before each student reads the test sentences onto the tape, he or she fills out a test sheet containing the questions. (See Table 13.)

■13
ORAL READING TEST SHEET: ENGLISH FOR GERMANS

Class_____   Hour_____

My name is _____.
1. Where is the dog?
2. He's right behind the house.
3. I think he is tangled in the cord.

On Table 13, nine different phonemes that would prove difficult for a German have been underscored. Thus, a German learning English would be tested on these conflict points (assuming that these phonemes had been adequate drilled previously). The specific items would not be underlined for the person being tested; the underscoring would appear only on the answer sheet to remind the teacher of the test's focus. Tables 14 and 15 are further illustrations of simple recombination sentences that might be used to test oral reading achievement.

■14
ORAL READING TEST SHEET: SPANISH

Me llamo_____.
1. El burro es un animal popular.
2. Las muchachas son muy bonitas.
3. Tenemos que comer ahora.
4. ¿Dónde está un vaso?

348

Ich heisse_____.
1. *Holen Sie sofort Ihren Hut.*
2. *Tragen Sie diesen Mantel?*
3. *Das kleine Kind lacht nicht.*
4. *Wo ist mein Zimmer?*

Testing the Ability to Do Silent Reading

The ultimate goal of reading is to develop in students the ability to read directly, rapidly, and silently—that is, to draw meaning directly from the printed page without having to look up several words per page in a bilingual dictionary. This presumes that students have developed the ability to guess the meaning of unfamiliar words from the contextual clues supplied by the more familiar words. It also presumes that they have acquired a considerable repertoire of high-frequency lexical items as a part of their passive or recognitional vocabulary. Further, if the silent reading is not to proceed at a snail's pace, then the recognition of words must be rapid. Therefore, speed of recognition can enter into the testing process, and the administering of timed tests is justified. If too much time is allowed, many students can puzzle out the answers by a slow, deliberate process of elimination. But normal or near-normal reading requires an instantaneous grasp of meaning. Thus the student who can get the most items right in the shortest period of time is likely to be the best reader, assuming the test is well constructed. Table 16 illustrates various formats for testing silent reading. To conserve space the examples are given in English. Points of interference are indicated for each of the commonly taught European languages.

■16

READING: TYPES OF ACHIEVEMENT TESTS

A. *Translation—target language to English. (Maximum interference from English)*
B. *Completion tests with multiple choice.*
  1. *Choice of correct structural item.*
    My father _____ in the shoe factory every day until 4:00 o'clock. (German)
    a. *is working*   c. *does work*
    b. *works*   d. *working*
  2. *Emphasis upon phonology.*
    I could not tell what time it was because I had broken my _____. (Spanish)
    a. *welch*   c. *watch*
    b. *wash*   d. *wortch*
  3. *Choice of correct vocabulary item.*
    We need an objective appraisal; therefore, we want this material to be read carefully by several _____ persons.
    a. *uninterested*   c. *distraught*
    b. *uninteresting*   d. *disinterested*

4. *Choice of correct idiom.*

   Grandma became furious when she could not get the thread through the _____ *of the needle. (French)*

   a. *cat*   c. *tick*

   b. *eye*   d. *cut*

C. *Multiple choice tests.*

   1. *Reading selection with paraphrase answers. (Graded material would be used according to level.)*

      Captain Holt banked his heavily laden transport sharply to the left. The huge jet swept past inches from his upturned wing tip. In a moment Holt knew that he had averted a major air disaster. But his evasive action had cost him air speed, and the turbulence raised by the jetliner threw him into a wingover. His ship and all on board were doomed.

      Which of the following most nearly summarizes what happened?

      a. *Two airplanes collided.*

      b. *Two airplanes narrowly missed collision and both landed safely.*

      c. *Two airplanes narrowly missed collision, but one crashed.*

      d. *A transport plane and a passenger plane signaled to each other.*

   2. *Substituting the correct synonym for the underlined words.*

      I'm in a real spot, John; what do you suggest?

      a. *I'm having difficulties.*

      b. *I'm in a significant location.*

      c. *I'm in a position of importance.*

      d. *I'm downtown.*

   3. *Transformation of morphological or syntactical items.*

      I must go there tomorrow.

      (Which of the following refers correctly to the past?)

      a. *I musted to go there yesterday.*

      b. *I should have gone there yesterday.*

      c. *I have gone there yesterday.*

      d. *I had to go there yesterday.*

D. *Timed reading followed by written summarization in the foreign language (only at more advanced levels).*

   1. *Students read a selection that they can reasonably be expected to understand. (This means a selection that contains very little new vocabulary and practically no new structures or syntactical arrangements.) Students are allowed to read the material over as often as they are able within (say) a 20-minute period. They are not allowed to take notes.*

   2. *After the predetermined period of time has elapsed, the teacher collects the reading selections and distributes the test sheets. The students are then told to summarize the plot of the story using direct, simple language. The target foreign language would be used both in the reading and the summarization of content.*

E. *Timed reading followed by written summarization in English.*

   (Use the same procedures as above except that students are allowed to write their. answers in English.)

TESTING ACHIEVEMENT IN SPEAKING

Among the four skills, the testing of oral production presents the greatest number of practical problems for the classroom teacher. Not only is the teacher confronted with difficulties in eliciting the desired responses, he/she is also faced with the question of how to evaluate those responses objectively. Listening and reading skills can be evaluated with a high degree of

350

objectivity. The other productive skill (writing) presents some problems in the area of objective scoring, but these are not nearly so severe as is the case with oral production.

The eliciting of written responses is much simpler, both from the standpoint of test design and the mechanics of administering the test. The other three skills can be largely tested with pencil and paper. Only oral *reading* necessitates student recording, and for this the stimuli are the unequivocal graphic symbols. With oral *production,* on the other hand, other stimuli must be used if the test is to retain its purity. And once the appropriate stimuli have been devised as test questions, the teacher must find a means of recording each student's responses and of checking each set of responses as objectively as possible.

The Language Laboratory and Oral Testing

Ideally, the school would have a language laboratory with tape recorders for every student in the class so that each student's response could be recorded onto tape for subsequent correction. Also, under ideal conditions, the student's tape will be paused while the test questions are playing from the console and will move only when the students are responding. Thus, after all students have been tested, the teacher can play back each tape and hear only the student's name and his/her responses to the test stimuli. This technique cuts correction time in half since the teacher does not have to listen to the recorded question as he/she evaluates the student responses. However, although few schools are likely to have the needed equipment for proceeding in this manner, the testing of oral production need not be abandoned. With two tape recorders and a separate room, it is possible to accomplish the same end if extra personnel are available on the testing days. Students are sent one at a time to the testing room. The questions are played on the one tape recorder and the answers (only) are recorded on a second recorder (along with the student's name). If pictorial stimuli are used, one tape recorder will suffice. Naturally, if an entire class is to be tested in this way, the questions will have to be very brief (less than a minute) and the administration will have to be efficiently organized. Also, since all students will be inactive most of the period, it is advisable to have arranged for assignments that students can do on their own during the time that they are not being tested.

Testing Techniques for Oral Production

Testing phonology in the area of oral production can involve simple mimicry. Utterances are played on one recorder; and the student, speaking into the microphone of a second machine, is required to mimic the native speaker. The utterances will contain, of course, the critical phonemes upon which the student is being tested.

Morphological and syntactical items can be tested by adapting the pattern-drill format to the testing situation. Thus students will hear a foreign language utterance and will be required to transform or recombine what they hear.

351

Examples: *(Directions in English: stimuli in foreign language)*
Directions: Answer the following sentences, changing each verb to the past tense.
Stimulus: Every day I go to the store ; what did I do yesterday ?
Response: Yesterday you went to the store.
Stimulus: Every day I eat lunch here ; what did I do yesterday ?
Response: Yesterday you ate lunch here.
Directions: Change each of the following sentences into contrary-to-fact statements.
Stimulus: If I am early, I do it.
Response: If I were early, I would do it.
Directions: Change the nouns in the following sentences to pronouns and make all necessary word-order changes.
Stimulus: Give Mary the book.
Response: Give it to her.
Stimulus: Bring your father the papers.
Response: Bring them to him.

The essential difference between the drill format and the test format is that the latter does not include the correct response. In achievement testing, it is presumed that the student has been exposed to all aspects of the test items in the course of studying the language. This includes the directions as well as the stimuli. If students err because they are unfamiliar with the instructions, then the test is invalid.

Testing Vocabulary for Oral Production

Vocabulary (and phonology) can be tested with the highest degree of purity if pictorial stimuli are used. At the simplest level, a series of objects can be shown each of which is labeled with a number. The student simply reads the number and identifies the object in the picture. At a slightly more complex level, the pictures can portray a series of actions or qualities for which the student must supply an oral comment.

Examples:
Directions: Tell what is happening.
Stimulus:

Response: The boy is running.
 Stimulus:

Response: The girl is sleeping.
Directions: Tell what the person or object is like.
 Stimulus:

Response: The girl is <u>pretty</u>. *or* She is <u>pretty</u>. *or*
She's a <u>pretty</u> girl. *or* other acceptable response
 Stimulus:

Response: The building is <u>tall</u>. *or*
That's a <u>tall</u> building. *or* other acceptable response

Testing Free Oral Expression

Fluency and free expression are the ultimate goals of oral production. It appears that these can best be tested by means of selected visuals. A series of simple line drawings that tell a story are used as stimuli. Students describe orally what is happening (or what has happened, what will happen, and so on) and, within a time limit, record their description on tape. In the laboratory, the drawings can be projected onto a screen on the front wall; in individual testing, the same test booklet can be used with each student. Also, the possibility of utilizing motion pictures in the foreign language for oral testing should not be overlooked. With this technique, the students see an action series on the screen, which is narrated in simple language. When the film has been played once, it is rewound and replayed silently. On the second showing the students supply their own narrations, which are recorded on tape. (Here, of course, special laboratory facilities are required.)

In all cases involving spontaneous oral production, the tapes are graded for fluency, correctness, sophistication of language, and quantity of information. Thus it often is difficult to choose between the cautious student who makes a series of grammatically accurate comments in infantile but precise language and the intrepid student who supplies more information in a more mature manner but with a number of errors. Obviously, a large element of subjective judgment unavoidably enters into the grading of free oral production.

TESTING ACHIEVEMENT IN WRITING

Many of the techniques used for testing oral production can also be adapted for testing written production. Dictations can serve for testing spelling ability (that is, the relationship between phonemes and graphemes). Some of the transformation and completion exercises discussed in earlier chapters can also be used to test written command of morphology and syntax. Similarly, a series of pictorial stimuli can be utilized to elicit direct written expression as can motion pictures that are viewed and then summarized briefly in writing. At the more advanced levels, written compositions can follow reading assignments in the form of simple plot summaries or comments upon characters in a story or novel. However, the more difficult the reading assignment is, the more questionable is the purity of the writing test. Similarly, written compositions that ask for even simple literary criticisms are highly impure tests of *either* reading or writing ability. American students who read English perfectly well are often unable to engage in simple literary criticisms involving American and English literature. To expect the same students to read a foreign language and to write perceptive compositions about the relative literary merits of a given selection in the foreign language is highly unrealistic for all but a handful of American high school students. For these few, perhaps some sort of advanced placement testing is in order. For the vast majority, however, testing would seem most appropriately to focus upon measuring the extent to which a student can write reasonably mature sentences and paragraphs about nonabstract content.

354

TESTING FOR COMMUNICATIVE COMPETENCE

The previous sections on the testing of student achievement relate largely to measures of *linguistic* competence. However, as was noted above, the ability to perform adequately with respect to discrete linguistic elements is no proof of an individual's ability to perform in a real communications situation. Thus, measures of linguistic competence can be regarded as indicators of student control over certain prerequisite skills or of their having gained certain specific insights that are potentially useful for receiving and conveying information via the target language. For those who wish to know whether students can, in fact, apply their language training for communicative purposes, a different kind of testing is needed— that is, tests that measure the *quality of the message* rather than the *accuracy of the medium,* that focus on meaning rather than form, on content rather than style. In recent years, various investigators have suggested a variety of techniques for assessing a student's ability to give and receive messages in simulated communication contexts.[4]

Communicative Competence in Speaking

In administering such a test the student is first told in general terms about the overall purpose of the test. For example, "The purpose of the test is to determine how well you can make yourself understood in _____ (name of language). Do not worry about speaking flawlessly, but rather concentrate on making yourself understood. Your performance will be judged on how much information you convey and how smoothly you do it. Best results are usually obtained in an informal atmosphere. So, relax and do the best you can." The general instructions are then followed with instructions for various kinds of oral communication. Bartz suggests categories such as "Relating Information," "Oral Description," "Interview for Giving Information," and "Interview for Getting Information."[5]

Relating information. The student is given a list of facts about a situation involving people and events in the target culture. This is done in English. The student is instructed to read the paragraph through several times. The student is then handed a list of the pertinent facts contained in the paragraph. With the aid of the list he/she is then to pretend to be talking to a native and to try, in as natural a way as possible, to convey the meaning of the paragraph by means of the target language. The student is told that he/she can ask for help with an occasional word and that the occasional substitution of an English word is permissible.

---

[4] Sandra Savignon, "Talking with My Son: An Example of Communicative Competence," In Frank Grittner (ed.), *Careers, Communication and Culture,* Skokie, Ill., National Textbook Company, 1974, pp. 26–39. See also, Walter H. Bartz, *A Study of the Relationship of Certain Learner Factors with the Ability to Communicate in a Second Language (German) for the Development of Measures of Communicative Competence,* unpublished PhD dissertation, Ohio State University, 1973, pp. 141–156.

[5] Bartz, op. cit., pp. 141–142.

Oral description. The student is handed a picture or a series of pictures and is asked to describe the situation depicted there in English. After having exhausted his/her ability to describe what is there in English, the student is then asked to describe the situation in the target foreign language.

Interview for giving information. In this test the teacher asks the student to play the role of someone being interviewed in the foreign language. The teacher pretends to be unable to communicate in any other way than by means of the foreign language. The teacher then asks a series of planned personal questions about the student, who is told to answer in a natural way giving as much information as possible.

Interview for getting information. In this test the roles are reversed. That is, the student is to interview the teacher, who again represents a native speaker. The interview is to be conducted in as natural a manner as possible and in the foreign language only. The student is instructed to begin with a self-introduction and to end with some appropriate terminating remarks. The teacher pretends to understand only the target language. The student can take notes and is expected at the end of the interview to write up in English a report on what he/she found out about the person interviewed. A listing of minimal desired information can be given to the student with the suggestion that even more information about the "native speaker" would be desirable.

In interpreting the tests of oral communicative competence, it is helpful to have certain categories for judging student performance. A standard evaluation sheet can also be of value in summarizing the points of strength and weakness that the student demonstrates when he/she attempts to communicate in the target language. The items given below are examples of the kinds of rating scales and evaluation sheets that can be used to advantage in evaluating students' communicative attempts.

■17

EVALUATION SHEET
COMMUNICATIVE COMPETENCE IN SPEAKING

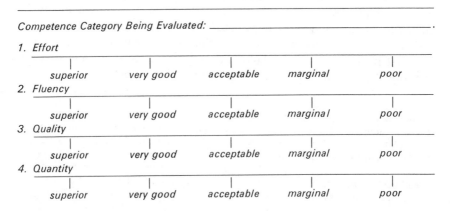

Competence Category Being Evaluated: _____.

1. *Effort*

| | superior | very good | acceptable | marginal | poor |

2. *Fluency*

| | superior | very good | acceptable | marginal | poor |

3. *Quality*

| | superior | very good | acceptable | marginal | poor |

4. *Quantity*

| | superior | very good | acceptable | marginal | poor |

1. *Effort.* Communicative effort has to do with the apparent willingness of the student to make himself/herself understood. The student does not withdraw and give up easily, but keeps trying to communicate despite apparent failure. (See Table 17.)

Interpretation of scale:

Poor: Student is listless; appears not to care if message is properly conveyed.

Marginal: Student is slightly attentive; will express what comes easily, but appears unwilling to put forth any special effort.

Acceptable: Student is alert; tries to complete the communications task and may add something not specifically called for.

Very good: Student is interested; makes a concerted effort to communicate and goes well beyond what the task requires.

Superior: Student is enthusiastic; makes an extremely active effort to communicate using a wide variety of means, verbal and non-verbal, to express himself/herself.

2. *Fluency.* Communicative fluency related to ease, logical continuity, and naturalness of delivery. Lack of fluency is characterized by hesitance, constant restatement, groping for the correct utterance, and so on.

Interpretation of scale:

Poor: Delivery is constantly hesitant and halting with a very large number of unnatural pauses and fragmented utterances.

Marginal: Delivery is often hesitant and halting with quite a few unnatural pauses and fragmented utterances.

Acceptable: Delivery is occasionally hesitant and halting with a few unnatural pauses and fragmented utterances.

Very good: Delivery is seldom hesitant or halting and seems fairly smooth and effortless.

Superior: Delivery is never hesitant or halting. It is smooth and nearly effortless, approaching near-native delivery.

3. *Quality.* Communicative quality refers to the naturalness and appropriateness of the utterances that the student uses in the given communications situation.

Interpretation of scale:

Poor: Delivery is characterized by a constant flow of incomplete statements, inappropriate expressions, and isolated words with only a few short complete utterances.

Marginal: Delivery is characterized by quite a few incomplete statements, inappropriate expressions, and isolated words with some short, complete utterances.

Acceptable: Delivery is characterized by some incomplete statements, an occasional inappropriate expression and a few isolated words with many short, complete utterances.

Very good: Delivery is characterized by very few incomplete statements, inappropriate expressions or isolated words with mostly complete utterances.

Superior: Delivery is characterized by complete utterances, appropriate expressions and the use of isolated words only where appropriate.

4. *Quantity.* Communicative quantity refers to the amount of information conveyed by the student in the course of carrying out the communications task.

Interpretation of scale:

    Poor: Student conveys very little of the information called for in the communications task. Nearly all the relevant facts are omitted.

  Marginal: Student conveys some of the information called for in the communications task. A large number of relevant facts are omitted.

Acceptable: Student conveys much of the information called for in the communications task. Many of the relevant facts are included.

Very good: Student conveys most of the information called for in the communications task. Nearly all of the relevant facts are included.

  Superior: Student conveys all the information called for in the communications task. All relevant facts are included.

Communicative Competance in Listening

A situation requiring listening skill is simulated in some manner. For example, a short tape of a telephone conversation in the foreign language can be prepared with instructions such as the following: "You are alone in the house and the telephone rings. The person on the other end of the line speaks only the target language. He has an important message that must be

■18

TEACHER EVALUATION SHEET
COMMUNICATIVE COMPETENCE IN LISTENING

Check list of points for scoring.

1	a friend called	1.	_____
2	name, Kohl	2.	_____
3	was in a hurry	3.	_____
4	arriving by train	4.	_____
5	in afternoon	5.	_____
6	at 4:00 p.m.	6.	_____
7	not coming by plane	7.	_____
8	don't go to airport	8.	_____
9	don't go to depot	9.	_____
10	will be at Hotel Kaiser	10.	_____
11	on Brennerstrasse	11.	_____
12	with business colleague	12.	_____
13	until 7:30 p.m.	13.	_____
14	will eat dinner there	14.	_____
15	don't wait with dinner	15.	_____
16	meet Kohl in lobby	16.	_____
17	between 7:30 and 8:00 p.m.	17.	_____

358

relayed to the head of the house. The person is calling long distance and must leave soon. Therefore, he cannot call back." The student then listens to the tape, which explains (in the foreign language) that plans have changed. (See Table 18.)

The student is instructed to listen to the foreign language message and to take notes on it in English. The message is then written up in English

Sample tape script (translated into English) of "phone message" from Mr. Kohl to Mr. Klein.

Please listen closely. This is Heinrich Kohl, a friend of Mr. Klein. I have to catch a train in a few minutes. Tell Mr. Klein that I will be arriving by train at four o'clock this afternoon instead of coming by plane in the evening. So, he should *not* pick me up at the airport. Instead, I will be at the Kaiser Hotel on Brennerstrasse until 7 :30 p.m. I will be meeting there with a business colleague and will be having dinner with him, so don't wait dinner for me. I'll be waiting for Mr. Klein in the lobby of the Kaiser Hotel between 7 : 30 and 8 : 00 p.m. I have to rush off now ; the train is about to leave.

TESTING READING COMPREHENSION BY MEANS OF THE CLOZE PROCEDURES AND THE INPUT TEST[6]

The cloze procedures offer a simple, objective way of assessing reading comprehension directly. Almost any reading passage can be easily adapted to the cloze-test format. A commonly recommended procedure is to omit every fifth word in a reading selection of appropriate difficulty. The following is an example translated from Spanish :

THE STROLL

In hispanoamerica the stroll _____ a very common custom. _____ the afternoon, toward the _____ of six or seven _____ people go to the _____ or to main street. _____ boys chat in groups _____ the corner or in _____ street. The girls, also _____ groups, stroll slowly around _____ square. Upon passing the _____, the boys greet them _____ begin to converse openly _____ them.

The test is administered by having the student fill in the correct word for each blank. In the most stringent application for scoring cloze-test results, the teacher accepts only the exact word that had been deleted from the original passage. A more liberal scoring method is to accept any response that makes sense contextually. Experience with cloze testing suggests that the more liberal approach is best for the classroom situation. From the instructional standpoint, it makes sense to reward students for supplying any contextually acceptable response. Inasmuch as the teacher

---

[6] Oscar Ozete, *Assessing Reading Comprehension in Spanish as a Foreign Language: An Information-Process Approach*, unpublished PhD dissertation, Indiana University, 1974. This section is based on Ozete's research into testing of reading in the foreign language.

is attempting to help students learn the art of intelligent guessing as an integral part of reading instruction, it would seem wise to offer all possible encouragement to this effort in the testing process.

It is assumed that the cloze test measures much more than the ability of the student to guess. For example, the student must understand the overall message of the paragraph and must have learned most of the lexical items in order to perform adequately. From the pedagogical standpoint, cloze procedures offer several advantages. First, it is possible to convert portions of regular reading lessons into test items rapidly and easily. Thus, good cloze tests can be prepared in a fraction of the time needed for comparable true/ false or multiple choice tests. Secondly, cloze tests of paragraph lengths can be scored rapidly by anyone who knows the language (although true/false and multiple choice tests can be scored somewhat faster). Thirdly, cloze tests are not dependent on students' skill in interpreting and answering questions; the test is a rather direct measure of a student's ability to deal with meaningful material on the printed page.

The input test is a variation of the cloze procedures. The input test provides that every fifth lexical item be in the form of a choice between the correct response and a distractor. The format for the input test applied to the example of "The Stroll" given above would look like this:

In hispanoamerica the stroll $\begin{smallmatrix}has\\is\end{smallmatrix}$ a very common custom. $\begin{smallmatrix}In\\Also\end{smallmatrix}$ the afternoon,

toward the $\begin{smallmatrix}hour\\day\end{smallmatrix}$ of six or seven $\begin{smallmatrix}constant\\young\end{smallmatrix}$ people go to the $\begin{smallmatrix}square\\ever\end{smallmatrix}$ or to the main street. (and so on)

The input test is different from the cloze test in that there is little interruption of the normal reading act due to the fact that the correct answer is readily accessible to the reader. Also, there is no need for the student to write out a word since the reader is asked to do no more than mark one of the two choices. In practice the input test appears to be a reliable indicator of the reader's readiness to cope with the difficulty level of a given reading passage. Data from a study conducted by Ozete indicated that the input test can be used effectively for measuring the reading skill of beginning students.[7] However, the cloze test appears to be somewhat more suitable for use with advanced students.

EVALUATING THE TEXTBOOK FOR BEGINNING LEVELS

Although a few people have found ways to teach a foreign language successfully during the first two years without the aid of a commercially produced text, the vast majority of language teachers seem convinced that the textbook is an essential instructional tool. Thus, since the text assumes such importance in determining local curricula, it seems advisable to

[7] Ibid., pp. 70–75.

exercise great care in its selection. This, in turn, implies the need for selective criteria. During the late 1960s such criteria were developed. However, in the opinion of many people, past criteria have been excessively biased in favor of a particular methodological school. The criteria presented below attempt to minimize penalties against a given *text* on the basis of a particular theoretical orientation or lack thereof. Care has been taken to accomodate diversity and to avoid narrow adherence to any given party line. It is, perhaps, self-evident that evaluative criteria of any kind are only a partial help in selecting a text series. The careful personal examination and evaluation of materials would, ideally, be supplemented with field testing of text components in the classroom situation. For comparing a number of texts, a 5-point scale can be devised on the order of the instrument suggested above for evaluating communicative competence in speaking. The points can be charted for each book with respect to each of the 15 criteria given below.

Textbook Evaluative Criteria[8]

1   Skill Development : *Is provision made for learning all four skills ?*
Yes—Students practice all four skills, though not necessarily to the same degree.
No —One (or more) of the four skills is largely neglected.

2   Listening Comprehension : *Does the text contain appropriate listening comprehension material ?*
Yes—Specific listening comprehension material is present throughout the text; utterances are short, natural, and of high frequency in the target language.
No —Specific listening comprehension material is sporadic or missing; utterances are too long, unnatural, or uncommon.

3   Pronunciation : *Is pronunciation dealt with satisfactorily ?*
Yes—Pronunciation and the sound system are dealt with explicitly, either in a pronunciation unit or on a unit-by-unit basis throughout the text; sufficient attention is paid to close "equivalents" in English and the target language and to those sounds that are difficult for Americans; stress and intonation are considered.
No —Pronunciation and the sound system are to be learned indirectly, they are never dealt with explicitly; the sound system is dealt with, but insufficient attention is paid to near-equivalents in and to problem sounds in the target language; stress and intonation are not considered.

4   Speaking : *Is appropriate conversational material present ?*
Yes—Oral practice material is available throughout the text; utterances are short, natural, and concentrate on basic structures.
No —Material for developing oral skills is sporadic or missing; material

8 These criteria are based on items developed by Frank M. Grittner and Sam Welty, "Beginning German Textbooks for the High School Level (1969–1973) : A Descriptive Evaluation," *Modern Language Journal* 57 (November 1974), pp. 314–322. See subsequent issues of *Modern Language Journal* for other evaluations of foreign language textbooks.

contains lengthy or seldom-used utterances and structures.

5   Reading : *Is adequate opportunity provided for practising reading skill ?*

    Yes—Reading material derives organically from the unit; reading material is not overburdened with new vocabulary; reading material aims at comprehension of the written word rather than translation.

    No —Reading material does not relate to the unit; reading material demands learning too much vocabulary; reading material is largely an exercise in translating rather than direct comprehension of the written word.

6   Writing : *Is adequate opportunity provided for practising the writing skill ?*

    Yes—Writing exercises develop progressively through the book; exercises are varied and emphasize recombination of previously learned material; exercises lead to a degree of self-expression appropriate to the instructional level.

    No —Writing exercises do not develop progressively; very few different types of exercises are available; exercises call for excessive amount of new vocabulary or structures; exercises do not lead to self-expression.

7   Grammar : *Is grammar dealt with satisfactorily ?*

    Yes—Basic grammar is accurately presented; provision is made for sufficient practice before proceeding to new structures; the amount of grammar is about right for the intended group of students.

    No —Grammar is described incompletely or faulty; grammatical principles are seldom or never summarized; insufficient drill opportunity is afforded before introducing new structures; there is too much or too little grammar.

8   Vocabulary : *Is the vocabulary in the text appropriate and adequately presented ?*

    Yes—Vocabulary is appropriate to the needs and interests of the intended group of students; vocabulary is introduced in context; vocabulary is summarized by chapter in the form of lists, glossaries, or indexes.

    No —Vocabulary is too difficult for the intended students or irrelevant to their interests; vocabulary is presented without context; vocabulary items are inadequately summarized by chapter.

9   Culture : *Does the book present suitable cultural material ?*

    Yes—Examples of culture both in the fine arts sense and the anthropological sense are presented; the material is organically related to the rest of the unit.

    No —There is a one-sided or minimal emphasis on culture; the cultural material does not relate to the rest of the unit.

10   Drills and Exercises : *Are drills and exercises varied and numerous ?*

    Yes—The book contains a wide variety of drills and exercises; drills and exercises are numerous enough to minimize the need for teacher-devised material.

    No —The book utilizes the same types of practice material throughout the text; the kinds *of exercises are so few in number and so limited in scope that teacher-written material is necessary.*

11   Length : *Are the text and its units realistic in terms of the amount of material presented ?*

    Yes—The text can be completed by most high school students in one year; the units are short enough to maintain student interest and afford a feeling of progress.

    No —One or more of the above is missing.

12   Flexibility : *Is the text flexible and adaptable ?*
        *Yes—The text makes provision for a variety of student interests, abilities
            and learning styles.*
        No —The text makes no such provision.
13   Supplementary Materials : *Are basic supplementary materials available ?*
        *Yes—Teacher's edition or manual, workbook, audio materials, visuals,
            tests and quizzes.*
        No —One or more of the above is missing.
14   Suggested Supplementary Activities : *Are suggestions made for
        supplementary activities ?*
        *Yes—Suggestions are made for supplementing the text with such things
            as films, games, songs, slides, crossword puzzles, field trips, student-
            created skits, letter writing and cooking.*
        No —No such suggestions are made.

BIBLIOGRAPHY

Born, Warren C. (ed.), *Goals Clarification: Curriculum Teaching, Evaluation,*
Middlebury, Vt., Northeast Conference, 1975.

Lafayette, Robert C., and Renate Schulz, "Evaluating Cultural Learnings,"
in Robert C. Lafayette (ed.), *The Cultural Revolution in Foreign Language
Teaching,* Skokie, Ill., National Textbook Company, 1975, pp. 104–118.

Moskowitz, Gertrude, "The Effects of Training Foreign Language Teachers in
Interaction Analysis," *Foreign Language Annals* 1 (March 1968,) pp. 218–238.

Paquette, F. André, and Suzanne Tollinger (eds.), *A Handbook on Foreign
Language Classroom Testing: French, German, Italian, Russian, Spanish,*
New York, Modern Language Association, 1968.
According to the editors, "This *Handbook* has been produced to help the classroom teacher make efficient use of tests. It contains discussions of the main
purposes tests can serve. It treats the principle kinds of testing devices that seem
to be especially useful for those purposes in the context of foreign-language
teaching." The 17-page bibliography is one of the most extensive available with
respect to foreign language testing.

Tursi, Joseph A. (ed.), "Foreign Language Attitude Questionnaire," in *Foreign
Languages and the "New" Student,* Middlebury, Vt., Northeast Conference, 1970.
A comprehensive instrument for measuring students' attitudes toward the
foreign language program. Questionnaire forms can be ordered in quantity from
the Northeast Conference, Box 623, Middlebury, Vt. 05753.

Valette, Rebecca, *Modern Language Testing,* New York, Harcourt Brace
Jovanovich 1976.
This is a very useful handbook containing a large number of model test items
along with clearly stated directions for constructing foreign language tests.

Proficency Tests and Other Materials

Common Concepts Foreign Language Tests, California Test Bureau, Del Monte
Research Park, Monterey, Calif. 93940.

363

MLA Cooperative Foreign Language Tests, Educational Testing Service, Princeton, N.J. 08540.

New York Regents Exams, University of the State of New York, State Education Department, Albany, N.Y. 12224.

Pimsleur Modern Foreign Language Proficiency Tests, New York, Harcourt Brace Jovanovich.

INDEX

365

366

367